Frommer

P9-APY-927

Puerto Rico

8th Edition

by Darwin Porter & Danforth Prince

Here's what the critics say about Frommer's:

"Amazingly easy to use. Very portable, very complete."

—*Booklist*

"Detailed, accurate, and easy-to-read information for all price ranges."
—*Glamour Magazine*

"Hotel information is close to encyclopedic."

—*Des Moines Sunday Register*

"Frommer's Guides have a way of giving you a real feel for a place."
—*Knight Ridder Newspapers*

WILEY

Wiley Publishing, Inc.

About the Author

A team of veteran travel writers, **Darwin Porter** and **Danforth Prince** have produced numerous titles for Frommer's including best selling guides to Italy, France, the Caribbean, England, and Germany. Porter is also a noted Hollywood biographer, and his recent releases include *Howard Hughes: Hell's Angel* and *Brando Unzipped*. He is a newspaper columnist on popular culture as well as a radio commentator, with broadcasts heard in all 50 states. Prince, formerly of the *New York Times* Paris bureau, is the president of Blood Moon Productions and other media-related firms.

Published by:

Wiley Publishing, Inc.

111 River St.
Hoboken, NJ 07030-5774

ISBN-13: 978-0-471-78740-2
ISBN-10: 0-471-78740-X

Editor: Stephen Bassman
Production Editor: Jana M. Stefanciosa
Cartographer: Guy Ruggiero
Photo Editor: Richard Fox
Production by Wiley Indianapolis Composition Services

Front cover photo: Navio Beach on Vieques Island
Back cover photo: Detail of building in Old San Juan

For information on our other products and services or to obtain technical support, please contact our Customer Care Department within the U.S. at 800/762-2974, outside the U.S. at 317/572-3993 or fax 317/572-4002.

Wiley also publishes its books in a variety of electronic formats. Some content that appears in print may not be available in electronic formats.

Manufactured in the United States of America

5   4   3   2

Contents

List of Maps

An Invitation to the Reader

In researching this book, we discovered many wonderful places—hotels, restaurants, shops, and more. We're sure you'll find others. Please tell us about them, so we can share the information with your fellow travelers in upcoming editions. If you were disappointed with a recommendation, we'd love to know that, too. Please write to:

Frommer's Puerto Rico, 8th Edition
Wiley Publishing, Inc. • 111 River St. • Hoboken, NJ 07030-5774

An Additional Note

Please be advised that travel information is subject to change at any time—and this is especially true of prices. We therefore suggest that you write or call ahead for confirmation when making your travel plans. The authors, editors, and publisher cannot be held responsible for the experiences of readers while traveling. Your safety is important to us, however, so we encourage you to stay alert and be aware of your surroundings. Keep a close eye on cameras, purses, and wallets, all favorite targets of thieves and pickpockets.

Other Great Guides for Your Trip:

Frommer's Caribbean

Frommer's Caribbean Ports of Call

Caribbean for Dummies

Frommer's Cruises & Ports of Call

The Unofficial Guide to Cruises

Cruise Vacations For Dummies

Frommer's Star Ratings, Icons & Abbreviations

Every hotel, restaurant, and attraction listing in this guide has been ranked for quality, value, service, amenities, and special features using a **star-rating system.** In country, state, and regional guides, we also rate towns and regions to help you narrow down your choices and budget your time accordingly. Hotels and restaurants are rated on a scale of zero (recommended) to three stars (exceptional). Attractions, shopping, nightlife, towns, and regions are rated according to the following scale: zero stars (recommended), one star (highly recommended), two stars (very highly recommended), and three stars (must-see).

In addition to the star-rating system, we also use **eight feature icons** that point you to the great deals, in-the-know advice, and unique experiences that separate travelers from tourists. Throughout the book, look for:

Finds	Special finds—those places only insiders know about
Fun Fact	Fun facts—details that make travelers more informed and their trips more fun
Kids	Best bets for kids and advice for the whole family
Moments	Special moments—those experiences that memories are made of
Overrated	Places or experiences not worth your time or money
Tips	Insider tips—great ways to save time and money
Value	Great values—where to get the best deals
Warning	Warning—traveler's advisories are usually in effect

The following **abbreviations** are used for credit cards:

AE	American Express	DISC	Discover	V	Visa
DC	Diners Club	MC	MasterCard		

Frommers.com

Now that you have the guidebook to a great trip, visit our website at **www.frommers.com** for travel information on more than 3,000 destinations. With features updated regularly, we give you instant access to the most current trip-planning information available. At Frommers.com, you'll also find the best prices on airfares, accommodations, and car rentals—and you can even book travel online through our travel booking partners. At Frommers.com, you'll also find the following:

- Online updates to our most popular guidebooks
- Vacation sweepstakes and contest giveaways
- Newsletter highlighting the hottest travel trends
- Online travel message boards with featured travel discussions

What's New in Puerto Rico

The dynamic island explodes with change year after year. Today's grand resort might be swept away in a hurricane, or last winter's hot restaurant dining choice might be a sea of empty tables this season. Even beaches come and go. Here are some of the latest developments.

WHERE TO STAY IN SAN JUAN Just outside the Old Town of San Juan, **Caribe Hilton** (© **800/HILTONS** or 787/721-0303), has inaugurated its most luxurious living choices with 168 new luxury villas opening onto views of the Condado Lagoon. Studios as well as one- or two-bedroom suites are up for grabs, each with a kitchen and private balcony.

WHERE TO DINE IN SAN JUAN In the swanky **Ritz-Carlton San Juan Spa & Casino,** the most succulent steaks are being served at **Prime 787** (© **787/ 253-1700**), in deluxe surroundings. Its "Kobe Flat Iron" steak is hailed as the finest cut being offered in the Caribbean today. In Old San Juan, and giving Il Perugino a run for its money, **Sofia** (© **787/721-0396**) has burst on the scene with its finely honed Italian cuisine. It is especially notable for its fresh seafood and its paella that uses linguine instead of rice. When you tire of a constant diet of Puerto Rican fare, you can head for **Fatty's** (© **787/586-6925**), which brings a taste of Jamaica, along with reggae music, to San Juan. Chefs turn out marvelous jerk dishes, especially chicken, fish, and shrimp.

SAN JUAN AFTER DARK The hottest rendezvous spot in Old Town is the **Sake Sushi Bar** (© **787/977-1082**), on the upper floor of an old building near the cruise-ship docks. In a comfortable setting, a sophisticated crowd of locals, expats, and visitors gather here to eat, dance, and listen to the music. The joint really jumps after midnight.

WHERE TO STAY IN DORADO The grand **Hyatt Dorado Beach Resort & Country Club** closed in May 2006 and has no immediate plans to reopen under new management. This is a shame; we once recommended the hotel for everything from family vacations to honeymoons. Fortunately, the country club's tennis courts and legendary golf courses are slated to remain open indefinitely, and you can still dine at two of the hotel's restaurants, Hacienda del Sol and Zafra. Call © **787/796-1234** for updates. See p. 171.

WHERE TO STAY IN RIO GRANDE Coated in luxury, **Sol Melia Paradisus** (© **866/43-MELIA**) is a new 582-room hotel that rates five stars for deluxe living with every accommodation an elegant suite. It is Puerto Rico's first and only all-inclusive, all-suite resort. Seemingly everything is here from first-class spa treatments to six restaurants with the most varied hotel cuisine on island. You may never leave the grounds. But if you do, there are two 18-hole golf courses adjacent to the hotel at the **Coco Beach**

Golf and Country Club (© 787/657-2000). Four 9-hole loops fan out from the Caribbean's largest clubhouse.

WHERE TO PLAY GOLF IN PONCE

The best golf course, a 27-holer, along the southern coast has opened here. **Costa Caribe Golf & Country Club** (© 787/848-1000) offers beautifully landscaped holes with vistas of ocean and mountain. This course is one of golf architect Bruce Besse's best.

WHERE TO STAY IN SAN GERMAN

At long last this historic city has a good place to stay. A fine country inn, **Villa Del Rey** (© 787/642-2627) has opened with spacious and attractively furnished bedrooms. There's also a good open-air restaurant featuring regional dishes.

WHERE TO STAY IN RINCON   One

of the best beachfront resorts has opened here, a secluded hideaway, **Rincón Beach Resort** (© 866/598-0009 or 787/589-9000). The staff is the most helpful along the coast, and the open-air Brasas Restaurant serves a savory cuisine. Guest rooms are spacious and well furnished with a tropical decor.

WHERE TO STAY AT PALMAS DEL MAR   The long-dormant resort on the

eastern coast has come back. This time it's called **Four Points by Sheraton Palmas del Mar Resort** (© 787/850-6000), offering 107 well-furnished bedrooms in a setting of parks, golf, and tennis. A casino and an "infinity pool" are also on the grounds, along with a varied international cuisine, even a wine and cigar bar.

WHERE TO STAY ON VIEQUES

Imbued with Philippe Starck designs, **Bravo Beach Hotel** (© 787/741-1128) lies only 30 feet (9m) from the beach. It's our preferred nest on this offshore island, complete with a dramatic decor—lots of white—and ultimate comfort, with the island's best on-site restaurant.

WHERE TO DINE ON VIEQUES

The best tapas in Puerto Rico are served at the oddly named **bbh** (© 787/741-1128), an open-air restaurant at the swanky Bravo Beach Hotel. The tapas are uniformly luscious, prepared with the finest of ingredients. A taste delight.

The Best of Puerto Rico

It's only the size of Connecticut, but Puerto Rico pulsates with more life than any other island in the Caribbean. To the beat of bomba, there's a party going on here 24 hours a day.

The 4 million people who live here believe that having fun is one of the reasons they were born on this dazzling but troubled island. One of the most popular tourist destinations south of Florida raises the rainbow flag to a diverse heritage, beginning with the early settlers, the Taíno Indians. Their culture later gave way to African and Spanish influences.

That Puerto Rico maintains its culture or identity is just short of a miracle. Its big brother to the north—that is, the United States—dominates the island's economy but not its soul. Most Puerto Ricans maintain a love-hate relationship with the States. Although an independence-minded political party favors breaking away completely, the majority of Puerto Ricans, when faced with a decision at the voting polls, don't want to take such a drastic step into the unknown.

Even though millions have fled Puerto Rico to find work in industrial cities of the north, for many the "heart's devotion" (to steal a phrase from the song "America" in *West Side Story*) still belongs to the native island. On every plane arriving at Luis Muñoz Marín International Airport in San Juan, *Neoyorkinos* (as expats are called) burst into spontaneous applause the moment the aircraft touches their native land.

Much of the island lives in poverty, but Puerto Ricans have a lot to boast about, including 260 miles of sandy beaches; the third-largest underground cave system on earth; and the world's largest radio telescope, which sends signals into outer space 24 hours a day, hoping ET will call in for a "close encounter." And don't forget its lush Caribbean forests, including the only rainforest (El Yunque) on U.S. territory. There are an astonishing *nine* protected nature reserves on this so-called "Island of Enchantment," with species of wildlife you won't find anywhere else in the world.

Of course, everything on island is not always enchanting. The drug trade and a rising crime rate are troubling. As one gas station attendant bluntly informed us, "You Americans should not wear your expensive jewelry to Puerto Rico because we'll have to take it away from you."

The Puerto Rican writer René Marqués calls his island schizophrenic. "Puerto Rico has two languages," he claims, "and two citizenships, two basic philosophies of life, two flags, two anthems, two loyalties."

A clue to the Puerto Rican soul is reflected in the national anthem, "La Borinqueña." Most national anthems around the world sing of military muscle and a triumph over enemies. Not so "La Borinqueña." It sings of "a flowering garden of exquisite magic . . . the daughter of the sea and the sun." Get to know this garden and the people who call it home.

1 The Best Beaches

White sandy beaches put Puerto Rico and its offshore islands on tourist maps in the first place. Many other Caribbean destinations have only jagged coral outcroppings or black volcanic-sand beaches that get very hot in the noonday sun. The best beaches are labeled on the "Puerto Rico" map on p. 18.

- **Best for Singles (Straight & Gay):** Sandwiched between the Condado and Isla Verde beaches along San Juan's beachfront, **Ocean Park Beach** attracts more adults and less of the family trade. Only Isla Verde beach to the east matches Ocean Park for its broad beach and good swimming. The people-watching here is nothing compared to the well-stuffed bikinis (both male and female) found on South Miami Beach or Rio de Janeiro. However, for the Caribbean, Ocean Park is as good as it gets. Because many gay boardinghouses lie in Ocean Park, a lot of the beach here is frequented by gay young men, mainly from New York. However, straight people looking to meet someone while wearing swimwear will find plenty of lookers (and perhaps takers). See "Diving, Fishing, Tennis & Other Outdoor Pursuits," in chapter 7.

- **Best Beach for Families:** Winning without contest, **Luquillo Beach,** 30 miles (42km) east of San Juan, attracts both local families, mainly from San Juan, and visitors from Condado and Isla Verde beaches in San Juan. Beach buffs heading for Luquillo know they will get better sands and clearer waters there than in San Juan. The vast sandy beach opens onto a crescent-shaped bay edged by a coconut grove. Coral reefs protect the crystal-clear lagoon from the often rough Atlantic waters that can buffet the northern coast, making Luquillo a good place for young children to swim. Much photographed because of its white sands, Luquillo also has tent sites and other facilities, including picnic areas with changing rooms, lockers, and showers. See "Luquillo Beach" in chapter 8.

- **Best for Swimming:** Whereas on much of the northwest coast of Puerto Rico, rough Atlantic waters often deter bathers but attract surfers (see below), the south coast waters are calmer. On the south coast, **Playa de Ponce,** outside Ponce, Puerto Rico's second-largest city, consists of a long strip of beautiful white sand that opens onto the tranquil waters of the Caribbean. Less crowded than Condado and Luquillo, Playa de Ponce is an ideal place to swim year-round in clearer, less polluted waters than those along the more heavily populated northern coastline. See "Ponce" in chapter 9.

- **Best for Scenery:** In the southwestern corner of Puerto Rico, **Boquerón Beach** lies in a section of the island called the Cape Cod of Puerto Rico. The beach town of Boquerón itself, filled with colorful scenery, stands at the heart of a 3-mile (4.8km) bay, with palm-fringed white sand curving away on both sides. Enjoy this panoramic vista and sample vignettes of local life; fisherfolk, sailors, and scuba divers are also attracted to this beach, where fresh oysters are shucked on the spot, doused with Tabasco, and sold at various ramshackle shacks. You can see that there are plenty of interesting photo ops at this beach. While enjoying the scenery and the sands, you can take a break and order a regional ice cream at one of the stands. It's made with sweet corn and dusted with paprika. Sound awful?

Try it: It's good. See "The Southwest Coast" in chapter 10.

- **Best for Windsurfing:** Rincón's winter surf, especially at **Playa Higüero,** puts Malibu to shame. Today surfers from all over the world are attracted to Rincón, which they have dubbed "Little Malibu." From Borinquén Point south to Rincón, nearly all the beaches along the western coast are ideal for surfing from November to April. As the windsurfing capital of the Caribbean, the Rincón area was put on the map when it was the site of the 1968 world surfing championships. Some of the 16-foot (4.9m) breakers here equal those on the north shore of Oahu. See "Rincón" in chapter 10.

- **Best Beaches for Being Alone:** The main island is filled with isolated sandy coves that only the locals seem to know about. The best, all guaranteed to delight the escapist in you, stretch between Cabo Rojo (the southwesterly tip of Puerto Rico) all the way east to Ponce. Beginning in the west, directly east of Cabo Rojo, you'll discover **Rosado Beach, Santa Beach, Caña Gorda Beach,** and **Tamarindo Beach.** Access to many of these is limited because of poor roads, but the effort is worth it. Be sure to bring the necessary supplies. See the box, "Puerto Rico's Secret Beaches," in chapter 10.

- **Best for Snorkeling:** For snorkeling, we prefer to escape from the Puerto Rican mainland altogether, heading for the isolated beaches of the offshore islands of **Vieques** and **Culebra,** part of the Spanish Virgin Islands. In Vieques alone there are some 40 beaches, most of them officially unnamed even though U.S. sailors once stationed on the island have nicknamed their favorites—everything from Green Beach to Orchid. The best beach for snorkeling on Vieques is **Playa Esperanza,** especially that spot in front of the Trade Winds Guesthouse. Another favorite location, which we discovered when directed there by a Navy SEAL, is across the little harbor at **Cayo de Afuera.** This site gives you the best preview of dramatic (and living) antler coral. Nurse sharks and the occasional manatee also hang out here. See "Vieques" in chapter 12.

On the neighboring island of Culebra, the beaches are less visited by snorkelers, even though they open onto coral reefs and clear waters. The snorkeling is not so hot at the island's most frequented beach, Flamenco Beach. But all you have to do is take a 15- to 20-minute hike from the parking lot at Flamenco over the hill to **Playa Carlos Rosario,** which offers some of the best snorkeling in Puerto Rico. A barrier reef virtually envelops the beach, and you can snorkel all day. For other great snorkeling, you can walk along the cliffs south of here for about a quarter-mile (.4km) to a place called **"The Wall,"** which has 40-foot (12m) drop-offs, rainbow-hued fish, and other delights. See "Culebra" in chapter 12.

2 The Best Hotel Beaches

- **El San Juan Hotel & Casino** (San Juan; © **787/791-1000**): This posh resort occupies the choicest beachfront real estate at Isla Verde Beach, one of the finest in Puerto Rico. Ideal for swimming, the golden sands near the airport evoke South Miami Beach. Picnic tables are found here, and the beach is also good for snorkeling. But it is mostly the sands themselves that provide the attraction—that and all the many facilities of El San Juan resort itself. See p. 92.

- **Copamarina Beach Resort** (Caña Gorda; ☎ **787/821-0505**) lies west of Ponce, Puerto Rico's second-largest city. A laid-back retreat, the resort opens onto one of the best and least crowded beaches in southwestern Puerto Rico. This appealing beach is set a quarter-mile (.4km) south of Guánica at the edge of a government-protected marshland known for its rich bird life. Its pale beige sand fronts a backdrop of *bohíos* (thatched huts), where you can retreat from the noonday sun. See p. 213.

3 The Best Scuba Diving

With the continental shelf surrounding it on three sides, Puerto Rico has an abundance of coral reefs, caves, sea walls, and trenches for divers of all experience levels to explore. See "The Active Vacation Planner" in chapter 2.

- **Metropolitan San Juan:** This easy **beach dive off the Condado district** in San Juan is not as spectacular as other dives mentioned here, but it's certainly more convenient. Lava reefs sculptured with caverns, tunnels, and overhangs provide hiding areas for schools of snapper, grunts, and copper sweepers. In the active breeding grounds of the inner and outer reefs, divers of all levels can mingle with an impressive array of small tropical fish—French angels, jacks, bluehead wrasse, butterfly fish, sergeant majors, and more—along with sea horses, arrow crabs, coral shrimp, octopuses, batfish, and flying gunards. Visibility is about 10 to 20 feet (3–6m). The Condado reef is also ideal for resort courses, certification courses, and night dives. See "Diving, Fishing, Tennis & Other Outdoor Pursuits" in chapter 7.

- **Mona Island:** Mona Island, 40 miles (64km) west of the city of Mayagüez in western Puerto Rico, is the Caribbean version of the Galápagos Islands. Renowned for its pirate tales, cave-pocked cliffs, 3-foot-long (.9m) iguanas, and other natural wonders, its waters are among the cleanest in Puerto Rico, with horizontal visibility at times exceeding 200 feet (61m). More than 270 species of fish have been found in Mona waters, including more than 60 reef-dwelling species. Larger marine animals, such as sea turtles, whales, dolphins, and marlins, visit the region during migrations. Various types of coral reefs, underwater caverns, drop-offs, and deep vertical walls ring the island. The most accessible reef dives are along the southern and western shores. Getting there is a pain, however. You must brave a 5-hour boat ride across the often rough Mona Passage. See the box, "Mona Island: The Galápagos of Puerto Rico," in chapter 9.

- **Southern Puerto Rico:** The continental shelf drops off precipitously several miles off the southern coast, producing a dramatic wall 20 miles (32km) long and teeming with marine life. Compared favorably to the wall in the Cayman Islands, this Puerto Rican version has become the Caribbean's newest world-class dive destination. Paralleling the coast from the seaside village of La Parguera to the city of Ponce, the wall descends in slopes and sheer drops from 60 to 120 feet (18–37m) before disappearing into 1,500 feet (457m) of sea. Scored with valleys and deep trenches, it is cloaked in immense gardens of staghorn and elkhorn coral, deep-water gorgonians, and other exquisite coral formations. Visibility can exceed 100 feet (30m). There are more than 50 dive sites around Parguera alone. See "The Southwest Coast" in chapter 10.

• **Fajardo:** This coastal town in eastern Puerto Rico offers divers the opportunity to explore reefs, caverns, mini-walls, and channels near a string of palm-tufted islets. The reefs are decked in an array of corals ranging from delicate gorgonians to immense coral heads. Visibility usually exceeds 50 feet (15m). Divers can hand-feed many of the reef fish that inhabit the corals. Sand channels and a unique double-barrier reef surround Palomino Island, where bandtailed puffers and parrotfish harems are frequently sighted. Cayo Diablo, farther to the east, provides a treasure box of corals and marine animals, from green moray eels and barracudas to octopuses and occasional manatees. See "Las Croabas" in chapter 11.

• **Humacao Region:** South of Fajardo are some 24 dive sites in a 5-mile (8km) radius off the shore. Overhangs, caves, and tunnels perch in 60 feet (18m) of water along mile-long (1.6km) Basslet Reef, where dolphins visit in spring. The Cracks, a jigsaw of caves, alleyways, and boulders, hosts an abundance of goby-cleaning stations and a number of lobsters. With visibility often exceeding 100 feet (30m), the Reserve offers a clear look at corals. At the Drift, divers float along with nurse sharks and angelfish into a valley of swim-throughs and ledges. For the experienced diver, Red Hog is the newest site in the area, with a panoramic wall that drops from 80 to 1,160 feet (24–354m). See "Palmas del Mar" in chapter 11.

4 The Best Snorkeling

Puerto Rico offers top-notch snorkeling even though freshwater run-offs from tropical outbursts feeding into the sea can momentarily cloud the ocean's waters. In most places, when conditions are right, visibility extends from 50 to 75 feet (15–23m).

• **Mona Island:** This remote island off the west coast of Puerto Rico (see "The Best Scuba Diving," above) also offers the best snorkeling possibilities. The reefs here, the most pristine in Puerto Rico, are home to a wide variety of rainbow-hued fish, turtles, octopuses, moray eels, rays, puffers, and clownfish: the single largest concentration of reef fish life in Puerto Rico. You must bring your snorkeling equipment to the island, however, as there are no rentals available once you are here. See the box, "Mona Island: The Galápagos of Puerto Rico," in chapter 9.

• **Caja de Muertos:** The best snorkeling off the coast of Ponce is on the uninhabited coast island of Caja de Muertos ("Coffin Island"). This isla got its name from an 18th-century French writer who noted that the island's shape resembled a cadaver in a coffin. Over the years there have been fanciful legends about the island, including tales of necrophilia, star-crossed lovers, and, of course, piracy. Island Adventures will take you to this remote spot for a full day's outing, with plenty of snorkeling. See "Ponce" in chapter 9.

• **Fajardo's Playa Escondido & La Cordillera:** On the eastern coast of Puerto Rico, the clear waters along the beachfront are the best on mainland

Puerto Rico for snorkeling. The best beach here for snorkeling is Playa Escondido, although the marine wildlife refuge known as La Cordillera right off the coast is even more alluring. See "Las Croabas" in chapter 11.

• Vieques & Culebra: For a quick preview of the underwater possibilities, refer to "The Best Beaches," earlier in this chapter. For more information, see chapter 12.

5 The Best Golf & Tennis

• **Westin Rio Mar Golf Course** (Palmer; © 787/888-6000): A 45-minute drive from San Juan on the northeast coast, the 6,145-yard (5,619m) Rio Mar Golf Course is shorter than those at both Palmas del Mar and Dorado East. One avid golfer recommended it to "those whose games and egos have been bruised by the other two courses." Wind here can seriously influence the outcome of your game. The greens fees are a lot lower than those of its two major competitors. See p. 146.

• **Hyatt Resort at Dorado** (Hyatt Dorado Beach Resort & Country Club; © 800/233-1234 or 787/796-1234): With 72 holes, Dorado has the highest concentration of golf on the island. Two courses—East and West—belong to the Hyatt. Dorado East is our favorite. Designed by Robert Trent Jones, Sr., it was the site of the Senior PGA Tournament of Champions throughout the 1990s. True tennis buffs head here, too. The Dorado courts are the best on the island, and both hotels sponsor tennis weeks and offer special tennis

packages. The Hyatt Dorado Beach Resort & Country Club weighs in with seven Laykold courts, two of them lighted. See p. 171. *Note:* This hotel is closing as we go to print, but its golf courses and tennis courts will remain open.

• **El Conquistador Resort & Golden Door Spa** (Las Croabas; © 800/468-5228 or 787/863-1000): This sprawling resort east of San Juan is one of the island's finest tennis retreats, with seven Har-Tru courts and a pro on hand to offer guidance and advice. If you don't have a partner, the hotel will find one for you. Only guests of the hotel are allowed to play here. See p. 223.

• **Palmas del Mar Country Club** (Humacao; © 787/285-2256): Lying on the southeast coast on the grounds of a former coconut plantation, the Palmas del Mar resort boasts the second-leading course in Puerto Rico—a par-72, 6,803-yard (6,221m) layout designed by Gary Player. Crack golfers consider holes 11 through 15 the toughest five successive holes in the Caribbean. See p. 226.

6 The Best Hikes

Bring your boots. Puerto Rico's mountainous interior offers ample opportunity for hiking and climbing, with many trails presenting spectacular panoramas at the least-expected moments. See "The Active Vacation Planner" in chapter 2 for detailed information.

• **El Yunque** (© 787/888-1880 for information): Containing the only tropical rainforest on U.S. soil, this Caribbean National Forest east of San Juan offers a number of walking and hiking trails. The rugged El Toro trail passes through four different forest systems en route to the 3,523-foot (1,074m) Pico El Toro, the highest peak in the forest. The El Yunque trail leads to three of the recreation area's most panoramic lookouts, and the Big Tree Trail is an easy walk to La Mina Falls. Just off the main road is La Coca Falls, a sheet of water cascading down mossy cliffs. See "El Yunque" in chapter 8.

- **Guánica State Forest** (© 787/724-3724 for information): At the opposite extreme of El Yunque's lush and wet rainforest, Guánica State Forest's climate is dry and arid, the Arizona-like landscape riddled with cacti. The area, cut off from the Cordillera Central mountain range, gets little rainfall. Yet it's home to some 50% of all the island's terrestrial bird species, including the rare Puerto Rican nightjar, once thought to be extinct. The forest has 36 miles (58km) of trails through four forest types. We prefer the mile-long (1.6km) Cueva Trail, where hikers look for the endangered bufo lemur toad, another species once thought to be extinct but still jumping in this area. Within the forest, El Portal Tropical Forest Center offers 10,000 square feet (929 sq. m) of exhibition space and provides information. See "Ponce" in chapter 9.

- **Mona Island:** Off the western coast of Puerto Rico, this fascinating island noted for its scuba-diving sites provides hiking opportunities found nowhere else in the Caribbean. Called the "Galápagos of Puerto Rico" because of its unique wildlife, Mona is home to giant iguanas and three species of endangered sea turtles. Some 20 endangered animals also have been spotted here. Eco-tourists like to hike among Mona's mangrove forests, coral reefs, cliffs, and complex honeycomb of caves, ever on the alert for the diversity of both plant and animal life, including 417 plant and tree species, some of which are unique and 78 of which are rare or endangered. More than 100 bird species (two unique) have been documented. Hikers can camp at Mona for $10 per night. Contact the **Puerto Rico Department of Natural Resources** (© 787/721-5495) for more information. See the box, "Mona Island: The Galápagos of Puerto Rico," in chapter 9.

7 The Best Natural Wonders

- **El Yunque** (© 787/888-1880): Forty-five minutes by road east of San Juan in the Luquillo Mountains and protected by the U.S. Forest Service, El Yunque is Puerto Rico's greatest natural attraction. Some 100 billion gallons of rain fall annually on this home to four forest types containing 240 species of tropical trees. Families can walk one of the dozens of trails that wind past waterfalls, dwarf vegetation, and miniature flowers, while the island's colorful parrots fly overhead. You can hear the sound of Puerto Rico's mascot, the *coquí,* a small frog. See "El Yunque" in chapter 8.

- **Río Camuy Caves** (© 787/898-3100): Some 2½ hours west of San Juan, visitors board a tram to descend into this forest-filled sinkhole at the mouth of the Clara Cave. They walk the footpaths of a 170-foot-high (52m) cave to a deeper sinkhole. Once they're inside, a 45-minute tour helps everyone, including kids, learn to differentiate stalactites from stalagmites. At the Pueblos sinkhole, a platform overlooks the Camuy River, passing through a network of cave tunnels. See "Arecibo & Camuy" in chapter 8.

- **Las Cabezas de San Juan Nature Reserve** (© **787/722-5882**): This 316-acre (128-hectare) nature reserve about 45 minutes from San Juan encompasses seven different ecological systems, including forestland, mangroves, lagoons, beaches, cliffs, and offshore coral reefs. Five days a week (Wed–Sun), the park staff conducts tours in Spanish and English, the latter at 2pm only. Each tour lasts 2½ hours and is conducted with electric trolleys that traverse most of the park. Tours end with a climb to the top of the still-working, 19th-century lighthouse for views over Puerto Rico's eastern coast and nearby Caribbean islands. Call to reserve space before going, as bookings are based on stringent restrictions as to the number of persons who can tour the park without damage to its landscape or ecology. See the box, "To the Lighthouse: Exploring Las Cabezas de San Juan Nature Reserve," in chapter 11.

8 The Best Family Resorts

Puerto Rico has a bounty of attractions, natural wonders, and resorts that welcome families who choose to play together. Here are some of the best.

- **Condado Plaza Hotel & Casino** (San Juan; © **800/468-8588** or 787/721-1000): This resort offers Camp Taíno, a regular program of activities and special events for children ages 5 to 12. The cost of $25 per child includes lunch. The main pool has a kids' water slide that starts in a Spanish castle turret, plus a toddler pool. For teenagers, the hotel has a video game room, tennis courts, and various organized activities. For the whole family, the resort offers two pools and opens onto a public beach. It also has the best collection of restaurants of any hotel on the Condado. See p. 84.
- **El San Juan Hotel & Casino** (San Juan; © **787/791-1000**): The grandest hotel in Puerto Rico lies on Isla Verde, the less-famous strip of beach connected to the Condado. Its Kids Klub features trained counselors and group activities for the 5- to 12-year-old set. A daily fee of $40 buys lunch and an array of activities. The hotel opens onto a good beachfront and has some of the best restaurants in San Juan. See p. 92.
- **El Conquistador Resort & Golden Door Spa** (Las Croabas; © **800/468-5228** or 787/863-1000): Located 31 miles (50km) east of San Juan, this resort offers Camp Coquí on Palomino Island for children 3 to 12 years of age. The hotel's free water taxi takes kids to the island for a half or full day of watersports and nature hikes. This resort has some of the best facilities and restaurants in eastern Puerto Rico. See p. 223.

9 The Best Honeymoon Resorts

- **El San Juan Hotel & Casino** (San Juan; © **787/791-1000**): If you want Vegas-style shows, gambling, nightlife, great restaurants, and the most famous beach in Puerto Rico, El San Juan is at your disposal. It has the most glamorous lobby in the Caribbean and is set on 12 acres (4.9 hectares) of Isla Verde, a strip of beach connected to the Condado. Options include a suite in the main tower with a whirlpool or your own private casita with a sunken Roman bath. The best deal is a package for 3 nights. A lot of freebies are thrown in, including champagne and tropical fruit, daily tennis, one dinner, continental breakfast, and two massages. See p. 92.

- **Ponce Hilton & Casino** (Ponce; ✆ **800/HILTONS** or 787/259-7676): A first-class act at Puerto Rico's "second city" on the south coast, this sprawling resort is set in an 80-acre (32-hectare) garden. On-site amenities include a casino and disco, plus a whirlpool, tennis courts, and a fitness room. The two restaurants serve the best food on the south coast. Five suites are ideal for honeymoons. A per-night package includes a bottle of champagne, truffles, chocolates, and fresh strawberries, as well as breakfast daily, plus $25 in casino chips. You also receive a coupon granting 50% off on your next visit. See p. 188.
- **Horned Dorset Primavera Hotel** (Rincón; ✆ **800/633-1857** or 787/ 823-4030): The most romantic place for a honeymoon on the island (unless you stay in a private villa somewhere), this small, tranquil estate lies on the Mona Passage in western Puerto Rico, a pocket of posh where privacy is almost guaranteed. Accommodations are luxurious in the Spanish neocolonial style. The property opens onto a long, secluded beach of white sand. There are no phones, TVs, or radios in the rooms to interfere with the soft sounds of pillow talk. This is a retreat for adults only, with no facilities for children. Seven-night packages, with all meals included and round-trip transfers from the airport, are featured. See p. 203.
- **El Conquistador Resort & Golden Door Spa** (Las Croabas; ✆ **800/ 468-5228** or 787/863-1000): If you're looking for good food and diversions rather than a tranquil retreat, El Conquistador is the best big-time resort on the island. Atop a 300-foot (91m) bluff in eastern Puerto Rico, it has virtually everything for outdoor play, including golf and tennis, but when you want seclusion, you can post the PRIVADO sign and the world is yours. Honeymoon packages, based on 3 nights and 4 days, include a fruit basket and champagne, one dinner in the room, two massages, and all breakfasts. See p. 223.

10 The Best Big Resort Hotels

- **Ritz-Carlton San Juan Hotel, Spa & Casino** (San Juan; ✆ **800/241-3333** or 787/253-1700): At last Puerto Rico has a Ritz-Carlton, and this truly deluxe, oceanfront property is one of the island's most spectacular resorts. Guests are pampered in a setting of elegance and beautifully furnished guest rooms. Hotel dining is second only to that at El San Juan, and a European-style spa features 11 treatments "for body and beauty." See p. 94.
- **El San Juan Hotel & Casino** (San Juan; ✆ **787/791-1000**): An opulent circular lobby sets the haute style at the Caribbean's most elegant resort. From its location along Isla Verde Beach, it houses some of the capital's finest restaurants and is the city's major entertainment venue. Guest rooms are tropically designed and maintained in state-of-the-art condition. See p. 92.
- **Westin Rio Mar Beach Golf Resort & Spa** (Rio Grande; ✆ **800/ WESTIN-1** or 787/888-6000): This $180-million 481-acre (195-hectare) resort, 19 miles (31km) east of the San Juan airport, is one of the three largest hotels in Puerto Rico. Despite its size, personal service and style are hallmarks of the property. Twelve

restaurants and lounges boast an array of cuisines. Along with its proximity to two golf courses, entertainment, such as an extensive program of live music, is a key ingredient in the hotel's success. See p. 176.

- **El Conquistador Resort & Golden Door Spa** (Las Croabas; © **800/ 468-5228** or 787/863-1000): The finest resort in Puerto Rico, this is a world-class destination—a sybaritic haven for golfers, honeymooners, families, and anyone else. Three intimate "villages" combine with one grand hotel, draped along 300-foot (91m) bluffs overlooking both the Atlantic and the Caribbean at Puerto Rico's northeastern tip. The 500 landscaped acres (202 hectares) include tennis courts, an 18-hole Arthur Hills–designed championship golf course, and a marina filled with yachts and charter boats. See p. 223.

11 The Best Moderately Priced Hotels

- **Gallery Inn at Galería San Juan** (San Juan; © **787/722-1808**): The most whimsically bohemian hotel in the Caribbean sits in the heart of the historic city. Once the home of an aristocratic Spanish family, it is today filled with verdant courtyards and adorned with sculptures, silk screens, and original paintings. Staying in one of the comfortable rooms here is like living in an art gallery. See p. 82.

- **At Wind Chimes Inn** (San Juan; © **800/946-3244** or 787/727- 4153): This renovated and restored Spanish manor house, a favorite with families, is one of the best guesthouses in the Condado district. The inn offers spacious rooms with kitchens, lies only a short block from Puerto Rico's most famous beach, and also features a pool. See p. 88.

- **Copamarina Beach Resort** (Caña Gorda; © **787/821-0505**): Near Ponce, this resort was once the private vacation retreat of local cement barons—the de Castro family. Today it's been converted into one of the best beach hotels along Puerto Rico's southern shore. In fact, its beach is one of the best in the area. Set in a palm grove, the resort is handsomely decorated and comfortably furnished, with a swimming pool and two tennis courts. See p. 213.

- **Lemontree Waterfront Suites** (Rincón; © **787/823-6452**): On a sandy beach at the windsurfing capital of the Caribbean, this colony offers large apartments with kitchenettes, ideal for families who like to prepare some of their own meals. See p. 204.

- **Hacienda Tamarindo** (Vieques; © **787/741-0420**): On the site of a 1990s nightclub, this expanded inn has style, flair, charm, and a desirable location—just inland from a great white sandy beach. Built around a massive 2-century-old tamarind tree and operated by a couple from Vermont, the inn has comfortable and appealing accommodations, which are often furnished with antiques. The welcome is warm. See p. 236.

12 The Best Attractions

- **The Historic District of Old San Juan:** There's nothing like it in the Caribbean. Partially enclosed by old walls dating from the 17th century, Old San Juan was designated a U.S. National Historic Zone in 1950.

Some 400 massively restored buildings fill this district, which is chockablock with tree-shaded squares, monuments, and open-air cafes as well as shops, restaurants, and bars. If you're interested in history, there is no better stroll in the West Indies. See "Seeing the Sights" in chapter 7.

- **Castillo de San Felipe del Morro** (Old San Juan): In Old San Juan and nicknamed El Morro, this fort was originally built in 1540. It guards the bay from a rocky promontory on the northwestern tip of the old city. Rich in history and legend, the site covers enough territory to accommodate a 9-hole golf course. See p. 128.

- **The Historic District of Ponce:** Second only to Old San Juan in terms of historical significance, the central district of Ponce is a blend of Ponce Creole and Art Deco building styles, dating mainly from the 1890s to the 1930s. One street, Calle Isabel, offers an array of Ponceño architectural styles, which often incorporate neoclassical details. The city underwent a massive restoration preceding the celebration of its 300th anniversary in 1996. See "Ponce" in chapter 9.

- **Museo de Arte de Ponce** (Ponce): This museum has the finest collection of European and Latin American art in the Caribbean. The building was designed by Edward Durell Stone, who also designed the Museum of Modern Art in New York City. Contemporary works by Puerto Ricans are displayed, as well as works by an array of old masters, including Renaissance and baroque pieces from Italy. See p. 181.

- **Tropical Agriculture Research Station:** These tropical gardens contain one of the largest collections of tropical species intended for practical use. These include cacao, fruit trees, spices, timbers, and ornamentals. Adjacent to the Mayagüez campus of the University of Puerto Rico, the site attracts botanists from around the world. See "Mayagüez" in chapter 9.

- **The City of San Germán:** In the southwestern corner of Puerto Rico and founded in 1512, this small town is Puerto Rico's second-oldest city. Thanks to a breadth of architectural styles, San Germán is also the second Puerto Rican city (after San Juan) to be included in the National Register of Historic Places. Buildings, monuments, and plazas fill a 36-acre (15-hectare) historic zone. Today's residents descend from the smugglers, poets, priests, and politicians who once lived here in "the city of hills," so-called because of the mountainous location. See "San Germán" in chapter 9.

- **Iglesia Porta Coeli** (San Germán): The main attraction of this ancient town is the oldest church in the New World. It was originally built by Dominican friars in 1606. The church resembles a working chapel, although Mass is held here only three times a year. Along the sides of the church are treasures gathered from all over the world. See "San Germán" in chapter 9.

13 The Best Restaurants

- **Aquaviva** (San Juan; ℂ 787/722-0665): Dauntingly stylish, this is one of the grand new restaurants of Puerto Rico, specializing in a Latin nouvelle cuisine with fresh seafood a specialty. You can count on the best catch of the day—the prime specimens—which are then prepared with consummate skill. See p. 105.

- **Barú** (San Juan; ℂ 787/977-7107): Fashionable and popular, this is a creative showcase for a fusion Caribbean and Mediterranean cuisine, occupying stately looking premises in the Old Town. Sterling craftsmanship marks a menu that includes, for example, five different kinds of carpaccio. See p. 105.

- **Parrot Club** (San Juan; ✆ 787/ 725-7370): This addition to the San Juan scene has already been acclaimed as one of the finest and most innovative restaurants on the island. Its chef serves a Nuevo Latino cuisine that is a happy medley of Puerto Rican delights, drawing upon the Spanish, African, and even Taíno influences of the island. Menu items are based on updated interpretations of old-fashioned regional dishes— everything from *criolla*-styled flank steak to a pan-seared tuna served with a sauce of dark rum and essence of oranges. See p. 107.

- **Ramiro's** (San Juan; ✆ 787/ 721-9049): Chef Jesús Ramiro has some of the most innovative cookery along the Condado beachfront strip, along with the city's best wine list. Ramiro has made his culinary reputation with such dishes as quail stuffed with lamb in a port sauce and lamb loin in a tamarind coriander sauce, both equally delectable. His dessert menu is two pages long and includes the town's best soufflés. His death-by-chocolate mousse on a green grape leaf is equaled only by his caramelized fresh mango napoleon. See p. 116.

- **Ajili Mójili** (San Juan; ✆ 787/ 725-9195): On the Condado beachfront, Ajili Mójili provides the most refined interpretation of classic Puerto Rican cookery on the island.

Locals find it evocative of the food they enjoyed at their mother's table, one example being *mofongos*—green plantains stuffed with veal, chicken, shrimp, or pork. The chefs take that cliché dish *arroz con pollo* (stewed chicken with saffron rice) and raise it to celestial levels. The restaurant takes its name from the lemon-garlic sweet chile salsa that's traditionally served here with fish or meat. See p. 116.

- **Mark's at the Meliá** (Ponce; ✆ 787/284-6275): Mark French has elevated Puerto Rican dishes to a new high at this endearing restaurant that also serves an impeccable international cuisine. He took over what was a backwater and turned the place into an enclave of refined dining with such imaginative and good-tasting dishes as tamarind barbecued lamb with yucca mojo. See p. 189.

- **La Cava** (in the Ponce Hilton, Ponce; ✆ 787/259-7676): The stellar restaurant of this first-class hotel, La Cava was designed to resemble a 19th-century coffee plantation. It's the most elegant restaurant along the southern tier, and it serves delectable international cuisine. From the ever-changing menu, you are likely to be served everything from grilled lamb sausage on a bed of couscous to tuna loin seared with sesame oil. See p. 189.

- **bbh** (Vieques; ✆ 787/741-1128): The best tapas in all of Puerto Rico are served at this restaurant at the elegant Bravo Beach Hotel. Tapas "by the sea" include everything from Jamaican jerk chicken to seared ahi tuna. See p. 241.

14 The Best Offbeat Travel Experiences

- **Attending a Cockfight:** Although a brutal sport that many find distasteful, cockfighting is legal in Puerto Rico and has its devotees. The most

authentic cockfights are in the town of Salinas in the southeast. But it's not necessary to go that far to witness one of these bouts. Three fights a week are held at the **Coliseo Gallistico,** Route 37 (© **787/791-6005**), in San Juan. Betting is heavy when these roosters take to the ring. See "San Juan After Dark" in chapter 8.

- **Diving off Mona Island** (Mayagüez): Surrounded by some of the most beautiful coral reefs in the Caribbean, Mona Island has the most pristine, extensive, and well-developed reefs in Puerto Rican waters. In fact, they have been nominated as a U.S. National Marine Sanctuary. The tropical marine ecosystem around Mona includes patch reefs, black coral, spore and groove systems, underwater caverns, deepwater sponges, fringing reefs, and algal reefs. The lush environment attracts octopuses, lobster, queen conch, rays, barracuda, snapper, jack, grunt, angelfish, trunkfish, filefish, butterfly fish, dolphin, parrotfish, tuna, flying fish, and more. The crystal waters afford exceptional horizontal vision from 150 to 200 feet (46–61m), as well as good views down to the shipwrecks that mark the site—including some Hispanic galleons. Five species of whales visit the island's offshore waters. See the box, "Mona Island: The Galápagos of Puerto Rico," in chapter 9.

- **Visiting Vieques & Culebra:** Puerto Rico's offshore islands—still relatively undiscovered by the modern world—remain an offbeat adventure, and they've got great beaches, too. The most developed is Vieques, which attracts visitors with its gorgeous stretches of sand with picnic facilities and shade trees. It is an ideal retreat for snorkelers and tranquillity seekers. The beaches are nearly always deserted, even though they are among the Caribbean's loveliest. Nearly three-quarters of the island is owned by the Fish & Wildlife

Service. The even-less-developed Culebra has a wildlife refuge, coral reefs, and Playa Flamenco, another of the Caribbean's finest beaches. And is it ever sleepy here! See chapter 12.

- **Spending the Evening at Mosquito (Phosphorescent) Bay** (Vieques Island): At any time except when there's a full moon, you can swim in glowing waters lit by dinoflagellates called *pyrodiniums* (whirling fire). These creatures light up the waters like fireflies, and swimming among them is one of the most unusual things to do anywhere—truly a magical, almost psychedelic experience. It's estimated that a gallon of bay water might contain about three-quarters of a million of these little glowing creatures. See chapter 12.

- **Sampling the Island's Nosh Pits:** Think of Puerto Rico as one gigantic fast-food joint, for no other island in the Caribbean offers such a delectable array of road-side eats. Snack food lies around virtually every turn in the road. As you drive throughout the island, stop and take your pick of the road-side dives. They may look junky, even trashy, but the food is often a delight—and cheap, too.

  You'll find succulent barbecued pig, *pastelillos* (pastry turnovers filled with meat, cheese, or seafood), *surullitos* (deep-fried cornmeal sticks), *alcapurrias* (a filling of fish or meat in a deep-fried casing of finely grated green plantains and taro root), *bacalaitos* (deep-fried codfish fritters), *papas rellenas* (stuffed potatoes), and *arañitas* ("little spiders"—actually, deep-fried clusters of shredded green plantains).

  You don't have to go far for barbecued pig—just head to the roadside food stands in Luquillo Beach, to the east of San Juan. It makes for a great picnic at the beach.

A truck stop, **Café Restaurant La Nueva Union,** 35 miles (56km) west of San Juan at the junction of Carretera 2 and Highway 22 between Arecibo and Hatillo, serves the most succulent traditional fare. Sample its fresh octopus salad, its meaty goat stew, and definitely its *guisados* (beef stew). Don't leave without an order of coconut flan.

If you make it all the way around the island to La Parguera, stop at **El Quenepo,** a lunch wagon parked under a towering *quenepa* (a tropical fruit tree) on Route 116 between routes 304 and 324. You can usually spot it by a line of cars letting passengers out to sample the delights from its crowded postage-stamp kitchen. El Quenepo offers a vast array of Puerto Rican specialties, many of which you may never have sampled before: cold codfish soup, even a green-bean omelet, and *piononos* (a "mountain" composed of fried eggs, plantain strips, and seasoned meat filling).

2

Planning Your Trip to Puerto Rico

This chapter discusses the where, when, and how of your trip to Puerto Rico—everything required to plan your trip and get it on the road. Here we've concentrated on what you need to do *before* you go.

1 The Regions in Brief

Although the many geological divisions of Puerto Rico might not be immediately apparent to the ordinary visitor, its people take great pride in the island's diversity. The most important geological and political divisions are detailed below.

SAN JUAN

The largest and best-preserved complex of Spanish colonial architecture in the Caribbean, Old San Juan (founded in 1521) is the oldest capital city under the U.S. flag. Once a lynchpin of Spanish dominance in the Caribbean, it has three major fortresses, miles of solidly built stone ramparts, a charming collection of antique buildings, and a modern business center. The city's economy is the most stable and solid in all of Latin America.

San Juan is the site of the official home and office of the governor of Puerto Rico (La Fortaleza), the 16th-century residence of Ponce de León's family, and several of the oldest places of Christian worship in the Western Hemisphere. Its bars, restaurants, shops, and nightclubs attract an animated group of fans. In recent years, the old city has become surrounded by densely populated modern buildings, including an ultramodern airport, which makes San Juan one of the most dynamic cities in the West Indies.

THE NORTHWEST: ARECIBO, RIO CAMUY, RINCON & MORE

A fertile area with many rivers bringing valuable water for irrigation from the high mountains of the Cordillera, the northwest also offers abundant opportunities for sightseeing. The region's districts include the following:

AGUADILLA Christopher Columbus landed near Aguadilla during his second voyage to the New World in 1493. Today the town has a busy airport, fine beaches, and a growing tourism-based infrastructure. It is also the center of Puerto Rico's lace-making industry, a craft imported here many centuries ago by immigrants from Spain, Holland, and Belgium.

ARECIBO Located on the northern coastline a 2-hour drive west of San Juan, Arecibo was originally founded in 1556. Although little remains of its original architecture, the town is well known to physicists and astronomers around the world because of the radar/radio-telescope that fills a concave depression between six of the region's hills. Equal in size to 13 football fields and operated jointly by the National Science Foundation and Cornell University, it studies the shape and formation of the galaxies by deciphering radio waves from space.

Puerto Rico

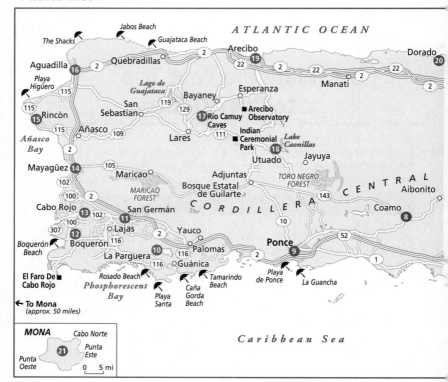

RINCON   Named after the 16th-century landowner Don Gonzalo Rincón, who donated its site to the poor of his district, the tiny town of Rincón is famous throughout Puerto Rico for its world-class surfing and beautiful beaches. The lighthouse that warns ships and boats away from dangerous offshore reefs is one of the most powerful on Puerto Rico.

RIO CAMUY CAVE PARK   Located near Arecibo, this park's greatest attraction is underground, where a network of rivers and caves provides some of the most enjoyable spelunking in the world. At its heart lies one of the largest known underground rivers. Aboveground, the park covers 300 acres (121 hectares).

UTUADO   Small and nestled amid the hills of the interior, Utuado is famous as the center of the hillbilly culture of Puerto Rico. Some of Puerto Rico's finest mountain musicians have come from Utuado and mention the town in many of their ballads. The surrounding landscape is sculpted with caves and lushly covered with a variety of tropical plants and trees.

DORADO & THE NORTH COAST

Playa Dorado, directly east of San Juan at Dorado, is actually a term for a total of six white-sand beaches along the northern coast, reached by a series of winding roads. Dorado is the island's oldest resort town, the center of golf, casinos, and a

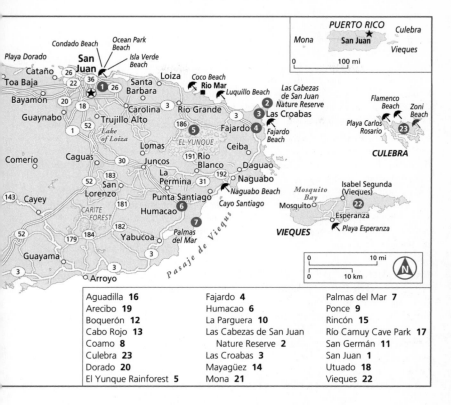

PUERTO RICO

Mona   San Juan   Culebra

Vieques

0   100 mi

Aguadilla **16**	Fajardo **4**	Palmas del Mar **7**
Arecibo **19**	Humacao **6**	Ponce **9**
Boquerón **12**	La Parguera **10**	Rincón **15**
Cabo Rojo **13**	Las Cabezas de San Juan	Río Camuy Cave Park **17**
Coamo **8**	Nature Reserve **2**	San Germán **11**
Culebra **23**	Las Croabas **3**	San Juan **1**
Dorado **20**	Mayagüez **14**	Utuado **18**
El Yunque Rainforest **5**	Mona **21**	Vieques **22**

once-major Hyatt resort that's closing as we go to print (p. 171). Luckily, the Hyatt's golf courses will remain open: 72 holes of golf, the greatest concentration in the Caribbean—all designed by Robert Trent Jones, Sr. The complex is quite family-friendly, with its Camp Coquí, which offers programs for children ages 3 to 12.

Another big resort poised to gain from the closing of the Hyatt Dorado: Wyndham El Conquistador Resort & Country Club at Palomino Island, a private island paradise with sandy beaches and recreational facilities. This resort lies near Las Croabas, a fishing village on the northeastern tip of Puerto Rico's north coast.

Challenging the El Conquistador is the Westin Rio Mar Beach Resort, Country Club & Ocean Villas, which lies 19 miles (31km) to the east of the Luis Muñoz Marín International Airport.

THE NORTHEAST: EL YUNQUE, A NATURE RESERVE & FAJARDO

The capital city of San Juan (see above) dominates Puerto Rico's northeast. Despite the region's congestion, there are still many remote areas, including some of the island's most important nature reserves. Among the region's most popular towns, parks, and attractions are the following:

EL YUNQUE The rainforest in the Luquillo Mountains, 25 miles (40km) east of San Juan, El Yunque is a favorite escape from the capital. Teeming with plant and animal life, it is a sprawling tropical forest (actually a national forest) whose ecosystems are strictly protected. Some 100 billion gallons of rainwater fall here each year, allowing about 250 species of trees and flowers to flourish.

FAJARDO Small and sleepy, this town was originally established as a supply depot for the many pirates who plied the nearby waters. Today, a host of private yachts bob at anchor in its harbor, and the many offshore cays provide visitors with secluded beaches. From Fajardo, ferryboats make choppy but frequent runs to the offshore islands of Vieques and Culebra.

LAS CABEZAS DE SAN JUAN NATURE RESERVE About an hour's drive from San Juan, this is one of the island's newest ecological refuges. It was established in 1991 on 316 acres (128 hectares) of forest, mangrove swamp, offshore cays, coral reefs, and freshwater lagoons—a representative sampling of virtually every ecosystem on Puerto Rico. There is a visitor center, a 19th-century lighthouse (El Faro) that still works, and ample opportunity to forget the pressures of urban life.

THE SOUTHWEST: PONCE, MAYAGÜEZ, SAN GERMAN & MORE

One of Puerto Rico's most beautiful regions, the southwest is rich in local lore, civic pride, and natural wonders.

BOQUERON Famous for the beauty of its beach and the abundant birds and wildlife in the nearby Boquerón Forest Reserve, this sleepy village is now ripe for large-scale tourism-related development. During the early 19th century, the island's most-feared pirate, Roberto Cofresi, terrorized the Puerto Rican coastline from a secret lair in a cave nearby.

CABO ROJO Established in 1772, Cabo Rojo reached the peak of its prosperity during the 19th century, when immigrants from around the Mediterranean, fleeing revolutions in their own countries, arrived to establish sugar-cane plantations. Today, cattle graze peacefully on land originally devoted almost exclusively to sugar cane, and the area's many varieties of exotic birds draw bird-watchers from throughout North America. Even the offshore waters are fertile; it's estimated that nearly half of all the fish consumed on Puerto Rico are caught in waters near Cabo Rojo.

LA PARGUERA Named after a breed of snapper (*pargos*) that abounds in the waters nearby, La Parguera is a quiet coastal town best known for the phosphorescent waters of *La Bahía Fosforescente* (Phosphorescent Bay). Here, sheltered from the waves of the sea, billions of plankton (luminescent dinoflagellates) glow dimly when they are disturbed by movements of the water. The town comes alive on weekends, when crowds of young people from San Juan arrive to party the nights away. Filling modest rooming houses, they temporarily change the texture of the town as bands produce loud sessions of salsa music.

MAYAGÜEZ The third-largest city on Puerto Rico, Mayagüez is named after the *majagua*, the Amerindian word for a tree that grows abundantly in the area. Because of an earthquake that destroyed almost everything in town in 1917, few old buildings remain. The town is known as the commercial and industrial capital of Puerto Rico's western sector. Its botanical garden is among the finest on the island.

PONCE Puerto Rico's second-largest city, Ponce has always prided itself on its independence from the Spanish-derived laws and taxes that governed San Juan and the rest of the island. Long-ago home of some of the island's shrewdest traders, merchants, and smugglers, it is enjoying a renaissance as citizens and visitors rediscover its unique cultural and architectural charms. Located on Puerto Rico's southern coast, about 90 minutes by car from the capital, Ponce contains a handful of superb museums, one of the most charming main squares in the Caribbean, an ancient cathedral, dozens of authentically restored colonial-era buildings, and a number of outlying mansions and villas that, at the time of their construction, were among the most opulent on the island.

SAN GERMAN Located on the island's southwestern corner, small, sleepy, and historic San Germán was named after the second wife of Ferdinand of Spain, Germaine de Foix, whom he married in 1503. San Germán's central church, Iglesia Porta Coeli, was built in 1606. At one time, much of the populace was engaged in piracy, pillaging the ships that sailed off the nearby coastline. The central area of this village is still sought out for its many reminders of the island's Spanish heritage and colonial charm.

THE SOUTHEAST: PALMAS DEL MAR & MORE

The southeastern quadrant of Puerto Rico has some of the most heavily developed, as well as some of the least developed, sections of the island.

COAMO Although today Coamo is a bedroom community for San Juan, originally it was the site of two different Taíno communities. Founded in 1579, it now has a main square draped with bougainvillea and one of the best-known Catholic churches on Puerto Rico. Even more famous, however, are the mineral springs whose therapeutic warm waters helped President Franklin D. Roosevelt during his recovery from polio. (Some historians claim that these springs inspired the legend of the Fountain of

Youth, which in turn set Ponce de León off on his vain search of Florida.)

HUMACAO Because of its easy access to San Juan, this small, verdant inland town has increasingly become one of the capital's residential suburbs.

PALMAS DEL MAR This sprawling vacation and residential resort community is located near Humacao. A splendid golf course covers some of the grounds. Palmas del Mar is at the center of what has been called the "New American Riviera"— 3 miles (4.8km) of white-sand beaches on the eastern coast of the island. Palmas del Mar is the largest resort in Puerto Rico, lying to the south of Humacao on 2,800 acres (1,133 hectares) of a former coconut plantation—now devoted to luxury living and the sporting life.

The Equestrian Center at Palmas is the finest riding headquarters in Puerto Rico, with trails cutting through an old plantation and jungle along the beach. The resort is ideal for families and has a supervised summer activities program for children ages 5 to 12.

THE OFFSHORE ISLANDS: CULEBRA, VIEQUES & MORE

Few *norteamericanos* realize that Puerto Rico has at least four well-known islands and a multitude of tiny cays lying offshore. The most famous of these are:

CAYO SANTIAGO Lying off the southeastern coast is the small island of Cayo Santiago. Home to a group of about two dozen scientists and a community of rhesus monkeys originally imported from India, the island is a medical experimentation center run by the U.S. Public Health Service. Monkeys are studied in a "wild" but controlled environment both for insights into the behavioral sciences and for possible cures for such maladies as diabetes and arthritis. Casual visitors are not permitted on Cayo Santiago, but they can cruise along the shore and watch the monkeys.

CULEBRA & VIEQUES Located off the eastern coast, these two islands are among the most unsullied and untrammeled areas in the West Indies, even though Vieques is being belatedly discovered. Come here for sun, almost no scheduled activities, fresh seafood, clear waters, sandy beaches, and teeming coral reefs. Vieques is especially proud of its phosphorescent bay, Mosquito Bay.

MONA Remote, uninhabited, and teeming with bird life, this barren island off the western coast is ringed by soaring cliffs and finely textured white-sand beaches. The island has almost no facilities, so visitors seldom stay for more than a day of swimming and picnicking. The surrounding waters are legendary for their dangerous eddies, undertows, and sharks.

2 Visitor Information

For information before you leave home, visit **www.gotopuertorico.com** or contact one of the following **Puerto Rico Tourism Company** offices: 666 Fifth Ave., New York, NY 10013 (© **800/ 866-7827** or 212/586-6262); 3575 W. Cahuenga Blvd., Suite 620, Los Angeles, CA 90068 (© **800/866-7827** or 323/ 874-5991); or 901 Ponce de León Blvd., Suite 101, Coral Gables, FL 33134 (© **800/815-7391** or 305/445-9112); and in Puerto Rico, La Princesa Building, Paseo La Princesa 2, Old San Juan, PR 00902 (© **800/866-7827** or 787/721-2400).

In Canada contact the company at 230 Richmond St. W., #902, Toronto, ON M5V 1V6 (© **416/368-2680** or 800/667-0394).

One of the best Caribbean websites is **Caribbean-On-Line** (www.caribbean-on-line.com), a series of virtual guidebooks full of information on hotels, restaurants, and shopping, along with sights and detailed maps of the islands. The site also includes links to travel agents and cruise lines that are up on the Web.

Other helpful websites include **Municipality of Ponce** (www.ponceweb.org), **Municipality of Rincón** (www. rincon.org), **Municipality of Vieques** (www.vieques.com), **Welcome to Puerto Rico** (www.welcometopuertorico.org), **Discover Culebra** (www.culebra-island. com), and **Puerto Rico Travel Maps** (www.travelmaps.com).

You might also want to contact the U.S. State Department for background bulletins, which supply up-to-date information on crime, health concerns, import restrictions, and other travel matters. Write the **Superintendent of Documents, U.S. Government Printing Office,** Washington, DC 20402 (© **866/ 512-1800** or 202/512-1800).

A good travel agent can be a source of information. Make sure your agent is a member of the American Society of Travel Agents (ASTA). If you get poor service from an ASTA agent, you can write to the **ASTA—The American Society of Travel Agents,** 1101 King St., Alexandria, VA 22314 (© **703/739-2782;** www.astanet.com).

3 Entry Requirements & Customs

ENTRY REQUIREMENTS
DOCUMENTS Because Puerto Rico is a commonwealth, **U.S. citizens** coming from mainland destinations do not need any documents to enter Puerto Rico. It is the same as crossing from

Georgia into Florida. They do not need to carry proof of citizenship or to produce documents. However, because of new airport security measures, it is necessary to produce a government-issued photo ID (federal, state, or local) to board a plane; this is most often a driver's license.

Be sure to carry plenty of documentation. You might need to show a government-issued photo ID (federal, state, or local) at various airport checkpoints. Be sure that your ID is *up-to-date:* an expired driver's license or passport, for example, might keep you from boarding a plane.

Visitors from **other countries,** including Canada, need a valid passport to land in Puerto Rico. For those from countries requiring a visa to enter the U.S., the same visa is necessary to enter Puerto Rico, unless these nationals are coming directly from the U.S. mainland and have already cleared U.S. Immigration and Customs there.

VACCINATIONS Vaccinations are not required for entry to Puerto Rico if you're coming from the United States or Canada.

Infectious hepatitis has been reported on other Caribbean islands but less frequently on Puerto Rico. Consult your doctor about the advisability of getting a gamma-globulin shot before you leave home.

Typhoid, poliomyelitis, and tetanus are not common diseases on the island, and inoculations against them are recommended mainly to visitors who plan to rough it in the wilds. If you're staying in a regular Puerto Rican hotel, such preventive measures are generally not needed, but your doctor can advise you based on your destination and travel plans.

CUSTOMS

U.S. citizens do not need to clear Puerto Rican Customs upon arrival by plane or ship from the U.S. mainland. All non–U.S. citizens must clear Customs and are permitted to bring in items intended for their personal use, including tobacco, cameras, film, and a limited supply of liquor (usually 40 oz.).

WHAT YOU CAN TAKE HOME

U.S. CUSTOMS On departure, U.S.-bound travelers must have their luggage inspected by the U.S. Agriculture Department because laws prohibit bringing fruits and plants to the U.S. mainland. Fruits and vegetables are not allowed, but otherwise, you can bring back as many purchased goods as you want without paying duty.

For specifics on what you can bring back, download the invaluable free pamphlet *Know Before You Go* online at **www.cbp.gov.** (Click on "Travel," and then click on "Know Before You Go! Online Brochure.") Or contact the **U.S. Customs & Border Protection (CBP),** 1300 Pennsylvania Ave., NW, Washington, DC 20229 (✆ 877/287-8667) and request the pamphlet.

For a clear summary of **Canadian** rules, write for the booklet *I Declare,* issued by the **Canada Border Services Agency** (✆ 800/461-9999 in Canada, or 204/983-3500; www.cbsa-asfc.gc.ca). Canada allows its citizens a C$750 exemption, and you're allowed to bring back duty-free one carton of cigarettes, one can of tobacco, 40 imperial ounces of liquor, and 50 cigars. In addition, you're allowed to mail gifts to Canada valued at less than C$60 a day, provided they're unsolicited and don't contain alcohol or tobacco (write on the package "Unsolicited gift, under $60 value"). All valuables should be declared on the Y-38 form before departure from Canada, including serial numbers of valuables you already own, such as expensive foreign cameras. Note: The C$750 exemption can only be used once a year and only after an absence of 7 days.

U.K. citizens returning from **a non-E.U. country** have a customs allowance of: 200 cigarettes; 50 cigars; 250 grams of smoking tobacco; 2 liters of still table wine; 1 liter of spirits or strong liqueurs (over 22% volume); 2 liters of fortified wine, sparkling wine or other liqueurs; 60cc (ml) perfume; 250cc (ml) of toilet water; and £145 worth of all other goods, including gifts and souvenirs. People under 17 cannot have the tobacco or alcohol allowance. For more information, contact **HM Revenue & Customs** at ✆ **0845/010-9000** (from outside the U.K., 020/8929-0152), or consult their website at www.hmrc.gov.uk.

The duty-free allowance in **Australia** is A$900 or, for those under 18, A$450. Citizens can bring in 250 cigarettes or 250 grams of loose tobacco, and 2.25 liters of alcohol. If you're returning with valuables you already own, such as foreign-made cameras, you should file form B263. A helpful brochure available from Australian consulates or Customs offices is *Know Before You Go*. For more information, call the **Australian Customs Service** at ✆ **1300/363-263,** or log on to www.customs.gov.au.

The duty-free allowance for **New Zealand** is NZ$700. Citizens over 17 can bring in 200 cigarettes, 50 cigars, or 250 grams of tobacco (or a mixture of all three if their combined weight doesn't exceed 250g); plus 4.5 liters of wine and beer, or 1.125 liters of liquor. New Zealand currency does not carry import or export restrictions. Fill out a certificate of export, listing the valuables you are taking out of the country; that way, you can bring them back without paying duty. Most questions are answered in a free pamphlet available at New Zealand consulates and Customs offices: *New Zealand Customs Guide for Travellers, Notice no. 4.* For more information, contact **New Zealand Customs Service,** The Customhouse, 17–21 Whitmore St., Box 2218, Wellington (✆ **04/473-6099** or 0800/428-786; www.customs.govt.nz).

4 Money

CURRENCY The U.S. dollar is the coin of the realm. Keep in mind that once you leave Ponce or San Juan, you might have difficulty finding a place to exchange foreign money (unless you're staying at a large resort), so it's wise to handle your exchange needs before you head off into rural parts of Puerto Rico.

ATMs ATMs are linked to a network that most likely includes your bank at home. **Cirrus** (✆ **800/424-7787;** www.mastercard.com) and **Plus** (✆ **800/843-7587;** www.visa.com) are the two most popular networks in the U.S.; call or check online for ATM locations at your destination. Be sure you know your four-digit PIN before you leave home and be sure to find out your daily withdrawal limit before you depart. You can also get cash advances on your credit card at an ATM. Keep in mind that credit card companies try to protect themselves from theft by limiting the funds someone can withdraw away from home; it's therefore best to call your credit card company before you leave and let them know where you're going and how much you plan to spend. You'll get the best exchange rate if you withdraw money from an ATM, but keep in mind that many banks impose a fee every time a card is used at an ATM in a different city or bank. On top of this, the bank from which you withdraw cash may charge its own fee.

CURRENCY EXCHANGE The currency exchange facilities at any large international bank within Puerto Rico's larger cities can exchange non–U.S. currencies for dollars. You can also exchange money at the Luis Muñoz Marín International Airport. Also, you'll find foreign-exchange facilities in large hotels and at the many banks in Old San Juan or Avenida Ashford in Condado. In Ponce, look for foreign-exchange facilities at large resorts and at banks such as **Banco Popular,** Plaza Las Delicias (✆ **787/843-8000**).

TRAVELER'S CHECKS Traveler's checks are something of an anachronism from the days before the ATM made cash accessible at any time. Given the fees you'll pay for ATM use at banks other than your own, however, you might be better off with traveler's checks if you're withdrawing money often.

What Things Cost in Puerto Rico	US$	UK£	CD$
Taxi from Airport to Condado	13.00	6.85	14.90
Average Taxi Fare within San Juan	6.00	3.20	6.90
Typical Bus Fare within San Juan	25¢–50¢	13p–26p	29¢–57¢
Local Telephone Call	10¢	5p	11¢
Double Room at the Condado Plaza (very expensive)	350.00	184.00	401.00
Double Room at El Canario by the Lagoon (moderate)	115.00	60.50	132.00
Double Room at Wind Chimes Inn (inexpensive)	99.00	52.00	113.00
Lunch for One at Amadeus (moderate)	16.00	8.40	18.30
Lunch for One at Fatty's (inexpensive)	10.00	5.25	11.45
Dinner for One at Ramiro's (very expensive)	50.00	26.30	57.30
Dinner for One at Ostra Cosa (moderate)	26.00	13.70	29.80
Dinner for One at La Bombonera (inexpensive)	12.00	6.30	13.75
Bottle of Beer in a Bar	3.00	1.60	3.45
Glass of Wine in a Restaurant	4.00	2.10	4.60
Roll of ASA 100 Color Film (36 exp.)	8.50	4.50	9.75
Movie Ticket	5.00	2.60	5.75
Theater Ticket	15.00–75.00	7.90–39.45	17.20–85.95

You can get traveler's checks at almost any bank. **American Express** offers denominations of $20, $50, $100, $500, and (for cardholders only) $1,000. You'll pay a service charge ranging from 1% to 4%. You can also get American Express traveler's checks over the phone by calling 🕿 **800/221-7282;** Amex gold and platinum cardholders who use this number are exempt from the 1% fee.

Visa offers traveler's checks at Citibank locations nationwide, as well as at several other banks. The service charge ranges between 1.5% and 2%; checks come in denominations of $20, $50, $100, $500, and $1,000. Call 🕿 **800/732-1322** for information. AAA members can obtain Visa checks for a $9.95 fee (for checks, minimum of $300 up to $1,500) at most AAA offices or by calling 🕿 **866/339-3378. MasterCard** also offers traveler's checks. Call 🕿 **800/223-9920** for a location near you.

CREDIT CARDS Credit cards are invaluable when you're traveling. They are a safe way to carry money and provide a convenient record of all your expenses. You can also withdraw cash advances from your credit cards at any bank (though you'll start paying hefty interest on the advance the moment you receive the cash). At most banks, you don't even need to go to a teller; you can get a cash advance at the ATM if you know your PIN. If you've forgotten yours, or didn't even know you had one, call the number on the back of your credit card and ask the card issuer to send it to you. It usually takes 5 to 7 business days, though some banks will provide the number over the phone if you tell them your mother's maiden name or pass some other security clearance.

In San Juan and at all the big resorts on the island, even some of the smaller inns, credit cards are commonly accepted. However, as you tour through rural areas and if you intend to patronize small, out-of-the-way establishments, it's wise to carry sufficient amounts of the Yankee dollar. Visa and MasterCard are accepted most widely throughout Puerto Rico.

For tips and telephone numbers to call if your wallet is stolen or lost, go to "Lost & Found" in the "Fast Facts: Puerto Rico" section, later in this chapter.

5 When to Go

CLIMATE

Puerto Rico has one of the most unvarying climates in the world. Temperatures year-round range from 75 to 85°F (24–29°C). The island is wettest and hottest in August, averaging 81°F (27°C) and 7 inches of rain. San Juan and the northern coast seem to be cooler and wetter than Ponce and the southern coast. The coldest weather is in the high altitudes of the Cordillera, the site of Puerto Rico's lowest recorded temperature—39°F (4°C).

THE HURRICANE SEASON

The hurricane season, the curse of Puerto Rican weather, lasts—officially, at least—from June 1 to November 30. But there's no cause for panic. In general, satellite forecasts give adequate warnings so that precautions can be taken.

If you're heading to Puerto Rico during the hurricane season, you can call your local branch of the **National Weather Service** (listed in your phone directory under the U.S. Department of Commerce) for a weather forecast.

It'll cost 95¢ per query, but you can get information about the climate conditions in any city you plan to visit by calling ℂ **800/WEATHER.** When you're prompted, enter your Visa or MasterCard account number and then punch in the name of any of 1,000 cities worldwide whose weather is monitored by the **Weather Channel** (www.weather.com).

THE "SEASON"

In Puerto Rico, hotels charge their highest prices during the peak winter period from mid-December to mid-April, when visitors fleeing from cold northern climates flock to the islands. Winter is the driest season along the coasts but can be wet in mountainous areas.

If you plan to travel in the winter, make reservations 2 to 3 months in advance. At certain hotels it's almost impossible to book accommodations for Christmas and the month of February.

SAVING MONEY IN THE OFF SEASON

Puerto Rico is a year-round destination. The island's "off season" runs from late spring to late fall, when temperatures in the mid-80s (about 29°C) prevail throughout most of the region. Trade winds ensure comfortable days and nights, even in accommodations without air-conditioning. Although the noonday sun may raise the temperature to around 90°F (32°C), cool breezes usually make the morning, late afternoon, and evening

Average Temperatures on Puerto Rico

	Jan	Feb	Mar	Apr	May	June	July	Aug	Sept	Oct	Nov	Dec
Temp. (°F)	75	75	76	78	79	81	81	81	81	81	79	77
Temp. (°C)	25	24	24	24.4	25.6	26	27	27	27	27	27	26

more comfortable here than in many parts of the U.S. mainland.

Dollar for dollar, you'll spend less money by renting a summer house or fully equipped unit in Puerto Rico than you would on Cape Cod, Fire Island, Laguna Beach, or the coast of Maine.

The off season in Puerto Rico—roughly from mid-April to mid-December (rate schedules vary from hotel to hotel)—amounts to a summer sale. In most cases, hotel rates are slashed from 20% to a startling 60%. It's a bonanza for cost-conscious travelers, especially families who like to go on vacations together. In the chapters ahead, we'll spell out in dollars the specific amounts hotels charge during the off season.

OTHER OFF-SEASON ADVANTAGES

Although Puerto Rico may appear inviting in the winter to those who live in northern climates, there are many reasons your trip may be much more enjoyable if you go in the off season:

- After the winter hordes have left, a less-hurried way of life prevails. You'll have a better chance to appreciate the food, culture, and local customs.
- Swimming pools and beaches are less crowded—perhaps not crowded at all.
- Year-round resort facilities are offered, often at reduced rates, which may include snorkeling, boating, and scuba diving.
- To survive, resort boutiques often feature summer sales, hoping to clear the merchandise they didn't sell in February to accommodate stock they've ordered for the coming winter.
- You can often appear without a reservation at a top restaurant and get a table for dinner, a table that in winter would have required a reservation far in advance. Also, when waiters are less hurried, you get better service.

- The endless waiting game is over: no waiting for a rented car (only to be told none is available), no long wait for a golf course tee time, and quicker access to tennis courts and watersports.
- Some package-tour fares are as much as 20% lower, and individual excursion fares are also reduced between 5% and 10%.
- All accommodations and flights are much easier to book.
- Summer is an excellent time for family travel, not usually possible during the winter season.
- The very best of Puerto Rican attractions remain undiminished in the off season—sea, sand, and surf, with lots of sunshine.

OFF-SEASON DISADVANTAGES

Let's not paint too rosy a picture. Although the advantages of off-season travel far outweigh the disadvantages, there are nevertheless drawbacks to traveling in summer:

- You might be staying at a construction site. Hoteliers save their serious repairs and their major renovations until the off season, when they have fewer clients. That means you might wake up early in the morning to the sound of a hammer.
- Single tourists find the cruising better in winter, when there are more clients, especially the unattached. Families predominate in summer, and there are fewer chances to meet fellow singles than in the winter months.
- Services are often reduced. In the peak of winter, everything is fully operational. But in summer, many of the programs such as watersports might be curtailed. Also, not all restaurants and bars are fully operational at all resorts. For example, for lack of business, certain gourmet or

specialty dining rooms might be shut down until house count merits reopening them. In all, the general atmosphere is more laid-back when a hotel or resort might also be operating with a reduced staff. The summer staff will still be adequate to provide service for what's up and running.

HOLIDAYS

Puerto Rico has many public holidays when stores, offices, and schools are closed: New Year's Day, January 6 (Three Kings Day), Washington's Birthday, Good Friday, Memorial Day, July 4th, Labor Day, Thanksgiving, Veterans Day, and Christmas, plus such local holidays as Constitution Day (July 25) and Discovery Day (Nov 19). Remember, U.S. federal holidays are holidays in Puerto Rico, too.

PUERTO RICO CALENDAR OF EVENTS

January

Three Kings Day, islandwide. On this traditional gift-giving day in Puerto Rico, there are festivals with lively music, dancing, parades, puppet shows, caroling troubadours, and traditional feasts. January 6.

San Sebastián Street Festival, Calle San Sebastián in Old San Juan. Nightly celebrations with music, processions, crafts, and typical foods, as well as graphic arts and handicraft exhibitions. For more information, call ℂ 787/721-2400. Mid-January.

February

San Blas de Illescas Half Marathon, Coamo. International and local runners compete in a challenging 13-mile (21km) half-marathon in the hilly south-central town of Coamo. Call **Delta Phi Delta Fraternity** (ℂ 787/ 825-4077). Early February.

Coffee Harvest Festival, Maricao. Folk music, a parade of floats, typical foods, crafts, and demonstrations of coffee preparation in Maricao, a 1-hour drive east of Mayagüez. For more information, call ℂ **787/838-2290** or 787/267-5536. Second week of February.

Carnival Ponceño, Ponce. The island's Carnival celebrations feature float parades, dancing, and street parties. One of the most vibrant festivities is held in Ponce, known for its masqueraders wearing brightly painted horned masks. For more information, call ℂ **787/284-4141.** Mid-February.

Casals Festival, Performing Arts Center in San Juan. Sanjuaneros and visitors alike eagerly look forward to the annual Casals Festival, the Caribbean's most celebrated cultural event. When renowned cellist Casals died in Puerto Rico in 1973 at the age of 97, the Casals Festival was 16 years old and attracting the same class of performers who appeared at the Pablo Casals Festival in France, founded by Casals after World War II. When he moved to Puerto Rico in 1957 with his wife, Marta Casals Istomin (former artistic director of the John F. Kennedy Center for the Performing Arts), he founded not only this festival but also the Puerto Rico Symphony Orchestra to foster musical development on the island.

Ticket prices for the Casals Festival range from $30 to $40. A 50% discount is offered to students, people over 60, and persons with disabilities. Tickets are available through the **Performing Arts Center** in San Juan (ℂ 787/721-7727). Information is also available from the **Casals Festival** (ℂ 787/721-8370; www.festcasalspr. gobierno.pr). The festivities take place late February to early March.

March

Emancipation Day, islandwide. Commemoration of the emancipation of Puerto Rico's slaves in 1873, held at various venues. March 22.

April

Good Friday and Easter, islandwide. Celebrated with colorful ceremonies and processions. April 6 to April 8, 2007.

José de Diego Day, islandwide. Commemoration of the birthday of José de Diego, patriot, lawyer, writer, orator, and political leader who was the first president of the Puerto Rico House of Representatives under U.S. rule. April 17.

Sugar Harvest Festival, San Germán. This festival marks the end of the island's sugar harvest, with live music, crafts, and typical foods, as well as exhibitions of sugar-cane plants and past and present harvesting techniques. Late April.

May

Puerto Rican Danza Week *(Semana de la "Danza" Puertorriqueña),* Convento de los Dominicos, Old San Juan. This week commemorates what is, perhaps, the most expressive art form in the Puerto Rican culture: danza music and dance. Throughout Danza Week, live performances and conferences are held at Convento de los Dominicos's indoor patio. The building is located on Old San Juan's Cristo Street. For information, call *(€* **800/866-7827** or 787/721-2400. Second week of May

Heineken JazzFest, San Juan. The annual jazz celebration is staged at Parque Sixto Escobar. Each year a different jazz theme is featured. The open-air pavilion is in a scenic oceanfront location in the Puerta de Tierra section of San Juan, near the Hilton. For more information, call *(€* **787/ 277-9200.** End of May through the beginning of June.

June

San Juan Bautista Day, islandwide. Puerto Rico's capital and other cities celebrate the island's patron saint with weeklong festivities. At midnight, San-juaneros and others walk backward into the sea (or nearest body of water) three times to renew good luck for the coming year. June 24.

Aibonito Flower Festival, at Road 721 next to the City Hall Coliseum, in the central mountain town of Aibonito. This annual flower-competition festival features acres of lilies, anthuriums, carnations, roses, gardenias, and begonias. For more information, call *(€* **787/735-3871.** Last week in June and first week in July.

July

Luis Muñoz Rivera's Birthday, islandwide. A birthday celebration commemorating Luis Muñoz Rivera (1829–1916), statesman, journalist, poet, and resident commissioner in Washington, D.C. July 15.

El Gigante Marathon, Adjuntas. This 9¼-mile (15km) race starts at Puerta Bernasal and finishes at Plaza Pública. For more information call *(€* **787/ 829-3114.** Sunday before July 25.

Loíza Carnival. This annual folk and religious ceremony honors Loíza's patron saint, John *(Santiago)* the Apostle. Colorful processions take place, with costumes, masks, and *bomba* dancers (the bomba has a lively Afro-Caribbean dance rhythm). This jubilant celebration reflects the African and Spanish heritage of the region. For more information, call *(€* **787/ 876-3570.** Late July through early August.

August

Cuadragésimo Cuarto Torneo de Pesca Interclub del Caribe, Cangrejos Yacht Club. This international blue-marlin fishing tournament features crafts, music, local delicacies, and other activities. For more information, call *(€* **787/791-1015.** Mid-August.

International Billfish Tournament, at Club Náutico, San Juan. This is one of the premier game-fishing tournaments and the longest consecutively held bill-fish tournament in the world. Fishermen from many countries angle for blue marlin that can weigh up to 900 pounds (408 kilograms). For specific dates and information, call © 787/722-0177. Late August to early September.

October

La Raza Day (Columbus Day), islandwide. This day commemorates of Columbus's landing in the New World. October 12.

National Plantain Festival, Corozal. This annual festivity involves crafts, paintings, agricultural products, exhibition, and sale of plantain dishes; *neuva trova* music and folk ballet are performed. For more information, call © 787/859-3060. Mid-October.

November

Start of Baseball Season, in Hiram Bithorn Park in San Juan and throughout the island. Six Puerto Rican professional clubs compete. Professionals from North America also play here from December to January. For more information, contact **Professional Baseball of Puerto Rico** (© 787/765-6285). Early November.

Festival of Puerto Rican Music, San Juan. Annual classical and folk music festival. One of its highlights is a *cuatro*-playing contest. (A *cuatro* is a guitar-like instrument with 10 strings.) For more information, call © 787/721-5274. First week in November.

Jayuya Indian Festival, Jayuya. This fiesta features the culture and tradition of the island's original inhabitants, the Taíno Indians, and their music, food, and games. More than 100 artisans exhibit and sell their works. There is also a Miss Taíno Indian Pageant. For more information, call © 787/828-1241. Second week of November.

Puerto Rico Discovery Day, island-wide. This day commemorates the "discovery" by Columbus in 1493 of the already inhabited island of Puerto Rico. Columbus is thought to have come ashore at the northwestern municipality of Aguadilla, although the exact location is unknown. November 19.

December

Old San Juan's White Christmas Festival, Old San Juan. Special musical and artistic presentations take place in stores, with window displays. December 1 through January 12.

Bacardi Artisans' Fair, San Juan. The best and largest artisans' fair on the island features more than 100 artisans who turn out to exhibit and sell their wares. The fair includes shows for adults and children, a Puerto Rican troubadour contest, rides, and typical food and drink—all sold by nonprofit organizations. It is held on the grounds of the world's largest rum-manufacturing plant in Cataño, an industrial suburb set on a peninsula jutting into San Juan Bay. For more information, call © 787/788-1500. First two Sundays in December.

Las Mañanitas, Ponce. A religious procession that starts out from Lolita Tizol Street and moves toward the city's Catholic church, led by mariachis singing songs to honor Our Lady of Guadalupe, the city's patron saint. The lead song is the traditional Mexican birthday song, *Las Mañanitas.* There's a 6am Mass. For more information, contact **Ponce City Hall** (© 787/284-4141). December 12.

Lighting of the Town of Bethlehem, between San Cristóbal Fort and Plaza San Juan Bautista in Old San Juan. This is the time that the most dazzling Christmas lights go on, and many islanders themselves drive into San

Juan to see this dramatic lighting, the finest display of lights in the Caribbean at Christmas. During the Christmas season.

Hatillo Masks Festival, Hatillo. This tradition, celebrated since 1823, represents the biblical story of King Herod's ordering the death of all infant boys in an attempt to kill the baby Jesus. Men with colorful masks and costumes represent the soldiers, who run or ride through the town from early morning, looking for the children. Food, music, and crafts exhibits in the town square. For more information, call © **787/262-2093.** December 28.

YEAR-ROUND FESTIVALS

In addition to the individual events described above, Puerto Rico has two yearlong series of special events.

Many of Puerto Rico's most popular events are during the **Patron Saint Festivals** *(fiestas patronales)* in honor of the patron saint of each municipality. The festivities, held in each town's central plaza, include religious and costumed processions, games, local food, music, and dance.

At **Festival La Casita,** prominent Puerto Rican musicians, dance troupes, and orchestras perform; puppet shows are staged; and painters and sculptors display their works. It happens every Saturday at Puerto Rico Tourism's "La Casita" Tourism Information Center, Plaza Darsenas, across from Pier 1, Old San Juan.

For more information about all these events, contact the **Puerto Rico Tourism Company,** 666 Fifth Ave., New York, NY 10103 (© **800/ 866-7827** or 212/586-6262).

6 The Active Vacation Planner

Dorado Beach, Cerromar Beach, and Palmas del Mar are the chief centers for golf, tennis, and beach life. San Juan's hotels on the Condado–Isla Verde coast also generally offer a complete array of watersports.

BOATING & SAILING

The waters off Puerto Rico provide excellent boating in all seasons. Winds average 10 to 15 knots virtually year-round. Marinas provide facilities and services on par with any others in the Caribbean, and many have powerboats or sailboats for rent, crewed, or bareboat charter.

Major marinas include the **San Juan Bay Marina,** Fernandez Juncos Avenue (© 787/721-8062); **Marina Puerto Chico,** at Puerto Chico (© 787/863-0834); and **Marina de Salinas** (© 787/752-8484) in Salinas. The Caribbean's largest and most modern marina, **Puerto del Rey,** Route 3, Km 51.4 (© 787/860-1000), is located on the island's east coast, in Fajardo.

One of the sailing regattas in Puerto Rico is the Copa Velasco Regatta for ocean racing, at Palmas del Mar in Humacao.

For the typical visitor interested in watersports—not the serious yachter—

Beach Warning

Don't go walking along the beaches at night, even as tempting as it may be to do with your lover. Even if you find the secluded, hidden beach of your dreams, proceed with caution. On unguarded beaches, you will have no way to protect yourself or your valuables should you be approached by a robber or mugger, which happens frequently.

Camping in Puerto Rico

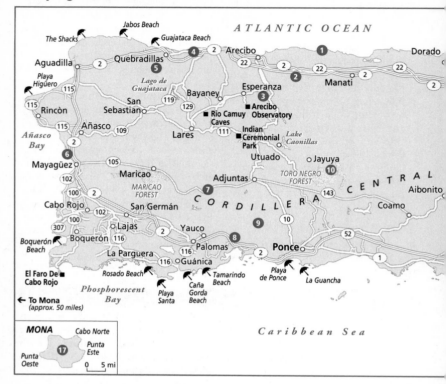

our favorite place for fun in the surf is the aptly named **San Juan Water Fun,** Isla Verde Beach in back of the Wyndham El San Juan Hotel and Casino, Avenida Isla Verde in Isla Verde, San Juan (✆ **787/644-2585**). Here you can rent everything from a two-seater kayak for $30 per hour to a banana boat that holds eight passengers and costs $15 per person for a 20-minute ride.

If you're staying in eastern Puerto Rico, the best place for watersports rentals is **Iguana Water Sports,** Westin Rio Mar Beach Resort, 6000 Rio Mar Blvd., Rio Grande (✆ **787/888-6000**), which has the island's best selection of small boats. Waverunners cost $100 per hour, and two-seat kayaks go for $35 per hour.

For more serious boating needs, we head for **Karolette Charter,** Palmas del Mar, AB-12 St., Route 3, Km 86.4, Humacao (✆ **787/850-7442**). You can be taken out on a snorkeling cruise for $107 per person for 4½ hours. More serious fishermen can book an entire boat, which holds six comfortably and costs $680 for 4½ hours or $840 for 6 hours.

CAMPING

Puerto Rico abounds in sandy beaches and forested hillsides that are suitable for erecting a tent. It is best and safest to camp only in the sites maintained by the government-sponsored **Companias de Parques Nacionales.** (See the map "Camping in Puerto Rico," above.) Some

Arroyo **12**	
Cambalache State Forest **2**	Monte Guilarte State Forest **7**
Carite State Forest **11**	Punta Maracayo **4**
Cerro Gordo **1**	Rio Abajo State Forest **3**
El Yunque Rainforest **13**	Seven Seas **14**
Flamenco Beach **15**	Sun Bay **16**
Guajataca State Forest **5**	Susua State Forest **8**
Isla de Mona Wildlife Refuge **17**	Toro Negro Forest Reserve **10**
Lago Lucchetti Wildlife Refuge **9**	Tres Hermanos Beach **6**

of these are simple places where you erect your own tent, although they are outfitted with electricity and running water; some are simple cabins, sometimes with fireplaces. Showers are communal. To stay at a campsite costs between $15 and $25 per night per tent. For more information and an application to rent one of the units or reserve a site, call © **787/622-5200.**

Many sites offer very basic cabins for rent. Each cabin is equipped with a full bathroom, a stove, a refrigerator, two beds, and a table and chairs. However, most of your cooking will probably be tastier if you do it outside at one of the on-site barbecues. In nearly all cases, you must provide your own sheets and towels.

You might want to camp along or near a lovely beach. On the western coast of Puerto Rico, the best camping site is **Tres Hermanos Beach,** which opens onto Anasco Bay, lying between Rincón to the north and Mayagüez to the south.

Heading west from San Juan en route to Isabella, there are two excellent beach camps: **Cerro Gordo,** east of the city of Arecibo, and **Punta Maracayo,** to the west of Arecibo, both reached along Route 22. The Atlantic waters here are turbulent, even in summer.

If you'd like to camp in the east of Puerto Rico, the finest site is the beach at **Seven Seas** to the south of Fajardo.

Take Me Out to the *Beisbol* Game

Baseball has a long, illustrious history in Puerto Rico. Imported around the turn of the 20th century by plantation owners as a leisure activity for workers, *beisbol* quickly caught fire, and local leagues have produced such major-league stars as Roberto Alomar, Bernie Williams, and the late great Roberto Clemente.

A top-notch league of six teams—featuring many rising professionals honing their skills during the winter months—begins its season in October and plays in ballparks throughout Puerto Rico. Many baseball fans from the U.S. mainland come down specifically to see these teams play. For a chance to see good baseball in a more intimate setting than is afforded in the U.S. major leagues, call **Professional Baseball of Puerto Rico** (© 787/765-6285) for information about professional games and, if available, a schedule.

Arroyo on the southern coast to the east of the town of Guayama is yet another site on mainland Puerto Rico that has both cabins and regular campsites, although this location is a bit bare-boned.

Both Culebra and Vieques offer camping by the beach. The best for camping on Culebra is **Flamenco Beach,** on the north shore. On Vieques, the best beach camping is at **Sun Bay,** on the island's south coast.

For information about camping on or near a beach, call © 787/721-2800.

Puerto Rico also allows camping in various state forests, provided that permits are obtained. Except for cabins at Monte Guilarte State Forest, which cost $20 per night, camping sites are available at $5 per person. For further information about permits, call the **forest service office** at San Juan Bay Marina (© 787/724-3724).

There are seven major on-island camping sites in various state forests: **Cambalache State Forest,** near Barceloneta; **Carite State Forest,** near Patillas; **Guajataca State Forest,** near Quebradillas; **Monte Guilarte State Forest,** near Adjuntas; **Susua State Forest,** near Yauco; **Río Abajo State Forest,** near

Arecibo; and our favorite, **Toro Negro Forest Reserve,** near Villaba, where you can camp in the shadow of Puerto Rico's highest peaks.

In addition, the **Caribbean National Forest/El Yunque** allows primitive camping within the rainforest. For more information, call © 787/888-1810.

It's also possible to camp at either of two wildlife refuges, **Isla de Mona Wildlife Refuge** (© 787/724-3724), lying some 50 miles (81km) off the rough seas of Mona Passage, and at **Lago Lucchetti Wildlife Refuge** (© 787/844-4660), between Yauco and Ponce.

The **Parks and Recreation Association of Puerto Rico** (© 787/721-2800) can provide you with a map and detailed instructions about how to reach all these sites.

DEEP-SEA FISHING

The offshore fishing here is top-notch! Allison tuna, white and blue marlin, sailfish, wahoo, dolphin, mackerel, and tarpon are some of the fish that can be caught in Puerto Rican waters, where some 30 world records have been broken.

Charter arrangements can be made through most major hotels and resorts. In

San Juan, **Benitez Fishing Charters** sets the standard by which to judge other captains (see "Diving, Fishing, Tennis & Other Outdoor Pursuits" in chapter 7). In Palmas del Mar, which has some of the best year-round fishing in the Caribbean, you'll find **Capt. Bill Burleson** (see "Palmas del Mar" in chapter 11).

GOLF

Home to 13 golf courses, including eight championship links, Puerto Rico is justifiably known as the "Scotland of the Caribbean." In fact, the 72 holes at the **Hyatt Dorado Beach Resort & Country Club** (p. 171) offer the greatest concentration of golf in the Caribbean. (*Note:* though the Hyatt is closing as we go to print, its golf courses and tennis courts will remain open.) The courses at the Hyatt are among the 25 best courses created by Robert Trent Jones, Sr. Jack Nicklaus rates the challenging 13th hole at the Hyatt Dorado as one of the top 10 in the world. See chapter 8 for more details.

On the southeast coast, crack golfers consider holes 11 through 15 at the **Golf Club at Palmas del Mar** (p. 226) to be the toughest 5 successive holes in the Caribbean. At **El Conquistador Resort & Golden Door Spa** (p. 223), the spectacular $250-million resort at Las Croabas east of San Juan, the course's 200-foot (61m) changes in elevation provide panoramic vistas. With the exception of the El Conquistador Resort and Country Club, these courses are open to the public. See chapter 11 for more details on the major golf clubs east of San Juan.

HIKING

The mountainous interior of Puerto Rico provides ample opportunities for hill climbing and nature treks. These are especially appealing because panoramas open at the least-expected moments, often revealing spectacular views of the distant sea.

The most popular, most beautiful, and most spectacular trekking spot is **El Yunque,** the sprawling "jungle" maintained by the U.S. Forest Service and the only rainforest on U.S. soil.

El Yunque is part of the **Caribbean National Forest,** which lies a 45-minute drive east of San Juan. More than 250 species of trees and some 200 types of ferns have been identified here. Some 60 species of birds inhabit El Yunque, including the increasingly rare Puerto Rican parrot. Such rare birds as the elfin woods warbler, the green mango hummingbird, and the Puerto Rican lizard-cuckoo live here.

Park rangers have clearly marked the trails that are ideal for walking. See "El Yunque" in chapter 8 for more details.

A lesser forest, but one that is still intriguing to visit, is the **Maricao State Forest,** near the coffee town of Maricao. This forest is in western Puerto Rico, east of the town of Mayagüez. For more details, see "Mayagüez" in chapter 8.

Ponce is the best center for exploring some of the greatest forest reserves in the Caribbean Basin, notably **Toro Negro Forest Reserve** with its **Lake Guineo** (the lake at the highest elevation on the island), the **Guánica State Forest,** ideal for hiking and bird-watching, and the **Carite Forest Reserve,** a 6,000-acre (2,428-hectare) park known for its dwarf forest. For more details, see "Ponce" in chapter 9.

Equally suitable for hiking are the protected lands (especially the **Río Camuy Cave Park**) whose topography is characterized as "karst"—that is, limestone riddled with caves, underground rivers, and natural crevasses and fissures. Although these regions pose additional risks and technical problems for trekkers, some people prefer the opportunities they provide for exploring the territory both above and below its surface. See "Arecibo & Camuy" in chapter 8 for details about the Río Camuy Caves.

For more information about any of the national forest reserves of Puerto Rico, call the **Department of Sports & Recreation** at © 787/721-2800.

Aventuras Tierra Adentro (© 787/766-0470; www.aventuraspr.com) offers the best island adventure tours, focusing on hiking through virgin forests, rock climbing, or cliff jumping. Four different adventures are offered, costing $150 per person, which includes transportation from San Juan. Most of the jaunts take place on weekends. Scuba Diving & Snorkeling

SCUBA DIVING The continental shelf, which surrounds Puerto Rico on three sides, is responsible for an abundance of coral reefs, caves, sea walls, and trenches for scuba diving and snorkeling.

Open-water reefs off the southeastern coast near **Humacao** are visited by migrating whales and manatees. Many caves are located near Isabela on the west coast. The **Great Trench,** off the island's south coast, is ideal for experienced open-water divers. Caves and the sea wall at **La Parguera** are also favorites. **Vieques** and **Culebra islands** have coral formations. **Mona Island** offers unspoiled reefs at depths averaging 80 feet (24m); seals are one of the attractions. Uninhabited islands, such as **Icacos,** off the northeastern coast near Fajardo, are also popular with both snorkelers and divers.

These sites are now within reach because many of Puerto Rico's dive operators and resorts offer packages that include daily or twice-daily dives, scuba equipment, instruction, and excursions to Puerto Rico's popular attractions.

In San Juan, **Caribe Aquatic Adventures** offers an array of sailing, scuba, and snorkeling trips, as well as boat charters and fishing (see "Diving, Fishing, Tennis & Other Outdoor Pursuits" in chapter 7).

Elsewhere on the island, several other companies offer scuba and snorkeling instruction. We provide details in each chapter.

SNORKELING Because of its over-population, the waters around San Juan aren't the most ideal for snorkeling. In fact, the entire north shore of Puerto Rico fronts the Atlantic, where the waters are often turbulent. Windsurfers—not snorkelers—gravitate to the waves and surf in the northwest.

The most ideal conditions for snorkeling in Puerto Rico are along the shores of the remote islands of **Vieques** and **Culebra** (see chapter 12).

The best snorkeling on the main island is found near the town of **Fajardo,** to the east of San Juan and along the tranquil eastern coast (see chapter 11).

The calm, glasslike quality of the clear Caribbean along the south shore is also ideal for snorkeling. The most developed tourist mecca here is the city of Ponce. Few rivers empty their muddy waters into the sea along the south coast, resulting in gin-clear waters offshore. You can snorkel off the coast without having to go on a boat trip. One good place is at **Playa La Parguera,** where you can rent snorkeling equipment from kiosks along the beach. This beach lies east of the town of Guánica, to the east of Ponce. Here tropical fish add to the brightness of the water, which is generally turquoise. The addition of mangrove cays in the area also makes La Parguera more alluring for snorkelers. Another good spot for snorkelers is **Caja de Muertos** off the coast of Ponce. Here a lagoon coral reef boasts a large number of fish species (see chapter 9).

SURFING

Puerto Rico's northwest beaches attract surfers from around the world. Called the "Hawaii of the East," Puerto Rico has hosted a number of international competitions. October through February are the best surfing months, but the sport is enjoyed in Puerto Rico from August through April. The most popular areas are from Isabela around Punta Borinquén to Rincón—at beaches such as Wilderness, Surfers, Crashboat, Los Turbos in Vega Baja, Pine Grove in Isla Verde, and La Pared in Luquillo. Surfboards are available at many watersports shops.

International competitions held in Puerto Rico have included the 1968 and 1988 World Amateur Surfing Championships, the annual Caribbean Cup Surfing Championship, and the 1989 and 1990 Budweiser Puerto Rico Surfing Challenge events.

TENNIS

Puerto Rico has approximately 100 major tennis courts. Many are at hotels and resorts; others are in public parks throughout the island. Several paradores also have courts. A number of courts are lighted for nighttime play.

In San Juan, the **Caribe Hilton** and the **Condado Plaza Hotel & Casino** have tennis courts. Also in the area are the **public courts** at the San Juan Central Municipal Park. See chapter 7. The **Hyatt Dorado Beach Resort & Country Club** maintains a total of 21 courts. (*Note:* The property is closing as we go to print, but the golf courses and tennis courts will remain open.) See chapter 8.

WINDSURFING

The best windsurfing is found at Punta Las Marias in the Greater San Juan metropolitan area. Other spots on the island for windsurfing include Santa Isabel, Guanica, and La Parguera in the south; Jobos and Shacks in the northwest, and the island of Culebra off the eastern coast. The best advice and equipment rental is available at **Velauno,** Calle Loíza 2430, Punta Las Marias in San Juan (*©* **787/ 728-8716**).

7 Travel Insurance

If you're buying travel insurance, expect to pay between 5% and 8% of the vacation itself. You can get estimates from various providers through **InsureMyTrip. com.** Enter your trip cost and dates, your age, and other information, for prices from more than a dozen companies.

TRIP-CANCELLATION INSURANCE

Trip-cancellation insurance will help retrieve your money if you have to back out of a trip or depart early, or if your travel supplier goes bankrupt. Permissible reasons for trip cancellation can range from sickness to natural disasters. In this unstable world, trip-cancellation insurance is a good buy if you're purchasing tickets well in advance—who knows what the state of the world, or of your airline, will be in 9 months? Insurance policy details vary, so read the fine print and make sure that your airline or cruise line is on the list of carriers covered in case of bankruptcy. A

good resource is **"Travel Guard Alerts,"** a list of companies considered high-risk by Travel Guard International (see website below). Protect yourself further by paying for the insurance with a credit card—by law, consumers can get their money back on goods and services not received if they report the loss within 60 days after the charge is listed on their credit card statement.

Note: Many tour operators, particularly those offering trips to remote or high-risk areas, include insurance in the total trip cost or can arrange insurance policies through a partnering provider, which is a convenient and often cost-effective way for the traveler to obtain insurance. Make sure the tour company is a reputable one, however, and be aware that some experts suggest you avoid buying insurance from the tour or cruise company you're traveling with. They contend it's more secure to buy from a "third party" than to put all your money in one place.

For more information, contact one of the following recommended insurers: **Access America** (© 866/807-3982; www.accessamerica.com); **Travel Guard International** (© 800/826-4919; www.travelguard.com); **Travel Insured International** (© 800/243-3174; www.travelinsured.com); and **Travelex Insurance Services** (© 888/457-4602; www.travelex-insurance.com).

MEDICAL INSURANCE

Most health insurance policies cover you if you get sick away from home, but they are not likely to provide for medical evacuation in case of life-threatening injury or illness. It's a good idea to buy a travel insurance policy that provides for **emergency medical evacuation.** If you have to buy a one-way same-day ticket home and forfeit your nonrefundable round-trip ticket, you might be out big bucks. And the cost of a flying ambulance could wipe out your life's savings.

Check with your insurer, particularly if you're insured by an HMO, about the extent of its coverage while you're overseas. With the exception of certain HMOs and Medicare/Medicaid, your medical insurance should cover medical treatment—even hospital care—overseas. However, most out-of-country hospitals make you pay your bills upfront, and they send you a refund after you've returned home and filed the necessary paperwork.

If you require additional insurance, try one of the following companies:

- **MEDEX International** (© 888/MEDEX-00 or 410/453-6300; fax 410/453-6301; www.medexassist.com)
- **Travel Assistance International** (© 800/821-2828; www.travelassistance.com); for general information on services, call the company's Worldwide Assistance Services, Inc. at © **800/777-8710.**
- **The Divers Alert Network (DAN)** (© **800/446-2671** or 919/684-2948; www.diversalertnetwork.org)

LOST-LUGGAGE INSURANCE

On domestic flights, checked baggage is covered up to $2,500 per ticketed passenger. On international flights (including U.S. portions of international trips), baggage coverage is limited to approximately $9.07 per pound, up to approximately $635 per checked bag. If you plan to check items more valuable than what's covered by the standard liability, see if your homeowner's policy covers your valuables; get baggage insurance as part of your comprehensive travel-insurance package. Don't buy insurance at the airport, where it's usually overpriced. Be sure to take any valuables or irreplaceable items with you in your carry-on luggage, because many valuables (including books, money, and electronics) aren't covered by airline policies.

If your luggage is lost, immediately file a lost-luggage claim at the airport, detailing the luggage contents. Most airlines require that you report delayed, damaged, or lost baggage within 4 hours of arrival. The airlines are required to deliver luggage, once found, directly to your house or destination free.

8 Health & Safety

STAYING HEALTHY

Puerto Rico poses no major health problem for most travelers. If you have a chronic condition, however, you should check with your doctor before visiting the islands. For conditions such as epilepsy,

diabetes, or heart problems, wear a **MedicAlert Identification Tag** (© **800/825-3785;** www.medicalert.org), which will immediately alert doctors to your condition and give them access to your records through MedicAlert's 24-hour hot line.

Warning   **Dengue Fever**

Although mosquitoes are a nuisance, they do not carry malaria in Puerto Rico. However, after a long absence, the dreaded dengue fever has returned to Puerto Rico. The disease is transmitted by the Aede mosquito, and its symptoms include fever, headaches, pain in the muscles and joints, skin blisters, and hemorrhaging. Most of its victims lack any defense against it. You should wear bug spray at all times, especially on beaches and on the islands of Vieques and Culebra.

Finding a good doctor in Puerto Rico is easy, and most speak English. See "Fast Facts: Puerto Rico" later in this chapter for the locations of hospitals.

If you worry about getting sick away from home, consider purchasing **medical travel insurance** and carry your ID card in your purse or wallet. In most cases, your existing health plan will provide the coverage you need. See "Travel Insurance," above, for more information.

Contact the **International Association for Medical Assistance to Travelers (IAMAT)** (© 716/754-4883 or, in Canada, 416/652-0137; www.iamat.org) for tips on travel and health concerns in the countries you're visiting, and for lists of local, English-speaking doctors. The United States **Centers for Disease Control and Prevention** (© 800/311-3435; www.cdc.gov) provides up-to-date information on health hazards by region or country and offers tips on food safety. The website **www.tripprep.com**, sponsored by a consortium of travel medicine practitioners, may also offer helpful advice on traveling abroad. You can find listings of reliable clinics overseas at the **International Society of Travel Medicine** (www.istm.org).

It's best to stick to **bottled mineral water** here. Although tap water is said to be safe to drink, many visitors experience diarrhea, even if they follow the usual precautions. The illness usually passes quickly without medication if you eat simply prepared food and drink only mineral water until you recover. If symptoms persist, consult a doctor.

The **sun** can be brutal, especially if you haven't been exposed to it in some time. Experts advise that you limit your time on the beach the first day. If you do overexpose yourself, stay out of the sun until you recover. If your exposure is followed by fever or chills, a headache, or a feeling of nausea or dizziness, see a doctor.

Sandflies (or "no-see-ums") are one of the biggest insect menaces in Puerto Rico. They appear mainly in the early evening, and even if you can't see these tiny bugs, you sure can "feel-um," as any native Puerto Rican will attest. Screens can't keep them out, so you'll need to use your favorite insect repellent.

Hookworm and other **intestinal parasites** are relatively common in the Caribbean, though you are less likely to be affected in Puerto Rico than on other islands. Hookworm can be contracted by just walking barefoot on an infected beach. *Schistosomiasis* (also called *bilharzia*), caused by a parasitic fluke, can be contracted by submerging your feet in rivers and lakes infested with a certain species of snail.

Puerto Rico has been especially hard hit by **AIDS.** Exercise *at least* the same caution in choosing your sexual partners, and in practicing safe sex, as you would at home.

STAYING SAFE

The U.S. State Department issues no special travel advisories for the Commonwealth of Puerto Rico, the way it might for, say, the more troubled island of Jamaica. However, there are problems in Puerto Rico, especially muggings along San Juan's Condado and Isla Verde beaches. Auto theft and cars getting broken into are other major problems. Do not leave valuables in cars, even when the doors are locked.

Take precautions about leaving valuables on the beach, and exercise extreme care if you're searching for a remote beach where there's no one in sight. The only person lurking nearby might be someone not interested in surf and sand but a robber waiting to make off with your possessions.

Avoid wandering around the darkened and relatively deserted alleys and small streets of San Juan's Old Town at night, especially a section called El Callejón, near the intersection of calles San Sebastián and Tanca. Be especially careful along the narrow alley that connects this intersection with Calle Norzagaray. The district attracts more drug dealers than any other spot in Puerto Rico. A number of muggings also occur in Old Town's Cementerio de San Juan.

9 Specialized Travel Resources

TRAVELERS WITH DISABILITIES

Most disabilities shouldn't stop anyone from traveling. There are more options and resources out there today than ever before.

The Americans with Disabilities Act is enforced as strictly in Puerto Rico as it is on the U.S. mainland—in fact, a telling example of the act's enforcement can be found in Ponce, where the sightseeing trolleys are equipped with ramps and extra balustrades to accommodate travelers with disabilities. Unfortunately, hotels rarely give much publicity to the facilities they offer persons with disabilities, so it's always wise to contact the hotel directly, in advance, if you need special facilities. Tourist offices usually have little data about such matters.

You can obtain a free copy of *Air Transportation of Handicapped Persons,* published by the U.S. Department of Transportation. Write for *Free Advisory Circular No. AC12032,* Distribution Unit, U.S. Department of Transportation, Publications Division, 3341Q 75 Ave., Landover, MD 20785. No phone requests are accepted, but you can write for a copy of the publication or download it for free at http://isddc.dot.gov.

The U.S. National Park Service offers a Golden Access Passport that gives free lifetime entrance to U.S. national parks, including those in Puerto Rico, for persons who are blind or permanently disabled, regardless of age. You can pick up a Golden Access Passport at any NPS entrance fee area by showing proof of medically determined disability and eligibility for receiving benefits under federal law. Besides free entry, the Golden Access Passport also offers a 50% discount on federal-use fees charged for such facilities as camping, swimming, parking, boat launching, and tours. For more information, go to www.nps.gov/fees_passes.htm or call © 888/467-2757.

Many travel agencies offer customized tours and itineraries for travelers with disabilities. **Flying Wheels Travel** (© 507/451-5005; www.flyingwheelstravel.com) offers escorted tours and cruises that emphasize sports and private tours in minivans with lifts. **Access-Able Travel Source** (© 303/232-2979; www.access-able.com) offers extensive access information and advice for traveling around the world with disabilities. **Accessible Journeys** (© 800/846-4537 or 610/521-0339; www.disabilitytravel.com) caters specifically to slow walkers and wheelchair travelers and their families and friends.

Organizations that offer assistance to disabled travelers include **MossRehab**

(800/CALL-MOSS; www.mossresource net.org), which provides a library of accessible-travel resources online; the **American Foundation for the Blind (AFB)** (© 800/232-5463 or 212/502-7600; www.afb.org), a referral resource for the blind or visually impaired that includes information on traveling with Seeing Eye dogs; and **SATH** (Society for Accessible Travel & Hospitality) (© 212/447-7284; www.sath.org; annual membership fees: $45 adults, $30 seniors and students), which offers a wealth of travel resources for all types of disabilities and informed recommendations on destinations, access guides, travel agents, tour operators, vehicle rentals, and companion services. **AirAmbulanceCard.com** is now partnered with SATH and allows you to pre-select top-notch hospitals in case of an emergency for $195 a year ($295 per family), among other benefits.

For more information specifically targeted to travelers with disabilities, the community website **iCan** (www.ican online.net) has destination guides and several regular columns on accessible travel. Also check out the quarterly magazine *Emerging Horizons* (www.emerging horizons.com; $14.95 per year, $19.95 outside the U.S.); and *Open World* magazine, published by SATH (see above; subscription: $13 per year, $21 outside the U.S.).

A tip for British travelers: The **Royal Association for Disability and Rehabilitation (RADAR),** Unit 12, City Forum, 250 City Rd., London, EC1V 8AF (© 020/7250-3222; fax 020/7250-0212; www.radar.org.uk), publishes information for travelers with disabilities.

GAY & LESBIAN TRAVELERS

Puerto Rico is the most gay-friendly destination in the Caribbean, with lots of accommodations, restaurants, clubs, and bars that actively cater to a gay clientele. A free monthly newsletter, *Puerto Rico Breeze,* lists items of interest to the island's gay community. It's distributed at the Atlantic Beach Hotel (p. 88) and many of the gay-friendly clubs mentioned in this book.

The **International Gay & Lesbian Travel Association (IGLTA;** © 800/448-8550 or 954/776-2626; www.iglta. org) links travelers up with gay-friendly hoteliers, tour operators, and airline and cruise-line representatives. It offers monthly newsletters, marketing mailings, and a membership directory that's updated once a year. Membership is $225 yearly, plus a $100 administration fee for new members.

Above and Beyond Tours (© 800/397-2681; www.abovebeyondtours.com) offers gay and lesbian tours worldwide and is the exclusive gay and lesbian tour operator for United Airlines.

Now, Voyager (© 800/255-6951; www.nowvoyager.com) is a San Francisco–based gay-owned and -operated travel service.

Olivia Cruises & Resorts (© 800/631-6277; www.olivia.com) charters entire resorts and ships for exclusive lesbian vacations and offers smaller group experiences for both gay and lesbian travelers. (In 2005, tennis great Martina Navratilova was named Olivia's official spokesperson.)

Gay.com Travel (© 800/929-2268 or 415/644-8044; www.gay.com/travel or www.outandabout.com), is an excellent online successor to the popular *Out & About* print magazine. It provides regularly updated information about gay-owned, gay-oriented, and gay-friendly lodging, dining, sightseeing, nightlife, and shopping establishments in every important destination worldwide. It also offers trip-planning information for gay and lesbian travelers for more than 50 destinations, along various themes, ranging from Sex & Travel to Vacations for Couples.

The following travel guides are available at many bookstores, or you can order them from any online bookseller: ***Spartacus International Gay Guide*** (Bruno Gmünder Verlag; www.spartacusworld. com/gayguide) and ***Odysseus: The International Gay Travel Planner*** (Odysseus Enterprises Ltd.), both good, annual, English-language guidebooks focused on gay men; and the ***Damron*** guides (www.damron.com), with separate, annual books for gay men and lesbians.

SENIOR TRAVEL

Mention the fact that you're a senior when you first make your travel reservations. All major airlines and many Puerto Rican hotels offer discounts for seniors.

Though much of the island's sporting and nightlife activity is geared toward youthful travelers, Puerto Rico also has much to offer the senior. The best source of information for seniors is the Puerto Rico Tourism Company (see "Visitor Information," earlier in this chapter), or, if you're staying in a large resort hotel, talk to the activities director or the concierge.

Members of **AARP,** 601 E St. NW, Washington, DC 20049 (℗ **888/687-2277** or 202/434-2277; www.aarp.org), get discounts on hotels, airfares, and car rentals. AARP offers members a wide range of benefits, including *AARP: The Magazine* and a monthly newsletter. Anyone over 50 can join.

The **U.S. National Park Service** offers a **Golden Age Passport** that gives seniors 62 years or older lifetime entrance to U.S. national parks for a one-time processing fee of $10. The pass must be purchased in person at any NPS facility that charges an entrance fee. Besides free entry, a Golden Age Passport also offers a 50% discount on federal-use fees charged for such facilities as camping, swimming, parking, boat launching, and tours. For more information, click onto www.nps.gov or call ℗ **888/467-2757.**

Grand Circle Travel (℗ **800/221-2610** or 617/350-7500; fax 617/346-6700; www.gct.com) offers package deals for the 50-plus market, mostly of the tour-bus variety, with free trips thrown in for those who organize groups of 10 or more.

SAGA Holidays (℗ **800/343-0273;** www.sagaholidays.com) offers tours and cruises for those 50 and older. SAGA also offers a number of single-traveler tours.

Recommended publications offering travel resources and discounts for seniors include: the quarterly magazine *Travel 50 & Beyond* (www.travel50andbeyond.com); *Travel Unlimited: Uncommon Adventures for the Mature Traveler* (Avalon); *101 Tips for Mature Travelers,* available from Grand Circle Travel (℗ **800/221-2610** or 800/959-0405; www.gct.com); and *Unbelievably Good Deals and Great Adventures That You Absolutely Can't Get Unless You're Over 50* (McGraw-Hill), by Joann Rattner Heilman.

10 Getting There: Flying to Puerto Rico

Puerto Rico is by far the most accessible of the Caribbean islands, with frequent airline service. It's also the major airline hub of the Caribbean Basin.

THE AIRLINES

With San Juan as its hub for the entire Caribbean, **American Airlines** (℗ **800/433-7300;** www.aa.com) offers nonstop daily flights to San Juan from Baltimore, Boston, Chicago, Dallas–Fort Worth, Hartford, Los Angeles, Miami, Newark, New York (JFK), Orlando, Philadelphia, Tampa, Fort Lauderdale, and Washington (Dulles), plus flights to San Juan from both Montreal and Toronto with changes in Chicago or Miami.

Delta (℗ **800/221-1212;** www.delta. com) has three daily nonstop flights from Atlanta Monday to Friday, six nonstop on Saturday, and six nonstop on Sunday. Flights into Atlanta from around the world are frequent, with excellent connections from points throughout Delta's network in the South and Southwest. The airline's subsidiary, **Song** (© 800/FLY-SONG; www.flysong.com), flies daily from Orlando, Florida, and JFK New York to San Juan.

United Airlines (© 800/241-6522; www.united.com) offers daily nonstop flights from Chicago to San Juan. **Northwest/KLM** (© 800/225-2525; www.nwa.com) has one daily nonstop flight to San Juan from Detroit, as well as at least two (and sometimes more) direct flights to San Juan from Detroit and five flights from Newark. United also offers flights to San Juan from both Memphis and Minneapolis, with a schedule that varies according to the season and the day of the week.

US Airways (© 800/428-4322; www.usairways.com) has several daily direct flights between Charlotte, N.C., and San Juan. The airline also offers three daily nonstop flights to San Juan from Philadelphia, and one daily nonstop Saturday and Sunday flight to San Juan from Pittsburgh.

Continental Airlines (© 800/525-0280 or 787/890-2990; www.continental.com) flies nonstop daily from Newark, Houston, and Cleveland. The airline also flies from Newark direct to the northwestern airport outside Aguadilla should you wish to begin your tour of Puerto Rico in the west. In winter, service is increased to daily flights. **JetBlue** (© 800/538-2583; www.jetblue.com) flies two times a day from New York's JFK airport to San Juan. The airline also serves 20 other U.S. cities, including Boston, Las Vegas, San Diego, and Seattle. **Spirit Air** (© 800/772-7117 or 787/772-7117;

www.spiritair.com) offers two daily nonstop flights from Orlando, and one from Fort Lauderdale to San Juan.

Canadians can fly **Air Canada** (© 800/426-7000; www.aircanada.com) from either Montreal or Toronto to San Juan.

Puerto Rico is the major transportation hub of the Caribbean, with the best connections for getting anywhere in the island. In addition to American Eagle (see below), **Cape Air** (© 800/352-0714 or 787/253-1121; www.flycapeair.com) links two of the major islands of the U.S. Virgin Islands, St. Thomas and St. Croix, as well as Tortola in the B.V.I., with San Juan.

Seaborne Airlines (© 888/FLY-TOUR; www.flyseaborne.com) offers daily links between St. Croix and St. Thomas with San Juan. The one-way cost from the U.S. Virgin Islands to Puerto Rico is $146 per person. The planes are small and frequent, carrying 15 to 19 passengers. Often there are more than 50 flights a day.

LIAT (© 787/791-0800) provides an air link to the Lesser Antilles islands.

British travelers can take a **British Airways** (© 0870/850-9850 in the U.K., or 800/247-9297 in the U.S.; www.ba.com) weekly flight direct from London to San Juan on Sunday. **Lufthansa** (© 01/805-838-426 in Germany, or 800/399-LUFT in the U.S.; www.luftansa-usa.com) passengers can fly on Saturday (one weekly flight) from Frankfurt to San Juan via USAir from Philadelphia. And **Iberia** (© 902-400-500 in Spain, or 800/772-4642 in the U.S.; www.iberia.com) has two weekly flights from Madrid to San Juan, leaving on Thursday and Saturday.

11 Package Deals & Group Tours

PACKAGE DEALS FOR THE INDEPENDENT TRAVELER

Before you start your search for the lowest airfare, you might want to consider booking your flight as part of a travel package such as an escorted tour or a package tour. What you lose in adventure, you'll gain in time and money saved when you book accommodations, and maybe even food and entertainment, along with your flight.

Package tours are not the same thing as escorted tours. With a package tour, you travel independently but pay a group rate. Packages usually include airfare, a choice of hotels, and car rentals, and packagers often offer several options at different prices. In many cases, a package that includes airfare, hotel, and transportation to and from the airport will cost you less than just the hotel alone would have, had you booked it yourself. That's because packages are sold in bulk to tour operators—who resell them to the public at a cost that drastically undercuts standard rates.

One good source of package deals is the airlines themselves. Most major airlines offer air/land packages, including **American Airlines Vacations** (℃ 800/321-2121; www.aavacations.com), **Delta Vacations** (℃ 800/221-6666; www.deltavacations.com), **US Airways Vacations** (℃ 800/455-0123; www.usairwaysvacations.com), **Continental Airlines Vacations** (℃ 800/301-3800; www.covacations.com), and **United Vacations** (℃ 888/854-3899; www.unitedvacations.com).

Vacation Together (℃ 877/444-4547; www.vacationtogether.com) allows you to search for and book packages offered by a number of tour operators and airlines. The **United States Tour Operators Association's** website (www.ustoa.com) has a search engine that allows you to look for operators that offer packages to a specific destination. Travel packages are also listed in the travel section of your local Sunday newspaper. **Liberty Travel** (℃ 888/271-1584; www.libertytravel.com), one of the biggest packagers in the Northeast, often runs full-page ads in Sunday papers. Or check ads in the national travel magazines such as *Arthur Frommer's Budget Travel Magazine,*

Travel & Leisure, National Geographic Traveler, and *Condé Nast Traveler.*

To save time comparing the price and value of all the package tours out there, consider calling **TourScan Inc.** (℃ 800/962-2080; www.tourscan.com). Every season the company gathers and computerizes the contents of about 200 brochures containing 10,000 different vacations in the Caribbean. Write to TourScan for their catalogs, costing $4 each, the price of which is credited to any TourScan vacation.

Other options for general independent packages include:

Just-A-Vacation (℃ 800/683-6313 or 301/559-0510; www.justavacation.com), specializes in all-inclusive upscale resorts in Puerto Rico.

AAA Island Tours, 1759 Pinero Ave., Summit Hills, San Juan (℃ 787/793-3688; www.aaaislandtours.com), offers some good packages ranging from 2 days to 2 weeks.

ESCORTED GENERAL-INTEREST TOURS

An escorted tour is a structured group tour with a group leader. The price usually includes everything from airfare to hotel, meals, tours, admission costs, and local transportation.

Puerto Rico Tours, Condo Inter-Suite, Suite 5M, on Isla Verde in San Juan (℃ 787/306-1540 or 787/791-5479; www.puertorico-tours.com), offers specially conducted private sightseeing tours of Puerto Rico, including trips to the rainforest, Luquillo Beach, the caves of Camuy, and other attractions, such as a restored Taíno Indian village.

Backstage Partners (℃ 787/791-0099; www.backstagepartners.com) offers customized tours that take in a wide range of island attractions, including eco-tours, deep-sea fishing, scuba diving and snorkeling, safaris, and golf packages.

Value Great Discounts through the LeLoLai VIP Program

With San Juan's **LeLoLai VIPs** (Value in Puerto Rico) free program, you can enjoy the equivalent of up to $250 in travel benefits. You'll get discounts on admission to folklore shows, guided tours of historic sites and natural attractions, lodgings, meals, shopping, activities, and more. Of course, most of the experiences linked to LeLoLai are of the rather touristy type, but it can still be worth joining the program.

With membership, the ***paradores puertorriqueños,*** the island's modestly priced network of country inns, give cardholders 10% to 20% lower room rates Monday through Thursday. Discounts of 10% to 20% are offered at many restaurants, from San Juan's toniest hotels to several *mesones gastronómicos,* government-sanctioned restaurants that serve Puerto Rican fare. Shopping discounts are offered at many stores and boutiques, and, best yet, cardholders get 10% to 20% discounts at many island attractions.

The card also entitles you to free admission to some of the island's folklore shows. At press time, the pass included *Jolgorio,* presented every Wednesday at 8pm at the Caribe Terrace of the Caribe Hilton, although the specifics might change by the time you arrive in Puerto Rico.

For more information about this card, call (📞 **787/722-1709** or go to the Centro de Información Turística, Plaza Darsenas, Old San Juan. Although you can call for details before you leave home, you can only sign up for this program once you reach Puerto Rico. Many hotel packages include participation in this program as part of their offerings.

Other leading escorted tour operators include **Atlantic San Juan Tours** (📞 787/644-9841; www.puertorico excursions.com), which helps you take in all the major sights of the island from Ponce to El Yunque; and **Sunshine Tours** (📞 866/785-3636; www.puerto-rico-sunshinetours.com), which covers much the same ground as the others. **Legends of Puerto Rico** (📞 787/605-9060; www.legendsofpr.com), hosts personalized tours, specializing in entertaining cultural and nature adventure tours.

12 For the Cruise-Ship Traveler

Miami is the cruise capital of the world, but San Juan is second. Unless you have never visited Miami and would like to include it as part of your extended Caribbean itinerary, there is justification in flying directly to San Juan by plane and beginning your cruise here. It puts you immediately in the Caribbean, which means you save a 2-day ocean voyage just to get here. Instead of sailing from Florida, you can spend the time getting to know Puerto Rico.

Consult a good travel agent for the latest offerings. Some of the most likely contenders include the following: **Ambassador Tours,** 50 First St., Suite 610, San Francisco, CA 94104 (📞 **800/989-9000** or 415/357-9876; www.ambassadortours.com); **Cruises One,** 1415 NW 62 St., Suite 205, Fort Lauderdale, FL 33309

(© **800/832-3592** or 954/958-3700; www.cruiseone.com); **Cruises of Distinction,** 4557 Woodward Ave., Bloomfield Hills, MI 48304 (© **800/634-3445;** www.cruisesofdistinction.com); **Cruises Only,** 1011 E. Colonial Dr., Orlando, FL 32808 (© **800/242-9000** or 407/898-5353; www.cruisesonly.com); **Kelly Cruises,** 1315 W. 22nd St., Suite 105, Oak Brook, IL 60521 (© **800/837-7447** or 630/990-1111; www.kellycruises.com); and **Hartford Holidays Travel,** 129 Hillside Ave., Williston Park, NY 11596 (© **800/828-4813** or 516/746-6670; www.hartfordholidays.com). Any of these providers stay tuned to last-minute price wars brewing among such megacarriers as Carnival, Princess, Royal Caribbean, and Holland America, as well as such low-budget contenders as Premier.

Vacations to Go, 1502 Augusta Dr., Suite 415, Houston, TX 77057 (© **800/338-4962** or 713/974-2121; www.vacationstogo.com), provides catalogs and information on discount cruises through the Caribbean, as well as the Atlantic and Mediterranean.

THE CRUISE LINES

Here's a brief rundown of some of the cruise lines that serve San Juan and the Caribbean. For detailed information, pick up a copy of one of our companion guides in this series, *Frommer's Caribbean Cruises and Ports of Call, Frommer's Caribbean Ports of Call,* or *Unofficial Guide to Cruises.*

- **Carnival Cruise Lines** (© **888/CARNIVAL** or 305/599-2200; www.carnival.com), a specialist in the maintenance of some of the biggest and most brightly decorated ships afloat, is the richest, boldest, brashest, and most successful mass-market cruise line in the world. Many of its vessels depart from Florida or Caribbean ports that include, among others, San Juan, Galveston, Miami,

Tampa, and New York. One of the ships, *Carnival Destiny* defines San Juan as its home port, from which 7-day excursions are made to such southern Caribbean ports as St. Thomas, Antigua, Aruba, Dominica, Barbados, Tortola, Martinique, Grenada, St. Lucia, and St. Kitts. If you prefer to depart from one of the ports of Florida (especially Miami), know in advance that many of the company's cruises make San Juan a focal point of their stopovers. Most of the company's Caribbean cruises offer good value, last between 4 and 8 days, and feature nonstop activities, lots of glitter, and the hustle and bustle of armies of clients and crew members embarking and disembarking at every port. Cuisine and party-colored drinks are plentiful, although with vessels of this size, they are, by necessity, mass-produced. The overall atmosphere is comparable to that of a floating theme park with hordes of visitors, loaded with whimsy, and with lots of emphasis on partying in a style you might have expected in Atlantic City. Lots of single passengers, some of them with gleams in their eye, opt for this line, and some actually get lucky. Despite the presence of lots of unattached or loosely attached adults, the line makes special efforts to amuse and entertain children between 2 and 17.

- **Celebrity Cruises** (© **800/647-2251** or 800/722-5941; www.celebrity.com) maintains eight medium-to-large ships offering cruises of between 7 and 10 nights to such ports as Key West; Grand Cayman; St. Thomas; Aruba, St. Lucia; and Cozumel, Mexico, among others. Passengers interested in maximum exposure to Puerto Rico usually opt to cruise aboard *Galaxy,* a 77,713-ton megaship that's based (Dec–Mar) in

San Juan, and which embarks every week throughout the year for tours to such southern Caribbean islands as Barbados, St. Kitts, and Aruba.

Despite a merger of Celebrity with the larger and better-financed Royal Caribbean International, Celebrity maintains its own identity and corporate structure within the larger framework. The niche this line has created is unpretentious but classy, several notches above mass market, but with pricing that's nonetheless relatively competitive. Accommodations are roomy and well equipped, and the cuisine is among the most intensely cultivated of any of its competitors afloat.

- **Costa Cruise Lines** (© **800/462-6782** or 954/266-5600; www.costacruises.com), the U.S.-based branch of an Italian cruise line that has thrived for about a century, maintains hefty-to-megasize vessels that are newer than those of many other lines afloat. Two of these offer virtually identical jaunts through the western and eastern Caribbean on alternate weeks, each of them departing from Fort Lauderdale, Florida. Ports of call during the eastern Caribbean itineraries of both vessels include a stopover in San Juan, followed by visits to St. Thomas, Catalina Island (a private island off the coast of the Dominican Republic known for its beaches), and Cozumel. There is an Italian flavor and lots of Italian design onboard here, and an atmosphere of relaxed indulgence. The ships—*CostaMagica* and *CostaMediterranea*—feature tame versions of ancient Roman Bacchanalia, as well as such celebrations as *Festa Italiana,* and focaccia and pizza parties by the pool.
- **Princess Cruises** (© **800/PRINCESS;** www.princess.com) has a large and far-flung fleet that totals 12 mega-vessels. The ships cruise at various times of the year through Caribbean and Bahamian waters, sometimes with stops at San Juan as part of the itinerary. The *Sun Princess* sails from Fort Lauderdale on roundtrip 10-night cruises that variously cover the eastern and the south Caribbean. Princess is one of the very few lines in the world to offer luxury accommodations and upscale service as a standard feature aboard its megaships. These usually carry a smaller number of passengers than similarly sized vessels on less elegant lines. The company's clientele is upscale, with an average passenger age of 55 or over. A respectable percentage of the staff is British.
- **Radisson Seven Seas Cruises** (© **800/285-1835** or 954/776-6123; www.rssc.com) is noted for the level of glamour and prestige that permeates its cruises. It sends all three of its ships—the *Seven Seas Mariner, Seven Seas Voyager,* and *Seven Seas Navigator*—into the Caribbean on a regular basis. The *Mariner,* carrying 700 passengers, is an all-suite vessel, and the *Navigator* carries 490 passengers on luxe cruises. The *Voyager* is a newer version of the all-suite *Mariner.* Cruises are relatively expensive compared to those offered by less prestigious lines, and roam freely, with less allegiance to a fixed home port than many other vessels.
- **Royal Caribbean International** (© **800/327-6700** or 305/539-6000; www.royalcaribbean.com) leads the industry in the development of megaships. Most of this company's 20 or so vessels weigh in at around 73,000 tons, are among the largest of any line afloat, and represent a roster of floating hardware that's more impressive than that of many

national navies. Marketed as a mainstream mass-market cruise line whose components have been fine-tuned through endless repetition, the line encourages a restrained house-party theme that's somehow a bit less frenetic than that found aboard the more raucous megaships of other cruise lines, including Carnival. The company is well run, and there are enough onboard activities to suit virtually any taste and age level. Though accommodations and accouterments are more than adequate, they are not upscale, and cabins aboard some of the line's older vessels tend to be a bit more cramped than the industry norm. Using either Florida ports or San Juan as their home port, RCI ships call regularly at such oft-visited ports as St. Thomas, Ocho Rios, Sint Maarten, Grand Cayman, St. Croix, and Curaçao. Most of the company's cruises last for 4 to 7 days. If Puerto Rico is the focal point of your itinerary, your best bet is *Adventure of the Seas* or *Serenade of the Seas,* offering 7-night cruises through the southern and eastern Caribbean regions, using San Juan as a base. Royal Caribbean is the only cruise line in the business that owns, outright, two tropical beaches (one in The Bahamas, the other along an isolated peninsula in northern Haiti) whose sands and watersports facilities are the focus of many of the company's Caribbean cruises.

13 Getting Around

BY PLANE

Cape Air (© **800/352-0714** or 787/253-1121; www.flycapeair.com) flies from Luis Muñoz Marín International Airport to Mayagüez, Ponce, and Vieques several times a day. They also offer many flights daily to St. Thomas, St. Croix, and Tortola. **American Eagle** (© **800/433-7300** or 800/981-4757) is the leader of the short-haul carriers, offering service to 37 destinations in the Caribbean and The Bahamas.

BY RENTAL CAR

There is good news and bad news about driving in Puerto Rico. First, the good news. Puerto Rico offers some of the most scenic drives in all the Caribbean. Driving around and discovering its little hidden beaches, coastal towns, mountain villages, vast forests, and national parks is reason enough to visit the island. In fact, if you want to explore the island in any depth, driving a private car is about the only way, as public transportation is woefully inadequate.

Of course, if you want to stay only in San Juan, having a car is not necessary. You can get around San Juan on foot or by bus, taxi, and in some cases, hotel minivan.

Now the bad news. Renting a car and driving in Puerto Rico, depending on the routes you take, can lead to a number of frustrating experiences, as our readers relate to us year after year. These readers point out that local drivers are often dangerous, as evidenced by the number of fenders with bashed-in sides. The older coastal highways provide the most scenic routes but are often congested. Some of the roads, especially in the mountainous interior, are just too narrow for automobiles. If you do rent a car, proceed with caution along these poorly paved and maintained roads, which most often follow circuitous routes. Cliffslides or landslides are not uncommon.

Some local agencies may tempt you with special reduced prices. But if you're planning to tour the island by car, you won't find any local branches that will help you if you experience trouble. And some of the agencies widely advertising low-cost deals won't take credit cards and want cash in advance. Also, watch out for "hidden" extra costs, which sometimes proliferate among the smaller and not very well-known firms, and difficulties connected with resolving insurance claims.

If you do rent a vehicle, it's best to stick with the old reliables: **Avis** (② **800/ 331-1212** or 787/791-2500; www.avis. com), **Budget** (② **800/472-3325** or 787/ 791-3685; www.budget.com), or **Hertz** (② **800/654-3131** or 787/791-0840; www.hertz.com). Each of these companies offers minivan transport to its office and car depot. Be alert to the minimum-age requirements for car rentals in Puerto Rico. Both Avis and Hertz require that renters be 25 or older; at Budget, renters must be 21 or older, but those between the ages of 21 and 24 pay a $10 to $25 daily surcharge to the agreed-upon rental fee.

Added security comes from an antitheft double-locking mechanism that has been installed in most of the rental cars available in Puerto Rico. Car theft is common in Puerto Rico, so extra precautions are always needed.

Distances are often posted in kilometers rather than miles (1km = 0.62 mile), but speed limits are displayed in miles per hour.

INSURANCE   Each company offers an optional collision-damage waiver priced at around $15 to $40 a day. Purchasing the waiver eliminates most or all of the financial responsibility you would face in case of an accident. With it, you can simply go home, leaving the rental company to sort it all out. Without it, you would be liable for up to the full value of the car in case it was damaged. Paying for the rental with certain credit or charge cards sometimes eliminates the need to buy this extra insurance. Also, your own

automobile insurance policy might cover some or all of the damages. You should check with both your own insurer and your credit card issuers before leaving home. (See "Travel Insurance" earlier in this chapter.)

GASOLINE   There is usually an abundant supply of gasoline in Puerto Rico, especially on the outskirts of San Juan, where you'll see all the familiar signs, such as Mobil. Gasoline stations are also plentiful along the main arteries traversing the island. However, if you're going to remote areas of the island, especially on Sunday, it's advisable to start out with a full tank. *Note:* In Puerto Rico, gasoline is sold by the liter, not by the gallon. The cost of gasoline is often somewhat cheaper than in the United States. A liter usually sells for 53¢, which comes to about $2.02 per gallon.

DRIVING RULES   Driving rules can be a source of some confusion. Speed limits are often not posted on the island, but when they are, they're given in miles per hour. For example, the limit on the San Juan–Ponce *autopista* (expressway) is 70 mph. Speed limits elsewhere, notably in heavily populated residential areas, are much lower. Because you're not likely to know what the actual speed limit is in some of these areas, it's best to confine your speed to no more than 30 mph. The highway department places *lomas* (speed bumps) at strategic points to deter speeders. Sometimes these are called "sleeping policemen."

Like U.S. and Canadian motorists, Puerto Ricans drive on the right side of the road.

ROAD MAPS   One of the best and most detailed road maps of Puerto Rico is published by **International Travel Maps** and distributed in the United States by Rand McNally. It's available in some bookstores and is a good investment at

$9.95. The ***Gousha Puerto Rico Road Map,*** available in the United States and Canada, has a good street map of San Juan but lacks detailed information about minor highways on the island and is very similar to the map of Puerto Rico distributed free at tourist offices.

BREAKDOWNS & ASSISTANCE
All the major towns and cities have garages that will come to your assistance and tow your vehicle for repairs if necessary. There's no national emergency number to call in the event of a mechanical breakdown. If you have a rental car, call the rental company first. Usually, someone there will bring motor assistance to you. If your car requires extensive repairs because of a mechanical failure, a new one will be sent to replace it.

BY PUBLIC TRANSPORTATION
Cars and minibuses known as *públicos* provide low-cost transportation around the island. Their license plates have the letters "P" or "PD" following the numbers. They serve all the main towns of Puerto Rico; passengers are let off and picked up along the way, both at designated stops and when someone flags them down. Rates are set by the Public Service Commission. *Públicos* usually operate during daylight hours, departing from the main plaza (central square) of a town.

Information about público routes between San Juan and Mayagüez is available at **Lineas Sultana,** Calle Esteban González 898, Urbanización Santa Rita, Río Piedras (**(C) 787/765-9377**). Information about público routes between San Juan and Ponce is available from **Choferes Unidos de Ponce,** Terminal de Carros Públicos, Calle Vive in Ponce (**(C) 787/764-0540**).

Fares vary according to whether the público will make a detour to pick up or drop off a passenger at a specific locale. (If you want to deviate from the predetermined routes, you'll pay more than if you wait for a público beside the main highway.) Fares from San Juan to Mayagüez range from $20 to $40; from San Juan to Ponce, from $20 to $40. Be warned that although prices of públicos are low, the routes are slow, with frequent stops, often erratic routing, and lots of inconvenience.

14 Tips on Accommodations

HOTELS & RESORTS
There is no rigid classification of Puerto Rican hotels. The word "deluxe" is often used—or misused—when "first class" might be a more appropriate term. We've presented fairly detailed descriptions of the hotels in this book, so you'll get an idea of what to expect once you're there.

Even in the real deluxe and first-class properties, however, don't expect top-rate service and efficiency. The slow tropical pace is what folks mean when they talk about "island time."

Ask detailed questions when booking a room. Entertainment in Puerto Rico is often alfresco, so light sleepers obviously won't want a room directly over a steel band. In general, back rooms cost less than oceanfront rooms, and lower rooms cost less than upper-floor units. Always ascertain whether transfers (which can be expensive) are included. And make sure that you know exactly what is free and what costs money. Some resorts seem to charge every time you breathe and might end up costing more than a deluxe hotel that includes most everything in the price.

Also factor in transportation costs, which can mount quickly if you stay 5 days to a week. If you want to go to the beach every day, it might be wise to book a hotel on the Condado and not stay in romantic Old San Juan, from which you'll spend a lot of time and money transferring back and forth between your hotel and the beach.

Most hotels in Puerto Rico are on the windward side of the island, with lots of waves, undertow, and surf. If a glasslike smooth sea is imperative for your stay, you can book on the leeward (eastern shore) or Caribbean (southeast coast) sides, which are better for snorkeling. The major centers in these areas are the resort complex of Palmas del Mar and the "second city" of Ponce.

MAP VS. AP, OR DO YOU WANT TO GO CP OR EP?

All resorts offer a **European Plan (EP)** rate, which means you pay for the price of a room. That leaves you free to dine around at night at various other resorts or restaurants without restriction. Another plan preferred by many is the **Continental Plan (CP),** which means you get your room and a continental breakfast of juice, coffee, bread, jam, and so on, included in a set price. This plan is preferred by many because most guests don't like to "dine around" at breakfast time.

Another major option is the **Modified American Plan (MAP),** which includes breakfast and one main meal of the day, either lunch or dinner. The final choice is the **American Plan (AP),** which includes breakfast, lunch, and dinner.

At certain resorts you will save money by booking either the MAP or AP because discounts are granted. If you dine a la carte for lunch and dinner at various restaurants, your final dining bill will no doubt be much higher than if you stayed on the MAP or AP.

These plans might save you money, but if as part of your holiday you like to eat in various places, you might be disappointed. You face the same dining room every night, unless the resort you're staying at has many different restaurants on the dining plan. Often they don't. Many resorts have a lot of specialty restaurants, serving, say, Japanese cuisine, but these more expensive restaurants are not included in MAP or AP; rather, they charge a la carte prices.

One option is to ask if your hotel has a dine-around plan. You might still keep costs in check, but you can avoid a culinary rut by taking your meals in some other restaurants if your hotel has such a plan. Such plans are rare in Puerto Rico, which does not specialize in all-inclusive resorts the way that Jamaica and some other islands do.

Before booking a room, check with a good travel agent or investigate on your own what you are likely to save by booking in on a dining plan. Under certain circumstances in winter, you might not have a choice if MAP is dictated as a requirement for staying there. It pays to investigate, of course.

PUERTO RICAN GUESTHOUSES

A unique type of accommodations is the guesthouse, where Puerto Ricans themselves usually stay when they travel. Ranging in size from 7 to 25 rooms, they offer a familial atmosphere. Many are on or near the beach; some have pools or sun decks, and a number serve meals.

In Puerto Rico, however, the term "guesthouse" has many meanings. Some guesthouses are like simple motels built around pools. Others have small individual cottages with their own kitchenettes, constructed around a main building in which you'll often find a bar and a restaurant serving local food. Some are surprisingly comfortable, often with private bathrooms and swimming pools. You may or may not have air-conditioning. The rooms are sometimes cooled by ceiling fans or by the trade winds blowing through open windows at night.

For value, the guesthouse can't be topped. If you stay at a guesthouse, you can journey over to a big beach resort and use its seaside facilities for only a small fee. Although bereft of frills, the guesthouses we've recommended are clean and safe for families or single women. However, the cheapest ones are not places where you'd want to spend a lot of time because of their modest furnishings.

For further information on guesthouses, contact the **Puerto Rico Tourism Company,** 666 Fifth Ave., New York, NY 10013 (© **800/866-7827** or 212/586-6262).

PARADORES

In an effort to lure travelers beyond the hotels and casinos of San Juan's historic district to the tranquil natural beauty of the island's countryside, the Puerto Rico Tourism Company offers *paradores puertorriqueños* (charming country inns) which are comfortable bases for exploring the island's varied attractions. Vacationers seeking a peaceful idyll can also choose from several privately owned and operated guesthouses.

Using Spain's *parador* system as a model, the Puerto Rico Tourism Company established the paradores in 1973 to encourage tourism across the island. Each of the paradores is situated in a historic place or site of unusual scenic beauty and must meet high standards of service and cleanliness. (See the map "Paradores & Country Inns of Puerto Rico" on p. 53.)

Some of the paradores are located in the mountains and others by the sea. Most have pools, and all offer excellent Puerto Rican cuisine. Many are within easy driving distance of San Juan.

Our favorite paradores are all in western Puerto Rico (see chapter 10). **Parador Posada Porlamar** in La Parguera gives you a taste of the good life in a simple fishing village. For a plantation ambience and an evocation of the Puerto Rico of colonial times, there is the **Parador Hacienda Gripiñas** at Jayuya, some 30 miles (48km) southwest of San Juan; it was a former coffee plantation. **Parador Vistamar,** at Quebradillas, one of the largest paradores in Puerto Rico,

enjoys a mountain location with beautiful gardens of tropical flowers.

VILLAS & VACATION HOMES

You can often secure good deals in Puerto Rico by renting privately owned villas and vacation homes.

Almost every villa has a staff, or at least a maid who comes in a few days a week. Villas also provide the essentials of home life, including bed linen and cooking paraphernalia. Condos usually come with a reception desk and are often comparable to life in a suite at a big resort hotel. Nearly every condo complex has a swimming pool, and some have more than one.

Private apartments are rented either with or without maid service. This is more of a no-frills option than the villas and condos. An apartment might not be in a building with a swimming pool, and it might not have a front desk to help you. Among the major categories of vacation homes, cottages offer the most freewheeling way to live. Most cottages are fairly simple, many opening in an ideal fashion onto a beach, whereas others may be clustered around a communal pool. Many contain no more than a simple bedroom together with a small kitchen and bathroom. For the peak winter season, reservations should be made at least 5 or 6 months in advance.

Dozens of agents throughout the United States and Canada offer these types of rentals (see "Rental Agencies," below, for some recommendations). You can also write to local tourist-information offices, which can advise you on vacation-home rentals.

Travel experts agree that savings, especially for a family of three to six people, or two or three couples, can range from 50% to 60% over what a hotel would cost. If there are only two in your party, these savings probably don't apply.

Paradores & Country Inns of Puerto Rico

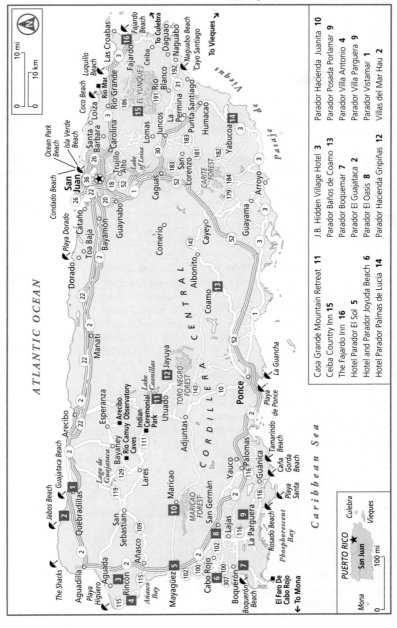

Casa Grande Mountain Retreat **11**
Ceiba Country Inn **15**
The Fajardo Inn **16**
Hotel Parador El Sol **5**
Hotel and Parador Joyuda Beach **6**
Hotel Parador Palmas de Lucía **14**

J.B. Hidden Village Hotel **3**
Parador Baños de Coamo **13**
Parador Boquemar **7**
Parador El Guajataca **2**
Parador El Oasis **8**
Parador Hacienda Gripiñas **12**

Parador Hacienda Juanita **10**
Parador Posada Porlamar **9**
Parador Villa Antonio **4**
Parador Villa Parguera **9**
Parador Vistamar **1**
Villas del Mar Hau **2**

RENTAL AGENCIES

Agencies specializing in renting properties in Puerto Rico include:

- **VHR, Worldwide,** 235 Kensington Ave., Norwood, NJ 07648 (© **800/ 633-3284** or 201/767-9393; www. vhrww.com), offers the most comprehensive portfolio of luxury villas, condominiums, resort suites, and apartments for rent in the Caribbean, including complete packages for airfare and car rentals.

- **Hideaways Aficionado,** 767 Islington St., Portsmouth, NH 03801 (© **800/843-4433** or 603/430-4433; www.hideaways.com), provides a 144-page guide with illustrations of its accommodations so that you can get an idea of what you're renting. Most villas come with maid service. You can also ask this travel club about discounts on plane fares and car rentals.

15 Recommended Reading

HISTORY

Carrion, Artura Morales. *Puerto Rico: A Political and Cultural History.* This is one of the best major overviews of Puerto Rican history and culture.

Golding, Morton. *A Short History of Puerto Rico.* This book suits those who want their history readable and condensed.

Honychurch, Reginald. *The Caribbean People.* In three volumes, this is a well-balanced account written by one of the so-called new historians of the Caribbean.

Scarano, Francisco A. *Sugar and Slavery in Puerto Rico: The Plantation Economy of Ponce, 1800–1850.* Scarano produces a scholarly study of an agrarian region of Puerto Rico far removed from the Spanish-controlled capital of San Juan.

POLITICS

Carr, Ramon. *Puerto Rico: A Colonial Experiment.* Carr offers one of the most insightful views of island politics, which has been called the national religion of Puerto Rico.

Johnson, Roberta. *Puerto Rico: Commonwealth or Colony?* This book attempts to answer the title's provocative question.

Perusse, Roland I. *The United States and Puerto Rico: Breaking the Bonds of Economic Colonialism.* This book traces the history of trade relations in Puerto Rico, the second-largest Western trading partner of the United States, after Canada. It is a cultural and economic survey with a strongly politicized point of view.

Williams, Byron. *Puerto Rico: Commonwealth, State, or Nation?* This book offers a pointed discussion of the major Puerto Rican self-determination movements.

FAST FACTS: Puerto Rico

American Express See "Fast Facts: San Juan" in chapter 4.

Area Code The telephone area code for Puerto Rico is **787**. For calls on the island, the area code is not used.

ATM Networks See "Money," earlier in this chapter.

Banks All major U.S. banks have branches on Puerto Rico; their hours are 8am to 2:30pm Monday through Friday and 9:45am to noon on Saturday.

Business Hours Regular business hours are Monday through Friday from 8am to 5pm. Shopping hours vary considerably. Regular shopping hours are Monday through Thursday and Saturday from 9am to 6pm. On Friday, stores have a long day: 9am to 9pm. Many stores also open on Sunday from 11am to 5pm.

Camera & Film It's important to protect your camera not only from theft but also from saltwater and sand; furthermore, your camera can become over-heated and any film it contains can be ruined if left in the sun or locked in the trunk of a car. See "Fast Facts: San Juan" in chapter 4.

Car Rentals See "Getting Around," earlier in this chapter.

Climate See "When to Go," earlier in this chapter.

Currency See "Money," earlier in this chapter.

Customs See "Entry Requirements & Customs," earlier in this chapter.

Driving Rules See "Getting Around," earlier in this chapter.

Drugs A branch of the Federal Narcotics Strike Force is permanently stationed on Puerto Rico, where illegal drugs and narcotics are a problem. Convictions for possession of marijuana can bring severe penalties, ranging from 2 to 10 years in prison for a first offense. Possession of hard drugs, such as cocaine or heroin, can lead to 15 years or more in prison.

Drugstores It's a good idea to carry enough prescription medications with you to last the duration of your stay. If you're going into the hinterlands, take along the medicines you'll need. If you need any additional medications, you'll find many drugstores in San Juan and other leading cities. One of the most centrally located pharmacies in Old San Juan is the **Puerto Rican Drug Co.,** Calle San Francisco 157 (© **787/725-2202**); it's open daily from 7:30am to 9:30pm.

Electricity The electricity is 110 volts AC, as it is in the continental United States and Canada.

Embassies & Consulates Because Puerto Rico is part of the United States, there is no U.S. embassy or consulate. Instead, there are branches of all the principal U.S. federal agencies. Canada has no embassy or consulate either. There are no special provisions or agencies catering to British travel needs in Puerto Rico, nor are there agencies serving citizens of Australia or New Zealand.

Emergencies In an emergency, dial © **911**. Or call the local police (© **787/343-2020**), fire department (© **787/343-2330**), ambulance (© **787/343-2550**), or medical assistance (© **787/754-3535**).

Gambling In addition to **casino gambling** at major Puerto Rico resorts, the country also has a **lottery,** for which tickets can be purchased at hundreds of kiosks, stores, and shops around the island. The major casino gambling on the island is Caribbean stud poker, blackjack, roulette, and craps, along with thousands of slot machines. Under Puerto Rican law, alcoholic beverages cannot be served in a casino.

Healthcare Medical-care facilities, including excellent hospitals and clinics, in Puerto Rico are on par with those in the United States. Hotels can arrange for a doctor in case of an emergency. Most major U.S. health insurance plans are recognized here, but it's advisable to check with your carrier or insurance agent before your trip, because medical attention is very expensive. See "Health & Safety," earlier in this chapter.

Holidays See "When to Go," earlier in this chapter.

Hospitals In a medical emergency, call © **911. Ashford Presbyterian Community Hospital,** Av. Ashford 1451, San Juan (© **787/721-2160**), maintains 24-hour emergency service. Service is also provided at **Clinica Las Americas,** Franklin Delano Roosevelt Ave. 400, Hato Rey (© **787/765-1919**), and at **Puerto Rico Medical Center,** Av. Americo Miranda, Río Piedras (© **787/777-3535**).

Information See "Visitor Information," earlier in this chapter.

Internet Access Public access to the Internet is available at some large-scale resorts; the staff often provides access from their own computers. Another place to try is **Cybernet,** Av. Ashford Condado 1128 (© **787/724-4033**), which is open Monday to Thursday from 9am to 11pm, Friday and Saturday from 9am to midnight, and Sunday from 10am to 10pm. It charges $4 for 20 minutes, $5 for 35 minutes, $7 for 50 minutes, and $9 for 65 minutes.

Language English is understood at the big resorts and in most of San Juan. Out in the island, Spanish is still *numero uno.*

Lost & Found Be sure to tell all of your credit card companies the minute you discover your wallet has been lost or stolen, and file a report at the nearest police precinct. Your credit card company or insurer may require a police report number or record of the loss. Most credit card companies have an emergency toll-free number to call if your card is lost or stolen; they may be able to wire you a cash advance immediately or deliver an emergency credit card in a day or two. Visa's U.S. emergency number is © **800/847-2911** or 410/581-9994. American Express cardholders and traveler's check holders should call © **800/221-7282.** MasterCard holders should call © **800/307-7309** or 636/722-7111. For other credit cards, call the toll-free number directory at © **800/555-1212.**

If you need emergency cash over the weekend when all banks and American Express offices are closed, you can have money wired to you via **Western Union** (© **800/325-6000;** www.westernunion.com). **Travelers Express/MoneyGram** is the largest company in the U.S. for money orders. You can transfer funds either online or by phone in about 10 minutes (© **800/MONEYGRAM;** www.money gram.com).

Identity theft or fraud are potential complications of losing your wallet, especially if you've lost your driver's license along with your cash and credit cards. Notify the major credit-reporting bureaus immediately; placing a fraud alert on your records may protect you against liability for criminal activity. The three major U.S. credit-reporting agencies are **Equifax** (© **800/766-0008;** www.equifax.com), **Experian** (© **888/397-3742;** www.experian.com), and **Trans-Union** (© **800/680-7289;** www.transunion.com). Finally, if you've lost all forms of photo ID call your airline and explain the situation; they might allow you to board the plane if you have a copy of your passport or birth certificate and a copy of the police report you've filed.

Liquor Laws You must be 18 years of age to purchase liquor in stores or buy drinks in hotels, bars, and restaurants.

Maps See "Getting Around," earlier in this chapter.

Marriage Requirements There are no residency requirements for getting married in Puerto Rico. You need parental consent if either of you is under 18. Blood tests are required, although a test conducted in your home country within 10 days of the ceremony will suffice. A doctor must sign the license after an examination of the bride and groom. For complete details, contact the **Commonwealth of Puerto Rico Health Department,** Demographic Register, Franklin Delano Roosevelt Ave., Hato Rey (P.O. Box 11854), San Juan, PR 00910 (© **787/728-7980**).

Newspapers & Magazines **The San Juan Star,** a daily English-language newspaper, has been called the *"International Herald Tribune"* of the Caribbean." It concentrates extensively on news from the United States. You can also pick up copies of *USA Today* at most news kiosks. If you read Spanish, you might enjoy *El Nuevo Día,* the most popular local tabloid. Few significant magazines are published on Puerto Rico, but *Time* and *Newsweek* are available at most newsstands.

Passports See "Visitor Information," earlier in this chapter.

Pets To bring your pet in, you must produce a health certificate from a U.S. mainland veterinarian and show proof of vaccination against rabies. Very few hotels allow animals, so check in advance.

Postal Services Because the U.S. Postal Service is responsible for handling mail on Puerto Rico, the regulations and tariffs are the same as on the mainland United States. Stamps can be purchased at any post office, all of which are open Monday through Friday from 8am to 5pm. Saturday hours are from 8am to noon (closed Sun). As on the mainland, you can purchase stamps at vending machines in airports, stores, and hotels. First-class letters to addresses within Puerto Rico, the United States, and its territories cost 39¢; postcards, 24¢. Letters and postcards to Canada both cost 60¢ for the first half-ounce. Letters and postcards to other countries cost 80¢ for the first half-ounce.

Safety Crime exists here as it does everywhere. Use common sense and take precautions. Muggings are commonplace on the Condado and Isla Verde beaches, so you might want to confine your moonlit beach nights to the fenced-in and guarded areas around some of the major hotels. The countryside of Puerto Rico is safer than San Juan, but caution is always in order. Avoid narrow country roads and isolated beaches, night or day.

Smoking Antismoking regulation is less stringent here than it is on the U.S. mainland. Anyone over 18 can smoke in any bar here. Smoking is permitted in restaurants, within designated sections, but not necessarily everywhere. Most hotels have smoking and nonsmoking rooms.

Taxes All hotel rooms in Puerto Rico are subject to a tax, which is not included in the rates given in this book. At casino hotels, the tax is 11%; at noncasino hotels, it's 9%. At country inns you pay a 7% tax. Most hotels also add a 10% service charge. If they don't, you're expected to tip for services rendered. When you're booking a room, it's always best to inquire about these added charges. There is no airport departure tax.

Telephone & Fax Coin-operated phones can be found throughout the island, with a particularly dense concentration in San Juan. After depositing your coins, you can dial a seven-digit number at the sound of the dial tone. If you're calling long distance within Puerto Rico, add a **1** before the numbers. When you're placing a call to the U.S. mainland or to anywhere else overseas, preface the number with **011**. An operator (or a recorded voice) will tell you how much money to deposit, although you'll probably find it more practical to use a calling card issued by such long-distance carriers as Sprint, AT&T, or MCI. Public phones that allow credit cards such as American Express, Visa, or MasterCard to be inserted or "swiped" through a magnetic slot are rare on the island. Most of these are located at the San Juan airport. Most phone booths contain printed instructions for dialing. Local calls are 35¢. Most Puerto Ricans buy phone cards valid for between 15 and 100 units. The 30-unit card costs $14; the 60-unit card, $28. The card provides an even less expensive and usually more convenient way of calling within Puerto Rico or to the U.S. mainland. They are for sale in most drugstores and gift shops on the island.

Most hotels can send a telex or fax for you and bill the costs to your room, and in some cases, they'll even send a fax for a nonguest if you agree to pay a charge. Barring that, several agencies in San Juan will send a fax anywhere you want for a fee. Many are associated with print shops/photocopy stands.

Time Puerto Rico is on Atlantic Standard Time, which is 1 hour later than Eastern Standard Time. Puerto Rico does not go on daylight saving time, however, so the time here is the same year-round.

Tipping Tipping is expected here, so hand over the money as you would on the U.S. mainland. That usually means 15% in restaurants, 10% in bars, and 10% to 15% for taxi drivers, hairdressers, and other services, depending on the quality of the service rendered. Tip a porter, either at the airport or at your hotel, $1 per bag. The U.S. government imposes income tax on waitstaff and other service-industry workers whose income is tip-based according to the gross receipts of their employers; therefore, if you don't tip them, those workers could end up paying tax anyway.

Visitor Information See "Visitor Information," earlier in this chapter.

Water See "Health & Safety," earlier in this chapter.

Weights & Measures There's a mixed bag of measurements in Puerto Rico. Because of its Spanish tradition, most weights (meat and poultry) and measures (gasoline and road distances) are metric. But because of the U.S. presence, speed limits appear in miles per hour and liquids such as beer are sold by the ounce.

3

Suggested Puerto Rico Itineraries

It would be fun to get "lost" on the island of Puerto Rico, wandering about at your leisure, discovering unspoiled villages and remote mountain hamlets off the beaten path. But few of us have such a generous amount of time in the speeded-up 21st century. Vacations are getting shorter, and you'll need a "lean-and-mean" schedule if you want to experience the best of any destination—even a small one like Puerto Rico—in a ridiculously short amount of time.

Try our "Best of Puerto Rico in One Week" tour, or our "Best of Puerto Rico in Two Weeks" if you have more time. If you've been to Puerto Rico before and have already visited San Juan and El Yunque, you may want to take a more esoteric drive, following the trail of the Panoramic Route.

Puerto Rico has some good highways along the coast but as you venture deeper into the heartland, driving conditions become more difficult. Take along a detailed road map, and remember to blow your horn as you turn dangerous curves in the mountains.

The itineraries that follow take you to some major attractions with some surprise discoveries. The pace may be a bit breathless, so skip a town or sight occasionally for some chill-out time—after all, you're on vacation. Of course, you can use any of these itineraries as a jumping-off point for your own custom-made trip that more closely matches your interests. See chapter 1, "The Best of Puerto Rico," for some ideas.

1 The Best of Puerto Rico in 1 Week

If you budget your time carefully, you can see some of the major highlights of Puerto Rico in just 1 week. Naturally, most of your time will be spent in **San Juan,** the capital, but you'll also have time to visit **El Yunque** (a rainforest) and the most famous beach in Puerto Rico, **Luquillo.** There will also be time for days spent in **Ponce,** Puerto Rico's second city, the historic town of **San Germán,** and a side trip to offshore **Mona Island.**

Days ❶ & ❷: San Juan 🏝🏝🏝

Take a flight that arrives in San Juan as early as possible on **Day 1.** Check into your hotel and head for the nearest cafe for a pick-me-up coffee and a pastry before sightseeing. First, head for San Juan's Old

Town. For orientation purposes, you can take our 2-hour walking tour, which will cover all the highlights, including forts and churches. Have lunch at one of the many little taverns in Old San Juan. The city is also one of the shopping meccas of the

Suggested Puerto Rico Itineraries

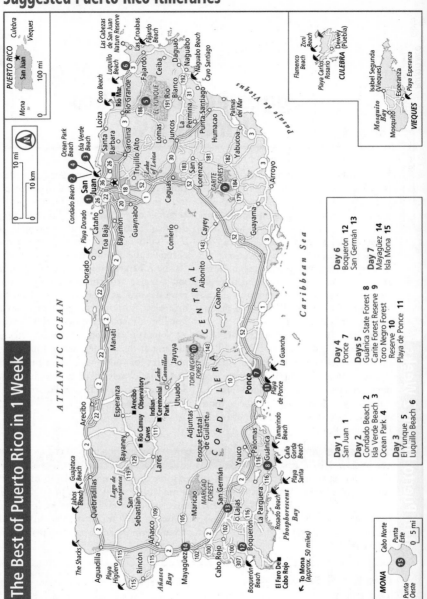

The Best of Puerto Rico in 1 Week

Day 1
San Juan **1**

Day 2
Condado Beach **2**
Isla Verde Beach **3**
Ocean Park **4**

Day 3
El Yunque **5**
Luquillo Beach **6**

Day 4
Ponce **7**

Days 5
Guánica State Forest **8**
Carite Forest Reserve **9**
Toro Negro Forest
Reserve **10**
Playa de Ponce **11**

Day 6
Boquerón **12**
San Germán **13**

Day 7
Mayagüez **14**
Isla Mona **15**

The Best of Puerto Rico in 2 Weeks

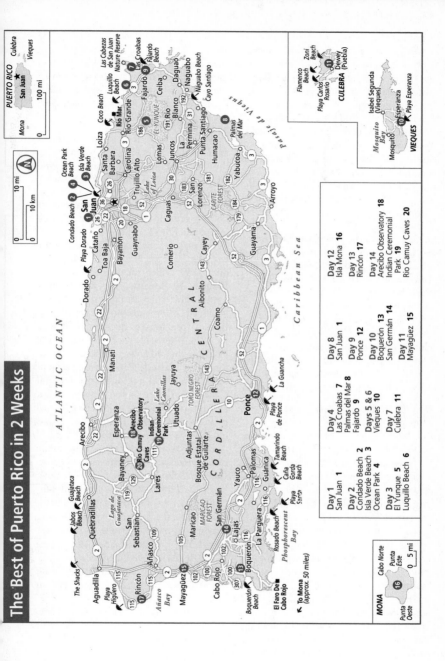

Day 1
San Juan **1**

Day 2
Condado Beach **2**
Isla Verde Beach **3**
Ocean Park **4**

Day 3
El Yunque **5**
Luquillo Beach **6**

Day 4
Las Croabas **7**
Palmas del Mar **8**
Fajardo **9**

Days 5 & 6
Vieques **10**

Day 7
Culebra **11**

Day 8
San Juan **1**

Day 9
Ponce **12**

Day 10
Boquerón **13**
San Germán **14**

Day 11
Mayagüez **15**

Day 12
Isla Mona **16**

Day 13
Rincón **17**

Day 14
Arecibo Observatory **18**
Indian Ceremonial
Park **19**
Rio Camuy Caves **20**

Caribbean with bargains galore. Allow about 2 hours of shopping before returning to your hotel room for a much-needed rest. In the early evening, select a typical Puerto Rican restaurant, preferably one with music, and soak up island atmosphere while enjoying good regional dishes.

On **Day 2,** with shopping and sightseeing behind you, enjoy the sports activities and/or beaches of the Greater San Juan area. See the "Diving, Fishing, Tennis & Other Pursuits" section beginning on p. 145. Of course, there's nothing wrong with spending a day at the beach. For many visitors, that's why they came to San Juan in the first place. Depending on the location of your hotel, the finest beaches are **Condado Beach** (p. 145), **Isla Verde Beach** (p. 145), and **Ocean Park Beach** (p. 145). Since you're likely to be better rested on your second day in town, enjoy some of the nightlife of the capital, either bar hopping, taking in the club or music scene, or going casino gambling. San Juan is one of the nightlife capitals of the Caribbean. See the "San Juan After Dark" section, beginning on p. 158.

Day ❸: El Yunque 🍃🍃🍃 and Luquillo Beach 🍃🍃🍃

While still based in San Juan, drive east for 25 miles (40km) to **El Yunque** for a morning visit. This 28,000-acre (11,331-hectare) attraction is the only tropical rainforest in the U.S. National Forest Service system. Stop first at **El Portal Tropical Forest Center** (p. 172) for maps and guidance. You're faced with a choice of hiking trails or else driving through. Unless you engage in extensive hiking, you can see some of the forest's greatest beauty in time for lunch.

After a visit to the rainforest, head north toward the town of Rio Grande and follow the signs to **Luquillo Beach** in the east. There are many roadside signs and kiosks where you can enjoy a tasty but inexpensive lunch. Shaded by tall coconut palms, the beach is crowded on weekends.

Surfing, kayaking, diving, and snorkeling are just some of the activities you can enjoy here, along with the golden sands of the beach itself. There are also refreshment stands and a bathhouse as well as toilets. Return west to San Juan for a final night.

Days ❹ & ❺: Ponce 🍃🍃

Leave San Juan on the morning of **Day 4** and drive 75 miles (121km) southwest to the city of **Ponce,** the island's "second city." Take Route 1 south to Highway 52, then continue south and west to Ponce, following the road signs. Allow at least 1½ hours for the drive. Once in Ponce, check into a hotel for 2 nights.

For orientation and to see the historic city, see "Walking Tour: Old San Juan," on p. 139, which includes a stopover at **Parque de Bombas,** the famous firehouse. The chief attraction of Ponce, which could easily absorb 2 hours of your time, is the **Museo de Arte de Ponce** (p. 181). After some shopping and a local lunch in the old town, spend the rest of the day at **Playa de Ponce,** a long strip of white sand opening onto the tranquil Caribbean. Return to Ponce for the night, perhaps gambling and enjoying entertainment at the **Ponce Hilton & Casino** (p. 188) even if you're not staying here.

On the morning of **Day 5,** drive to the major attractions in the environs, especially **Guánica State Forest,** west of Ponce along Route 2. This is the best-preserved subtropical ecosystem on the planet, and you'll want to spend at least 2 hours here, taking in some of the 750 plants and rare tree species that grow here. For coverage, see p. 182. If you secured the makings of a picnic lunch, you can enjoy it at the **Carite Forest Reserve** (p. 183), which lies an hour's drive east of Ponce along Route 52. The forest borders a lake of the same name.

Now you have a choice. You can visit yet another forest reserve, **Toro Negro Forest Reserve** (p. 183), a 7,200-acre (2,914-hectare) park, straddling the highest peak of the Cordillera Central, or else head for **Playa de Ponce** to get in some more serious beaching before nightfall. If you opted for the forest reserve, you can take in the most beautiful lake of Puerto Rico—and also its loftiest. **Lake Guineo** records the lowest temperatures on island. Many hiking possibilities are available from this lake site. Return to Ponce for the night.

Day ⑥: Boquerón & San Germán 𝓰𝓰

On **Day 6,** leave Ponce early in the morning, driving 34 miles (55km) west to the historic city of San Germán. Coverage begins on p. 197. Before lunch, you'll have time to take in the town's major attractions, including **Iglesia Porta Coeli** and **San Germán de Auxerre.** Have lunch in San Germán.

In the early afternoon you can head southwest to the town of **Boquerón,** 34 miles (55km) west of Ponce where you can spend the night. There are several moderately priced places to stay here. If you want to explore, you can go south to **El Faro de Cabo Rojo,** a lighthouse at Puerto Rico's southernmost corner. Or else you can do as much as other visitors do, and spend the rest of the day on a great beach, **Boquerón Beach** with its golden sands. After a seafood dinner and perhaps some music from an island band, you can turn in for the night.

Day ⑦: Mayagüez 𝓰 & Isla Mona 𝓰𝓰𝓰

You have a choice on this day. Both of them involve an overnight in Mayagüez,

the "third city" of Puerto Rico. We'd recommend a trip to Mona Island (see below). If that proves too difficult to arrange, have a leisurely day on the Puerto Rican mainland. In the morning before leaving the Boquerón area, explore the **Refugio Nacional Cabo Rojo** (p. 196), which has the best bird-watching on island. After that, continue north along Route 12 until you reach the city of Mayagüez where you can overnight. Once here you can explore the **Tropical Agriculture Research Station** (p. 192) and also pay an afternoon visit to **Maricao State Forest** (p. 192). There is a picnic area here which would make an idyllic spot for lunch. Coverage of the forest reserve is on p. 192. We recommend that you spend the rest of the day enjoying the beaches that lie north of Mayagüez on the way to Rincón. **Punta Higüero** is a local favorite. Return to Mayagüez for the night.

If you can arrange boat transport to **Mona Island** (p. 194), we suggest you skip all these Mayagüez activities and spend the day on this uninhabited island, called "the Galápagos of Puerto Rico." The island is inhabited by giant iguanas and three species of endangered sea turtles, among other wildlife. You'll have to return to Mayagüez for the night unless you plan to camp out.

The following morning, you'll find that it's only a 98-mile (158km) drive northeast back to San Juan, the hub of all the island's major transportation.

2 The Best of Puerto Rico in 2 Weeks

This tour, the longest in this series, is also the most recommended. It encapsulates the very essence of the island—you might label it "Puerto Rico In a Nutshell." Because of the island's small size, you can visit not only its three major cities (**San Juan, Ponce,** and **Mayagüez**) but also its greatest attraction, the **El Yunque** rainforest; its finest beach (**Luquillo**); its offshore islands (**Mona, Vieques,** and **Culebra**); and even its most intriguing man-made attractions, such as the alien-hunting **Arecibo Observatory.** To start, follow the first 3 days of the "Best of Puerto Rico in One Week" itinerary above (San Juan on Days 1 and 2, El Yunque and Luquillo Beach on Day 3), then head to Las Croabas to begin Day 4.

Day ❹: Las Croabas & Palmas del Mar

The northeast corner of Puerto Rico is filled with sports and attractions and is deserving of at least a day of your time, especially if you like outdoor pursuits. We'd recommend that you check into **El Conquistador Resort & Golden Door Spa** (p. 223) for the day, taking advantage of its vast array of facilities and restaurants, as well as its health club, spa, children's programs, and watersports equipment.

Using the resort as a base, you can explore **Las Cabezas de San Juan Nature Reserve** (p. 222), with its famous lighthouse, "El Faro." Boaters are attracted to **Puerto del Rey** (the Caribbean's largest and most modern marina), and beach buffs flock to such strips of white sand as **Playa Seven Seas** or **Playa Escondido** ("Hidden Beach"). See p. 222 for more coverage of these sandy strips.

If you can tear yourself away from Las Croabas for a few hours, you can also drive down to Fajardo and the nearby resort of **Palmas del Mar** where you can participate in the best-organized sporting activities in eastern Puerto Rico, ranging from vast tennis courts to scuba diving and golf, along with deep-sea fishing (see coverage beginning on p. 225). Palmas also has 3 miles (4.8km) of exceptional white sandy beaches, all open to the public. There are also a large number of places for lunch at the resort and several good seafood restaurants at the port of **Fajardo.**

If you can't afford the prices of El Conquistador, consider an overnight stay at one of the small inns in the area. See "Paradores of Eastern Puerto Rico," p. 228.

Days ❺ & ❻: Vieques ☞

Regardless of where you based for the night, arrive early at the port of Fajardo on Puerto Rico's eastern coast for a 1-hour ferryboat ride to the island of **Vieques,** the largest of the so-called Spanish Virgin Islands (it is, in fact, a U.S. territory). Check into a hotel here for 2 nights. Resorts and small inns come in all price ranges (coverage of hotels begins on p. 235).

A stopover in Vieques might be the most idyllic spot in your vacation, as the island offers 40 beautiful white sandy beaches, all open to the public. See **"The Best Beaches,"** with coverage beginning on p. 232. Lazy days in the sun aren't the only activities on island. You can tour the luminous waters of **Phosphorescent Bay,** join mountain bike excursions, go fishing from a kayak, take snorkeling trips, or go scuba diving. You can more or less forget about man-made attractions unless you want to visit **Fort Conde de Mirasol Museum** (p. 234). At night Vieques offers a wide choices of bars and good restaurants, the best available on any of Puerto Rico's offshore islands.

Day ❼: Culebra ☞

Should you have come down with island fever, you can return to the port of Fajardo and take another ferry for an overnight stopover on the island of Culebra, which is far more offbeat and undiscovered than Vieques. It's the way the Caribbean used to be back in the '50s. All the inns are relatively simple, as are the restaurants, each of which specializes in seafood. At least Culebra will be kind to your wallet, although you won't live in luxury.

Like Vieques, Culebra is chock-full of white sandy beaches, and you can explore the **Culebra Wildlife Refuge** (p. 244). Also snorkel here, or kayak, fish, sail, or hike. *Tip:* The best way to explore the island is to rent and drive a jeep—though most visitors prefer to hang out for the day on one of Culebra's beaches. Our preferred beach for the day? It's the mile-long (1.6km) **Flamenco Beach.** The next morning return by ferry to the port of Fajardo for a continuation of our tour.

Day ❽: San Juan ✦✦✦

On the morning of **Day 8,** leave Culebra by taking a ferryboat back to the port of Fajardo. From here, drive west to San Juan for an overnight stopover. Since the city is so vast and so filled with amusements, try to use the time to mop up all the shopping, attractions, and nightlife options you missed on your first visit. Review chapter 7 for all the possible options, including outdoor pursuits, awaiting for you. You can more or less fashion an itinerary on this day to suit your individual interests (shopping, beaches, sightseeing, and so forth).

Day ❾: Ponce ✦✦

On the morning of **Day 9,** leave San Juan and drive south to Ponce, the chief city on the southern coast. Follow the suggestions as outlined in Day 4 of "The Best of Puerto Rico in One Week" (above), adding a few excursions from Day 5 if you have time.

Day ❿: Boquerón & San Germán ✦✦

Follow the suggestions for Day 6 of "The Best of Puerto Rico in One Week," above.

Day ⓫: Mayagüez ✦

For suggestions, refer to Day 7 in "The Best of Puerto Rico in One Week," above. However, save a separate day for Isla Mona (see below), which richly deserves it.

Day ⓬: Isla Mona ✦✦✦

Boat excursions over to this island are not as organized as they should be, but it's worth the trouble to get to Mona, even enduring a difficult sea crossing across Pasaje de la Mona. Coverage begins on p. 194. Most visitors use Mayagüez (see above) as their base for exploring Mona Island, returning to the mainland for the night. Other more adventurous travelers camp out on the island. Lying some 50 miles (80km) off the Puerto Rican

mainland, Mona has been called the Jurassic Park of the Caribbean.

A nature reserve since 1919, Mona has been uninhabited for the past half-century except for day-trippers. Living here is every species from fish-eating bats to wild goats and pigs, and especially giant iguanas. The environment is beautiful, but potentially hostile because of its wildness. A deputy from the Department of Natural Resources is on hand to offer advice and guidance. There are toilets and saltwater showers at Playa Sardinera. Return to Mayagüez in the evening.

Day ⓭: Rincón

On the morning of Day 13, drive north from Mayagüez into Rincón, the windsurfing capital of the Caribbean. You'll find a number of accommodations, ranging from a deluxe resort to simple inns. Coverage begins on p. 203. Even if you're not a windsurfer, you are likely to enjoy the laid-back beach life on the westernmost point of the island. Rincón's **Playa Higüero** (p. 202) is one of the finest surfing spots in the world, and there is also good snorkeling nearby, even winter whale-watching. Many outdoor pursuits, including fun cruises and fishing, are offered to visitors. There is also nearby golf. Rincón abounds in bars and seafood taverns. The day will pass quickly.

Day ⓮: Arecibo ✦, Indian Ceremonial Park & Rio Camuy Caves ✦✦✦

As you head east for your return to San Juan, you can take in three wonders of Puerto Rico. The **Observatorio de Arecibo** (p. 166) is the world's largest and most sensitive radar/radio-telescope, searching for extraterrestrial life in the universe beyond. In Karst Country, the **Indian Ceremonial Park** at Caguaña (p. 169) was built by the Taíno Indians a thousand years ago. The grandest attraction of all, the **Rio Camuy Caves** (p. 166) contains the third-largest underground river in the world. With proper timing, all three of these attractions can be explored in 1 day, with time still left for the final drive back into San Juan. Arm yourself with a good map and explore our coverage of these attractions in chapter 8 before heading here. Following your visits, continue to San Juan at a distance of some 68 miles (109km) to the west.

3 Puerto Rico for Families

Puerto Ricans love their **niños,** and places all over the island are kid-friendly. The nature of the island itself, with its parks, beach-studded seaside resorts, and amusement centers virtually invite you for a family outing. Don't forget that picnic lunch.

Days ❶ & ❷: San Juan 𝕲𝕲𝕲

The historic old city of San Juan has more to offer children than any other Caribbean capital. The walled Old Town doesn't exactly look as if built by Walt himself, but it's the most fun for kids to enjoy. They like to hop on and off the Old Town Trolley as they explore forts, a kiddie museum designed just for them, or look at the world's most stunning collection of mounted butterflies. Begin with our walking tour of Old San Juan (p. 139) in the morning, with special visits to **Castillo de San Felipe del Morro** (p. 128) and **Fort San Cristóbal** (p. 130). If you have time for only one such visit, make it El Morro with its tunnels, vaults, look-out points, dungeons, and ramps. For lunch, join other Puerto Rican families at **La Bombonera** (p. 144), even if it's only for a sandwich. The best baked goods in Old Town are sold here.

After lunch, take the kids for a half-day at one of the **beaches** along the Condado or Isla Verde. Refer to "The Beaches" in chapter 7 for more details.

On the morning of **Day 2,** return to San Juan's Old Town for a visit to the **Museo del Niño (Children's Museum,** p. 139). With its many interactive exhibits, this is the only museum in Puerto Rico devoted to children. Afterward, drop in to call on the **Butterfly People** (p. 150). Although all the stunningly beautiful and mounted winged creatures are for sale, the store is a virtual museum of butterflies. Before leaving San Juan, let your kids enjoy a burger at the most typically American restaurant here, **El Patio de Sam** (p. 159).

For your remaining afternoon in San Juan, head for one of the beaches again, either on the Condado or Isla Verde. Or else spend the afternoon at the **Time Out Family Amusement Center** (p. 139), the largest of its type in Puerto Rico and the most popular for family outings on the island. Return to San Juan for the night.

Day ❸: El Yunque 𝕲𝕲𝕲 and Luquillo Beach 𝕲𝕲𝕲

While still based in San Juan, journey east for a day to two of the island's biggest attractions: **El Yunque** rainforest and the island's most famous and best beach, **Luquillo.** For suggestions, refer to Day 3 above, "The Best of Puerto Rico in One Week."

Day ❹: Ponce 𝕲𝕲

On the morning of **Day 4,** leave San Juan early in the morning for a scenic drive southwest to the second city of Ponce, a distance of 75 miles (121km). This is one of the most kid-friendly destinations on the island, and you can take our walking tour for a preview of the city's history and its old streets. See p. 178 for directions. Adults will want to slip into the major attraction, **Museo de Arte de Ponce** (p. 181), and hopefully your kids will find something to interest them here, too.

After lunch, take the brood to the **Parque de Bombas,** with its famous firehouse (p. 182). After that, head for an afternoon at the beach at **Playa de Ponce** (p. 186), a long strip of white sand. When the sun starts to set, stroll along the public boardwalk, **La Guancha** (p. 186) south of the city. This is like a more wholesome version of New York's Coney Island and is often mobbed with families. There are snack bars galore. Overnight in Ponce.

Day ❺: Guánica, La Parguera & Boquerón

The entire family can enjoy a tour of the southwest corner of Puerto Rico, lying to the immediate west of Ponce. Your first stop could be **Guánica** (p. 182), 21 miles (34km) west of Ponce. This is a world-designated biosphere reserve adjacent to Guánica's dry forest, home to some 100 species of birds. The beach here is ideal for swimming and snorkeling, and boat trips can be arranged to **Gilligan's Island** (yes, the same name as that old TV sitcom). Part of the forest reserve, the island is a series of mangrove and sandy cays off the Caña Gorda peninsula. In or near Guánica, you can select your hotel for the night. The best choices for families are **Copamarina Beach Resort** (p. 213) or **Mary Lee's by the Sea** (p. 213).

After lunch at your hotel, you can continue immediately west to **La Parguera** (p. 209), a fishing village 26 miles (42km) west of Ponce. The little town is known for its beaches and for its diving. After an hour or so visit, you can continue west to **Boquerón** (p. 208), a little beach town near the western edge of a forest reserve. Its public beach here is one of the safest for children in the area. At some point before the afternoon fades, you can drive down to **El Faro de Cabo Rojo,** with its famous lighthouse at the southernmost corner of Puerto Rico.

Day ❻: Mayagüez ๛ & Rincón

On the morning of **Day 6,** continue north along the western coast to the largest city in the west coast, the old port of Mayagüez (coverage begins on p. 191), which has seen a greater day. Now in sad decline, it nonetheless makes a good stopover. South of the city you approach one of the west coast's best beaches, **Boquerón Beach,** with a strip of white sand and fine snorkeling. Consider a 2-hour beach layover for your children before continuing into the city to see the **Tropical Agriculture Research Station** (p. 192), one of the greatest tropical gardens in the Caribbean.

Afterward, pick up the makings of a picnic and enjoy it at one of the outdoor tables in the **Maricao State Forest** (p. 192), with its hiking trails and observation tower. A trip to Maricao will give your family a chance to explore some of the interior of the mountainous island—not just the coastline.

After a visit, head back to Mayagüez and continue up the coast to Rincón for the night. There are plenty of accommodations here in all price ranges. Coverage begins on p. 200. Many of the beaches, though scenic, are not suitable for swimming for young children, but are idyllic for windsurfers. There are many seafood restaurants in the area, which would be a fine way for the entire family to end their exploration of the west coast.

Day ❼: Arecibo ๛, Indian Ceremonial Park & Rio Camuy Caves ๛๛๛

For your final day, you can take in three major island attractions on your drive east back to San Juan and its transportation hub. For details, refer to Day 14 under "The Best of San Juan in Two Weeks."

4 La Ruta Panorámica in 2 Days

"The Panoramic Route"—called *La Ruta Panorámica* by Puerto Ricans—winds its way through the Central Mountains in the heart of the island for some 100 miles (161km). This is the most scenic drive in the Caribbean. The mountains are the home of the *jíbaro*—we'd call them hillbillies—who still live an agricultural life far removed from the rest of industrial Puerto Rico. Expect winding, twisting roads, and don't forget to blow your horn as you turn blind curves. After rainstorms, there are frequent washouts. Although locals speed by you as if in a race car, it's advisable for newcomers to go no more than 25 mph (40kmph). In spite of some difficulties, it's worth the effort to cross through the Cordillera Central's dramatic peaks and valleys. The Cordillera mountains rise more than 4,000 feet (1,219m) in some places. You'll pass by **Cerro de Punta,** which at 4,389 feet (1,338m) is the highest in Puerto Rico. From these mountains came music and even literature that helped define Puerto Rico.

Day ❶: From Carite Forest ☀ to Jayuya

Leave San Juan early in the morning for the drive south, taking Highway 52 to exit 32, which will take you to Route 184, also heading south. Stay on 184 as it cuts right through the most scenic parts of the **Carite Forest Reserve.** Roadside grills tempt with the succulent *lechón* (roasted pig) sold at the area's famous *lechoneras. Sanjuaneros* flock here on weekends to enjoy the cool mountain breezes and the grills, even dance halls that line 184. There are also cool swimming holes throughout the forest and recreation areas. For more information, refer to Carite Forest Reserve (p. 183).

Highway 184 leads into Route 179 which you can follow out of the forest reserve (signposts lead to **Lago Carite,** the largest lake in the forest). To continue west along the route, follow the signs northwest to the town of Cayey. The surrounding area is called the "Switzerland of Puerto Rico," and many *sanjuaneros* use it as their vacation homes.

Once at Cayey, follow Route 1 south to Route 7722. On Route 7722, turn right on Route 722 which leads directly into **Aibonito.**

You'll feel you've wandered back into a time capsule, especially in the Aibonito town center with its main plaza and historic church. Only the most adventurous hike the **Cañon de San Cristóbal,** a canyon lying between Aibonito and Barranquitas. Scenically, it's beautiful but can be dangerous without a guide (visitors have been killed here). With its waterfalls and forbidding cliffs, it's a thrill but risky. San Cristóbal is cut 500 feet (152m) into the Cordillera Central and lies some 5 miles (8km) north of Aibonito.

In Aibonito, there are many cafeterias around the main plaza, our favorite being **Café Sandoval's,** Calle Muñoz Rivera 34 (✆ **787/857-3475**). Here you can pick up the makings for a picnic lunch to be enjoyed at the Reserve Forestal Toro Negro (see below).

Leave Aibonito and follow the signs toward our next stopover, **Toro Negro Forest Reserve** and **Lake Guineo** (for complete details see p. 183). The forest reserve lies to the west and is reached by heading west on Route 723, which becomes Route 143 as it winds its way to the reserve.

We find the panoramic views from this forest reserve the most impressive along the Ruta Panorámica. The most popular area is the Recreativa Doña Juana, with its short trails and stream-fed swimming pool. You can enjoy your picnic in this section. At the pool are changing rooms, toilets, and showers. It is open only April to September Saturday and Sunday from 9am to 5pm, charging $1.

In the eastern side of the forest is the famous **Doña Juana Waterfall** (Rte. 149, 41.5km) cascading 120 feet (37m) over a rock-strewn cliff.

There is a **Visitors Center** at Route 143, 32.4km (© 787/867-3040), offering you a trail map; it's open daily from 8am to 4pm. There are no supplies in the park so bring mosquito repellent and bottled water.

After a day of sightseeing, you can seek accommodations for the night. We'd suggest you head for the little town of **Jayuya,** in the foothills of Cerro Punta, only a half-hour drive off Ruta Panorámica. Our recommendation of an inn is **Parador Hacienda Gripiñas** (p. 215). From Route 143 cut north along Route 149 and then turn west at the junction of Route 144 signposted into Jayuya.

Day ❷: Utuado, Adjuntas & Maricao

The next morning leave Jayuya in the morning, cutting south on Route 44, then northwest along Route 140 (which becomes Rte. 111), following the signs into the town of **Utuado,** site of another well-known parador, **Casa Grande Mountain Retreat** (p. 216), which could have made another stopover for you if you chose not to spend the night at Jayuya. For more details on the town, see p. 214.

With its Spanish-styled central plaza, Utuado still reflects its colonial roots, although it was once inhabited by the Taíno Indians. Most visitors arrive here to explore the **Indian Ceremonial Park** at Caguaña (p. 217). This is the largest site of Taíno ruins in Puerto Rico.

After wandering around the town for an hour or two, head for our next stopover, the coffee-exporting town of **Adjuntas.** Follow the curvy Route 10 south, a grand panoramic ride but tricky.

Once again, you confront a colonial-inspired central plaza and can spend another hour or two exploring the narrow streets.

This town has an **Oficina de Turismo** at the Town Hall (Ayuntamiento) on a corner of the main square (© 787/ 829-5000), open Monday to Friday 8am to 4:30pm.

Adjuntas is known as "the town of the sleeping giant," because of its silhouette created by the enveloping mountains. In addition to coffee, it is also the "orange capital" of the island. This is not the most idyllic stopover along Ruta Panorámica because of all the heavy traffic, especially trucks, picking up coffee or citrus shipments.

Ruta Panorámica winds south (follow the signs) to **Bosque Estatal de Guilarte,** the beauty spot of the area. Composed of 3,600 acres (1,457 hectares), most of Guilarte is rainforest (hardly El Yunque, however). Sierra palms dot the forest, and **Lago Garzas,** a lake, is popular with fishermen. If you purchased the makings of a picnic lunch in Adjuntas, you can enjoy it in a sheltered area at the junction of Route 518 and Route 131, complete with cooking grills and toilets. You can climb a trail that takes you to the peak of **Monte Guilarte** at 3,950 feet (1,204m).

After a visit, head north again along Route 518, traveling west to our final stopover at **Maricao.** This winding road changes its number so many times you'll lose track; follow the signposts to Maricao and not the route numbers and you won't go wrong.

For details on the **Maricao State Forest,** see p. 192 under Mayagüez. This is the largest state forest on the island, and you can spend all day exploring it. The coffee-producing town is the smallest municipality in Puerto Rico. It lies at the far western end of Ruta Panorámica, and is an idyllic retreat for exploring, as it's surrounded by mountain gorges, old bridges, terraced houses, rushing streams of cold water, and enough switchback roads to challenge the most skilled of alpine drivers.

Since there are picnic areas in the forest, we suggest you take lunch here surrounded by mountain peaks. You can pick up food at **El Buen Café** (© 787/ **838-4198**), on the main plaza of Maricao, ordering sandwiches and drinks or else plates of *comida criolla,* local island dishes. It's open Monday from 6am to 3pm, Tuesday and Wednesday 6am to 10pm, and Thursday to Sunday 6am to midnight.

There is a **Visitor Center** at Route 120, Km 16.2 (© **787/838-1040**), which will provide maps of the forest and even hook you up with a private guide if you want to do more extensive exploring. Hours are Monday to Friday 7am to 3:30pm and Saturday and Sunday 8am to 3:30pm. If you climb **Torre de Observación,** you can take in a panoramic sweep of the entire western half of Puerto Rico. It is open daily from 8am to 4pm (free admission).

The best place for overnighting in the area is **Parador Hacienda Juanita** (p. 196), or else you can continue west into Mayagüez for the night. After the tour of the panoramic route, you can continue from Mayagüez to San Juan, a distance of 98 miles (158km) to the northeast.

4

Getting to Know San Juan

All but a handful of visitors arrive in San Juan, the capital city. It is the political base, economic powerhouse, and cultural center of the island, and it's home to about one-third of all Puerto Ricans.

The second-oldest city in the Americas (behind Santo Domingo in the Dominican Republic), this metropolis presents two different faces. On one hand, the charming historic district, Old San Juan, is strongly reminiscent of the Spanish Empire. On the other hand, modern expressways outside the historic district cut through urban sprawl to link towering concrete buildings and beachfront hotels resembling those of Miami Beach.

Old San Juan is a 7-square-block area that was once completely enclosed by a wall erected by the Spanish with slave labor. The most powerful fortress in the Caribbean, this fortified city repeatedly held off would-be attackers. By the 19th century, however, it had become one of the Caribbean's most charming residential and commercial districts. Today it's a setting for restaurants and shops. Most of the major resort hotels are located nearby, along the Condado beachfront and at Isla Verde (see chapter 5).

1 Orientation

ARRIVING BY PLANE & GETTING FROM THE AIRPORT INTO THE CITY

Visitors from overseas arrive at **Luis Muñoz Marín International Airport** (© 787/ 791-1014), the major transportation center of the Caribbean. The airport is on the easternmost side of the city, rather inconvenient to nearly all hotels except the resorts and small inns at Isla Verde.

The airport offers services such as a tourist-information center, restaurants, hair stylists, coin lockers for storing luggage, bookstores, banks, currency-exchange kiosks, and a bar (open daily 9am–8pm) that offers Puerto Rican rums.

BY TAXI   Some of the larger hotels send vans to pick up airport passengers and transport them to various properties along the beachfront. It's wise to find out if your hotel offers this service when making a reservation. If your hotel doesn't have shuttle service between the airport and its precincts, you'll have to get there on your own steam—most likely by taxi. Dozens of taxis line up outside the airport to meet arriving flights, so you rarely have to wait. Fares can vary widely, depending on traffic conditions. Again depending on traffic, figure on about a 30-minute drive from the airport to your hotel along the Condado.

Although technically cabdrivers should turn on their meters, more often than not they'll quote a flat rate before starting out. The rate system seems effective and fair, and if you're caught in impenetrable traffic, it might actually work to your advantage. The island's **Tourist Transportation Division** (© 787/999-2100), establishes flat rates

San Juan Orientation

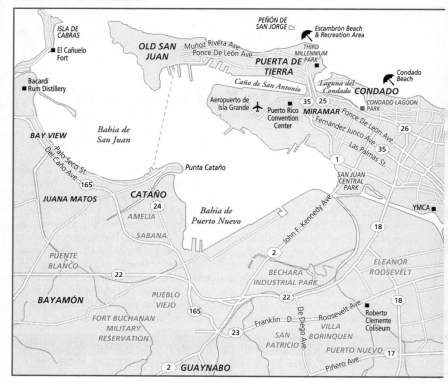

between the Luis Muñoz Marín International Airport and major tourist zones as listed here: From the airport to any hotel in Isla Verde, the fee is $8; to any hotel in the Condado district, the charge is $12; and to any hotel in Old San Juan, the cost is $16. Normal tipping supplements of between 10% and 15% of these fares are appreciated.

BY MINIVAN OR LIMOUSINE   A wide variety of vehicles at the San Juan airport call themselves *limosinas* (their Spanish name). For limousine service, **Bracero Limousine (© 787/253-8053)** offers cars with drivers that will meet you and your entourage at the arrivals terminal for luxurious, private transportation to your hotel. Transport to virtually anywhere in San Juan ranges from $85 to $125; transport to points throughout the island varies from $55 per hour in a sedan carrying four passengers to $75 per hour in a limousine with six passengers. Ideally, transport should be arranged in advance, so that a car and driver can be waiting for you near the arrivals terminal.

BY CAR   All the major car-rental companies have kiosks at the airport. Although it's possible to rent a car once you arrive, your best bet is to reserve one before you leave home. See the "Getting Around" section of chapter 2 for details.

To drive into the city, head west along Route 26, which becomes Route 25 as it enters Old San Juan. If you stay on Route 25 (also called Av. Muñoz Rivera), you'll have the best view of the ocean and the monumental city walls.

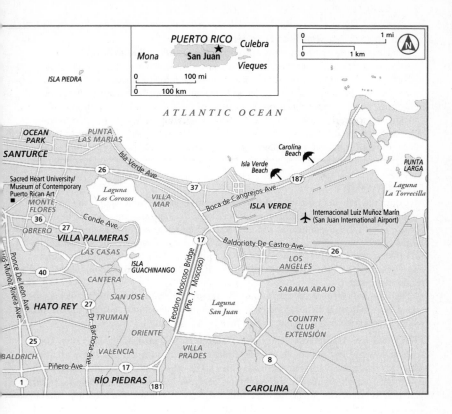

Just before you reach the capitol building, turn left between the Natural Resources Department and the modern House of Representatives office building. Go 2 blocks, until you reach the intersection of Paseo de Covadonga, and then take a right past the Treasury Building, and park your car in the **Covadonga Parking Garage** (© 787/ 7222-337) on the left. The garage is open 24 hours; the first hour costs $1, the second hour 65¢, and 24 hours costs $16.

BY BUS   Those with little luggage can take the A5 bus, which runs to the center of the city.

BY BIKE   Rentals are available at **Hot Dog Cycling,** Av. Isla Verde 5916 (© 787/ 982-5344), open Monday to Saturday 9am to 6pm. Charges for rentals are $15 per half-day, $25 for a full day.

VISITOR INFORMATION

Tourist information is available at the **Luís Muñoz Marín Airport** (© 787/791- 1014) daily from 9am to 10pm. Another office is at **La Casita,** Pier 1, Old San Juan (© 787/722-1709), open Saturday to Wednesday 9am to 8pm, Thursday and Friday 8:30am to 6:30pm.

San Juan Mass-Transit: Tren Urbano

Tren Urbano, the first mass-transit project in the history of Puerto Rico, opened in 2005, linking San Juan to its suburbs such as Santurce, Bayamón, and Guaynabo. Costing $1.55 billion, the system provides an easy mode of transportation to the most congested areas of metropolitan San Juan. During rush hour (5–9am and 3–6pm), the train operates every 5 minutes; otherwise, it runs every 10 minutes. There is no service daily from 11pm to 5am. The fare is $1.50 one-way. From the airport, it's possible to take the AMA-B40 bus to Tren Urbano, a 30-minute ride. For more information, call ℂ **866/900-1284;** www.ati.gobierno.pr.

CITY LAYOUT

Metropolitan San Juan includes the old walled city on San Juan Island; the city center on San Juan Island (called Puerta de Tierra), containing the capitol building; Santurce, on a larger peninsula, which is reached by causeway bridges from San Juan Island (the lagoon-front section here is called Miramar); Condado, the narrow peninsula that stretches from San Juan Island to Santurce; Hato Rey, the business center; Río Piedras, site of the University of Puerto Rico; and Bayamón, an industrial and residential quarter.

The Condado strip of beachfront hotels, restaurants, casinos, and nightclubs is separated from Miramar by a lagoon. Isla Verde, another resort area, is near the airport, which is separated from the rest of San Juan by an isthmus.

FINDING AN ADDRESS   Finding an address in San Juan isn't always easy. You'll have to contend not only with missing street signs and numbers but also with street addresses that appear sometimes in English and at other times in Spanish. The most common Spanish terms for thoroughfares are *calle* (street) and *avenida* (avenue). When it is used, the street number follows the street name; for example, the El Convento hotel is located at Calle del Cristo 100, in Old San Juan. Locating a building in Old San Juan is relatively easy. The area is only 7 square blocks, so by walking around, it's possible to locate most addresses.

STREET MAPS   *Qué Pasa?,* the monthly tourist magazine distributed free by the tourist office, contains accurate, easy-to-read maps of San Juan and the Condado that pinpoint the major attractions.

NEIGHBORHOODS IN BRIEF

OLD SAN JUAN This is the most historic area in the West Indies. Filled with Spanish colonial architecture and under constant restoration, it lies on the western end of an islet. It's encircled by water; on the north is the Atlantic Ocean and on the south and west is the tranquil San Juan Bay. Ponte San Antonio bridge connects the Old Town with "mainland" Puerto Rico. Ramparts and old Spanish fortresses form its outer walls.

PUERTA DE TIERRA Translated as "gateway to the land" or "gateway to the island," Puerta de Tierra lies just east of the old city walls of San Juan. It is split by Avenida Ponce de León and interconnects Old San Juan with the Puerto Rican "mainland." Founded by freed black slaves, the settlement today functions as the island's administrative center and is the site of military and government buildings, including the capitol and various U.S. naval reserves.

MIRAMAR Miramar is an upscale residential neighborhood across the bridge from Puerta de Tierra. Yachts anchor in its waters on the bay side of Ponte Isla Grande, and some of the finest homes in Puerto Rico are found here. It's also the site of Isla Grande Airport, where you can board flights to the islands of Vieques and Culebra.

CONDADO Linked to Puerta de Tierra and Old San Juan by a bridge built in 1910, the Condado was once known as the Riviera of the Caribbean, enjoying a voguish reputation in the 1920s. This beach-bordering district is wedged between the Atlantic Ocean and several large inland bodies of water, including the lakelike Los Corozos and Lagunas Condado. Over the years the area has declined. It is now a cliché to compare it to Miami Beach. But like Miami Beach, the Condado is making major improvements, although many parts of it remain seedy and in need of restoration. The *putas* (prostitutes), pimps, and drug dealers are still here, but there are many fine deluxe hotels as well. Much of the Condado architecture today is viewed as "kitsch," the way Art Deco on Miami Beach is prized. The area is especially popular with gays, but straights also flock here, especially those attracted to the beaches during cruise-ship stopovers. Much of the Condado has been turned into timeshare condos.

OCEAN PARK Dividing the competitive beach resort areas of the Condado and Isla Verde, Ocean Park is a beachfront residential neighborhood that's sometimes plagued by flooding, especially during hurricanes. It's completely built up today with houses that are smaller and more spread out than those in the Condado district. Beaches here are slightly less crowded than those at Condado or Isla Verde. Because several gay guesthouses are located here, some of the beaches of Ocean Park are popular with gay men.

VILLA PALMERAS Villa Palmeras is a residential sector and business area of San Juan, an eastern extension of the Santurce district. Its far-eastern frontier opens onto Laguna Los Corozos. On the eastern side of the water is the international airport. From the Old Town, Route 26 east takes you to this district.

ISLA VERDE East of the Condado, en route to the airport, Isla Verde—technically known as the "Carolina" section of San Juan—is the chief rival of the Condado. Because much of the Condado is in need of massive rejuvenation, many of the great resorts have fled east to Isla Verde, which has better, cleaner beaches. Don't come here for history or romance. Two features put Isla Verde on the tourist map: some of San Juan's best beaches and its most deluxe hotels. This district appeals to travelers who like a hotel to be a virtual theme park, with everything under one roof—entertainment, vast selections of dining, convenient shopping, pools, and an array of planned activities. Isla Verde is the Las Vegas of San Juan. The area roughly lies between Ocean Park and the San Juan airport. When visitors get tired of all this glamour and glitz, they can taxi into Old San Juan for museum hopping and shopping.

HATO REY Situated to the south of the Martín Peña canal, this area was a marsh until landfill and concrete changed it forever. Today it is the Wall Street of the West Indies, filled with many high-rises, a large federal complex, and many business and banking offices.

RIO PIEDRAS South of Hato Rey and Santurce, this is the site of the University of Puerto Rico. It's dominated by the landmark Roosevelt Bell Tower, named for Theodore Roosevelt, who donated the money for its construction. The main thoroughfare is Paseo de Diego, site of a popular local produce market. The Agricultural Experimental Station of Puerto Rico maintains a botanical garden that includes many tropical plants, including 125 species of palms.

BAYAMON The San Juan sprawl has reached this once-distant southwestern suburb, which was once farmland. Some 207,000 people and nearly 200 factories are now located in this large district. Bus no. 46 from the center of San Juan runs out here.

2 Getting Around

BY TAXI   Except for a handful of important, high-profile tourist routes, public taxis are metered within San Juan (or should be). Normal tipping supplements of between 10% and 15% are appreciated. Passengers traveling between most other destinations within greater San Juan are charged by meter readings. The initial charge is $1, plus 10¢ for each ¹⁄₁₆ mile (.1km) and 50¢ for every suitcase, with a minimum fare of $3. These rates apply to conventional *taxis turisticos,* which are usually white-painted vehicles with official logos on their doors. Owned by a medley of individual outfitters within San Juan, they maintain standards that are higher than those of the cheaper but more erratic and inconvenient *públicos,* which are described in chapter 2. Call the **PSC** (✆ 787/756-1443) to request information or to report any irregularities.

Taxis are invariably lined up outside the entrance to most of the island's hotels, and if they're not, a staff member can almost always call one for you. But if you want to arrange a taxi on your own, call the **Rochdale Cab Company** (✆ 787/721-1900) or the **Mejor Cab Company** (✆ 787/723-2460).

You'll have to negotiate a fare with the driver, usually at a flat rate, for trips to far-flung destinations within Puerto Rico.

BY BUS   The **Metropolitan Bus Authority** (✆ 787/767-7979 for route information) operates buses in the greater San Juan area. Bus stops are marked by upright metal signs or yellow posts that say PARADA. There's one bus terminal in the dock area and another at the Plaza de Colón. A typical fare is 25¢ to 50¢.

Most of the large hotels of the Condado and Isla Verde maintain air-conditioned buses that make free shuttle runs into Old San Juan. Clients are usually deposited at the Plaza de Colón. Public buses also make the run along the Condado, stopping at clearly designated bus stops placed near the major hotels. Public buses usually deposit their clients at the Plaza Colón and the main bus terminal across the street from the Cataño ferryboat pier. This section of Old San Juan is the starting point for many of the city's metropolitan bus routes.

Here are some useful public bus routes: Bus no. B21 goes from the Plaza de Colón along the Condado, eventually reaching the commercial section of San Juan, Hato Rey; bus no. A7 passes from Old San Juan to the Condado and goes on to Avenida Isla Verde; and no. A5 heads for Avenida de Diego in the Condado district, then makes a long run to Isla Verde and the airport.

ON FOOT   This is the only way to explore Old San Juan. All the major attractions can easily be covered in a day. If you're going from Old San Juan to Isla Verde, however, you'll need to rely on public transportation.

BY TROLLEY   When you tire of walking around Old San Juan, you can board one of the free trolleys that run through the historic area. Departure points are the Marina and La Puntilla, but you can board along the route by flagging the trolley down (wave at it and signal for it to stop) or by waiting at any of the clearly designated stopping points. Relax and enjoy the sights as the trolleys rumble through the old and narrow streets.

BY RENTAL CAR   See "Getting Around" in chapter 2 for details—including some reasons you shouldn't plan to drive in Puerto Rico.

BY FERRY   The **Acua Expreso** (✆ 787/729-8714) connects Old San Juan with the industrial and residential community of Cataño, across the bay. Ferries depart daily every 30 minutes from 6am to 9pm. The one-way fare to Cataño is 50¢. Departures are from the San Juan Terminal at pier number 2 in Old San Juan. However, it's best to avoid rush hours because hundreds of locals who work in town use this ferry. The ride lasts 6 minutes.

FAST FACTS: San Juan

Airport See "Arriving by Plane & Getting from the Airport into the City," earlier in this chapter.

American Express The agency is represented in San Juan by **Bithorn Travel,** Isla Verde Mall (✆ **787/791-0914**). The office is open Monday to Friday from 9am to 5pm.

Banks Most U.S. banks have branches with ATMs in San Juan, and are open Monday to Friday 8:30am to 4pm. Bank branches in malls are open Saturday 8:30am to 6pm and Sunday 9am to 3pm.

Bus Information For information about bus routes in San Juan, call ✆ **787/729-1512.**

Camera & Film **Cinefoto** (✆ **787/753-7238**), located in the Plaza Las Americas Shopping Mall in Hato Rey, offers a wide variety of photographic supplies. The shop is open Monday through Saturday from 9am to 9pm.

Car Rentals See "Getting Around" in chapter 2. If you want to reserve after you've arrived in Puerto Rico, call **Avis** (✆ **787/791-2500**), **Budget** (✆ **787/791-0600**), or **Hertz** (✆ **787/791-0840**).

Consulates **Britain** has a consulate at Av. Chardón 350 (✆ **787/758-9828**) at Hato Rey, open Monday to Friday 9am to 1pm and 2 to 5pm. The consulate for **Canada** is at Av. Ponce de León 273 (✆ **787/759-6629**), also at Hato Rey and open only by appointment.

Currency Exchange The unit of currency is the U.S. dollar. Most banks provide currency exchange, and you can also exchange money at the **Luis Muñoz Marín International Airport.** See "Money" in chapter 2.

Drugstores One of the most centrally located pharmacies is **Puerto Rican Drug Co.,** Calle San Francisco 157 (✆ **787/725-2202**), in Old San Juan. It's open Monday to Friday from 7:30am to 9:30pm, Saturday 8am to 9:30pm, and Sunday 8:30am to 7:30pm. **Walgreens,** Av. Ashford 1130, Condado (✆ **787/725-1510**), is open 24 hours.

Emergencies In an emergency, dial © **911.** Or call the local police (© **787/726-7020**), fire department (© **787/722-1120**), ambulance (© **787/343-2550**), or medical assistance (© **787/754-2222**).

Eyeglasses Services are available at **Pearle Vision Express,** Plaza Las Americas Shopping Mall (© **787/753-1033**). Hours are Monday to Saturday from 9am to 9pm and Sunday from 11am to 5pm.

Hospitals **Ashford Presbyterian Community Hospital,** Av. Ashford 1451 (© **787/721-2160**), maintains a 24-hour emergency room.

Information See "Visitor Information," earlier in this chapter.

Internet Access Try **CyberNet Café,** Av. Ashford 1128 (© **787/724-4033**) on the Condado, charging $5 for 35 minutes or $7 for 50 minutes. Open Monday to Saturday 9am to 11pm, Sunday 10am to 11pm.

Maps See "City Layout," earlier in this chapter.

Police Call © **787/726-7020** for the local police.

Post Office In San Juan, the **General Post Office** is at Av. F.D. Roosevelt 585 (© **787/622-1758**). If you don't know your address in San Juan, you can ask that your mail be sent here "c/o General Delivery." This main branch is open Monday to Friday from 5:30am to 6pm, Saturday from 6am to 2pm. A letter from Puerto Rico to the U.S. mainland will arrive in about 4 days. See "Fast Facts: Puerto Rico," in chapter 2, for more information.

Restrooms Restrooms are not public facilities accessible from the street. It's necessary to enter a hotel lobby, cafe, or restaurant to gain access to a toilet. Fortunately, large-scale hotels are familiar with this situation, and someone looking for a restroom usually isn't challenged during his or her pursuit.

Safety At night, exercise extreme caution when walking along the back streets of San Juan, and don't venture onto the unguarded public stretches of the Condado and Isla Verde beaches at night. All these areas are favorite targets for muggings.

Salons Most of San Juan's large resort hotels, including the Condado Plaza, the Marriott, and the Sheraton Old San Juan Hotel, maintain hair salons.

Taxis See "Getting Around," earlier in this chapter.

Telephone & Fax Many public telephones are available at **World Service Telephone (AT&T),** Pier 1, Old San Juan (© **787/721-2520**). To send a fax, go to **Eagle Print,** F. D. Roosevelt Blvd. 1229, Puerto Nuevo (© **787/782-7830**). For more information, see "Fast Facts: Puerto Rico" in chapter 2.

Tourist Offices See "Visitor Information," earlier in this chapter.

5

Where to Stay in San Juan

Whatever your preferences in accommodations—a beachfront resort or a place in historic Old San Juan, sumptuous luxury or an inexpensive base from which to see the sights—you can find a perfect fit in San Juan.

In addition to checking the recommendations listed here, you might want to contact a travel agent; there are package deals galore that can save you money and match you with an establishment that meets your requirements. See "Packages for the Independent Traveler," in chapter 2.

Before talking to a travel agent, you should refer to our comments about how to select a room in Puerto Rico. See "Tips on Choosing your Accommodations" in chapter 2. You should also refer to "Packages for the Independent Traveler" in the

same chapter, particularly if you're planning to book a deal with all your meals included.

Not all hotels here have air-conditioned rooms. We've pointed them out in the recommendations below. If air-conditioning is important to you, make sure "A/C" appears after "*In room:*" at the end of the listing.

If you prefer shopping and historic sights to the beach, then Old San Juan might be your preferred nest. The highrise resort hotels lie primarily along the Condado beach strip and the equally good sands of Isla Verde. The hotels along Condado and Isla Verde attract the cruise-ship and casino crowds. The hotels away from the beach in San Juan, in such sections as Santurce, are primarily for business clients.

TAXES & SERVICE CHARGES

All hotel rooms in Puerto Rico are subject to a tax that is not included in the rates given in this book. At casino hotels, the tax is 11%; at non-casino hotels, it's 9%. At country inns you pay a 7% tax. Most hotels also add a 10% service charge. If they don't, you're expected to tip for services rendered. When you're booking a room, it's a good idea to ask about these charges.

MAKING RESERVATIONS

You can make accommodations reservations via telephone, mail, fax, and, in some cases, the Internet. If you're booking into a chain hotel, such as a Hilton, you can easily make your reservations by calling the chain's toll-free numbers in many countries. We provide the North American toll-free numbers in this book.

You can usually cancel a room reservation 1 week ahead of time and get a full refund. A few places will return your money on cancellations up to 3 days before the reservation date; others won't return any of your deposit, even if you cancel far in advance. It's best to clarify this issue when you make your reservation. If booking by mail, include a stamped, self-addressed envelope with your payment so that the hotel can easily send you a receipt and confirmation.

If you arrive without a reservation, you need to begin your search for a room as early in the day as possible. If you arrive late at night and without a reservation, you might have to take what you can get, often in a price range much higher than you'd like.

San Juan has become a year-round destination, and summers are no longer as tranquil as they used to be. Nonetheless, hotels still have lower occupancy from mid-April to mid-December. Off-season discounts, which can be substantial, are often granted at the resort hotels during this slower period.

1 Old San Juan

Old San Juan is 1½ miles (2.4km) from the beach. You should choose a hotel here if you're more interested in shopping and attractions than you are in watersports. For the locations of hotels in Old San Juan, see the map on p. 81.

EXPENSIVE

El Convento ☆☆   Puerto Rico's most famous hotel came majestically back to life when it was restored and reopened in 1997, and it continues to offer some of the most charming and historic hotel experiences anywhere in the Caribbean. As one observer put it, El Convento "is an exquisitely wrought David on an island of otherwise glitzy Goliaths." Built in 1651 in the heart of the old city, it was the New World's first Carmelite convent, but over the years it played many roles, from a dance hall to a flophouse to a parking lot for garbage trucks. It first opened as a hotel in 1962.

The midsize accommodations include Spanish-style furnishings, throw rugs, beamed ceilings, paneling, and Andalusian terra-cotta floor tiles. Each unit contains king-size, queen-size, or two double or twin beds, fitted with fine linen. The small bathrooms, with tub/shower combinations, contain scales and second phones. For the ultimate in luxury, ask for Gloria Vanderbilt's restored suite or ask for no. 508, a corner room with panoramic views. Although the facilities here aren't as diverse as those of some resorts on the Condado or in Isla Verde, this hotel's sweeping charm and Old Town location usually compensate. The hotel has its own "beach club," although it's not on the beach itself. But it has arrangements with a nearby hotel where guests can enjoy beach facilities. The lower two floors feature a collection of shops, bars, and restaurants. The so-called pool here is accessible via the 4th floor, and it measures only about 6'×10' (1.8m×3m)—very small, but personalized, charming, and endearing because of its view over the facade of the nearby cathedral. There's a Jacuzzi immediately adjacent to the pool and a big sun terrace.

Calle del Cristo 100, San Juan, PR 00901. ✆ 800/468-2779 or 787/723-9020. Fax 787/721-2877. www.elconvento. com. 68 units. Winter $355–$410 double, from $650 suite; off season $225–$285 double. Rates include continental breakfast. AE, DC, DISC, MC, V. Parking $15. Bus: Old Town trolley. **Amenities:** 4 restaurants; 3 bars; small rooftop plunge pool; fitness center; Jacuzzi; massage; laundry service; dry cleaning; rooms for those w/limited mobility. *In room:* A/C, TV, dataport, coffeemaker, hair dryer, iron, safe.

Sheraton Old San Juan Hotel & Casino ☆   Opened in 1997, this dignified, nine-story, waterfront hotel was part of a $100-million renovation of San Juan's cruise-port facilities. The hotel has an unusual and desirable position between buildings erected by the Spanish monarchs in the 19th century and the city's busiest and most modern cruise-ship terminals. Most of the major cruise ships dock nearby, making this a worthwhile choice if you want to spend time in San Juan before boarding a ship. On

Old San Juan Accommodations & Dining

ATLANTIC OCEAN

SAN JUAN

area of detail

Castillo de San Felipe del Morro

El Campo del Morro

Cementerio de San Juan

Murallas de San Juan

ATLANTIC OCEAN

Fuerte San Cristobal

Muralles de San Juan

N

0   1/10 mile
0   100 meters

Calle del Morro

Norzagaray

Plaza San José

Del Cristo

Calle San Sebastian

de Valle

Calle Sol

Calle Luna

C. J. J. Acosta

Calle O'Donell

C. Tamarindo

C. Capilla

Calle Tanca

Calle San Justo

Plaza de Colon

Plaza de Armas

Calle San Jose

Calle Cruz

Calle San Francisco

Calle Fortaleza

Calle Tetuan

Paseo de la Princesa

Calle Presidio

Calle Puntillo

El Arsenal

Calle Recinto

Ave. Munoz Rivera

Ave. Ponce de Leon

Paseo de Covadonga

Ave. Fernandez Juncos

de Muelle

Calle Contreras

Calle Marina

Calle Allen

Calle Braumbaugh

25

38

25

1

20

21 to 26

28

7

3

4 5

6

2

1

8

9 10

11

12

13

14 15

16 17

18 19

DINING ◆

Al Dente **12**	El Picoteo **5**
Amadeus **4**	Fatty's **16**
Aquaviva **26**	Il Perugino **1**
Barú **6**	La Bombonera **10**
Bossa Nova **24**	La Chaumière **19**
Café Berlin **17**	La Mallorquina **9**
Café Bohemia **3**	La Querencia **22**
Café Puerto Rico **18**	Makarios **27**
Carli Café Concierto **11**	Ostra Cosa **2**
Casa Borinquen **4**	Parrot Club **25**
Dragonfly **26**	Patio del Nispero **3**
El Buen Samaritano **8**	Sofia **15**
El Jibarito **13**	Tantra **23**
El Patio de Sam **5**	Trois Cent Onze **21**
	Yeyos **14**

ACCOMMODATIONS ■

El Convento **3**
Gallery Inn at Galleria San Juan **7**
Hotel Milano **20**
Sheraton Old San Juan Hotel & Casino **28**

ⓘ Information   City Walls

81

days when cruise ships pull into port, the hotel's lobby and bars are likely to be jammed with passengers stretching their legs after a few days at sea.

Although the pastel building is modern, iron railings and exterior detailing convey a sense of colonial San Juan. The triangular shape of the building encircles an inner courtyard that floods light into the tasteful and comfortable bedrooms, each of which has two phone lines and a modem connection for laptop computers. Other than that, the smallish rooms lack character. Each room has a compact bathroom with a shower stall. Think of a Holiday Inn geared for business travelers. If you want Old Town character and atmosphere, head for El Convento (see above) instead. Most of the lobby level here is devoted to a mammoth casino. The upscale dining room serves perfectly fine, if unremarkable, international cuisine, with some regional specialties.

Calle Brumbaugh 100, San Juan, PR 00902. ✆ **787/721-5100**. Fax 787/721-1111. www.sheraton.com. 240 units. Winter $240–$345 double, $295–$395 suite; off season $135–$215 double, $190–$290 suite. AE, DC, DISC, MC, V. Free self-parking; valet parking $12. Bus: A7. **Amenities:** Restaurant; 3 bars; outdoor pool; fitness center; Jacuzzi; car-rental desk; business center; room service (6:30am–11:30pm); nonsmoking rooms; casino; rooms for those w/limited mobility. *In room:* A/C, TV, dataport, minibar, coffeemaker, hair dryer, iron, safe.

MODERATE

Gallery Inn at Galería San Juan ☞ *(Finds)* This hotel's location and ambience are unbeatable, though the nearest beach is a 15-minute ride away. Set on a hilltop in Old Town, with a sweeping sea view, this unusual hotel contains a maze of verdant courtyards. In the 1700s it was the home of an aristocratic Spanish family. Today it's the most whimsically bohemian hotel in the Caribbean. Jan D'Esopo and Manuco Gandia created this inn out of their art studio. They cast bronze in their studio when not attending to their collection of birds, including macaws and cockatoos. The entire inn is covered with clay and bronze figures as well as other original art. We suggest booking one of the least expensive doubles; even the cheapest units are fairly roomy and attractively furnished, with good beds.

Note to lovers: The honeymoon suite has a Jacuzzi on a private balcony with a panoramic view of El Morro. From the rooftop terrace, there is a 360-degree view of the historic Old Town and the port. This is the highest point in San Juan and the most idyllic place to enjoy a breeze at twilight and a glass of wine.

Calle Norzagaray 204–206, San Juan, PR 00901. ✆ **787/722-1808**. Fax 787/977-3929. www.thegalleryinn.com. 22 units (some with shower only). Year-round $175–$270 double; $350 suite. Rates include continental breakfast. AE, DC, MC, V. There are 6 free parking spaces, plus parking on the street. Bus: Old Town Trolley. **Amenities:** Breakfast room. *In room:* A/C, dataport, hair dryer.

Hotel Milano This Old Town hotel was created in April 1999 from a 1920s warehouse. You enter a wood-sheathed lobby at the lower, less desirable end of Calle Fortaleza before ascending to one of the clean, well-lit bedrooms. Despite its location in historic Old Town, there's not much charm about this place. The simple, modern rooms have cruise-ship-style decor and unremarkable views. The more expensive accommodations contain small refrigerators and dataports.

The building's fifth floor (the elevator goes only to the fourth floor) contains an alfresco Italian and Puerto Rican restaurant called the Panoramic, which has views of San Juan's harbor.

Calle Fortaleza 307, San Juan, PR 00901. ✆ **877/729-9050** or 787/729-9050. Fax 787/722-3379. www.hotel milanopr.com. 30 units. Winter $90–$165 double; off season $80–$145 double. Rates include continental breakfast. AE, MC, V. Bus: Old Town trolley. **Amenities:** Restaurant; bar; nonsmoking rooms; rooms for those w/limited mobility. *In room:* A/C, TV, dataport (in some), fridge, hair dryer.

2 Puerta de Tierra

Stay in Puerta de Tierra only if you have a desire to be at either the Caribe Hilton or the Normandie Hotel. When you stay in Puerta de Tierra, you're sandwiched halfway between Old San Juan and the Condado, but you're not getting the advantages of staying right in the heart of either. For the location of hotels in Puerta de Tierra, see the map on p. 85.

Caribe Hilton ✦✦✦   Thanks to rivers of money poured into its radical renovation, this deluxe hotel is one of the most up-to-date spa and convention hotels in San Juan. Because of an unusual configuration of natural barriers and legal maneuverings, the hotel has the only private beach on the island (and the only garden incorporating an antique naval installation: the semi-ruined colonial Fort San Gerónimo). Because this beachfront hotel was the first Hilton ever built outside the U.S. mainland (in 1949), the chain considers it its most historic property. The Caribe's size (17 acres/6.8 hectares of parks and gardens) and sprawling facilities often attract conventions and tour groups. Only the Condado Plaza and the El San Juan rival it for nonstop activity.

Rooms have been radically upgraded. Variations in price are related to the views outside and the amenities within. Each room has a larger-than-expected bathroom with a tub/shower combo as well as comfortable, tropical-inspired furniture. In the Caribe Terrace Bar, you can order the bartender's celebrated piña colada, which was once enjoyed by movie legends Joan Crawford and Errol Flynn. An oceanfront spa and fitness center is the only beachside spa in Puerto Rico. It features such tantalizing delights as couples massages, body wraps, hydrotherapy tub treatments, and soothing cucumber sun therapies.

Hilton operates the largest casino in the Caribbean on the grounds here. The best place to stay here is in one of the 158 new luxury villas with more than 1,500 square feet (139 sq. m) of space, all part of the Condado Lagoon Villas. Up for grabs are studios or one- or two-bedroom luxury accommodations, each with spectacular views of the Condado Lagoon and the Atlantic Ocean. Each comes with a kitchen, private balcony, and a marble bathroom with Jacuzzi. Winter rates are $335 in a studio for two, rising to $445 in a one-bedroom suite, and topping at $545 in a two-bedroom suite. Off-season rates are $285 studio, $395 one-bedroom suite, and $495 two-bedroom suite. All the services of the Caribe Hilton's main hotel are provided to guests of the villas.

Calle Los Rosales, San Juan, PR 00901. ℰ 800/HILTONS or 787/721-0303. Fax 787/725-8849. www.caribe.hilton. com. 646 units. Winter $370–$400 double; off season $265–$300 double; year-round $500–$1,200 suite. Children 16 and under stay free in parent's room (maximum 4 people per room). AE, DC, DISC, MC, V. Self-parking $15; valet parking $20. Bus: B21. **Amenities:** 5 restaurants; 2 bars; outdoor pool; health club; spa; children's activities and playground; business center (7am–7pm weekdays, 8am–5pm weekends); limited room service; babysitting; laundry service; dry cleaning; nonsmoking rooms; casino; rooms for those w/limited mobility. *In room:* A/C, TV, dataport, minibar, hair dryer, iron, safe.

Normandie Hotel   It isn't as well accessorized as its nearby competitor the Hilton, but for a clientele of mostly business travelers, it doesn't really matter. One guest, however, found the Hilton bright and festive, the Normandie "dark and haunting." The hotel first opened in 1939 and remains one of the purest examples of Art Deco architecture in Puerto Rico. Originally built for a Parisian cancan dancer by her tycoon husband, the building has a curve-sided design that was inspired by the famous French ocean liner, *Le Normandie.* The gardens are not particularly extensive, and the beach is unexceptional. But several multimillion-dollar renovations (the last was done in

2000 after devastation by a 1998 hurricane) have given the place a conservative, vaguely historical charm. Bedrooms are tastefully outfitted, each with a neatly tiled tub-and-shower bathroom. The lobby retains its original Art Deco zest, soaring upward into an atrium whose centerpiece is a bubbling aquarium.

Av. Muñoz-Rivera, San Juan, PR 00919. 📞 **877/987-2929** or 787/729-2929. Fax 787/729-3083. www.normandiepr. com. 175 units. Winter $169–$189 double; off season $130–$145 double. AE, DC, DISC, MC, V. Parking $10. Bus: A5 or B21. **Amenities:** Restaurant; bar; pool; health club; 24-hr. room service; babysitting; laundry service; dry cleaning; rooms for those w/limited mobility. *In room:* A/C, TV, dataport, coffeemaker, hair dryer, iron, safe.

3 Condado

Once the Condado area was filled with the residences of the very wealthy, but all that changed with the construction of the Puerto Rico Convention Center. Private villas gave way to high-rise hotel blocks, restaurants, and nightclubs. The Condado shopping area, along Ashford and Magdalena avenues, has an extraordinary number of boutiques. There are good bus connections into Old San Juan, and taxis are plentiful. For the locations of hotels in Condado, see the map on p. 85.

VERY EXPENSIVE

Condado Plaza Hotel & Casino 𝓡 𝘒𝘪𝘥𝘴   This is one of the busiest hotels on Puerto Rico, with enough facilities and restaurants to keep a visitor occupied for weeks. It's a favorite of business travelers, tour groups, and conventions, but it also attracts independent travelers. Families appreciate the extensive children's programs, some of the best on the island. The Caribe Hilton at Puerto de Tierra is its major rival, and we prefer that hotel's style and flair. It has two minor and rather unattractive swimming pools, and lots of security-related tension between the sunbathing area around those two pools and the narrow sands of the not-so-great beach that the hotel shares with the public. Because the beach is small the pools tend to be overcrowded with hotel guests. The rooms, however, all have private terraces and are spacious, bright, and airy, fitted with deluxe beds and mattresses, either king-size or doubles, but most often twins. The good-size bathrooms contain tub/shower combinations. The complex's best section, the Plaza Club, has 80 units (including five duplex suites), a VIP lounge for guests, and private check-in/checkout.

Only Hotel El San Juan has a larger choice of dining options. This place is known for creating restaurants with culinary diversity. The hotel's premier restaurant, a hot ticket on San Juan's dining scene, is Cobia, winner of several culinary awards.

Av. Ashford 999, San Juan, PR 00907. 📞 **800/468-8588** or 787/721-1000. Fax 787/721-1260. www.luxuryresorts. com. 570 units. Winter $350–$599 double, $685–$2,000 suite; off season $150–$400 double, $450–$1,400 suite. AE, DC, DISC, MC, V. Self-parking $10; Valet parking $15. Bus: C10 or B21. **Amenities:** 5 restaurants; 3 bars; 3 outdoor pools; 2 tennis courts; health club; spa; 3 Jacuzzis; watersports equipment; children's programs; car-rental desk; business center; salon; 24-hr. room service; laundry service; dry cleaning; nonsmoking rooms; casino; rooms for those w/limited mobility. *In room:* A/C, TV, minibar, coffeemaker, hair dryer, iron, safe.

San Juan Marriott Resort & Stellaris Casino 𝓡   It's the tallest building on the Condado, a 21-story landmark that Marriott spent staggering sums to renovate after a deadly fire gutted the premises in 1989. The current building packs lots of postmodern style, and one of the best beaches on the Condado is right outside. Furnishings in the soaring lobby were inspired by Chippendale. If there's a flaw, it's the decor of the comfortable but bland bedrooms, with pastel colors that look washed out when compared to the rich mahoganies and jewel tones of the rooms in the rival Condado Plaza

Puerta de Tierra, Miramar, Condado & Ocean Park Accommodations & Dining

ACCOMMODATIONS ■

Acacia Seaside Inn **31**
Aleli by the Sea **9**
At Wind Chimes Inn **32**
Atlantic Beach Hotel **18**
Beach Bouy Inn **35**
Best Western Hotel Pierre **30**
Caribe Hilton **2**
Casa del Caribe **26**
Comfort Inn **14**
El Canario by the Lagoon Hotel **15**
El Canario **21**
El Prado Inn **25**
Embassy Guest House Condado **17**
Holiday Inn Express **13**
Hostería del Mar **39**
Hotel Excelsior **5**
L'Habitation Beach Guesthouse **38**
Número 1 Guesthouse **36**
Park Plaza Normandie **1**
Radisson Ambassador Plaza Hotel & Casino **24**
Regency Hotel **4**
San Juan Beach Hotel **7**
San Juan Marriott Resort & Stellaris Casino **19**
Tres Palma **42**
Wyndham Condado Plaza Hotel & Casino **3**

DINING ◆

Ajili Mojili **10**
Augusto's Cuisine **5**
Café del Angel **8**
Café Madrid **34**
Café Mezzanine **24**
Chayote's **6**
Che's **43**
Cherry Blossom **19**
Cielito Lindo **11**
Cobia **3**
Don Tello **27**
Dunbar's **40**
La Casita Blanca **43**
La Casona **29**
La Scala **24**
Luigi's **33**
Madrid-San Juan **2**
Martino's **20**
Morton's of Chicago **2**
Palmera **2**
Pamela's **37**
Pikayo **28**
Ramiro's **12**
Repostería Kassalta **41**
Ristorante Tuscany **19**
Tony Roma's **3**
Urdin **16**
Via Appia **23**
Zabó **22**

0 1/10 mile
0 100 meters

85

(see above). The units are generally spacious, with good views of the water, and each comes with a tiled bathroom with a tub/shower combination.

Av. Ashford 1309, San Juan, PR 00907. © 800/228-9290 or 787/722-7000. Fax 787/722-6800. www.marriottpr.com. 525 units. Winter $265–$580 double, $730 suite; off season $174–$255 double, $350 suite. Suite rate includes breakfast. AE, DC, DISC, MC, V. Self-parking $14; valet parking $18. Bus: B21. **Amenities:** 3 restaurants; 3 bars; 2 pools; 2 tennis courts; health club; Jacuzzi; sauna; tour desk; car-rental desk; business center; 24-hr. room service; babysitting; laundry service; dry cleaning; casino; rooms for those w/limited mobility. *In room:* A/C, TV, dataport, minibar, coffeemaker, hair dryer, iron, safe.

EXPENSIVE

Radisson Ambassador Plaza Hotel & Casino ℱ   At the eastern edge of the Condado, a short walk from the beach, the Ambassador is now competitive with its more glamorous neighbors, after a local entrepreneur poured $40 million into its restoration in the '90s. Since then, it has evolved into a competent but not particularly exciting hotel. What's missing (especially at these prices) are the resort amenities associated with the Hilton, the Condado Plaza, the Ritz-Carlton, and the Hotel El San Juan. This hotel also lacks the sense of whimsy and fun that's so much a part of those glitzy competitors.

Accommodations are in a pair of towers, one of which is devoted to suites. The decor is inspired variously by 18th-century Versailles, 19th-century London, imperial China, and Art Deco California. However, despite the gaudy, glitzy overlay, the hotel used to be a Howard Johnson's, a fact that's evident in the relatively small size of the standard rooms. Each unit has a balcony with outdoor furniture. The beds (twins or doubles) are fitted with fine linen, and each bathroom has generous shelf space and a tub/shower combination.

Av. Ashford 1369, San Juan, PR 00907. © 800/333-3333 or 787/721-7300. Fax 787/723-6151. www.radisson.com. 233 units. Winter $190–$265 double, $305 suite; off season $149–$230 double, AE, DISC, MC, V. $189–$260 suite. Self-parking $8. Bus: B21 or C10. **Amenities:** 2 restaurants; 2 bars; rooftop pool; health club; limited room service; babysitting; laundry service; dry cleaning; casino; rooms for those w/limited mobility. *In room:* A/C, TV, coffeemaker, hair dryer, iron, safe (in suites).

MODERATE

Best Western Hotel Pierre ℱ *Value*   The seven-floor "Lucky Pierre" is one of San Juan's major bargains. It's 4 blocks from the beach and an easy drive to most major San Juan attractions if you rent a car. It's a small resort, with a large pool and deck in a setting of palm trees. The bedrooms, although hardly grand, have been remodeled. Each has a tiled bathroom with tub and shower. Its two restaurants are moderately priced and serve respectable cuisine.

Av. José De Diego 105, Condado, San Juan, PR 00914. © 800/528-1234 or 787/721-1200. Fax 787/721-3118. www. hotelpierresanjuan.com. 184 units. Winter $170–$230 double; off season $165–$200 double. AE, DC, DISC, MC, V. Children 11 and under stay free in parent's room. Bus: A5 or B21. **Amenities:** Restaurant; bar; outdoor pool; small health club; Jacuzzi; room service; babysitting; laundry service; dry cleaning; rooms for those w/limited mobility. *In room:* A/C, TV, dataport, coffeemaker, hair dryer, iron, safe.

Comfort Inn *Kids*   This family-oriented hotel rises seven stories above a residential neighborhood across the street from Condado Beach. The accommodations are small and not particularly imaginative in their decor. Each room has either one or two queen-size beds, and each has a tub-and-shower bathroom. Some rooms have sofas that convert into beds for children. There's a small swimming pool on the premises. The bars, restaurants, and facilities of the Condado neighborhood are within walking distance.

Calle Clemenceau 6, Condado, San Juan, PR 00907. © 800/858-7407 or 787/721-0170. www.comfortinn.com. 50 units. Winter $119 double, $170–$190 suite; off season $99 double, $139–$159 suite. AE, DC, DISC, MC, V. Parking $10. Bus: B21 or C10. **Amenities:** Outdoor pool; laundry service; dry cleaning; rooms for those w/limited mobility. *In room:* A/C, TV, hair dryer, iron, safe.

El Canario by the Lagoon Hotel   A relaxing, informal European-style hotel, El Canario is in a quiet residential neighborhood just a short block from Condado Beach. This is one of the better B&Bs in the area. The hotel is very much in the Condado styling, which evokes Miami Beach in the 1960s. The bedrooms are generous in size and have balconies. Most units have twin beds and sleek and contemporary bathrooms, with shower stalls and enough space to spread out your stuff. If the hotel doesn't have room for you, it can book you into its sibling properties, either El Canario Inn or El Canario by the Sea.

Calle Clemenceau 4, Condado, San Juan, PR 00907. © 800/533-2649 or 787/722-5058. Fax 787/723-8590. www. canariohotels.com. 44 units. Winter $120–$135 double; off season $95–$105 double. Rates include continental breakfast. AE, DC, DISC, MC, V. Bus: B21 or C10. **Amenities:** Tour desk; coin-operated laundry; nonsmoking rooms. *In room:* A/C, TV, safe.

Embassy Guest House Condado   Sandwiched between a vacant lot and a hamburger joint, this acceptable choice lies in a district heavily frequented by gay vacationers. The staff here is helpful and friendly, and restaurants, casinos, and nightlife are within easy walking distance; the famous Condado Beach lies just across the street. Guests usually stay here for economy. This is far from the luxury of Ritz-Carlton, but it offers a relaxed atmosphere—you could live in a swimsuit or shorts for your entire stay. The small bedrooms are simply furnished, many with rattan, and the small shower-only bathrooms are tiled. Each unit has a kitchenette or access to one. The most winning features are the rooftop sun deck, which has a view directly over the beach, and the pool and whirlpool.

Calle Seaview 1126, Condado, San Juan, PR 00907. © 787/725-8284 or 787/724-7440. Fax 787/725-2400. www. embassyguesthouse.com. 22 units (shower only). Winter $69–$149 double; off season $55–$95 double. AE, MC, V. Bus: B21. **Amenities:** Pool; whirlpool. *In room:* A/C, TV, kitchenette, coffeemaker, safe, ceiling fan.

San Juan Beach Hotel   This newly remodeled hotel is right on the oceanfront in the heart of the Condado. It lacks the style and facilities of some of its very expensive neighbors, but you can bask in the sun by the pool, have lunch or drinks on the sun deck, and dance the night away to live music in the Aqua Lounge and Restaurant. The on-site restaurant specializes in many Puerto Rican dishes, including *asopao* (the local gumbo), often made with shrimp and lobster. A selection of seafood is featured nightly. Shopping, sights, and island nightlife are within walking distance or just a short ride away. The rooms are classified as standard, superior, and deluxe. The deluxe rooms are larger than the others and open onto the beach; the superior rooms are slightly smaller than the deluxe rooms, and they are on the upper floors, overlooking the water. The standard rooms face the busy street and are a bit cramped. All the bathrooms are well maintained and medium in size, with adequate shelf space; each contains a shower and tub. The price seems rather high for what you get, but you must pay dearly for a beachfront Condado location, even though the shoreline adjacent to the hotel is rocky.

Av. Ashford 1045, San Juan, PR 00907. © 800/468-2040 or 787/723-8000. Fax 787/722-8230. www.sanjuanbeach hotel.com. 95 units. Winter $190–$230 double; off season $140–$165 double. AE, DC, DISC, MC, V. Parking $12. Bus: B21. **Amenities:** Restaurant; bar; pool; limited room service; laundry service; dry cleaning; rooms for those w/limited mobility. *In room:* A/C, TV, hair dryer, iron.

INEXPENSIVE

Acacia Seaside Inn *(Value)*   This inn, originally built as a private home in 1943 and transformed into a simple hotel in 1948, didn't become well known until the late 1960s, when its reasonable rates began to attract families with children and college students traveling in groups. It's a stucco-covered building with vaguely Spanish-colonial detailing on a residential street lined with similar structures. Each unit has simple, slightly battered furniture and a small shower-only bathroom. There's no pool and few amenities on-site, but the beach is only a 5-minute walk away.

Calle Taft 8, Condado, San Juan, PR 00911. © **787/725-0668.** Fax 787/728-0671. 15 units (shower only). $99–$140 double. AE, DISC, MC, V. Bus: A5 or B21. *In room:* A/C, TV, fridge (in some).

Aleli by the Sea *(Value)*   This is a lone budget holdout in a sea of expensive hotel options. Right on the Condado, it's a charming little guesthouse that opens onto the beach 1 block off Ashford Avenue. Most of the bedrooms, which are small to midsize, overlook the ocean, and all of them have rattan furnishings and compact, tiled, shower-only bathrooms. A pleasant touch is the second-floor terrace overlooking the Atlantic, where guests gather to watch the sunsets.

Calle Seaview 1125, Condado, San Juan, PR 00907. © **787/725-5313.** Fax 787/721-4744. 9 units (shower only). Winter $76–$114 double; off season $65–$103 double. AE, DISC, MC, V. Bus: B21 or C10. **Amenities:** Self-service laundry; communal kitchen. *In room:* A/C, TV, ceiling fan, no phone.

Atlantic Beach Hotel   This is the most famous gay hotel in Puerto Rico. Housed in a five-story building with vaguely Art Deco styling, the hotel is best known for its ground-floor indoor/outdoor bar—the most visibly gay bar in Puerto Rico. It extends from the hotel lobby onto a wooden deck about 15 feet (4.6m) above the sands of Condado Beach. The units are simple cubicles, all nonsmoking, with stripped-down but serviceable and clean décor. Some of the rooms are smaller than others, but few of the short-term guests seem to mind—maybe because the place can have the spirit of a house party. Each unit has a small, shower-only bathroom with plumbing that might not always be in prime condition. There's an on-again, off-again in-house restaurant and the above-mentioned bar.

Several readers have written in to complain about the restrictive policy of not allowing a guest to take a visitor back to the bedrooms. One disgruntled patron wrote, "Lighten up, folks! We're big boys and can decide for ourselves who we want to bring up to our room." If you're going with a lover, fine. If you want to play with the locals, stay in another hotel.

Calle Vendig 1, Condado, San Juan, PR 00907. © **787/721-6900.** Fax 787/721-6917. www.atlanticbeachhotel.net. 36 units (shower only). Winter $130–$170 double; off season $89–$115 double. AE, DISC, MC, V. Bus: B21. **Amenities:** Restaurant; bar; laundry service; dry cleaning; rooms for those w/limited mobility. *In room:* A/C, TV, safe.

At Wind Chimes Inn *(Finds)* *(Kids)*   This restored and renovated Spanish manor, 1 short block from the beach and 3½ miles from the airport, is one of the best guesthouses on the Condado. Upon entering a tropical patio, you'll find tile tables surrounded by palm trees and bougainvillea. There's plenty of space on the deck and a covered lounge for relaxing, socializing, and eating breakfast. Dozens of decorative wind chimes add melody to the daily breezes. The good-size rooms offer a choice of size, beds, and kitchens; all contain ceiling fans and air-conditioning. Beds are comfortable and come in four sizes, ranging from twin to king-size. The shower-only bathrooms, though small, are efficiently laid out. Families like this place not only because of the accommodations and the affordable prices but because they can also prepare light meals here, cutting down on food costs.

Av. McLeary 1750, Condado, San Juan, PR 00911. ℂ 800/946-3244 or 787/727-4153. Fax 787/728-0671. www. atwindchimesinn.com. 22 units (shower only). Winter $99–$140 double, $135–$150 suite; off season $75–$125 double, $135 suite. AE, DISC, MC, V. Parking $5. Bus: B21 or A5. **Amenities:** Bar; outdoor pool; limited room service; rooms for those w/limited mobility. *In room:* A/C, TV, dataport, kitchen (in some).

Casa del Caribe *(Value)*   Don't expect the Ritz, but if you're looking for a bargain on the Condado, this is it. This renovated guesthouse was built in the 1940s, later expanded, and then totally refurbished with tropical decor. A very Puerto Rican ambience has been created, with emphasis on Latin hospitality and comfort. On a shady side street just off Ashford Avenue, behind a wall and garden, you'll discover Casa del Caribe's wraparound veranda. The small but cozy guest rooms have ceiling fans and air conditioners, and most feature original Puerto Rican art. The bedrooms are inviting, with comfortable furnishings and efficiently organized bathrooms. The front porch is a social center for guests, and you can also cook out at a barbecue area. The beach is a 2-minute walk away, and the hotel is also within walking distance of some megaresorts, with their glittering casinos.

Calle Caribe 57, El Condado, San Juan, PR 00907. ℂ 787/722-7139. Fax 787/723-2575. www.casadelcaribe.net. 13 units. Winter $75–$125 double; off season $65–$99 double. Rates include continental breakfast. AE, DISC, MC, V. Parking $5. Bus: B21. **Amenities:** Nonsmoking rooms; 1 room for those w/limited mobility. *In room:* A/C, TV, kitchen (in some).

El Canario Inn *(Value)*   Affiliated with El Canario by the Lagoon Hotel (see above), this little bed-and-breakfast, originally built as a private home, is one of the best values along the high-priced Condado strip. The location is just 1 block from the beach (you can walk there in your bathing suit). This well-established hotel lies directly on the landmark Ashford Avenue, center of Condado action, and is close to casinos, nightclubs, and many restaurants in all price ranges. Although surrounded by megaresorts, it is a simple inn, with rather small but comfortable rooms and good maintenance by a helpful staff. All units are nonsmoking and have a small, tiled, shower-only bathroom. You can relax on the hotel's patios or in the whirlpool area, which is surrounded by tropical foliage. There is no elevator.

Av. Ashford 1317, Condado, San Juan, PR 00907. ℂ 800/533-2649 or 787/722-3861. Fax 787/722-0391. www. canariohotels.com. 25 units (shower only). Winter $119–$134 double; off season $90–$100 double. Rates include a continental breakfast. AE, DC, MC, V. Bus: B21 or C10. *In room:* A/C, TV, safe.

Holiday Inn Express   This seven-story, white-painted structure, expanded in 2003, offers a desirable Condado location but without the towering prices of the grand resorts along the beach. The hotel is about a 2-minute walk from Condado Beach and is convenient to Old San Juan (a 15-min. drive) and the airport (a 20-min. drive). Most accommodations have two double beds (ideal for families) and ceiling fans, and each has a small bathroom with tub and shower. Many open onto balconies with water views. It's about a 5-minute walk to major casinos at the Condado Plaza and San Juan Marriott hotels (see earlier in this chapter).

Calle Marinao Ramirez Bages 1, Condado, San Juan, PR 00907. ℂ 888/465-4329 or 787/724-4160. Fax 787/721-2436. www.ichotels.com. 115 units. Winter $119–$139 double; off season $99–$109 double. Children 18 and under stay free in parent's room. Rates include continental breakfast. AE, DC, DISC, MC, V. Parking $10. Bus: B21. **Amenities:** Pool; health club; laundry service; dry cleaning. *In room:* A/C, TV, dataport, hair dryer, iron, safe.

4 Miramar

Miramar, a residential neighborhood, is very much a part of metropolitan San Juan, and a brisk 30-minute walk will take you where the action is. Regrettably, the beach is at least half a mile (.8km) away. For the location of hotels in Miramar, see the map on p. 85.

Hotel Excelsior   Handsome accommodations and good service are offered at this family-owned and -operated hotel. Some of the bedrooms have been refurbished; many have fully equipped kitchenettes, and each has two phones (one in the bathroom), marble vanities, and a tub/shower combo. Included in the rates are shoeshines, transportation to the nearby beach, and parking in the underground garage or the adjacent parking lot. A lot of your reaction to this hotel will depend on your room assignment. Some units on the same floor can vary in quality. If possible, ask to see the room before checking in. One disgruntled reader called the Excelsior "an overexaggerated dump."

Av. Ponce de León 801, San Juan, PR 00907. ℰ **800/298-4274** or 787/721-7400. Fax 787/723-0068. excelsior@ caribe.net. 140 units. Winter $105–$155 double, $240 suite; off season $90–$130 double, $240 suite. Children 12 and under stay free in parent's room; cribs free. AE, DC, DISC, MC, V. Bus: 1, 2, A3, or A5. **Amenities:** 2 restaurants; outdoor pool; health club; limited room service; babysitting; laundry service; dry cleaning; rooms for those w/limited mobility. *In room:* A/C, TV, dataport, hair dryer, safe.

5 Santurce & Ocean Park

Less fashionable (and a bit less expensive) than their nearest neighbors Condado (to the west) and Isla Verde (to the east), Santurce and Ocean Park are wedged into a modern, not particularly beautiful neighborhood that's bisected with lots of roaring traffic arteries and commercial enterprises. Lots of Sanjuaneros come here to work in the district's many offices and to eat in its many restaurants. The coastal subdivision of Ocean Park is a bit more fashionable than landlocked Santurce, but with the beach never more than a 20-minute walk away, few of Santurce's residents seem to mind. For the location of hotels in Santurce and Ocean Park, see the map "Puerta de Tierra, Miramar, Condado & Ocean Park Accommodations & Dining" on p. 85.

MODERATE

Hosteria del Mar ℛ   Lying a few blocks from the Condado casinos and right on the beach are the white walls of this distinctive landmark. It's in a residential seaside community that's popular with locals looking for beach action on weekends. The hotel boasts medium-size oceanview rooms. Those on the second floor have balconies; those on the first floor open onto patios. The decor is invitingly tropical, with wicker furniture, good beds, pastel prints, and ceiling fans. The bathrooms are small but efficient, some with shower, some with tub only. The most popular unit is no. 201, with a king-size bed, private balcony, kitchenette, and a view of the beach; it's idyllic for a honeymoon. There's no pool, but a full-service restaurant here is known for its vegetarian, macrobiotic, and Puerto Rican plates, all freshly made. The place is simple, yet with its own elegance and warm hospitality.

Calle Tapía 1, Ocean Park, San Juan, PR 00911. ℰ **877/727-3302** or 787/727-3302. Fax 787/268-0772. hosteria@ caribe.net. 27 units. Winter $75–$227 double without ocean view, $96–$265 double with ocean view, $275 apt; off season $60–$110 double without ocean view, $125–$165 double with ocean view, $200 apt. Children 11 and under stay free in parent's room. AE, DC, DISC, MC, V. Bus: A5. **Amenities:** Restaurant; limited room service. *In room:* A/C, TV, dataport, kitchenette (in 3 units), coffeemaker (in some).

L'Habitation Beach Guesthouse   This small hotel sits on a tranquil tree-lined street with a sandy beach right in its backyard. Located only a few blocks from the Condado, this inn has a laid-back atmosphere. The good-size and well-maintained bedrooms have ceiling fans, comfortable beds, and fairly simple furnishings. The most spacious rooms are nos. 8 and 9, which also open onto ocean views. Each unit has a small, tiled, shower-only bathroom. Chairs and beverage service are provided in a private beach area, and guests can enjoy breakfast alfresco. You can also eat or drink on the breezy patio overlooking the sea. Ask for one of the bar's special margaritas.

Calle Italia 1957, Ocean Park, San Juan, PR 00911. ℭ **787/727-2499.** Fax 787/727-2599. www.habitationbeach.com. 10 units (shower only). Winter $75–$111 double; off season $60–$83 double. Extra person $20. Rates include continental breakfast. AE, DISC, MC, V. Free parking. Bus: T1. **Amenities:** Laundry service. *In room:* A/C, TV, coffeemaker, safe.

INEXPENSIVE

Número 1 Guest House 🏖🏖 *(Finds*   As a translation of its name implies, this is the best of the small-scale, low-rise guesthouses in Ocean Park. It was originally built in the 1950s as a private beach house in a prestigious residential neighborhood adjacent to the wide sands of Ocean Park Beach. A massive renovation transformed the place into the closest thing in Ocean Park to the kind of stylish boutique hotel you might find in an upscale California neighborhood. Much of this is thanks to the hardworking owner, Esther Feliciano, who cultivates within her walled compound a verdant garden replete with splashing fountains, a small swimming pool, and manicured shrubbery and palms. Stylish-looking bedrooms (all of which are nonsmoking) contain tile floors, wicker or rattan furniture, comfortable beds, and tiled, shower-only bathrooms. Some repeat clients, many of whom are gay, refer to it as their fantasy version of a private villa beside a superb and usually convivial beach. The staff can direct you to watersports emporiums nearby for virtually any tropical watersport. Although it lacks the staggering diversity of the big hotels of the nearby Condado or Isla Verde, some guests value its sense of intimacy and small-scale charm.

Calle Santa Ana 1, Ocean Park, San Juan, PR 00911. ℭ **866/726-5010** or 787/726-5010. Fax 787/727-5482. www.numero1guesthouse.com. 13 units (shower only). Winter $115–$185 double, $265 apt, $225 junior suite; off season $75–$115 double, $165 apt, $145 junior suite. $20 each additional occupant of a double room. Rates include continental breakfast. AE, MC, V. Bus: A5. **Amenities:** Restaurant; bar; outdoor pool; limited room service; rooms for those w/limited mobility. *In room:* A/C, TV, dataport, minibar, hair dryer, iron, safe, ceiling fan.

Oceana Beach Inn *(Finds*   About a block from the beach, this B&B deserves to be better known. This place is a comfortable, snug nest with helpful, friendly staff and clean, newly renovated rooms. Each efficiency has two double beds or two twin beds. Some units have small refrigerators, and each unit has a tiled bathroom with either a tub or a shower. You can enjoy the complimentary breakfast outdoors on the patio if you wish.

Av. McLeary 1853, Ocean Park, San Juan, PR 00911. ℭ **787/728-8119.** Fax 787/268-0037. 17 units (some shower only, some tub only). Winter $110–$125 double, $200 efficiency; off season $75–$85 double, $125 efficiency. Children 11 and under stay free in parent's room. Rates include continental breakfast. MC, V. Free parking. Bus: A5 or A7. **Amenities:** Restaurant; 1 room for those w/limited mobility. *In room:* A/C, TV, fridge, no phone.

Tres Palmas Inn *(Value*   Across the street from the ocean, this apartment-style guesthouse overlooks the surf. It's one of the best values for those seeking a beach vacation. The hotel is a lot like a B&B, lying between two main tourist destinations, the Condado to the west and Isla Verde to the east. If you don't want to swim in the ocean, try the hotel's pool, located in a secluded courtyard. You can also relax on the rooftop sun deck while soaking in the whirlpool. The medium-size bedrooms are simply but comfortably furnished, with rather standard motel items. Each guest room has a private entrance and a ceiling fan, and most have small refrigerators. Larger rooms also have small kitchens, and each unit has a small, tiled bathroom with either a tub or a shower.

Ocean Park Blvd. 2212, San Juan, PR 00913. © **888/290-2076** or 787/727-4617. Fax 787/727-5434. www. trespalmasinn.com. 18 units (some with shower only, some with tub only). Winter $87–$175 double; off season $81–$146 double. Rates include continental breakfast. AE, MC, V. Bus: A5 or A7. **Amenities:** Pool; 2 whirlpools; 1 room for those w/limited mobility. *In room:* A/C, TV, dataport, kitchen, fridge (in some), hair dryer, safe.

6 Isla Verde

Beach-bordered Isla Verde is closer to the airport than the Condado and Old San Juan. The hotels here are farther from Old San Juan than those in Miramar, Condado, and Ocean Park. It's a good choice if you don't mind the isolation and want to be near fairly good beaches. For the location of hotels in Isla Verde, see the map "Isla Verde Accommodations & Dining" on p. 93.

VERY EXPENSIVE

El San Juan Hotel & Casino ✦ *Kids*   This hotel is no longer the dazzler it once was. The Ritz-Carlton has taken the truly elite business, and The Water Club is even more sophisticated. Nonetheless, El San Juan Hotel is still a good choice for (well-to-do) families, with lots of activities for children. The beachfront hotel is surrounded by 350 palms, century-old banyans, and gardens. Its 2,099-foot (640m) sandy beach is the finest in the San Juan area. The hotel's river pool, with currents, cascades, and lagoons, evokes a jungle stream, and the lobby is the most opulent and memorable in the Caribbean. Entirely sheathed in red marble and hand-carved mahogany paneling, the public rooms stretch on almost endlessly.

The large, well-decorated rooms have intriguing touches of high-tech; each contains three phones and a VCR. Bedrooms are imbued with honey-hued woods and rattans and king-size or double beds. Bathrooms have all the amenities and tub/shower combos; a few feature Jacuzzis. About 150 of the units, designed as comfortable bungalows, are in the outer reaches of the garden. Known as casitas, they include Roman tubs, atrium showers, and access to the fern-lined paths of a tropical jungle a few steps away. A 17-story, $60-million wing with 120 suites, all oceanfront, was completed in 1998. The ultraluxury tower features 103 one- or two-bedroom units, eight garden suites, five governor's suites, and four presidential suites.

No other hotel in the Caribbean offers such a rich diversity of dining options and such high-quality food. Japanese, Italian, Mexican, and 24-hour American/Caribbean restaurants are just a few of the options.

Note: In recent years, readers have occasionally complained about maintenance in some of the bedrooms. If possible, ask to see your room before you check in.

Av. Isla Verde 6063, San Juan, PR 00979. © **787/791-1000.** Fax 787/791-0390. www.luxuryresorts.com. 382 units. Winter $315–$465 double, from $795 suite; off season $325–$475 double, from $585 suite. AE, DC, DISC, MC, V. Self-parking $10; valet parking $15. Bus: A5. **Amenities:** 7 restaurants; 4 bars; 2 outdoor pools; tennis; health club; spa; sauna and steam room; watersports equipment/rentals; children's programs; business center; 24-hr. room service; massage; babysitting; laundry service; dry cleaning; casino; rooms for those w/limited mobility. *In room:* A/C, TV/VCR, dataport, minibar, coffeemaker, hair dryer, iron, safe.

Inter-Continental San Juan Resort & Casino ✦   This resort competes with El San Juan Hotel & Casino (see above) next door, but here you'll get the sense of living

Isla Verde Accommodations & Dining

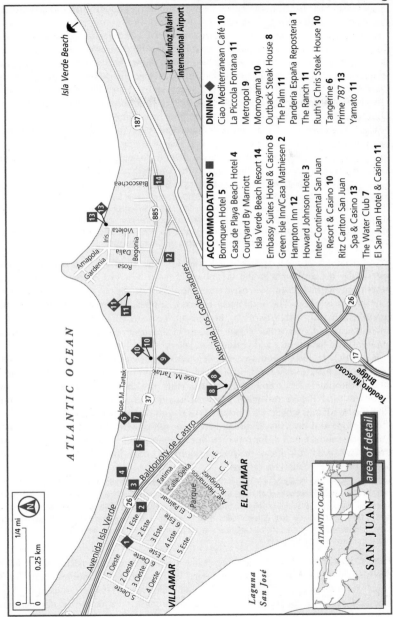

ACCOMMODATIONS ■

Borinquen Hotel **5**
Casa de Playa Beach Hotel **4**
Courtyard By Marriott
Isla Verde Beach Resort **14**
Embassy Suites Hotel & Casino **8**
Green Isle Inn/Casa Mathiesen **2**
Hampton Inn **12**
Howard Johnson Hotel **3**
Inter-Continental San Juan
Resort & Casino **10**
Ritz Carlton San Juan
Spa & Casino **13**
The Water Club **7**
El San Juan Hotel & Casino **11**

DINING ◆

Ciao Mediterranean Café **10**
La Piccola Fontana **11**
Metropol **9**
Momoyama **10**
Outback Steak House **8**
The Palm **11**
Pandería España Repostería **1**
The Ranch **11**
Ruth's Chris Steak House **10**
Tangerine **6**
Prime 787 **13**
Yamato **11**

93

in a sophisticated beach resort rather than a hotel where the sun rises and sets around the whims of high-rolling gamblers.

Most of the comfortable, medium-size rooms have balconies and terraces and tastefully conservative furnishings. Top-floor rooms are the most expensive, even though they lack balconies. Many bathrooms have power showerheads, deep tubs, and scales (though note that some suites don't have tubs). Especially desirable units are in the Plaza Club, a minihotel within the hotel that sports a private entrance, concierge service, complimentary food and beverage buffets, and suite/spa and beach facilities. Dining within any of this hotel's five restaurants merits attention; during a day at the beach, refreshments at **Ciao Mediterranean Café** 𝒢𝒢 (p. 126) are especially good (with faster service than the overworked waitresses working the beach). **Momoyama** 𝒢 (p. 125) serves excellent sushi but is most known for its teppanyaki, a Japanese cuisine that uses an iron griddle (a la Benihana in the United States).

Av. Isla Verde 5961, Isla Verde, PR 00979. ℂ 800/468-9076 or 787/791-6100. Fax 787/253-2510. www.ichotels group.com. 402 units. Winter $399–$545 double, $559–$910 suite; off season $209–$295 double, $360–$698 suite. Children 15 and under stay free in parent's room. AE, DC, DISC, MC, V. Self-parking $14; valet parking $20. Bus: A7, M7, or T1. **Amenities:** 6 restaurants; lounge; the Caribbean's largest free-form pool; whirlpool; health club; sauna; scuba diving; limo service; business center; 24-hr. room service; massage; babysitting; laundry service; dry cleaning; rooms for those w/limited mobility. *In room:* A/C, TV, dataport, minibar, coffeemaker, hair dryer, iron, safe.

Ritz-Carlton San Juan Spa & Casino 𝒢𝒢𝒢   The Ritz-Carlton is one of the most spectacular deluxe hotels in the Caribbean. Set on 8 acres (3.2 hectares) of prime beachfront, within a 5-minute drive from the airport, it appeals to both business travelers and vacationers. The hotel decor reflects Caribbean flavor and the Hispanic culture of the island, with artwork by prominent local artists. More visible, however, is an emphasis on Continental elegance. Some of the most opulent public areas feature wrought-iron balustrades and crystal chandeliers.

Beautifully furnished guest rooms open onto ocean views or the gardens of nearby condos. Rooms are very large, with excellent furnishings, fine linen, and dataports. The bathrooms are exceptionally plush, with tub/shower combinations, scales, bathrobes, and deluxe toiletries. Preferred accommodations are in the ninth-floor Ritz-Carlton Club, which has a private lounge and personal concierge staff.

The scope and diversity of dining here is second only to the El San Juan Hotel & Casino (see above), and as for top-shelf dining venues, the Ritz-Carlton has no equal. **Prime 787** (p. 123) is one of the finest restaurants in San Juan. The hotel also houses one of Puerto Rico's largest casinos.

Av. de los Gobernadores (State Rd.) 6961, no. 187, Isla Verde, PR 00979. ℂ 800/241-3333 or 787/253-1700. Fax 787/253-1777. www.ritzcarlton.com. 416 units. Winter $325–$439 double; off season $215–$399 double; year-round from $580 suite. AE, DC, DISC, MC, V. Self-parking $17; valet parking $22. Bus: A5, B40, or C45. **Amenities:** 5 restaurants; 3 bars; nightclub; large pool; 2 tennis courts; health club; spa; children's program; salon; 24-hr. room service; babysitting; laundry service; dry cleaning; Caribbean's largest casino; rooms for those w/limited mobility. *In room:* A/C, TV, dataport, minibar, hair dryer, safe.

The Water Club 𝒢𝒢𝒢   A refreshing change from the megachain resorts of San Juan, this ultrachic hotel is hip and contemporary. It's the city's only "boutique hotel" on a beach. We find much to praise at this small and exclusive hotel because of its highly personalized and well-trained staff. Although avant-garde, the design is not daringly provocative. Behind glass are "waterfalls," even on the elevators, and inventive theatrical-style lighting is used to bring the outdoors inside. The one-of-a-kind glass art doors are from Murano, the famed center of glassmaking outside Venice. Overlooking Isla

Family-Friendly Accommodations

At Wind Chimes Inn (p. 88)   Families like this hotel not only because of the accommodations and the affordable prices, but also because they can prepare meals here, cutting down on food costs.

Condado Plaza Hotel & Casino (p. 84)   For the family seeking an upmarket resort with lots of facilities, this is the best choice along the Condado. Its Camp Taíno is guided by experts and occupies children under 12 throughout the day for a fee. See "Especially for Kids" in chapter 7.

Courtyard by Marriott Isla Verde Beach Resort (see below)   This is an affordable option, and the kids will enjoy the Bananas Ice Cream Parlour, the game room, and Kids' Club activities for ages 3 through 11. Summer family packages can save you money and usually include coupons for pizza and banana sundaes.

El San Juan Hotel & Casino (p. 92)   This hotel, although expensive, offers more programs for children than any other hotel in Puerto Rico. Its supervised Kids' Klub provides daily activities—ranging from face painting to swimming lessons—for children 5 to 12 years of age.

Hampton Inn (p. 96)   For families seeking the kind of lodging values found on the mainland, this new hotel is highly desirable, as many of its rooms have two double beds. There's also a beautiful swimming pool in a tropical setting. Suites have microwaves and refrigerators.

Verde's best beach area, all the bedrooms are spacious and contain custom-designed beds positioned to face the ocean. Bathrooms are tiled and elegant, with tub/shower combinations. Unique features are the open-air 11th-floor exotic bar with the Caribbean's only rooftop fireplace. The pool is a level above; it's like swimming in an ocean in the sky.

Calle José M. Tartak 2, Isla Verde, Puerto Rico 00979. © 888/265-6699 or 787/253-3666. Fax 787/728-3610. www. waterclubsanjuan.com. 84 units. Winter $275–$330 double, $695 suite; off season $325–$400 double, $249–$309 suite. AE, DC, DISC, MC, V. Bus: T1 or A5. **Amenities:** 2 restaurants; 2 bars; outdoor rooftop pool; fitness center; Jacuzzi; limited room service; dry cleaning; nonsmoking rooms; rooms for those w/limited mobility. *In room:* A/C, TV, dataport, minibar, hair dryer, safe.

EXPENSIVE

Courtyard by Marriott Isla Verde Beach Resort ☆ *Kids*   This is affordable Caribbean at its best. Opening on Isla Verde Beach, close to the airport, the hotel has been completely refurbished with new facilities added, making it suitable for business travelers, families, or the random vacationer. The 12-floor hotel rises on the site of the old Crowne Plaza. It's a big, bustling place with many amenities and midsize and well-furnished bedrooms. Art Deco furnishings dominate, and there is plenty of comfort. The casino and lobby restaurants are filled with the sounds of Latin rhythms at night.

Boca de Cangrejos Avenida 7012, Isla Verde, PR 00979. © 800/791-2553 or 787/791-0404. Fax 787/791-2553. www.sjcourtyard.com/contact.html. 293 units. Winter $200–$265 double, $445 suite; off season $160–$220 double, $360 suite. AE, DC, DISC, MC, V. Bus: M7. **Amenities:** 3 restaurants; ice-cream parlor; bar; pool; fitness center; kids' club; business center; limited room service; laundry service; dry cleaning; casino. *In room:* A/C, TV, dataport, minibar, hair dryer, iron, safe.

Embassy Suites Hotel & Casino ⊛   The location is 2 blocks from the beach, and the hotel has its own water world, with waterfalls and reflecting ponds set against a backdrop of palms. As you enter, you're greeted with an aquarium, giving a tropical-resort aura to the place. The excellent accommodations are all suites, and they're comfortably furnished and roomy, with bedrooms separated from the living rooms. Each has a wet bar, a tub/shower combination bathroom, two phones, a safe, and a dining table. The most spacious suites are those with two double beds; each of the smaller suites is furnished with a king-size bed. The best view of the water is from units above the third floor. Two restaurants are on the premises, including the Embassy Grill, a low-key indoor/outdoor affair, and an independently managed Outback Steakhouse branch. There's also a small-scale casino on the property.

Calle José M. Tartak 8000, Isla Verde, San Juan, PR 00979. ℂ 800/362-2779 or 787/791-0505. Fax 787/791-0555. www.embassysuites.com. 299 suites. Winter $200–$400 1-bedroom suite, $409–$500 2-bedroom suite, $600 presidential suite; off season $170–$205 1-bedroom suite, $350 2-bedroom suite, $500 presidential suite. Rates include breakfast and free drinks 5:30–7:30pm. AE, DC, DISC, MC, V. Self-parking $10; valet parking $16. Bus: A5 or B21. **Amenities:** 2 restaurants; 3 bars; pool; health club; car-rental desk; business center; limited room service; laundry service; coin-operated laundry; dry cleaning; small casino; rooms for those w/limited mobility. *In room:* A/C, TV, wet bar (in suites), fridge, coffeemaker, hair dryer, iron, safe, microwave.

MODERATE

Hampton Inn *Kids*   Opened in 1997, this chain hotel is set across the busy avenue from Isla Verde's sandy beachfront, far enough away to keep costs down but within a leisurely 10-minute walk of the casinos and nightlife. Two towers, with four and five floors, hold the well-maintained, well-furnished, and comfortable bedrooms. There's no restaurant on the premises and no real garden; other than a whirlpool and a swimming pool with a swim-up bar, there are very few facilities or amenities. Because of its reasonable prices and location, however, this Isla Verde newcomer could be a good choice. Families are especially fond of staying here despite the fact that there are no special children's programs; many of the rooms have two double beds and suites have microwaves and refrigerators.

Av. Isla Verde 6530, Isla Verde, PR 00979. ℂ 800/HAMPTON or 787/791-8777. Fax 787/791-8757. 201 units. Winter $180 double, $250 suite; off season $119 double, $139 suite. Rates include breakfast bar. AE, DC, DISC, MC, V. Parking $5. Bus: A5 or C45. **Amenities:** Bar; pool; health club; whirlpool; babysitting; laundry service; dry cleaning; rooms for those w/limited mobility. *In room:* A/C, TV, fridge (in suites), coffeemaker, hair dryer, iron, microwave (in suites).

Howard Johnson Hotel   Rising eight stories above the busy traffic of Isla Verde, this chain hotel offers comfortable but small bedrooms, furnished simply with bland, modern furniture. They're done in typical motel style, with small but serviceable tub-and-shower bathrooms. Many guests carry a tote bag to the beach across the street, and then hit the bars and restaurants of the expensive hotels nearby. There's a restaurant and a pool. Though it's simple and not very personal, this is a good choice for the money.

Av. Isla Verde 4820, Isla Verde, PR 00979. ℂ 787/728-1300. Fax 787/727-7150. www.hojo.com. 115 units. Winter $145 double; off season $105 double; suite $125–$145 year-round. AE, MC, V. Parking $6.50. Bus: A5. **Amenities:** 2 restaurants; pool; health club; laundry service; dry cleaning; rooms for those w/limited mobility. *In room:* A/C, TV, fridge, coffeemaker, hair dryer, iron.

INEXPENSIVE

Borinquen Beach Inn *Value*   Lying just 1 block from the beach and a 5-minute drive from the airport, this is a good deal. This modest, one-story guesthouse has been popular with islanders and visitors for more than 2 decades. The unassuming white facade is in keeping with the plain interior decor, with its pastel-painted walls, communal lounge and kitchen, and small serving area where guests can order coffee. The rooms are small and plain, but they're clean and comfortable enough, and each has a small bathroom with a shower stall. The overall aura here is very laid-back, but the low prices and convenient location keep the place booked with holidaymakers year-round.

Av. Isla Verde 5451, Isla Verde, San Juan, PR 00979. (*) 866/728-8400 or 787/728-8400. Fax 787/268-2411. www. borinquenbeachinn.com. 12 units. Year-round $72–$90 double. AE, DC, DISC, MC, V. Free parking. Bus: A5. **Amenities:** Communal kitchen; 1 room for those w/limited mobility. *In room:* A/C, TV, no phone.

Casa de Playa Beach Hotel *(Finds)*
Jutting out over the sand on the mile-long (1.6km) Isla Verde beach, this bargain oasis is a find. If you're less interested in being in the center of San Juan than you are in spending time on the beach, check out this modest choice. The hotel consists of two, two-story buildings, with a porch around the second floor and a small garden in front. Furnishings are modest and functional but comfortable nonetheless. Each room has a tidily maintained, small bathroom with a tiled shower. Standard but inexpensive Italian food is served at a beach bar and restaurant. The hotel doesn't have everything—no pool, no room service—but the price is hard to beat in Isla Verde.

Av. Isla Verde 86, San Juan, PR 09979. (*) 800/916-2272 or 787/728-9779. Fax 787/727-1334. 21 units. Winter $115 double, $250 suite; off season $80 double, $200 suite. Children 9 and under stay free in parent's room. Rates include continental breakfast. AE, MC, V. Free parking. Bus: A5. **Amenities:** Restaurant; bar; 1 room for those w/limited mobility. *In room:* A/C, TV, fridge (in some), coffeemaker (in suites), safe.

Green Isle Inn/Casa Mathiesen
Across the busy avenue from the larger and much more expensive San Juan Grand Beach Resort & Casino, this is really two hotels in one. They stand side by side and charge the same prices. Both of them are equally comfortable, though modest. The beach is a 5-minute walk away, and each of the hotels has a pool. There are 25 rooms at the Green Isle. Casa Mathiesen is only slighter larger, with 29 units. The furnishings are summery, simple, and comfortable. Each has a tiled tub-and-shower bathroom.

Calle Uno 36, Villamar, Isla Verde, PR 00979. (*) 800/677-8860 or 787/726-8662. Fax 787/268-2415. www.coqui-inn. com. 54 units. Winter $70–$89 double; off season $58–$84 double. AE, DISC, MC, V. Free parking. Bus: A5. **Amenities:** Restaurant; bar; 2 small pools; laundry service; rooms for those w/limited mobility. *In room:* A/C, TV, kitchenette (in some), safe.

6

Where to Dine in San Juan

San Juan has the widest array of restaurants in the Caribbean. You can enjoy fine Continental, American, Italian, Chinese, Mexican, and Japanese cuisines, to name a few. In recent years, many restaurants have shown a greater appreciation for traditional Puerto Rican cooking, and local specialties now appear on the menus of numerous restaurants. When possible, many chefs enhance their dishes with native ingredients.

Many of San Juan's best restaurants are in the resort hotels along the Condado and at Isla Verde. There has been a restaurant explosion in San Juan in the past few years, but many of the newer ones are off the beaten tourist path, and some have not yet achieved the quality found at many of the older, more traditional restaurants.

Local seafood is generally in plentiful supply, but no restaurant guarantees that it will have fresh fish every night, especially during winter, when the sea can be too turbulent for fishing. In those cases, the chef relies on fresh or frozen fish flown in from Miami. If you want fresh fish caught in Puerto Rican waters, ask your server about the catch of the day. Make sure he or she can guarantee that the fish was recently caught rather than resting for a while in the icebox.

The restaurants listed in this chapter are classified first by area and then by price, using the following categories: **Very Expensive,** dinner from $40 per person; **Expensive,** dinner from $30 per person; **Moderate,** dinner from $20 per person; and **Inexpensive,** dinner under $20 per person. These categories reflect prices for an appetizer, a main course, a dessert, and a glass of wine.

1 Best Bets

- **Best Classic Creole Cooking** In his new location in Old Town's Museum of Art of Puerto Rico, Chef Wilo Benet at **Pikayo,** Av. José de Diego 299 (© 787/721-6194), holds forth. He's a master specialist in the *criolla* cooking of the colonial age, emphasizing the Spanish, Indian, and African elements in his unusual recipes.
- **Best Steakhouse** In the swanky Ritz-Carlton San Juan Hotel, **Prime 787,** Av. De los Gobernadores 6961 (© 787/253-1700), serves the most succulent steaks in Puerto Rico. Chefs specialize in U.S. prime and certified Angus beef prepared to order. Arguably its "Kobe Flat Iron" is the finest cut of beef you're likely to be served in the entire Caribbean Basin.
- **Best Food Value** The savory cookery of Brazil is today served at **Bossa Nova,** Calle Fortaleza 358 (© 787/722-0093). Its house specialty is reason enough to dine here: a Brazilian-style *Rodizio,* consisting of five different grilled meats.
- **Best Italian Restaurant** Across the street from Hotel El Covento, **Il Perugino,** Cristo St. 105 (© 787/722-5481), takes you on a culinary tour of sunny Italy. Plate

after plate of delectable northern Italian food is presented nightly—everything from grilled filets of fresh fish to succulent pastas. Service is first-rate, and the welcome warm.

- **Best French Cuisine**   Against a Moorish and Andalusian background, **Trois Cent Onze,** Calle Fortaleza 311 (© 787/725-7959), serves a classic French cuisine with many innovative overtones. Great attention is paid to color, flavor, and texture of each dish.
- **Best for a Romantic Dinner**   Out in Miramar, **Augusto's Cuisine,** in the Hotel Excelsior, Av. Ponce de León 801 (© 787/725-7700), lies on the 15th floor of this hotel, offering a stunning and panoramic view of San Juan at night. Not only that, it serves one of the best French and international cuisines in the Caribbean, backed up by an extensive wine list.
- **Best Nuevo Latino Cuisine**   **Parrot Club,** Calle Fortaleza 363 (© 787/725-7370), wows taste buds with its modern interpretation of Puerto Rican specialties. Even San Juan's mayor and the governor have made it their favorite. Husband-and-wife team Emilio Figueroa and Gigi Zafero borrow from a repertoire of Puerto Rican and Spanish recipes, and they also use Taíno and African influences in their cuisine. Their seviche is the best in town, and their Créole-style flank steak is worth the trek from Condado Beach.
- **Best Burgers**   Patrons freely admit that **El Patio de Sam,** Calle San Sebastián 102 (© 787/723-1149), is not always on target with its main dishes. But they agree on one thing: The hamburgers are the juiciest and most delectable in San Juan. The Old Town atmosphere is also intriguing—you almost expect to encounter Bogey and Bacall.
- **Best Asopao**   Soul food to Puerto Ricans, *asopao* is the regional gumbo, made in as many different ways as there are chefs on the island. Some versions are too thick to be called soup, such as the seafood variety at **La Bombonera,** Calle San Francisco 259 (© 787/722-0658), in San Juan's Old Town, which is more like a stew. One popular version of asopao includes pigeon peas, although the one with chicken is better known.
- **Best Spanish Cuisine**   You'd have to go all the way to Madrid to find Spanish food as well prepared as it is at **Ramiro's,** Av. Magdalena 1106 (© 787/721-9049). The chefs take full advantage of fresh island produce to create an innovative cuisine. In fact, the style is New Creole, although its roots are firmly planted in Spain. Their fresh fish and chargrilled meats are succulent, and any dessert with the strawberry-and-guava sauce is a sure palate pleaser.
- **Best Local Cuisine**   Devoted to *la cocina criolla,* the term for the often starchy local cuisine, **Ajili Mójili,** Av. Ashford 1006 (© 787/725-9195), features food that islanders might have enjoyed in their mama's kitchens. Try such specialties as *mofongos* (green plantains stuffed with veal, chicken, shrimp, or pork) or the most classic *arroz con pollo* (stewed chicken with saffron rice) in town.
- **Best Hotel Restaurant**   In 1997 *San Juan City Magazine* bestowed best hotel restaurant status on **Ristorante Tuscany** in the San Juan Marriott Resort, Av. Ashford 1309 (© 787/722-7000). It has continued to maintain high standards that won it the accolade in the first place. We've found it even better in the early 21st century than it was in the 1990s. The chef searches the markets for some of the best and freshest ingredients to whip into succulent northern Italian cuisine that is smooth and refined to the palate.

- **Best Late-Night Dining**   If you have hunger pangs late at night, forget the fast-food joints and head to **Amadeus,** Calle San Sebastián 106 in Old San Juan (© **787/722-8635**). It offers Caribbean ingredients deftly handled with a nouvelle twist. And it does so Tuesday through Sunday until midnight. An attractive, trendy, generally young crowd arrives late to feast on the refined cuisine, enjoying such delights as Cajun-grilled mahimahi.

- **Best Family Meals   Ciao Mediterranean Café,** in the Inter-Continental San Juan Resort & Casino, Av. Isla Verde 5961 (© **787/791-6100**), offers an excellent and reasonably priced menu. Many tables are placed on a private boardwalk adjacent to the beach. Pizza and pasta are favorite dishes, and you can also choose from a large selection of other Mediterranean fare.

- **Best Pizza**   At **Via Appia,** Av. Ashford 1350 (© **787/725-8711**), you should try the special: a delectable blend of sausages, onions, mushrooms, pepperoni, green pepper, and bubbling cheese. Or sample a pizza with meatballs or one with vegetarian ingredients.

- **Best Sunday Brunch**   Both locals and American visitors flock to **Palmera** at the Caribe Hilton, Calle Los Rosales (© **787/721-0303**), for its delectable all-you-can-eat Sunday brunch. Good food, glamour, and live music are combined here. The freshly prepared seafood alone is worth the set price, which includes champagne.

- **Best Aphrodisiac Cuisine**   Take someone special to **Ostra Cosa,** Calle del Cristo 154 (© **787/722-2672**), for a night of romance. Even if you aren't in the mood, the owner promises that you will be after consuming his dishes, which are "chock-full of aphrodisiacs." All the food is guaranteed to enhance your performance in the bedroom.

- **Best Ice Cream**   On a cobble-covered street in Old San Juan, **Ben & Jerry's,** Calle del Cristo 61 (© **787/977-6882**), is a block from the landmark cathedral, Catedral de San Juan, across from the entrance to the El Convento Hotel. This North American chain offers the best ice cream in San Juan. Any of the 32 flavors—10 of them low-fat—taste particularly good on hot, steamy days, when their names, such as Chubby Hubby and Phish Food, seem especially ironic and/or flavorful, depending on your point of view.

- **Best Drinks**   Even when we're just in San Juan waiting for plane connections and have time available, we take a taxi to Maria's, Calle del Cristo 204 (© 787/721-1678), in Old San Juan, for the coolest and most original drinks in the city. On a hot day, there is no finer place to enjoy a mixed-fruit frappé; a banana, pineapple, or chocolate frost; or an orange, papaya, or lime freeze.

2 Cocina Criolla & Kill-Devil Rum

Although Puerto Rican cooking is somewhat similar to both Spanish and Mexican cuisine, it has a unique style, using such indigenous seasonings and ingredients as coriander, papaya, cacao, *nispero* (a tropical fruit that's brown, juicy, and related to the kiwi), *apio* (a small African-derived tuber that's sort of a more pungent type of turnip), plantains, and *yampee* (a tuber that's similar to an apio, but bigger, growing as big as 5–10 lb.).

Cocina criolla (Creole cooking) can be traced back to the Arawaks and Taínos, the original inhabitants of the island, who thrived on a diet of corn, tropical fruit, and seafood. When Ponce de León arrived with Columbus in 1493, the Spanish added beef, pork, rice, wheat, and olive oil to the island's foodstuffs.

> ### ⟨Fun Fact⟩ **Strange Fruit**
>
> Reading of Capt. James Cook's explorations of the South Pacific in the late 1700s, West Indian planters were intrigued by his accounts of the **breadfruit tree,** which grew in abundance on Tahiti. Seeing it as a source of cheap food for their slaves, they beseeched King George III to sponsor an expedition to bring the trees to the Caribbean. In 1787 the king put Capt. William Bligh in command of HMS *Bounty* and sent him to do just that. One of Bligh's lieutenants was a former shipmate named Fletcher Christian. They became the leading actors in one of the great sea yarns when Christian overpowered Bligh, took over the *Bounty,* threw the breadfruit trees into the South Pacific Ocean, and disappeared into oblivion.
>
> Bligh survived by sailing the ship's open longboat 3,000 miles (4,830km) to the East Indies, where he hitched a ride back to England on a Dutch vessel. Later he was given command of another ship and sent to Tahiti to get more breadfruit. Although he succeeded on this second attempt, the whole operation went for naught when the West Indies slaves refused to eat the strange fruit of the new tree, preferring instead their old, familiar rice.
>
> Descendants of those trees still grow in the Caribbean, and the islanders prepare the head-size fruit in a number of ways. A thick green rind covers its starchy, sweet flesh whose flavor is evocative of a sweet potato. *Tostones*—fried green breadfruit slices—accompany most meat, fish, or poultry dishes served today in Puerto Rico.

The Spanish soon began planting sugar cane and importing slaves from Africa, who brought with them okra and taro (known in Puerto Rico as *yautia*). The mingling of flavors and ingredients passed from generation to generation among the different ethnic groups that settled on the island, resulting in the exotic blend of today's Puerto Rican cuisine.

APPETIZERS & SOUPS

Lunch and dinner generally begin with hot appetizers such as *bacalaitos,* crunchy cod fritters; *surullitos,* sweet and plump cornmeal fingers; and *empanadillas,* crescent-shaped turnovers filled with lobster, crab, conch, or beef.

Soups are also a popular beginning. There is a debate about whether one of the world's best-known soups, *frijoles negros,* is Cuban or Puerto Rican in origin. Wherever it started, black-bean soup makes a savory if filling opening to a meal. Another classic soup is *sopón de pollo con arroz*—chicken soup with rice—which manages to taste somewhat different in every restaurant. One traditional method of preparing this soup calls for large pieces of pumpkin and diced potatoes or *yautias* (the starchy root of a large-leaved tropical plant whose flesh is usually yellow or creamy white).

The third classic soup is *sopón de pescado* (fish soup), prepared with the head and tail intact. Again, this soup varies from restaurant to restaurant, and it may depend on the catch of the day. Traditionally, it is made with garlic and spices plus onions and tomatoes, the flavor enhanced by a tiny dash of vinegar and varying amount of sherry. *Caldo gallego* (Galician broth) is a dish imported from Spain's northwestern province of Galicia. It is prepared with salt pork, white beans, ham, and *berzas* (collard greens) or *grelos* (turnip greens), and the whole kettle is flavored with spicy *chorizos* (Spanish sausages).

Garbanzos (chickpeas) are often added to give flavor, body, and texture to Puerto Rican soups. One of the most authentic versions of this is *sopón de garbanzos con patas de cerdo* (chickpea soup with pigs' feet). Into this kettle is added a variety of ingredients, including pumpkin, chorizos, salt pork, chile peppers, cabbage, potatoes, tomatoes, and fresh cilantro leaves.

Not really a soup, the most traditional Puerto Rican dish is **asopao,** a hearty gumbo made with either chicken or shellfish. One well-known version, consumed when the food budget runs low, is *asopao de gandules* (pigeon peas asopao). Every Puerto Rican chef has his or her own recipe for asopao. *Asopao de pollo* (chicken asopao) takes a whole chicken, which is then flavored with spices such as oregano, garlic, and paprika, along with salt pork, cured ham, green peppers, chile peppers, onions, cilantro, olives, tomatoes, chorizos, and pimientos. For a final touch, green peas or asparagus might be added.

MAIN COURSES

The aroma that wafts from kitchens throughout Puerto Rico comes from adobo and sofrito—blends of herbs and spices that give many of the native foods their distinctive taste and color. Adobo, made by crushing together peppercorns, oregano, garlic, salt, olive oil, and lime juice or vinegar, is rubbed into meats before they are roasted. Sofrito, a potpourri of onions, garlic, and peppers browned in either olive oil or lard and colored with achiote (annatto seeds), imparts the bright yellow color to the island's rice, soups, and stews.

Stews loom large in the Puerto Rican diet. They are usually cooked in a *caldera* (heavy kettle). A popular one is *carne guisada puertorriqueña* (Puerto Rican beef stew). The ingredients that flavor the chunks of beef vary according to the cook's whims or whatever happens to be in the larder. These might include green peppers, sweet chile peppers, onions, garlic, cilantro, potatoes, olives stuffed with pimientos, or capers. Seeded raisins may be added on occasion.

Pastelon de carne, or **meat pies,** are the staple of many Puerto Rican dinners. Salt pork and ham are often used for the filling and are cooked in a *caldero* (small cauldron). This medley of meats and spices is covered with a pastry top and baked.

Other typical main dishes include fried beefsteak with onions *(carne frita con cebolla),* veal *(ternera)* a la parmesana, and roast leg of pork, fresh ham, lamb, or veal a la criolla. These roasted meats are cooked in the Creole style, flavored with adobo. *Chicharrónes*—fried pork with the crunchy skin left on top for added flavor—is very popular, especially around Christmastime.

Puerto Ricans also like such dishes as *sesos empanados* (breaded calves' brains), *riñones guisados* (calves' kidney stew), and *lengua rellena* (stuffed beef tongue).

A festive island dish is *lechón asado,* or **barbecued pig,** which is usually cooked for a party of 12 to 15. It is traditional for picnics and alfresco parties; one can sometimes catch the aroma of this dish wafting through the palm trees, a smell that must have been familiar to the Taíno peoples. The pig is basted with *jugo de naranja agria* (sour orange juice) and achiote coloring. Green plantains are peeled and roasted over hot stones, then served with the barbecued pig as a side dish. The traditional dressing served with the pig is *aji-li-mojili,* a sour garlic sauce. The sauce combines garlic, whole black peppercorns, and sweet seeded chile peppers, flavored further with vinegar, lime juice, salt, and olive oil.

Puerto Ricans adore **chicken,** which they flavor with various spices and seasonings. *Arroz con pollo* (chicken with rice) is the most popular chicken dish on the island, and it was brought long ago to the U.S. mainland. Other favorite preparations include *pollo al Jerez* (chicken in sherry), *pollo en agridulce* (sweet-and-sour chicken), and *pollitos asados à la parrilla* (broiled chickens).

Most visitors to the island prefer the **fresh fish** and **shellfish.** A popular dish is *mojo isleno* (fried fish with Puerto Rican sauce). The sauce is made with olives and olive oil, onions, pimientos, capers, tomato sauce, vinegar, and a flavoring of garlic and bay leaves. Fresh fish is often grilled and perhaps flavored with garlic and an overlay of freshly squeezed lime juice—a very tasty dinner indeed. Caribbean lobster is usually the most expensive item on any menu, followed by shrimp. Puerto Ricans often cook *camarones en cerveza* (shrimp in beer). Another delectable shellfish dish is *jueyes hervidos* (boiled crab).

Many tasty **egg dishes** are served, especially *tortilla española* (Spanish omelet), cooked with finely chopped onions, cubed potatoes, and olive oil.

The rich and fertile fields of Puerto Rico produce a wide variety of **vegetables.** A favorite is the **chayote,** a pear-shaped vegetable called *christophine* throughout most of the English-speaking Caribbean. Its delicately flavored flesh is often compared to that of summer squash.

Fried tostones are made with both **breadfruit** (see "Strange Fruit," above) and **plantains.** In fact, the plantain is the single most popular side dish served on the island. Plantains are a variety of banana that cannot be eaten raw. They are much coarser in texture than ordinary bananas and are harvested while green, then baked, fried, or boiled. When made into tostones, they are usually served as an appetizer with before-dinner drinks. Fried to a deep golden yellow, plantains may accompany fish, meat, or poultry dishes.

THE AROMA OF COFFEE

It is customary for most Puerto Ricans to end a meal with the strong, black aromatic coffee grown here. Originally imported from the nearby Dominican Republic, coffee beans have been produced in the island's high-altitude interior for more than 300 years and still rank among the island's leading exports.

Puerto Rican coffee, in the view of many connoisseurs, rivals that of the more highly touted product from Colombia. Coffee has several degrees of quality, of course, the lowest-ranking one being *café de primera,* which is typically served at the ordinary family table. The top category is called *café super premium.* Only three coffees in the world belong to super-premium class: Blue Mountain coffee of Jamaica, Kona coffee from Hawaii, and Puerto Rico's homegrown Alto Grande, coffee beans sought by coffee connoisseurs around the world. The best brand names for Puerto Rican coffee are Café Crema, Café Rico, Rioja, and Yaucono.

You can ask for your brew *puya* (unsweetened), *negrito con azúcar* (black and sweetened), *cortao* (black with a drop of milk), or *con leche* (with milk).

RUM: KILL-DEVIL OR WHISKEY-BELLY VENGEANCE

Rum is the national drink of Puerto Rico, and you can buy it in almost any shade. Because the island is the world's leading rum producer, it's little wonder that every Puerto Rican bartender worthy of the profession likes to concoct his or her own favorite rum libation. You can call for Puerto Rican rum in many mixed drinks such as rum Collins, rum sour, and rum screwdriver. The classic sangria, which is prepared in Spain with dry red wine, sugar, orange juice, and other ingredients, is often given a Puerto Rican twist with a hefty dose of rum.

Today's version of rum bears little resemblance to the raw, grainy beverage consumed by the renegades and pirates of Spain. Christopher Columbus brought sugar cane, from which rum is distilled, to the Caribbean on his second voyage to the New World, and in almost no time rum became the regional drink.

It is believed that Ponce de León introduced rum to Puerto Rico during his governorship, which began in 1508. In time, there emerged large sugar-cane plantations. From Puerto Rico and other West Indian islands, rum was shipped to colonial America, where it lent itself to such popular and hair-raising 18th-century drinks as Kill-Devil and Whiskey-Belly Vengeance. After the United States became a nation, rum was largely displaced as the drink of choice by whiskey, distilled from grain grown on the American plains.

It took almost a century before Puerto Rico's rum industry regained its former vigor. This occurred during a severe whiskey shortage in the United States at the end of World War II. By the 1950s, sales of rum had fallen off again, as more and different kinds of liquor had become available on the American market.

The local brew had been a questionable drink because of inferior distillation methods and quality. Recognizing this problem, the Puerto Rican government drew up rigid standards for producing, blending, and aging rum. Rum factories were outfitted with the most modern and sanitary equipment, and sales figures (encouraged by aggressive marketing campaigns) began to climb.

No one will ever agree on what "the best" rum is in the Caribbean. There are just too many of them to sample. Some are so esoteric as to be unavailable in your local liquor store. But if popular tastes mean anything, then Puerto Rican rums, especially Bacardi, head the list. There are 24 different rums from Puerto Rico sold in the United States under 11 brand names—not only Bacardi, but Ron Bocoy, Ronrico, Don Q, and many others.

Puerto Rican rums are generally light, gold, or dark. Usually white or silver in color, the biggest seller is light in body and dry in taste. Its subtle flavor and delicate aroma make it ideal for many mixed drinks, including the daiquiri, rum Collins, rum Mary, and rum and tonic or soda. It also goes with almost any fruit juice, or on the rocks with a slice of lemon or lime. Gold or amber rum is aromatic and full-bodied in taste. Aging in charred oak casks adds color to the rum.

Gold rums are usually aged longer for a deeper and more mellow flavor than light rums. They are increasingly popular on the rocks, straight up, or in certain mixed drinks in which extra flavor is desired—certainly in the famous piña colada, rum and Coke, or eggnog.

Dark rum is full-bodied with a deep, velvety, smooth taste and a complex flavor. It can be aged for as long as 15 years. You can enjoy it on the rocks, with tonic or soda, or in mixed drinks when you want the taste of rum to stand out.

3 Old San Juan

For the locations of Old San Juan restaurants, see the map "Old San Juan Accommodations & Dining" on p. 81.

EXPENSIVE

Aquaviva 🎔🎔 LATINO/SEAFOOD   The location is at the bottom of Calle Fortaleza, in Old San Juan, within a cool, turquoise-colored environment. Presiding above the sometimes frenetic bar action and dining room hubbub of this place are replicas of three *aquaviva* (jellyfish), quivering with illumination, each painstakingly manufactured from stained glass specifically for this site. Its owners spend a small fortune on publicity and promotion, making it one of the hottest restaurant tickets in Old San Juan.

Oysters and stiff drinks are served at the bar. Flowing from the open-to-view kitchens come dishes whose ingredients derive from the watery turquoise world that inspired this restaurant's color scheme. The best examples include six different seviches, including one made with mahimahi, mango juice, and lemons; and a different version from marlin and garlic. You might opt for a heaping tower composed of fried oysters, coco-flavored shrimp, fried octopus, and calamari. The best main courses include grilled fresh mahimahi with smoky shrimp, salsa, and coconut-poached yucca; seared medallions of halibut with a fondue of spinach and crabmeat; and a succulent version of paella garnished with seafood and pork sausage.

Calle Fortaleza 364. ℂ 787/722-0665. Reservations required. Main courses $16–$45. AE, MC, V. Lunch daily 11am–4pm; dinner Mon–Wed 6–11pm, Thurs–Sat 6pm–midnight, Sun 4–11pm. Bus: Old Town Trolley.

Barú 🎔 CARIBBEAN/MEDITERRANEAN   This is one of the most fashionable and popular of the imaginative new restaurants of Old San Juan, with an attractive and hard-playing clientele, some of whom might effectively compete for roles on the Hispanic soap operas. Named after an unspoiled island off the north coast of Colombia, a personal favorite of its Colombian-born owner, it occupies a stately looking high-ceilinged space capped with massive timbers, fronted with a hyper-convivial mahogany bar, and decorated with paintings by such Colombia-born artistic luminaries as Botéro.

Many dishes are deliberately conceived as something midway between an appetizer and a main-course platter, so it's hard to know how much, or how many courses, to order. If unsure, ask your waitperson to guide you. Menu items include an unusual choice of five different kinds of carpaccio (tuna, halibut, salmon, beef, or Serrano ham), presented in paper-thin and very small portions that are spread out like a few sheets of tissue paper on a pretentiously large plate. Seviche of mahimahi is appropriately tart, appealingly permeated with citrus; and the marinated lamb chops with a paprika and pineapple mojo sauce is flavorful. Other culinary creations include almond-encrusted goat cheese with Jamaican jerk mango dip and yucca chips, and sliced filet mignon. Regrettably, the place is not cheap, and service is well intentioned but disorganized as the youthful staff maneuvers as best it can through the packed-in crowd.

Calle San Sebastián 150. ℂ **787/977-7107.** Reservations recommended. Main courses $15–$28. AE, MC, V. Mon–Sat 6pm–3am; Sun 6pm–midnight. Bus: Old Town Trolley.

Bossa Nova 🎔 *Value* BRAZILIAN   Cozy, amicable, and unpretentious, this restaurant presents, night after night, one of the best food values in San Juan. Established in 2003 in a format that emulates a style of restaurant popular in Brazil and outfitted with masks fashioned from feathers from the rainforest and carved bas-reliefs of Brazilian dancers, it offers a convivial bar area near the entrance and an open-to-view grill from which derive many of the restaurant's specialties.

Your meal might begin with codfish fritters, succulent fried yucca served with hearts of palm and sausage, or turnovers stuffed with chunks of lobster and hearts of palm. The $29 house specialty is a Brazilian-style *rodizio* consisting of five kinds of grilled meat brought out to your table skewer by skewer and accompanied with Brazilian risotto, pastas, salads, french fries, fried plantains, fried cassava, and more—all are flavored with Brazilian-style vinaigrette sauce. If you happen to come on a Saturday, consider this place's weekly celebration of *feijoada completa,* a traditional hearty stew made from black beans and various meats served with white rice, collard greens, and at least in the version served here, with oranges.

Calle Fortaleza 358. Ⓒ 787/722-0093. Reservations not necessary. Main courses $18–$21; Brazilian *rodizio,* a full-fledged meal in itself, $29 per person. AE, MC, V. Mon–Sat 6pm–midnight. Bus: A5 or T1.

Carli Café Concierto ⚔ INTERNATIONAL   This stylish restaurant is owned by Carli Muñoz. The gold disc hanging on the wall attests to Carli's success in his previous role as a pianist for The Beach Boys. Nowadays, Carli entertains his dinner guests nightly with a combination of standards, romantic jazz, and original material on his grand piano. Diners can sit outside on the Plazoleta, where they can enjoy a panoramic view of the bay, or they can eat inside against a backdrop of a tasteful decor of terra-cotta walls and black marble tables. The chef tempts visitors with an imaginative international menu, including such delights as quail rockettes stuffed with dried fruits and sage. The filet of salmon and a mouthwatering rack of lamb are among the finest main dishes. The bar, with its mahogany and brass fittings, is an ideal spot to chill out.

Edificio Banco Popular, Calle Tetuán 206, off Plazoleta Rafael Carrión. Ⓒ 787/725-4927. Reservations recommended. Main courses $17–$36. AE, V. Mon–Fri 3:30–11pm; Sat 4–11:30pm. Bus: M2 or M3.

Il Perugino ⚔⚔ ITALIAN   Affiliated with the El Convento Hotel (p. 80), this is Puerto Rico's finest Italian restaurant, serving a cuisine that at times seems inspired. Located across from the hotel, the restaurant specializes in the cuisine of Umbria, that province of Italy adjoining Tuscany.

The chef and owner, Franco Seccarelli, hails from Umbria and insists that the classic dishes be authentic to his homeland. A special architectural feature of the restaurant is a converted dry well in the center which serves as a wine cellar. Service is impeccable and friendly.

Our favorite homemade pastas include black fettuccine with a shellfish ragout or ricotta and spinach gnocchetti with fresh tomatoes. For a starter, opt for the shrimp salad with grilled zucchini, a sublime dish, as is another salad made with scallops and porcini mushrooms. Among the meat and poultry dishes, Seccarelli shines with his pheasant breast alla Cacciatora and his pork filets flavored with an unusual combination of thyme and blueberries. Another dish we recently raved about was the rack of lamb with fresh herbs and a rich red-wine sauce. Desserts are also succulent and homemade.

Cristo St. 105. Ⓒ 787/722-5481. Reservations recommended. Main courses $18–$36. AE, DISC, MC, V. Thurs–Sat 11:30am–2:30pm; Tues–Sun 6:30–11pm. Bus: Old Town Trolley.

La Chaumière ⚔ CLASSIC FRENCH   The classic cuisine here has a loyal following of foodies. Just steps from the famous Tapía Theater, this restaurant has cafe-style decor in a greenhouse setting. You might begin with a Marseilles-style fish soup or a hearty country pâté, then follow with a perfectly prepared rack of baby lamb Provençal, filet mignon with béarnaise sauce, magret of duckling, or Dover sole meunière. Or you might choose the tender chateaubriand for two. Old standbys include chitterling sausage with red-wine sauce, veal Oscar, and oysters Rockefeller.

Calle Tetuán 367. (*C*) 787/722-3330. Reservations required. Main courses $24–$35. AE, MC, V. Mon–Sat 6pm–midnight. Closed July–Aug. Bus: Old Town Trolley.

Parrot Club *🍴🍴* NUEVO LATINO/CARIBBEAN   This bistro and bar, owned by husband-and-wife team Emilio Figueroa and Gigi Zafero, is one of the most sought-after restaurants in Old San Juan. Chef Roberto Treviño (a one-time *Iron Chef* contestant, vs. Mario Batali) cooks up Nuevo Latino cuisine that blends traditional Puerto Rican cookery with Spanish, Taíno, and African influences. It's set in a stately 1902 building that was originally a hair-tonic factory. Today you'll find a cheerful-looking dining room, where San Juan's mayor and the governor of Puerto Rico can sometimes be spotted, and a verdantly landscaped courtyard, where tables for at least 200 diners are scattered amid potted ferns, palms, and orchids. Live music, either Brazilian, salsa, or Latino jazz, is offered nightly as well as during the popular Sunday brunches.

Menu items are updated interpretations of old Puerto Rican specialties. They include an excellent seviche of halibut, salmon, tuna, and mahimahi; delicious crab cakes; criolla-style flank steak; and pan-seared tuna served with a sauce made from dark rum and essence of oranges. Everybody's favorite drink is a "Parrot Passion," made from lemon-flavored rum, triple sec, oranges, and passion fruit.

Calle Fortaleza 363. (*C*) 787/725-7370. Reservations not accepted. Main courses $18–$36 at dinner, $12–$20 at lunch. AE, DC, MC, V. Daily 11am–4pm and 6–11pm. Closed 2 weeks in Sept. Bus: Old Town Trolley.

Sofia *🍴* ITALIAN   Although our favorite Italian restaurant in Old Town San Juan remains Il Perugino, this challenger also serves a finely honed cuisine, though it's a bit pricey, especially if you opt for the fresh seafood. Its interior with its columns and arched doorways evokes a trattoria deep in the heart of Rome. Red colors and exposed brick, as well as an interior courtyard, aid in their impression. Service is first-rate, as are the market-fresh ingredients, and many of the specialties are quintessentially Italian. The chef is justifiably proud of his chopino Sofia, served for two people. It's like a paella but linguini is used instead of rice. The seared blackened tuna is also a perfect choice, and the classic saltimbocca alla romana (with veal and prosciutto flavored with sage and served in a buttery wine sauce) is another specialty. The beef dishes are good and tender, and are especially delectable when served in a chianti sauce. The pasta dishes are savory, and the pizza oven turns out lush, tasty pies.

Calle San Francisco 355. (*C*) 787/721-0396. Reservations recommended at night. Main courses $20–$42; pizzas $12–$14. AE, DC, MC, V. Mon–Fri 11am–2:30pm and 5–9pm (open to 10pm Fri); Sat 5–10pm.

Trois Cent Onze (311) *🍴🍴* FRENCH   When the French and Puerto Rican owners of this place renovated this building in 1999, they discovered some of the most beautiful Moorish-Andalusian tilework in San Juan's Old Town buried beneath layers of later coverings. Because of those tiles, and because of the delicate Andalusian-style iron rosette above the door, they wisely decided to retain the area's Moorish embellishments during the reconfiguration of their restaurant's decor. What you'll get today is the premier French restaurant of San Juan, replete with a zinc bar near the entrance, a soaring and richly beamed ceiling, and a decor like what you might have expected in the Casbah of old Tangiers. Your hosts are Christophe Gourdain and Zylma Perez, who are proud to recite the building's former use as the photography studio that developed many of Puerto Rico's earliest movies. Colors, textures, and flavors combine here

---

Tips **Take a Strong Coffee Break**

A coffee break in Old San Juan might last an afternoon. *Taza* (cup) after *taza* of Puerto Rico's rich brew might make you desert Jamaican Blue Mountain coffee or Hawaiian Kona forever. By law, Puerto Rican coffeehouses must serve coffee made from homegrown beans, most often from the mountains in the center of the island. For years we've taken our espresso—from early morning until our final "nightcap"—at **Cuatro Estaciones** (no phone), a rather ugly kiosk at the end of the bustling Plaza de Armas. You'll get a quick jolt from this tasty brew, which attracts local java heads day and night.

---

to produce an irresistible array of dishes. Menu items include a carpaccio of salmon marinated in citrus; sautéed sea scallops served with an almond-flavored butter sauce; mango and crabmeat salad; magret of duckling roasted with honey; and pork medallions served with caramelized onions, stewed white beans, and spicy *merguez* sausage.

Calle Fortaleza 311. © 787/725-7959. Reservations recommended. Main courses $19–$30. AE, MC, V. Tues–Thurs noon–2:30pm and 6:30–10pm; Fri–Sat noon–2:30pm and 6–11pm; Sun 5–10pm. Bus: Old Town Trolley, T2, or 2.

MODERATE

Al Dente SICILIAN/ITALIAN   Since the closing of some of its competitors in 2003, this is now the oldest continuously operated Italian restaurant in Puerto Rico, with a clientele that includes an awe-inspiring number of high-pressure lawyers, politicians, and judges every day at lunch, and a more leisurely crowd of friends and romantics every night at dinner. The venue includes a friendly and accommodating bar area near the entrance, a warm-toned color scheme of scarlets and blues, and a replica of a brightly painted Sicilian fishing boat—personally crafted by the owner—hanging on one of the walls. Sicily-born Giancarlo Amenta and his Puerto Rican wife Margie are the owners, fusing with skill the aesthetics of their respective countries. The relatively short list of culinary staples is enhanced with a changing array of daily specials, leading to a varied choice of dishes that's more varied than the relatively abbreviated menu might suggest. Your meal might include *osso buco*, house-made ravioli, rib-eye steak, several kinds of risotto (including versions with crayfish, Portobello mushrooms, or Parmesan cheese), calamari with polenta, and *arancini di spinachi fritti* (an old Sicilian specialty and one of the restaurant's bestsellers—spinach balls with rice, ricotta cheese, and pink sauce). Note the large-scale paintings that decorate the dining room. Executed by Margie Alcaraz Amenta herself, who will likely be on hand to greet you when you arrive, they're for sale, selling briskly at prices that range from between $2,000 and $4,500 each.

Calle Recinto Sur 309. © 787/723-7303. Reservations recommended. Main courses $16–$23. AE, MC, V. Mon–Fri noon–10:30pm; Sat noon–11pm. Bus: Old Town Trolley.

Amadeus ❀ CARIBBEAN   Housed in a brick-and-stone building that was constructed in the 18th century by a wealthy merchant, Amadeus offers Caribbean ingredients with a nouvelle twist. The appetizers alone are worth the trip here, especially the Amadeus dumplings with guava sauce and arrowroot fritters. And try the smoked-salmon-and-caviar pizza. One zesty specialty is pork scaloppine with sweet-and-sour sauce.

Calle San Sebastián 106 (across from the Iglesia de San José). © 787/722-8635. Reservations recommended. Main courses $8–$25. AE, DISC, MC, V. Mon 6pm–midnight; Tues–Sun 11am–midnight. Bus: Old Town Trolley, M2, M3, or A5.

Café Berlin INTERNATIONAL   Other than the hardworking staff, there's very little about this place that's particularly Hispanic. What you'll get is a corner of central Europe, identified by a *Jugendstil*-inspired sign, serving coffee, pastries, and a limited array of light platters, such as pasta, on tiny marble-top tables like what you'd expect in Vienna. Paintings, all of them for sale, are displayed on scarlet-colored walls, and lavishly caloric pastries are arranged behind glass display cases. More substantial, rib-sticking fare includes salmon in orange- and garlic-flavored herb broth, scallops in pesto sauce, and turkey breast Stroganoff.

Plaza de Colón 407. *C* 787/722-5205. Main courses $8–$19. AE, MC, V. Mon–Fri 10am–10pm; Sat–Sun 8am–10pm. Bus: Old Town Trolley.

Dragonfly *&&&* LATIN/ASIAN FUSION   At one of San Juan's hottest restaurants, the decor has been compared to that of a bordello in Old San Francisco. You pass through the beaded curtains into a world of red ceilings, fringed lamps, and gilded mirrors. The restaurant lies right across the street from the Parrot Club, and these two dining enclaves have put the newly named SoFo district (south of Calle Fortaleza in Old Town) on the culinary map. In the bar, the preferred cigarette is Marlboro and the most popular drink, a lethal "Dragon Punch." Night after night Dragonfly is the fun party place in town. Along with the latest gossip, you can enjoy live Latin jazz as background music.

An Authentic *Criolla* Restaurant

When you've had too many hotel meals or patronized too many first-class restaurants and want something authentic, head for **El Jibarito,** Calle del Sol 280 (*C* **787/725-8375**), where locals flock for food like their mamas used to make.

Set within a residential section of Old San Juan that's a few blocks removed from the showcase-style tourist haunts, this is a bustling local restaurant that's known to virtually everyone in the Old City for its avid loyalty to the kind of cuisine that many Sanjuaneros remember from their childhoods. Established as a testimonial to their rustic (*jíbaro*) backgrounds by Pedro and Aida Ruiz, it's a high-ceilinged, decent, and very clean enclave of brightly painted walls (mostly pinks and tones of green), paper napkins, solid porcelain, and completely unpretentious *criolla* cuisine. Menu items focus on rich, sometimes starchy, food that kept Puerto Rico alive throughout the early 20th century. Examples include fritters studded with pieces of seasoned pork; cube steak with onions; conch salad; oven-baked grouper; fried red snapper, chicken filets with garlic; and shrimps in garlic. A whopping portion of *mofongo* (chopped plantains with butter and seasonings) can be ordered as a folkloric side dish; and salad comes with every main course. Dessert might include a genuinely excellent wedge of coconut flan. Service is attentive, unpretentious, and extremely polite. Main courses cost $7.95 to $18 and are served daily from 10am to 9pm. American Express, Diners Club, MasterCard, and Visa are accepted.

This new-generation San Juan restaurant offers sexy cookery, such as seafood seviche scooped up with yucca, and plantain chips, *chicharrónes* (pork rinds), spicy crab cakes, and a host of other dishes, such as marinated grilled meats. We applaud the chefs for their use of root vegetables such as yucca. The red snapper and grouper are excellent, and we love the pumpkin and beans of every type. The barbecued lamb shanks are very hearty and filling. Ravioli, timbales, confits, cassoulets—it's a dizzy array of taste temptations.

Calle Fortaleza 364. Ⓒ 787/977-3886. Reservations required. Main courses $8–$30. AE, MC, V. Mon–Wed 6–11pm; Thurs–Sat 6pm–midnight. Bus: A5 or T1.

El Patio de Sam AMERICAN/PUERTO RICAN   Established in 1953, this joint has survived several generations of clients, who came here for booze, fantastic juicy burgers, Puerto Rican food, and dialogue. There is the unmistakable aura of pop, youth culture, Margaritaville, and college-age drinking ethos. The setting includes an exterior space with tables that overlook a historic statue of Ponce de León and a well-known church, and a labyrinth of dark, smoked-stained inner rooms with high-beamed ceilings and lots of potted plants. Dining usually occurs in a skylit garden-style courtyard in back where there is no view but a welcome sense of calm. In addition to those burgers, you can also order more sophisticated dishes such as Puerto Rican-style fried pork, seviche, shellfish paella, chicken and rice, and *churrasco* (Argentine-styled grilled meats).

Calle San Sebastián 102 (across from the Iglesia de San José). Ⓒ 787/723-1149. Sandwiches, burgers, and salads $9–$11; platters $13–$35. AE, DISC, MC, V. Daily noon–1am. Bus: Old Town Trolley.

El Picoteo ⚄ SPANISH   In the courtyard of the historic El Convento Hotel, this is the best place in Old Town to go for tapas and for heaping platters of seafood-studded paella. You get real Spanish flavor here, in such dishes as garbanzo salad, sausages, and seviche. Fresh octopus is also a delight as are the Spanish-style pizzas. Sanjuaneros along with visitors enjoy this informal place for lunch or a drink at the bar. Many spend the afternoon playing backgammon and sipping a pitcher of champagne-laced sangria. Dinner is festive, accompanied by salsa and lights in the courtyard. The menu has some 80 tapas from which to choose, the selection of imported Spanish cheeses is Old Town's finest, and the staff is politely charming.

In El Convento hotel, Calle del Cristo 100. Ⓒ 787/723-9202. Reservations recommended. Main courses $6–$17; paella $20–$35. AE, MC, V. Tues–Sun noon–midnight. Bus: Old Town Trolley.

La Mallorquina ⚄ PUERTO RICAN   Founded in 1848, this old favorite has been run by the Rojos family since 1900. If you look carefully at the floor adjacent to the old-fashioned mahogany bar, you'll see the building's original gray-and-white marble flooring, which the owners are laboriously restoring, square foot by square foot, to its original condition. Lunches here tend to attract local office workers; dinners are more cosmopolitan and more leisurely, with many residents of the Condado and other modern neighborhoods selecting this place specifically because of its old-fashioned, old-world charm.

The food has changed little here over the decades, with special emphasis on asopao made with rice and either chicken, shrimp, or lobster and shrimp. *Arroz con pollo* is almost as popular. Begin with either garlic soup or gazpacho, end with flan, and you'll have eaten a meal that's authentically Puerto Rican.

Calle San Justo 207. Ⓒ 787/722-3261. Reservations not accepted at lunch, recommended at dinner. Dinner main courses $15–$36 (highest price is for lobster). AE, MC, V. Mon–Sat 12:30–10pm. Closed Sept. Bus: Old Town Trolley.

La Querencia ✦ *Finds* PUERTO RICAN/INTERNATIONAL   Because of the many desirable restaurants that flank it, it's easy to overlook the charms of this one. Set within a 400-year-old town house, it offers an appealing mixture of elegance, restraint, and urban hip, all of it factored into a long and narrow format that includes an exotic and cozy bar (painted red) near the entrance, and a more formal forest-green dining room in back. The high ceiling and formal layout evokes a salon in a colonial governor's house. Surrounding you will be a collection of antique guitars and wind instruments. Separating the two areas is a skylit courtyard with an open view of the hardworking kitchens. You can opt to sit anywhere within this warren of rooms, but our preferences involve drinks and tapas in the red-painted bar area in front, surrounded by artwork and hints of Madrid during its *movida,* and candlelit meals in back. Your meal might begin delectably with a seviche of sea bass with orange zest; or sautéed shrimp with roasted pineapple, coconut flakes, and a rum-flavored vinaigrette. Main courses include a superb version of pork loin topped with cranberry sauce, served over caramelized apples, or a rack of lamb with red, black, and white bean ragout with fines herbs and puff pastry.

Calle Fortaleza 320. © 787/723-0357. Reservations recommended Sat–Sun. Main courses $16–$26. AE, DC, DISC, MC, V. Daily 6–11pm. Bus: Old Town Trolley, T2, or 2.

Makarios GREEK/LEBANESE   Set above a sometimes raucous cafe-bar, a few steps from Piers 1, 2, and 3 in Old San Juan, this is the only restaurant in Old San Juan that serves Lebanese and, to a lesser degree, Greek food. To reach it, you'll climb a flight of stairs immediately adjacent to the entrance to reach the second-floor dining room. Here, beneath a gracefully arched ceiling of a dining room trimmed in varnished wood, you can order good-tasting dishes that include baba ghanouj, hummus, falafel, baked halibut, salmon with honey-mustard dressing, grilled shrimp, grilled snapper, shish kabob, and couscous. As for the high-energy cafe on the establishment's street level, where blaring music manages to combine traditional Greek and Arabic music with the beats of highly danceable house and garage music, you might shun it completely, or find it absolutely fascinating, depending on your background and your point of view. There's a definite flavor of Middle Eastern energy here, replete with fast communications among the mostly Jerusalem-born staff. On Friday and Saturday there is belly dancing from 9 to 11pm.

Calle Tetuán 361. © 787/723-8653. Reservations not necessary. Main courses $15–$24. AE, DISC, MC, V. Daily noon–midnight (till 3am Fri–Sat). Bus: M2 or M3.

Ostra Cosa ✦ *Finds* ECLECTIC/SEAFOOD   This artfully promoted restaurant has a growing clientele that calls its ambience one of the most sensual and romantic in Old San Juan. Former advertising executive Alberto Nazario, a lifestyle guru who mingles New Age thinking with culinary techniques to promote love, devotion, and a heightened sexuality, created Ostra Cosa. Couples dine beneath a massive quenepe tree—waiters will tell you to hug the tree and make a wish—in a colonial courtyard surrounded by a 16th-century building that was once the home of the colony's governor. The atmosphere, enhanced by domesticated quail and chirping tree frogs, will make you feel far removed from the cares of the city. Featured foods are high in phosphorus, zinc, and flavor, designed to promote an "eat-up, dress-down experience." The seviche is superb; the small grilled (still-shelled) prawns were less thrilling (and a bit messy). But it is the conch, known as Caribbean Viagra, that rates "Wow!" or "Ay Ay Ay!"

Calle del Cristo 154. © 787/722-2672. Reservations recommended. Main courses $18–$29. AE, MC, V. Sun–Wed noon–10pm; Fri–Sat noon–11pm. Bus: Old Town Trolley.

Tantra ⓖ *Value* INDO-LATINO   Set in the heart of "restaurant row" on Calle Fortaleza, it has become famous for a sophisticated fusion of Latino with South Indian cuisine. Its chef and owner, Indian-born Ramesh Pillai, oversees a blend of slow-cooked tandoori cuisine from South India with Puerto Rico–derived spices, flavors, and ingredients. All of this occurs within a warm, candlelit environment that focuses on Indian handicrafts and Hindu and Buddhist symbols.

An appropriate way to begin a meal here is to order one of the best martinis we've ever had—a concoction flavored with cinnamon and cloves. Menu highlights include sesame masala-crusted sushi tuna with peanut sauce; fried coconut sesame jumbo shrimp with Indian noodles; chicken tikka masala with nan (flat bread); and rice and chicken rolls with passion-fruit sauce. One of the establishment's bestsellers is an absolutely brilliant version of tandoori chicken that combines the traditional Indian recipe with manchego and mozzarella cheese, guyaba fruit, guava-flavored dip, and nan.

Calle Fortaleza 356. ⓒ 787/977-8141. Reservations only for groups. Main courses $13–$19. AE, MC, V. Mon 3pm–3am; Tues–Sat noon–3pm; Sun noon–midnight. Bus: T1 or 2.

INEXPENSIVE

Café Bohemia INTERNATIONAL   Set within the street level of, but under independent management from, the landmark Hotel El Convento, this cafe presents the kind of irreverent aura you'd expect within a hip and arts-conscious cafe in Madrid. There are tables set up on an outdoor terrace, a welcome separation from the congested sidewalk and street outside, a rectangular and granite-topped bar area, and a dining area tucked between the massive columns of the El Convento's 400-year-old masonry. Menu items include sushi; a seviche of red snapper; steak au poivre, a carpaccio of beef tenderloin with Parmesan; shrimp Creole; and *yucafonga* (mashed cassava) stuffed with chicken, shrimp, or seafood. Despite the appeal of its food, many clients come here only for the drinks. Tuesday nights tends to attract, as promoted by the Café, a higher-than-usual percentage of gay clients.

Calle Cristo 100. ⓒ 787/723-9200. Reservations recommended. Main courses $17–$26. AE, MC, V. Daily 11am–2am. Bus: Old Town Trolley.

Casa Borinquen ⓖ *Finds* PUERTO RICAN   Set beside a (usually quiet) stretch of cobble-covered street in the uppermost altitudes of the Old City, this is a well-recommended and defiantly proud restaurant that's not in the least ashamed to proudly advertise its sense of Puerto Rican nationalism. It's the only restaurant in the Old Town with a famous work of art painted directly onto its concrete facade. It depicts the Puerto Rican separatist Don Pedro Albizu Campos, a Harvard-educated intellectual who was jailed as a revolutionary in the 1950s and who died in the 1960s. In the original, widely disseminated portrait, painted by the well-known local artist, Dennis Mario Rivera, he's pierced, in a style befitting San Sebastian himself, with arrows. In a restaurant this aggressively politicized, you naturally expect, and you get, a tremendous emphasis on Puerto Rican cuisine. We usually pass through the long and narrow dining room, then order a drink in the open-air courtyard bar in back before lunch or dinner at this place. Menu items are creative but deeply entrenched in Puerto Rican *(criolla)* traditions. Examples include pork ribs in guava-flavored barbecue sauce; filets of salmon in tamarind and caper sauce; mofongos stuffed with either chicken, shrimp, or shredded crab; pork sandwiches with sweet-potato fries; octopus salads; fish turnovers; seviche made from mahimahi and salmon; and Puerto Rican–style blood and chicken sausage. Other choices include eggplant lasagna with shrimp; shrimp in a piña colada sauce; and filet mignon with mushroom-flavored brandy sauce. There's live music presented here every Thursday (jazz) and Friday ("romantic bohemian") from around 9pm till closing.

Calle San Sebastián 109. ℂ 787/722-7070. Reservations recommended only on Thurs, Sat, and holidays. Main courses $14–$26. AE, MC, V. Mon–Sat 11:30am–11:30pm. Bus: Old Town Trolley.

Café Puerto Rico CREOLE/PUERTO RICAN   On the Plaza de Colón, this restaurant offers balconies overlooking one of the most charming of Old Town squares. The setting is colonial, with beamed ceilings and tile floors, and with ceiling fans whirling overhead. The menu features hearty regional fare. Tasty options include fried fish filet, paella, and lobster cooked as you like it. Eggplant parmigiana is an excellent vegetarian option, and you might also order eye round stuffed with ham in Creole sauce. Of course, if you're getting hungry during a day of strolling Old San Juan's windy streets, don't wait for dinner—you'll enjoy a lunch break here, too.

Calle O'Donnell 208. ℂ 787/724-2281. Main courses $9–$20. AE, MC, V. Mon–Sat 11:30am–11pm; Sun 11:30am–9pm. Bus: Old Town Trolley.

El Buen Samaritano PUERTO RICAN   Only the most experimental foreign tourists would venture in here, despite the fact that it provides lots of insights into the subculture of this thriving inner-city neighborhood. In fact, we have included this authentic little eatery to answer the often-posed question "Where do the locals dine?" It stands adjacent to the back door of city hall, near the corner of Calle San Justo, on one of our favorite "backwater" streets of the historic Old Town. Almost no English is spoken; it's as Creole and ethnic as anything on the island, and it contains no more than four well-scrubbed tables in a setting Hemingway would have praised. All the food is predictably filling and starchy, including roast pork with yellow rice and beans and filet of red snapper in pungent tomato sauce. The menu, which depends largely on what was available in the market that morning, is recited lethargically by a member of the family who owns the joint. Except during the midday crush, no one will mind if you opt for just a cup of thick Puerto Rican coffee, a beer, or a soda.

Calle Luna 255 (near Calle San Justo). ℂ 787/721-6184. Reservations not accepted. Platters and main courses $8–$15. AE, MC, V. Daily 8am–7pm. Bus: Old Town Trolley.

Fatty's JAMAICAN/WEST INDIAN   Amazingly, Puerto Rico didn't have a Jamaican restaurant until this dive opened. You'll know it's Jamaican when you see a picture of Bob Marley and the Jamaican flag displayed. Not only that, but reggae music plays in the background. The welcoming owner, "Fatty," is a great cook, turning out marvelous jerk dishes, especially chicken, fish, and shrimp. The chef is also known for curry chicken or a rice dish flavored with coconut milk. Chicken balls with curry sauce is another local favorite. Fried red snapper and conch in garlic sauce also win our praise.

Calle O'Donnell 102. ℂ 787/586-6925. Reservations not required. Main courses $5–$10. No credit cards. Thurs 9am–3pm; Fri–Wed 9am–3pm and 5:30–9pm. Bus: Old Town Trolley.

La Bombonera ℛℛ (Value) PUERTO RICAN   This place offers exceptional value in its homemade pastries, well-stuffed sandwiches, and endless cups of coffee—and it has done so since 1902. Its atmosphere evokes turn-of-the-20th-century Castille transplanted to the New World. The food is authentically Puerto Rican, homemade, and inexpensive, with regional dishes such as rice with squid, roast leg of pork, and seafood *asopao* (a thick rice soup). For dessert, you might select an apple, pineapple, or prune pie, or one of many types of flan. Service is polite, if a bit rushed, and the place fills up quickly at lunchtime.

Calle San Francisco 259. © 787/722-0658. Reservations recommended. American breakfast $4.50–$6.45; main courses $6–$18. AE, MC, V. Daily 7:30am–8pm. Bus: Old Town Trolley.

Patio del Nispero INTERNATIONAL   Surrounded by the soaring atrium of Old San Juan's most historic hotel, this restaurant provides a charming oasis of calm and quiet. Pots of verdant plants thrive under the direct sunlight of the open sky, and big canvas umbrellas shield diners from the rain. No one will mind if you order just a drink (the daiquiris are excellent) or a cup of coffee while resting after a tour of the Old Town or the cathedral next door. But if you want food, consider filet of red snapper with Creole sauce, chicken breast with chestnuts and mushrooms in cognac sauce, broiled veal chop with Marsala sauce, and one of a wide selection of desserts. Live music is featured 2 evenings a week.

In the El Convento hotel, Calle del Cristo 100. © 787/723-9020. Reservations not necessary. Sandwiches $9.50–$12; platters $14–$24. AE, DC, MC, V. Daily 11:30am–3:30pm. Bus: Old Town Trolley.

Yeyos *Value* PUERTO RICAN/CREOLE   You might decide to bypass the store next door, Condom World. This tiny little joint that has only eight tables is a real insider's place, and it serves decent food that's full of flavor under bare fluorescent bulbs. The spartan decor is more than compensated for by the really bargain food served in this working-class neighborhood. The breakfast served here is Old San Juan's most reasonable in price, complete with eggs, potatoes, and ham. For your main course, you could enjoy a generous helping of roast chicken or something light—such as codfish salad. Pork is smothered in onions and served with yellow rice, and you can also order *sancocho,* a robust meat-and-vegetable stew. Many dishes come with *mangú,* a plantain mash. The fixed-price menu is the town's greatest food buy. The place doesn't have a liquor license.

Calle San Francisco 353. © 787/725-9362. Breakfast $2–$3; main courses $5–$10; fixed-price menu $5. MC, V. Mon–Sat 6am–6pm. Bus: Old Town Trolley.

4 Puerta de Tierra

For the locations of restaurants in Puerta de Tierra, see the map "Puerta de Tierra, Miramar, Condado & Ocean Park Accommodations & Dining" on p. 85.

Madrid-San Juan SPANISH   This restaurant is the newest eatery within the megacompound known as the Caribe Hilton (p. 83). Its decor, especially that of its baronial-looking dining room in back, emulates that of a gracious and rather formal tasca in Spain, replete with Serrano hams hanging above the bar, a roster of oil paintings (many of which are for sale), a scarlet-covered dining room which you might have imagined as a *tableaux* within a still-life by Goya, and rack upon rack of wine. There's something big, generous, and well-mannered about this place, as a quick perusal of the list of tapas (both hot and cold) and the conventional lunch or dinner menu will quickly show. Highlights include piquillo peppers stuffed with pulverized codfish; fried plantain with smoked salmon; codfish fritters; *fabada asturianas* (a well-seasoned and soupy version of stew that combines fava beans, sausages, and ham); fried fresh anchovies; and chorizo sausages in red-wine sauce. Main courses include breast of chicken in garlic sauce; filet mignon with Manchego cheese and Serrano ham;

thin-sliced filets of beef with onions; *asopao de mariscos;* mofongo stuffed with shrimp; and halibut steak garnished with shrimp, mushrooms, and raisin sauce.

In the Caribe Hilton, Calle Los Rosales. ℂ 787/721-0303. Reservations recommended. Tapas $6.50–$15; main courses $21–$35. AE, DC, DISC, MC, V. Mon–Thurs 11:30am–midnight; Fri–Sun 11:30am–1am. Bus: B21.

Morton's of Chicago 🌟🌟 STEAKHOUSE   When it comes to steaks, Ruth's Chris Steak House in Isla Verde enjoys a slight edge, but otherwise Morton's is king of the steaks and other choice meats. The chain of gourmet steakhouses was founded in 1978 by Arnie Morton, former executive vice president of the *Playboy* empire. Beef lovers, from Al Gore to Liza Minnelli, know they'll get quality meats perfectly cooked at Morton's. Carts laden with everything from prime Midwestern beefsteaks to succulent lamb or veal chops are wheeled around for your selection. And Morton's has the island's best prime rib. This is a place where the bartenders make stiff drinks, and the waiters tempt you with their fresh fish, lobster, and chicken dishes. The vegetables here are among the freshest in the area. The house specialty is a 24-ounce porterhouse. Appetizers include perfectly cooked jumbo shrimp with cocktail sauce and smoked Pacific salmon. For dessert, we always gravitate to one of the soufflés, such as raspberry or Grand Marnier.

In the Caribe Hilton, Calle Los Rosales. ℂ **787/977-6262.** Reservations required. Main courses $20–$40. AE, DC, DISC, MC, V. Daily 5–11pm. Bus: B21.

Palmera 🌟 *Kids* INTERNATIONAL   Every Sunday the Hilton's brunch captivates the imagination of island residents and U.S. visitors with its combination of excellently prepared food, glamour, and entertainment. There's a clown to keep the children amused, as well as live music on the bandstand for anyone who cares to dance. Champagne is included in the price. Food is arranged at several different stations: Puerto Rican dishes, seafood, paella, ribs, cold cuts, steaks, pastas, and salads. Although Sunday is the most festive time to visit, Palmeras prides itself on serving the biggest and most elaborate breakfast buffet in Puerto Rico on any morning. Another lavish buffet is the Friday-night seafood fiesta. On other nights dinner is a la carte. Specialties include pastas, paellas–chicken, and cheese quesadillas, along with an array of other international food.

In the Caribe Hilton, Calle Los Rosales. ℂ **787/721-0303.** Reservations recommended for Sun brunch and Fri night. Breakfast buffet $18 daily, $30 Sun; lunch buffet $21 daily; main courses $12–$26. AE, DC, DISC, MC, V. Daily 6–11am, 12:30–3:30pm, and 5–11pm (until midnight Fri–Sat). Bus: 21.

5 Condado

For the locations of Condado restaurants, see the map "Puerta de Tierra, Miramar, Condado & Ocean Park Accommodations & Dining" on p. 85.

VERY EXPENSIVE

Pikayo 🌟🌟🌟 PUERTO RICAN/CAJUN   This is an ideal place to go for the next generation of Puerto Rican fusion cuisine. Pikayo not only keeps up with the latest culinary trends, it often sets them, thanks to the inspired guidance of owner and celebrity chef Wilo Benet. Formal but not stuffy, and winner of more culinary awards than virtually any other restaurant in Puerto Rico, Pikayo is a specialist in the *criolla cuisine* of the colonial age, emphasizing the Spanish, Indian, and African elements in its unusual recipes. Appetizers include a dazzling array of taste explosions: Try shrimp spring rolls with peanut sofrito sauce; crab cake with aioli; or perhaps a ripe plantain, goat-cheese, and onion tart. Main-course delights feature charred rare yellowfin tuna with onion *escabeche* and red-snapper filet with sweet-potato purée served with foie gras butter. Our favorite remains the grilled shrimp with polenta and barbecue sauce made with guava.

In the Museum of Art of Puerto Rico, Av. José de Diego 299. ℂ 787/721-6194. Reservations recommended. Main courses $28–$40; fixed-price menus $65. AE, DC, MC, V. Tues–Fri noon–3pm; Mon–Sat 6–11pm. Bus: M2, A7, or T1.

Ramiro's ✿ SPANISH/INTERNATIONAL   This restaurant boasts the most imaginative menu on the Condado. You might begin with breadfruit *mille-feuille* with local crabmeat and avocado. For your main course, any fresh fish or meat can be charcoal-grilled for you on request. Some of the latest specialties include grilled salmon on a bed of black rice and a Spanish prawn sauce, and a tantalizing roast duckling with a kumquat sauce. Among the many homemade desserts are caramelized mango on puff pastry with strawberry-and-guava sauce, and "four seasons" chocolate.

Av. Magdalena 1106. ℂ 787/721-9049. Reservations recommended off season, required in winter. Main courses $27–$39. AE, MC, V. Sun–Fri noon–3pm and 6:30–11pm; Sat 6–10pm. Bus: A7, T1, or M2.

EXPENSIVE

Ajili Mójili ✿ PUERTO RICAN/CREOLE   This restaurant serves *la cucina criolla,* the starchy, down-home cuisine that developed on the island a century ago. Though the building is quite modern, look for replicas of the crumbling brick walls you'd expect in Old San Juan and a bar that evokes Old Spain. Locals come here for a taste of the food they enjoyed at their mother's knee, like *mofongos* (green plantains stuffed with veal, chicken, shrimp, or pork), *arroz con pollo, medallones de cerdo encebollado* (pork loin sautéed with onions), *carne mechada* (beef rib-eye stuffed with ham), and *lechon asado con maposteado* (roast pork with rice and beans). Wash it all down with an ice-cold bottle of local beer. The staff will eagerly describe menu items in colloquial English.

Av. Ashford 1006. ℂ 787/725-9195. Reservations recommended. Main courses $18–$39; lunch $13–$26. AE, DISC, MC, V. Mon–Thurs 11:45am–3pm and 6–10pm; Fri noon–3pm and 6–11pm; Sat 11:45am–3:30pm and 6–11pm; Sun 12:30–4pm and 6–10pm. Bus: B21.

La Compostela ✿ INTERNATIONAL/SPANISH   Established by a Galician-born family, this pine-trimmed restaurant has gained a reputation as one of the best in the capital. The chef made his name on the roast peppers stuffed with salmon mousse. Equally delectable is duck with orange-and-ginger sauce or baby rack of lamb with fresh herbs. Any shellfish grilled in a brandy sauce is a sure winner. The chef also makes two savory versions of paella. The wine cellar, comprising some 10,000 bottles, is one of the most impressive in San Juan. A battalion of well-dressed waiters offers formal service.

Av. Condado 106. ℂ 787/724-6088. Reservations required. Main courses $24–$39. AE, DC, MC, V. Mon–Fri noon–3pm; Mon–Sat 6:30–10:30pm. Bus: M2.

Martino's ✿ NORTHERN ITALIAN   This restaurant offers some of the finest service on the Condado and a classic Italian cuisine, centered primarily in the north of Italy, especially Lombardy. Picture windows open onto views of the Atlantic and the night lights of the Condado. Appetizers include hot seafood antipasti and Caesar and spinach salads. The Caesar salad is made tableside with real panache. For a main course you can order one of the homemade pasta dishes or choose from such appetizing dishes as seafood suprême, vitello Martino (with shrimp), gnocchi with cream sauce and Parmesan, and filet mignon Monnalisa, which is flambéed at your table. In fact, almost any dish can receive a tableside flambé if you want. Good and reasonably priced wines add to the dining pleasure.

In the Diamond Palace Hotel & Casino, Av. Condado 55. ✆ **787/722-5256.** Reservations recommended. Main courses $20–$38. AE, MC, V. Daily 6–11:30pm. Bus: A7.

Ristorante Tuscany ✿✿ NORTHERN ITALIAN   This is the showcase restaurant of one of the most elaborate hotel reconstructions in the history of Puerto Rico, and the kitchen continues to rack up culinary awards. Notable entrees include grilled veal chops with shallots and glaze of Madeira, and grilled chicken breast in cream sauce with chestnuts, asparagus, and brandy, surrounded with fried artichokes. The seafood selections are excellent, especially the fresh red snapper sautéed in olive oil, garlic, parsley, and lemon juice. The risottos prepared al dente in the traditional northern Italian style are the finest on the island, especially the one made with seafood and herbs. The cold and hot appetizers are virtual meals unto themselves, with such favorites as grilled polenta with sausages or fresh clams and mussels simmered in herb-flavored tomato broth.

In the San Juan Marriott Resort, Av. Ashford 1309. ✆ **787/722-7000.** Reservations recommended. Main courses $20–$34. AE, DC, DISC, MC, V. Daily 6–11pm. Bus: B21.

Zabó ✿ AMERICAN/PUERTO RICAN/INTERNATIONAL   This restaurant enjoys citywide fame, thanks to its blend of bucolic charm and superb innovative food. It's set in a dignified villa that provides some low-rise dignity in a sea of skyscraping condos. The creative force here is owner and chef/culinary director Paul Carroll, who built the place from its origins as a simple deli into one of the most sought-after restaurants on the Condado. Menu items fuse the cuisines of the Mediterranean, the Pacific Rim, and the Caribbean into a collection that includes dishes such as blini stuffed with medallions of lobster with ginger, thyme, and beurre blanc; carpaccio of salmon with mesclun salad and balsamic vinegar; and baked chorizo stuffed with mushrooms, sherry, paprika, and cheddar. The black-bean soup is among the very best in Puerto Rico, served with parboiled cloves of garlic marinated in olive oil that melt in your mouth like candy.

Calle Candina 14 (entrance via alleyway leading from Av. Ashford between avenidas Washington and Cervantes). ✆ **787/725-9494.** Reservations recommended. Snacks $6; main courses $15–$35. AE, MC, V. Tues–Thurs 6–10pm; Fri–Sat 7–11pm. Bus: A7.

MODERATE

Most main courses in the restaurants below are at the low end of the price scale. These restaurants each have only two or three dishes that are expensive, almost invariably involving shellfish.

Cherry Blossom JAPANESE/STEAK/SEAFOOD   Set on the street level of the San Juan Marriott, with direct access to the busy pedestrian traffic of Avenida Ashford, this is one of the genuinely charming Japanese restaurants of the Condado. There are sections devoted to sushi, including a long bar where you can view the fish available that day, and to teppanyaki, where a corps of carefully trained chefs will fast-sear your meal on a sizzling griddle in front of you. The staff is charming, the food excellent.

In the San Juan Marriott Resort, Av. Ashford 1309. ✆ **787/723-7300.** Reservations recommended. Main courses $12–$23 at lunch, $19–$43 at dinner. AE, DC, MC, V. Mon–Fri 12:30–3pm; Mon–Sat 5:30–11pm; Sun noon–11pm. Bus: B21.

Luigi's 🦆🦆 ITALIAN/GENOVESE   There's a formal and even romantic atmosphere here at night. When chef-owner Luigi Sanguineti came to Puerto Rico from Genoa in the late 1980s, he liked the place so much he decided to bring "a little bit of Genoa" to the Old Town. After gaining a reputation as one of the island's foremost European chefs, Luigi finally opened his own place in 2000. Since then he's been delighting the palates of locals and visitors with high-quality Italian cuisine. Try the gnocchi with pesto or the eggplant lasagna, and perhaps start with a savory antipasto prepared by Luigi himself. His lobster ravioli is San Juan's finest, and another dish we like a lot is the shrimp risotto.

Diez de Andino 104. (℃) **787/977-0134.** Reservations recommended. Main courses $10–$28. AE, MC, V. Mon–Sat 11:30am–3pm and 6–10pm; Sun 1–7pm. Bus: B5.

Urdin 🦆🦆 PUERTO RICAN/INTERNATIONAL   Urdin is proud of its reputation as one of the capital's bright young restaurants. It occupies a low-slung, stucco-covered house set near a slew of competitors. Inside, a fanciful decor of postmodern, Caribbean-inspired accents and metal sculptures brings a touch of Latino New York. Popularity has brought an unexpected development to this highly visible restaurant: The bar is almost more popular than the food. Consequently, you're likely to find the bar area jam-packed every day between 6 and 10pm. Cliquish, heterosexual, and fashionable, some of this crowd eventually gravitates toward the tables. Yes, that was Ricky Martin we spotted here one evening. Filled with authentic Spanish flavor that's not necessarily geared to the palates of timid diners, the food is innovative, flavorful, strong, and earthy. For starters, there are baby eels Bilbaina style and Castilian lentil soup. Main courses include fresh filet of salmon in mustard sauce, filet of fish "Hollywood style" (with onions, raisins, and mango slices, served in white-wine sauce), and rack of lamb with orange sauce. One always-pleasing dish is piquillo peppers stuffed with seafood mousse and black-olive sauce. Savvy locals finish their meal with a slice of sweet-potato cheesecake. The staff can put a damper on (if they're sulky) or enhance (if they're welcoming) a meal here.

Av. Magdalena 1105. (℃) **787/724-0420.** Reservations recommended. Main courses $14–$27. AE, MC, V. Mon–Sat noon–3pm and 6–11pm. Bus: A7.

INEXPENSIVE
Café del Angel CREOLE/PUERTO RICAN   Don't come here for the decor. The juice bar up front looks like it was transported from Miami's Flagler Street in 1950, and the plastic green furniture won't compel you to get *Architectural Digest* on the phone. If indeed there is an "angel," as the cafe's name suggests, it is in the kitchen. The chef serves remarkably good food at affordable prices. The place has been in operation for more than a decade. Paintings and figures of its namesake angels decorate the dining room. Some 100 hungry diners can be fed here at one time, in a relaxed atmosphere that is welcoming and friendly. The service is also efficient. Prepare for some real island flavor, as in the traditional *mofongo relleno con camarones,* which is sautéed, mashed plantain with shrimp. You can order a generous helping of tender beefsteak sautéed with onions and peppers or a perfectly grilled chicken. *Pastel,* a kind of creamy polenta of cornmeal, is served with many dishes, and the fresh garlic bread is complimentary.

Av. Ashford 1106. (℃) **787/643-7594.** Reservations not necessary. Main courses $7–$20. AE, DC, MC, V. Wed–Mon 11am–10pm. Bus: B21.

Café Mezzanine INTERNATIONAL   This comfortable and cozy eatery for many years was the most famous Howard Johnson's in the Caribbean. It attracts some of the most prestigious politicians and financiers (many luminaries live nearby and consider it their neighborhood diner). Depending on the time of day, you can be served pancakes, omelets, muffins, hash browns, and sausages; or you can order lunch and dinner foods like fish fries, teriyaki steaks, clam platters, and an array of sandwiches and burgers, as well as typical Puerto Rican dishes.

In the Radisson Ambassador Plaza Hotel, Av. Ashford 1369. © **787/721-7300.** Reservations not necessary. Breakfast $7.25–$11; main courses $8–$21. AE, MC, V. Mon–Thurs 6:30am–2pm and 5–11pm; Fri–Sun 6:30am–11pm. Bus: B21 or C10.

Cielito Lindo MEXICAN   One of the most likable things about this restaurant is the way it retains low prices and an utter lack of pretension, despite the expensive Condado real estate that surrounds it. Something about it might remind you of a low-slung house in Puebla, Mexico, home of owner Jaime Pandal, who maintains a vigilant position from a perch at the cash register. Walls are outfitted with an intriguing mix of Mexican arts and crafts and ads for popular tequilas and beer. None of the selections has changed since the restaurant was founded, a policy that long-term clients find reassuring. The place is mobbed, especially on weekends, with those looking for heaping portions of well-prepared, standardized Mexican food. Examples include fajitas of steak or chicken; strips of filet steak sautéed with green peppers and onions, covered with tomatoes and spicy gravy; enchiladas of chicken or cheese, covered with cheese and served with sour cream; and several kinds of tacos.

Av. Magdalena 1108. © **787/723-5597.** Reservations recommended for dinner. Main courses $5–$20. AE, MC, V. Mon–Fri 11am–11pm; Sat–Sun 5–11pm. Bus: B21 or C10.

Tony Roma's BARBECUE   Efficient and unpretentious, this is Puerto Rico's busiest branch of the international chain and one of the least expensive restaurants in the Condado. It's well appreciated for its spicy barbecued food (the honey barbecue is not too fiery). Menu items include a wide range of barbecued dishes, such as chicken and several varieties of ribs, as well as hamburgers and the famous Tony Roma onion ring loaf. The most expensive item in the house, a combination platter containing several kinds of ribs with all the fixings, is a meal in itself that's a particularly good value in this high-priced neighborhood.

In the Condado Plaza Hotel, Av. Ashford 999. © **787/722-0322,** ext. 2623. Reservations not accepted. Main courses $11–$22. AE, DC, DISC, MC, V. Daily noon–midnight. Bus: B21 or C10.

Via Appia PIZZA/ITALIAN   A favorite of Sanjuaneros visiting Condado for the day, Via Appia offers food that's sometimes praiseworthy. Its pizzas are the best in the neighborhood. The chef's signature pizza, Via Appia, is a savory pie made with sausages, onions, mushrooms, pepperoni, green peppers, cheese, and spices. Vegetarians also have a pizza to call their own (made with whole-wheat dough, eggplant, mushrooms, green peppers, onions, tomatoes, and cheese). There's even a pizza with meatballs. Savory pasta dishes, including baked ziti, lasagna, and spaghetti, are also prepared with several of your favorite sauces. All of this can be washed down with sangria. During the day, freshly made salads and sandwiches are also available.

Av. Ashford 1350. © **787/725-8711.** Pizza and main courses $9–$16. AE, MC, V. Mon–Fri 11am–11pm; Sat–Sun 11am–midnight. Bus: B21 or C10.

6 Miramar

For the locations of restaurants in Miramar, see the map "Puerta de Tierra, Miramar, Condado & Ocean Park Accommodations & Dining" on p. 85.

Augusto's Cuisine ☆☆☆ FRENCH/INTERNATIONAL   With its European flair, this is one of the most elegant and glamorous restaurants in Puerto Rico. It is set on the lobby level of a 15-story hotel in Miramar. Menu items are concocted from strictly fresh ingredients, including such dishes as lobster risotto; rack of lamb with aromatic herbs and fresh garlic; an oft-changing cream-based soup of the day (one of the best is corn and fresh oyster soup); and a succulent version of medallions of veal Rossini style, prepared with foie gras and Madeira sauce. The wine list is one of the most extensive on the island.

In the Hotel Excelsior, Av. Ponce de León 801. © **787/725-7700**. Reservations recommended. Main courses $24–$38. AE, MC, V. Tues–Fri noon–3pm; Tues–Sat 7–9:30pm. Bus: T1.

Chayote's ☆ PUERTO RICAN/INTERNATIONAL   The cuisine of this restaurant is among the most innovative in San Juan. It draws local business leaders, government officials, and celebs like Sylvester Stallone and Melanie Griffith. It's an artsy, modern, basement-level bistro in a surprisingly obscure hotel (the Olimpo). The restaurant changes its menu every 3 months, but you might find appetizers like a yucca turnover stuffed with crabmeat and served with mango and papaya chutney, or ripe plantain stuffed with chicken and served with fresh tomato sauce. For a main dish, you might try red-snapper filet with citrus vinaigrette made of passion fruit, orange, and lemon. An exotic touch appears in the pork filet seasoned with dried fruits and spices in tamarind sauce and served with green banana and taro-root timbale. To finish off your meal, there's nothing better than the mango flan served with macerated strawberries.

In the Olimpo Hotel, Av. Miramar 603. © **787/722-9385**. Reservations recommended. Main courses $21–$28. AE, MC, V. Tues–Fri noon–2:30pm; Tues–Sat 7–10:30pm. Bus: B5.

7 Santurce & Ocean Park

For the locations of restaurants in Santurce and Ocean Park, see the map "Puerta de Tierra, Miramar, Condado & Ocean Park Accommodations & Dining" on p. 85.

VERY EXPENSIVE

La Casona ☆ SPANISH/INTERNATIONAL   In a turn-of-the-20th-century mansion surrounded by gardens, La Casona offers the kind of dining usually found in Madrid, complete with a strolling guitarist. The much-renovated but still charming place draws some of the most fashionable diners in Puerto Rico. Paella marinara, prepared for two or more, is a specialty, as is *zarzuela de mariscos* (seafood medley). Or you might select filet of grouper in Basque sauce, octopus vinaigrette, *osso buco*, or rack of lamb. Grilled red snapper is a specialty, and you can order it with almost any sauce you want, although the chef recommends one made from olive oil, herbs, lemon, and toasted garlic. The cuisine here has both flair and flavor.

Calle San Jorge 609 (at the corner of Av. Fernández Juncos). © **787/727-2717**. Reservations required. Main courses $25–$35. AE, DC, MC, V. Mon–Fri noon–3pm; Mon–Sat 6–11:30pm. Bus: 1.

EXPENSIVE

Pamela's ☆ CARIBBEAN FUSION/VEGETARIAN   A sense of cachet and style is very pronounced at this restaurant, a fact that's somewhat surprising considering its

My, what an inefficient way to fish.

Ring toss, good. Horseshoes, bad.

Faster! Faster! Faster!

We take care of the fiddly bits, from providing over 43,000 customer reviews of hotels, to helping you find our best fares, to giving you 24/7 customer service. So you can focus on the only thing that matters. Goofing off.

travelocity
You'll never roam alone.™

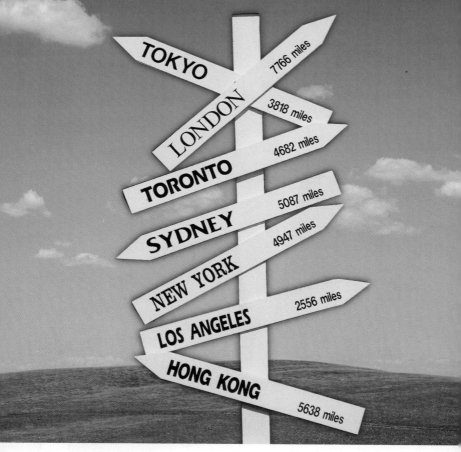

So many places, so little time?

Frommers.com

TOKYO — 7766 miles
LONDON — 3818 miles
TORONTO — 4682 miles
SYDNEY — 5087 miles
NEW YORK — 4947 miles
LOS ANGELES — 2556 miles
HONG KONG — 5638 miles

out-of-the-way location. Part of its allure derives from a sophisticated blend of Caribbean cuisines that combines local ingredients with Puerto Rican flair and a sense of New York style. Menu items include a salad that marries vine-ripened and oven-roasted tomatoes, each drizzled with a roasted-garlic-and-cilantro vinaigrette; club sandwiches stuffed with barbecued shrimp and cilantro-flavored mayonnaise; plantain-encrusted crab cakes with a spicy tomato-herb emulsion; and grilled island-spiced pork loin served with guava glaze and fresh local fruits. Beer and any of a wide array of party-colored drinks go well with this food.

In the Número 1 Guest House, Calle Santa Ana 1, Ocean Park. (C) **787/726-5010.** Reservations recommended. Sandwiches and salads at lunch $10–$14; main course platters $20–$29. AE, MC, V. Daily noon–3pm and 7–10:30pm. Tapas daily 3–7pm. Bus: A5.

INEXPENSIVE

Café Madrid *(finds* PUERTO RICAN   Come here to escape from the gloss and sheen of big-city, big-money tourism. Local residents promote this simple diner for its sense of workaday conviviality and low, low prices. Located on a narrow but busy street in a congested commercial neighborhood of Ocean Park, this joint has a battered facade with plastic lettering—signs that the inside is going to be very tacky. At first glance, that's partially true. But if you retain a sense of humor, you might begin to appreciate the Formica bar tops, rows of mismatched refrigerators, big-lettered menus over sizzling deep-fat fryers, and the kind of industrial accessories that Andy Warhol might have appreciated or even collected. It's been the domain of the Molina family since the 1930s, and the food has changed very little since then. Examples include roasted pork, sold either as a full-size meal platter or stuffed into a sandwich; several kinds of asopao and *carne frita* (fried meat); lasagna; and lots of empanadas. Roasted chicken, the signature dish, is an ongoing favorite.

Calle Loiza 100 (at the corner of Calle Las Flores). (C) **787/728-5250.** Reservations not accepted. Breakfast platters $3.50–$6; sandwiches $1.75–$5.95; lunch and dinner main courses $5–$10. MC, V. Daily 6am–10pm. Bus: B5 or T1.

Don Tello *(★ (finds* PUERTO RICAN   Right at the Santurce Market Square (Plaza del Mercado), this is a family-run restaurant serving an authentic criolla cuisine. All the locals call the owners, Jorge and Rosin, by their first names. In a casual atmosphere, diners dress informally, eat well, and don't pay a lot of money for the privilege. The service is excellent, and the ingredients are fresh and well prepared. The fish tastes among the freshest in San Juan. We've enjoyed the filet of sea bass in a plantain sauce, or a well-seasoned whole roasted sea bass. Grilled filet of mahimahi is another one of our favorites, as is the grilled filet of hake. You can also enjoy the traditional asopao of Puerto Rico, made with chicken, shrimp, lobster, or shellfish. A savory chicken stew is also served, as is a tender filet of steak roasted with onions.

Dos Hermanos 180, Santurce. (C) **787/724-5752.** Reservations recommended. Main courses $6–$13. AE, MC, V. Mon 11am–4pm; Tues–Sat 11am–10pm. Bus: 1.

Dunbar's INTERNATIONAL   Sprawling over at least five distinctly different dining and drinking areas, this is the busiest, most active, and most legendary bar and pub in Ocean Park. Painted an arresting shade of tangerine, it was established in 1982. The best way to navigate the labyrinth of Dunbar's is to wander through its various spaces: A large-screen TV room on the second floor attracts a macho, mostly North American crowd; a ground-floor pool room appeals to a deceptively affluent crowd of Spanish-speaking lawyers and doctors; and the various bars and cubbyholes ripple

> **Moments   Picnic Fare & Where to Eat It**
>
> Puerto Rico is usually ideal for picnicking year-round. The best place to fill a picnic basket is the **Repostería Kassalta** (see below), a cafeteria/bakery/deli with lots of goodies. Puerto Rican families often come here to order delicacies for their Sunday outings. The best places for a picnic are **Muñoz Marín Park,** along Las Américas Expressway, west of Avenida Piñro, and the **Botanical Gardens** operated by the University of Puerto Rico in the Río Piedras section.

with possibilities for making friends or influencing your romantic destiny. Well-prepared menu items pour out of the busy kitchens. Examples include thick sandwiches (Spanish chorizo sausage with roasted peppers is an ongoing favorite), omelets, pastas, and juicy steaks. French fries are made from vitamin-rich yams and conventional potatoes. Favorite drinks include (what else?) Sex on the Beach and lots of margaritas. Dunbar's was named, incidentally, after a particularly eccentric character in Joseph Heller's *Catch-22*.

Av. McLeary 1954. ✆ 787/728-2920. Reservations required Fri and Sun. Burgers and sandwiches $8.50–$13; main courses $11–$24. AE, DC, MC, V. Mon–Thurs 11:30am–midnight; Fri 11:30am–1am; Sat 5pm–1am; Sun 10am–midnight. Bus: A5 or A7.

Repostería Kassalta *Value* SPANISH/PUERTO RICAN   This is the most widely known of San Juan's cafeterias/bakeries/delicatessens. You'll enter a cavernous room flanked with sun-flooded windows and endless ranks of display cases filled with meats, sausages, and pastries appropriate to the season. Patrons line up to place their orders at a cash register, then carry their selections to one of the many tables. Knowledge of Spanish is helpful but not essential. Among the selections are steaming bowls of Puerto Rico's best caldo gallego, a hearty soup laden with collard greens, potatoes, and sausage slices, served in thick earthenware bowls with hunks of bread. Also popular are Cuban sandwiches (sliced pork, cheese, and fried bread), steak sandwiches, a savory octopus salad, and an assortment of perfectly cooked omelets. Paella Valenciano is a Sunday favorite.

Av. McLeary 1966. ✆ 787/727-7340. Reservations not accepted. Full American breakfast $3.50–$5; soups $3–$6; sandwiches $4.50–$6; platters $4–$22. AE, DC, MC, V. Daily 6am–10pm. Bus: A5.

8 Near Ocean Park

For the locations of these restaurants, see the map "Puerta de Tierra, Miramar, Condado & Ocean Park Accommodations & Dining" on p. 85.

Che's ARGENTINE/ITALIAN/INTERNATIONAL   Named after the Latino revolutionary Che Guevara, this place re-creates some of the color and drama of the Argentine pampas. It's about 2 miles (3.2km) east of Condado's resorts. Many of the specialties are grilled in the style preferred by cowherding gauchos. If you're not in the mood for highly seasoned flank steak or any of the grilled meats, you can choose from a variety of pastas and veal dishes. The meats here are very tender and well flavored.

Calle Caoba 35. ✆ 787/726-7202. Reservations recommended for lunch, required for dinner. Main courses $15–$30. AE, DC, DISC, MC, V. Sun–Thurs 11:30am–10:45pm; Fri–Sat noon–midnight. Bus: A5.

La Casita Blanca *Finds* CREOLE/PUERTO RICAN   Island politicians are said to have the best noses for good home cooking. We don't know if that is true or not, but one of their favorite places is this eatery. Governors or governor wannabes also come here to order excellent regional fare. This is a converted family home that opened its door to diners in the mid-1980s, and it's been a favorite of locals from all walks of Puerto Rican society ever since. In a popular barrio, it is off the tourist trail and best reached by taxi. You'll need to make a reservation for lunch but should have no trouble finding a table at dinner. The traditional Creole menu includes such delights as *guisado y arroz con gandule* (beef stew with rice and small beans), or *bacalao* (salt codfish with yucca). Guaranteed to put hair on your chest is *patita* (pigs' trotters in a Creole sauce). Veal with sautéed onions is popular, as is grilled red snapper or the chicken fricassee. A typical chicken asopao, a soupy rice stew, is also served. The fried plantains may make you forget french fries forever.

Calle Tapía 351. ✆ **787/726-5501.** Main courses $8–$16; Sun buffet $12–$13. MC, V. Mon–Thurs 11:30am–6:45pm; Fri–Sat 11:30am–9:30pm; Sun noon–4:30pm. Bus: C10 or C11.

9 Isla Verde

For the locations of restaurants in Isla Verde, see the map "Isla Verde Accommodations & Dining" on p. 93.

VERY EXPENSIVE

The Palm ✶✶ STEAK/SEAFOOD   The management of San Juan's most elegant hotel invited The Palm, a legendary New York steakhouse, to open a branch on the premises. The setting includes a stylish, masculine-looking saloon, where drinks are stiff, and a dining room with artfully simple linen-covered tables and caricatures of local personalities. If you've hit it big at the nearby casino, maybe you'll want to celebrate with The Palm's famous and famously pricey lobster. Otherwise, there's a tempting number of options, all served in gargantuan portions: jumbo lump crabmeat cocktail, Caesar salad, lamb chops with mint sauce, grilled halibut steak, prime porterhouse steak, and steak "a la stone," which finishes cooking on a sizzling platter directly atop your table. One thing is certain—you'll never go hungry here.

In El San Juan Hotel & Casino, Av. Isla Verde 6063. ✆ **787/791-1000.** Reservations recommended. Main courses $18–$40, except lobster, which is priced by the pound and can easily cost $22 per lb. or more. AE, DC, MC, V. Daily 5–11pm. Bus: A5.

Prime 787 ✶✶✶ STEAKHOUSE   This restaurant under the baton of the award-winning *chef de cuisine,* Simon Porter, is about as good as it gets in San Juan. Hailed by such gourmet magazines as *The Wine Spectator,* Prime 787 specializes in U.S. prime and certified Angus beef prepared to order. Of course, you can order a lot of other sublime dishes as well. Begin with such luxury items as Beluga caviar, an oyster platter, or foie gras and a black truffle cuisine. Although primarily a steakhouse, its chef also turns out delectable seafood, including a pan-seared sea bass topped with basil butter and served with sun-dried tomato dumplings. The prize tender beef steak, listed on the menu as "Kobe Flat Iron," is the finest cut of beef we've ever had on the island. Your meat comes with a wide array of sauces, ranging from Madagascar green-peppercorn sauce to cabernet shallot. The chef's soufflés are also San Juan's finest, especially the Grand Marnier version with kumquat vanilla cream.

In the Ritz-Carlton San Juan Hotel, Spa & Casino, Av. de los Gobernadores (State Rd.) 6961, no. 187, Isla Verde. ✆ **787/253-1700.** Reservations required. Main courses $28–$44; fixed-price menus $45, $55, $65, and $75. AE, DC, DISC, MC, V. Sun–Thurs 6–10:30pm; Fri–Sat 6–11pm. Bus: A5, B40, or C45.

> ### (Kids) Two Family-Friendly Restaurants
>
> **Palmera** (p. 115)   Located in the Caribe Hilton (p. 83), this place has a Sunday brunch—which is half price for children—with an all-you-can-eat buffet. There's even a clown on hand to keep the kids entertained.
>
> **Ciao Mediterranean Café** (p. 126)   Right on the beach, this is a family favorite that offers some of the best pizzas and pastas at Isla Verde. Prices are affordable, too.

Ruth's Chris Steak House 🍴🍴 STEAK   This Puerto Rican branch of one of the most famous steakhouse chains in the world presents macho food, especially steaks that are among the best beef dishes in San Juan. It obsessively focuses on big drinks and big steaks, grilled in the simplest possible way—usually just with salt, pepper, and a brush-over of butter. These are served within two dark blue, mahogany-trimmed dining rooms, separated by a saloon-style bar.

You might begin with barbecued shrimp, mushrooms stuffed with crabmeat, or seared ahi tuna. Or you might opt for a salad as an appetizer. Portions are large and very filling. Steaks are the finest from the U.S. cattle country. Examples include rib-eyes, veal chops, porterhouse, New York strips, and filet mignons. There's also roasted chicken, lobster, and a fresh catch of the day.

In the Inter-Continental San Juan Resort & Casino, Av. Isla Verde 187. ℂ **787/253-1717.** Reservations recommended. Main courses $32–$83. AE, DC, MC, V. Sun–Thurs 6–10pm; Fri–Sat 6–11pm. Bus: M7.

EXPENSIVE

La Piccola Fontana 🍴 NORTHERN ITALIAN   Right off the luxurious Palm Court in the El San Juan Hotel, this restaurant delivers plate after plate of delectable food nightly. From its white linen to its classically formal service, it enjoys a fine reputation. The food is straightforward, generous, and extremely well prepared. You'll dine in one of two neo-Palladian rooms whose wall frescoes depict Italy's ruins and landscapes. Menu items range from the appealingly simple (grilled filets of fish or grilled veal chops) to more elaborate dishes such as *tortellini San Daniele,* made with veal, prosciutto, cream, and sage; or *linguine scogliere,* with shrimp, clams, and seafood. Grilled medallions of filet mignon are served with braised arugula, Parmesan cheese, and balsamic vinegar.

In El San Juan Hotel & Casino, Av. Isla Verde 6063. ℂ **787/791-0966.** Reservations required. Main courses $18–$30. AE, MC, V. Daily 6–11pm. Bus: A5.

Tangerine 🍴🍴 EURO-ASIAN   This is the ultimate in chic Isla Verde dining, and it just happens to lie adjacent to the street-level reception area of The Water Club (see chapter 5). Hailed by many international food critics, it glows in its much-deserved praise. Minimalist, postmodern, and angular, and outfitted in monochromatic colors that include steel gray and navy blue, it has a prominent bar area in back, bubbling waterfalls, big-windowed views of the tropical landscapes outside, and an occasional and rather whimsical reference to the orange-colored fruit that gave the place its name.

Lighting radiates gently outward from the kind of ultraglam fixtures that makes ordinary-looking people look good and beautiful people look fabulous. Menu items include such appetizers (the restaurant rather coyly refers to them as "foreplay") as crispy Vietnamese lobster rolls with mango-based sweet chile and avocado-minted melon relish; or citrus-cured yellowfin tuna tartare. For a main course try the cassia-smoked breast of chicken with sweet-garlic potato purée or Asian-herbed crusted Colorado lamb chops with garlic-flavored mashed potatoes and a sauce made from goat cheese, pulverized cucumbers, plum-flavored sake, and yogurt. Dessert might be a lemon-lime crème brûlée.

Tartak St. 2. ℂ 787/728-3666. Reservations required. Main courses $21–$29. AE, DC, MC, V. Tues–Sat 6:30–11pm. Bus: T1 or A5.

Yamato ℱ JAPANESE   The artfully simple decor at Yamato shows the kind of modern urban minimalism that you might expect in an upscale California restaurant. Separate sections offer conventional seating at tables; at a countertop within view of a sushi display; or at seats around a hot grill where chefs shake, rattle, and sizzle their way through a fast but elaborate cooking ritual. Many visitors include at least some sushi with an entree such as beef sashimi with tataki sauce, shrimp tempura with noodle soup, filet mignon or chicken with shrimp or scallops, or several kinds of rice and noodle dishes.

In Wyndham El San Juan Hotel & Casino, Av. Isla Verde 6063. ℂ 787/791-1000. Reservations recommended. Sushi $2.50–$3 per piece; sushi and teppanyaki dinners $25–$43. AE, MC, V. Daily 6pm–midnight. Bus: A5.

MODERATE

Momoyama ℱ JAPANESE   Few other restaurants in Isla Verde are as indelibly associated with one dish: sushi pizza. The subject of rave reviews, it's made by deep-frying compressed rice into something akin to a pizza shell, which is layered with rows of salmon or tuna and garnished with fish roe, shaved ginger, and make-your-eyes-water wasabi. If you prefer your food cooked, you can head for one of several teppanyaki tables, where food is fast-cooked in front of you as part of a highly theatrical culinary show (think Benihana). Choices include chicken teriyaki with shrimp, soy-and-ginger chicken with filet mignon, and several kinds of tempura.

In the Inter-Continental San Juan Resort & Casino, Av. Isla Grande 187. ℂ 787/791-8883. Reservations recommended. Fixed-price lunches $12–$20; lunch and dinner main courses $18–$38. AE, DISC, MC, V. Mon–Fri noon–3pm and 5:30–11:30pm; Sat 5:30–11pm; Sun 11am–11pm. Bus: M7.

Outback Steakhouse 𝒱alue STEAK   This Puerto Rican branch of the two-fisted, Australian-themed restaurant chain occupies a dark-paneled room with booths positioned around a prominent bar area. Here you can study memorabilia devoted to the Land Down Under while ordering such drinks as a genuinely delicious Wallabee Darn. There's a simple steak-and-potato-with-salad special priced at $14, a cost-conscious meal in itself. But more appealing are some of the chain's signature dishes, such as a Bloomin' Onion (a batter-dipped deep-fried onion that fans out from its platter like a demented lotus and tastes delicious with beer); at least four kinds of steaks, including filet mignon; fish, including mahimahi and salmon; and our favorite of the lot, Alice Springs chicken, a breast of chicken layered with bacon, mushrooms, and cheese, and served with honey-mustard sauce and french fries.

In the Embassy Suites Hotel & Casino, Calle José M. Tartak 8000. ℂ 787/791-4679. Reservations not accepted. Main courses $14–$23. AE, MC, V. Mon–Thurs 5:30–10:30pm; Fri–Sat 5:30pm–midnight; Sun 3–10pm. Bus: M7.

The Ranch AMERICAN/STEAK   When the very posh El San Juan Hotel carved out a space for this irreverent, tongue-in-cheek eatery on its top (10th) floor, it was viewed as a radical departure from an otherwise grand collection of in-house restaurants. The result is likely to make you smile, especially if you have roots anywhere west of Ohio. You'll be greeted with a hearty "Howdy, partner" and the jangling of spurs from a crew of denim-clad cowboys as you enter a replica of a corral in the North American West. Banquettes and barstools are upholstered in faux cowhide; the decor is appropriately macho and rough-textured, and even the cowgirls on duty are likely to lasso anyone they find particularly appealing. The cowboys sing as they serve your steaks, barbecued ribs, country-fried steaks, Tex-Mex fajitas, and enchiladas. Food that's a bit less beefy includes seared red snapper with a cilantro-laced *pico de gallo* sauce. Especially succulent are soft-shell crabs layered in a pyramid with blue and yellow tortillas. And if you want to buy a souvenir pair of cowboy spurs, you'll find an intriguing collection of Western accessories and uniforms for sale outside. Consider beginning your meal with any of 20 kinds of tequila cocktails at the Tequila Bar, which lies a few steps away, on the same floor.

In El San Juan Hotel & Casino, Av. Isla Verde 6063. *C* **787/791-1000.** Reservations recommended at dinner Fri–Sat; otherwise, not necessary. Main courses $15–$32. AE, DC, DISC, MC, V. Tues–Thurs 5:30–11pm; Fri–Sat 5:30pm–midnight. Bus: A5.

INEXPENSIVE

Ciao Mediterranean Café 🎔🎔 *Kids* MEDITERRANEAN   This is the most charming restaurant in Isla Verde, and it is one of our enduring favorites. It's draped with bougainvillea and set directly on the sands, attracting both hotel guests and locals wandering in barefoot from the beach for delicious tropical drinks. The visual centerpiece is an open-air kitchen set within an oval-shaped bar. A crew of cheerfully animated chefs mingles good culinary technique with Latino theatricality.

Pizzas and pastas are popular here, and even more appealing are such dishes as seafood salad, wherein shrimp, scallops, calamari, peppers, onions, and lime juice create something you might expect in the south of Italy. *Kalamarakia tiganita* (Greek-style squid) consisting of battered and deep-fried squid served with ratatouille and spicy marinara sauce; rack of lamb with ratatouille, polenta, and Provençal herbs; and a mixed grill of seafood are evocative of what you'd expect in Marseilles, thanks to the roe-enhanced aioli and couscous. Compared to most of the restaurants around here, this cafe serves lighter fare that kids go for, especially in its selection of pizzas and pastas. The desserts are also some of the most luscious at Isla Verde, especially the ice cream.

In the Inter-Continental San Juan Resort & Casino, Av. Isla Grande. *C* **787/791-6100.** Reservations recommended for dinner. Pizzas and salads $8–$20; main courses $14–$30. AE, MC, V. Daily 11:30am–11pm. Bus: M7.

Tips **Eating Like a Sanjuanero**

To become a true Sanjuanero, you've got to learn to love *bacalaitos* (codfish fritters) and *alcapurrias* (meat-stuffed plantain fritters). The best of these are found at little fast-food stands on the **beaches of Piñones and Loiza,** east of the resorts of Isla Verde and the airport. Here you'll find rows of ramshackle shacks where women cook up these delicacies in time-blackened cauldrons over open fires.

Metropol CUBAN/PUERTO RICAN/INTERNATIONAL   This is part of a restaurant chain known for serving the island's best Cuban food, although the chefs prepare a much wider range of dishes. Metropol is the happiest blend of Cuban and Puerto Rican cuisine we've ever had. The black-bean soup is among the island's finest, served in the classic Havana style with a side dish of rice and chopped onions. Endless garlic bread accompanies most dinners, including Cornish game hen stuffed with Cuban rice and beans or perhaps marinated steak topped with a fried egg (reportedly Castro's favorite). Smoked chicken and chicken-fried steak are also heartily recommended; portions are huge. Plantains, yucca, and all that good stuff accompany most dishes. Finish with a choice of thin or firm custard. Most dishes are at the low end of the price scale.

Club Gallistico, Av. Isla Verde. ℭ **787/791-4046.** Main courses $10–$30. AE, MC, V. Daily 11:30am–11:30pm. Bus: C41, B42, or A5.

Panadería España Repostería SANDWICHES   The Panadería España makes San Juan's definitive Cuban sandwich—a cheap meal all on its own. The biggest sandwich weighs 3 pounds. Drinks and coffee are dispensed from behind a much-used bar. You can purchase an assortment of gourmet items from Spain, arranged as punctuation marks on shelves set against an otherwise all-white decor. The place has been serving simple breakfasts, drinks, coffee, and Cuban sandwiches virtually every day since it opened around 1970.

Centro Comercial Villamar, Marginal Baldoriti de Castro. ℭ **787/727-3860.** Reservations not necessary. Soups and tapas $4–$6; sandwiches $5–$8. AE, DISC, MC, V. Daily 6am–10pm. Bus: A5.

Exploring San Juan

The Spanish began to settle in the area now known as Old San Juan around 1521. At the outset, the city was called Puerto Rico ("Rich Port"), and the whole island was known as San Juan.

The streets are narrow and teeming with traffic, but a walk through Old San Juan—in Spanish, *El Viejo San Juan*—makes for a good stroll. Some visitors have likened it to a "Disney park with an Old World theme." Fast food and junk stores mar a lot of the beauty. Nonetheless, it's the biggest and best collection of historic buildings, stretching back 5

centuries, in all the Caribbean. You can do it in less than a day (see "Walking Tour: Old San Juan," later in this chapter). In this historic 7-square-block area of the western side of the city, you can see many of Puerto Rico's chief sightseeing attractions and do some shopping along the way.

On the other hand, you might want to plop down on the sand with a drink or get outside and play. "Diving, Fishing, Tennis & Other Outdoor Pursuits," later in this chapter, describes the beaches and sports in the San Juan area.

1 Seeing the Sights

SUGGESTED SAN JUAN ITINERARIES

IF YOU HAVE 1 DAY To make the most of a short stay, head straight for Old San Juan for an afternoon of sightseeing and shopping. Definitely schedule a visit to El Morro Fortress. Try to spend 2 hours at Condado Beach. Enjoy a Puerto Rican dinner at a local restaurant, listen to some salsa music, and enjoy a rum punch before retiring for the night.

IF YOU HAVE 2 DAYS On your first day, spend the morning shopping and sightseeing in Old San Juan. Schedule visits to El Morro and San Juan Cathedral and then relax on Condado Beach for the rest of the day. Enjoy a Puerto Rican dinner and some local music before retiring.

On your second day, spend the morning exploring El Yunque rainforest, a lush 28,000-acre (11,331-hectare) site east of San Juan. Schedule 2 or 3 hours at nearby Luquillo Beach, the finest beach in Puerto Rico. Buy lunch from an open-air kiosk. Return to San Juan for the evening and attend either a folk-culture show (if available) or a Las Vegas–style revue. Visit the casinos for some action before retiring.

We have outlined a walking tour of Old San Juan later in this chapter, but here is an introduction to some of the sights mentioned there, as well as others you might want to seek out.

FORTS

Castillo de San Felipe del Morro *(* *Kids* Called "El Morro," this fort stands on a rocky promontory dominating the entrance to San Juan Bay. Constructed in 1540,

Old San Juan Attractions

Aduana **29**
Alcaldía (City Hall) **20**
Antiguo Manicomio Insular **3**
Asilo de Beneficencia **4**
Capilla de Cristo **26**
Casa Blanca **12**
Casa del Callejón **31**
Castillo de San Felipe del Morro **1**
Catedral de San Juan **19**
Centro Nacional de Artes Populares y Artesanías **25**
City walls **23**
Cuartel de Ballajá **6**
El Arsenal **28**
El Convento **17**
Felisa Rincón de Gautier Museum **15**
Fort San Cristóbal **34**
Iglesia de San José **9**
La Casa del Libro **25**
La Casa Rosada **5**
La Fortaleza **22**
La Princesa **27**
Museo de Arte e Historia de San Juan **8**
Museo de las Américas **5**
Museo del Niño **18**
Museo Nuestras Raíces Africanas **10**

Museo Pablo Casals **11**
Parque de las Palomas **24**
Plaza de Armas **21**
Plaza de Colón **33**
Plaza de la Marina **30**
Plaza de las Monjas **16**
Plaza de San José **7**
Plaza del Quinto Centenario **7**
Plazuela de la Rogativa **13**
San Juan Cemetery **2**
San Juan Gate **14**
Teatro Tapia **32**

the original fort was a round tower, which can still be seen deep inside the lower levels of the castle. More walls and cannon-firing positions were added, and by 1787, the fortification attained the complex design you see today. This fortress was attacked repeatedly by both the English and the Dutch.

The U.S. National Park Service protects the fortifications of Old San Juan, which have been declared a World Heritage Site by the United Nations. With some of the most dramatic views in the Caribbean, you'll find El Morro an intriguing labyrinth of dungeons, barracks, vaults, lookouts, and ramps. Historical and background information is provided in a video in English and Spanish. The nearest parking is the underground facility beneath the Quincentennial Plaza at the Ballajá barracks (Cuartel de Ballajá) on Calle Norzagaray. Sometimes park rangers lead hour-long tours for free, although you can also visit on your own. With the purchase of a ticket here, you don't have to pay the admission for Fort San Cristóbal (see below) if you visit during the same day.

Before going into the citadel, you can visit the new $2-million **San Juan National Historic Site** (ⓒ 787/729-6960), which is open daily from 9am to 5pm, charging $3 for adults, $2 for seniors, and $1 for children 13 to 17 (free for 12 and under). The center is connected via two tunnels to **Fort San Cristóbal,** and was created from a strategic military base used in World War II. Visitors view a 12-minute film about the fortifications. A photo exhibit, a gift shop, and other exhibits are of interest.

At the end of Calle Norzagaray. ⓒ 787/729-6960. Admission $3 adults, $2 seniors and ages 13–17, free for children 12 and under. Daily 9am–5pm. Bus: A5, B21, or B40.

Fort San Cristóbal ⓡ This huge fortress, begun in 1634 and reengineered in the 1770s, is one of the largest ever built in the Americas by Spain. Its walls rise more than 150 feet (46m) above the sea—a marvel of military engineering. San Cristóbal protected San Juan against attackers coming by land as a partner to El Morro, to which it is linked by a half-mile (.8km) of monumental walls and bastions filled with cannon-firing positions. A complex system of tunnels and dry moats connects the center of San Cristóbal to its "outworks," defensive elements arranged layer after layer over a 27-acre (11-hectare) site. You'll get the idea if you look at the scale model on display. Like El Morro, the fort is administered and maintained by the U.S. National Park Service. Be sure to see the Garita del Diablo (the Devil's Sentry Box), one of the oldest parts of San Cristóbal's defenses, and famous in Puerto Rican legend. The devil himself, it is said, would snatch away sentinels at this lonely post at the edge of the sea. In 1898 the first shots of the Spanish-American War in Puerto Rico were fired by cannons on top of San Cristóbal during an artillery duel with a U.S. Navy fleet. Sometimes park rangers lead hour-long tours for free, and you can also visit on your own.

In the northeast corner of Old San Juan (uphill from Plaza de Colón on Calle Norzagaray). ⓒ 787/729-6960. Admission $3 adults, $1 ages 13–17, free for children 12 and under. Daily 9am–5pm. Bus: A5, B21, or B40; then the free trolley from Covadonga station to the top of the hill.

CHURCHES

Capilla de Cristo Cristo Chapel was built to commemorate what legend says was a miracle. In 1753 a young rider lost control of his horse in a race down this very street during the fiesta of St. John's Day and plunged over the precipice. Moved by the accident, the secretary of the city, Don Mateo Pratts, invoked Christ to save the youth, and he had the chapel built when his prayers were answered. Today it's a landmark in the old city and one of its best-known historical monuments. The chapel's gold and silver altar can be seen through its glass doors. Because the chapel is open only 1 day a week, most visitors have to settle for a view of its exterior.

Calle del Cristo (directly west of Paseo de la Princesa). (**C** 787/722-0700. Free admission. Tues 8am–5pm. Bus: Old Town Trolley.

Catedral de San Juan   This, the spiritual and architectural centerpiece of Old San Juan, as you see it in its present form, was begun in 1540 as a replacement for a thatch-roofed chapel that was blown apart by a hurricane in 1529. Chronically hampered by a lack of funds and a recurring series of military and weather-derived disasters, it slowly evolved into the gracefully vaulted, Gothic-inspired structure you see today. Among the many disasters to hit this cathedral are the following: In 1598 the Earl of Cumberland led the British navy in a looting spree, and in 1615 a hurricane blew away its roof. In 1908 the body of Ponce de León was disinterred from the nearby Iglesia de San José and placed in a marble tomb near the transept, where it remains today (see the box "Ponce de León: Man of Myth & Legend" in the appendix for more about Ponce de León). The cathedral also contains the wax-covered mummy of St. Pio, a Roman martyr persecuted and killed for his Christian faith. The mummy has been encased in a glass box ever since it was placed here in 1862. To the right of the mummy is a bizarre wooden replica of Mary with four swords stuck in her bosom. After all the looting and destruction over the centuries, the cathedral's great treasures, including gold and silver, are long gone, although many beautiful stained-glass windows remain. The cathedral faces Plaza de las Monjas (the Nuns' Square), a shady spot where you can rest.

Calle del Cristo 153 (at Caleta San Juan). (**C** 787/722-0861. Free admission. Mon–Sat 8am–5pm; Sun 8am–2pm. Bus: Old Town Trolley.

MUSEUMS

Many of the museums in Old San Juan close for lunch between 11:45am and 2pm, so schedule your activities accordingly if you intend to museum-hop.

Felisa Rincón de Gautier Museum   The most heralded woman of modern Puerto Rico served as the mayor of San Juan for 22 consecutive years, between 1946 and 1968. The museum that commemorates her memory is in a 300-year-old building a few blocks downhill from San Juan's cathedral, near one of the medieval gates (La Puerta San Juan) that pierces the walls of the Old City. The interior is devoted to the life and accomplishments of Felisa Rincón de Gautier, and proudly displays some of her personal furniture and artifacts, as well as 212 plaques, 308 certificates of merit,

---

Moments Joggers' Trail or Romantic Walk

El Morro Trail, a jogger's paradise, provides Old Town's most scenic views across the harbor. The first part of the trail extends to the San Juan Gate. The walk then goes by El Morro and eventually reaches a scenic area known as Bastion de Santa Barbara. The walk passes El Morro's well-preserved walls, and the trail ends at the entrance to the fortress. The walkway is designed to follow the undulating movement of the ocean, and sea grapes and tropical vegetation surround benches. The trail is romantic at night, when the walls of the fortress are illuminated. Stop at the tourist office for a map, and then set off on the adventure.

San Juan Attractions

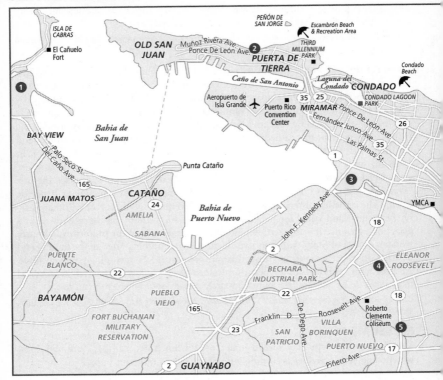

11 honorary doctorates, and 113 symbolic keys to other cities, such as Gary, Ind., and Perth Amboy, N.J. Her particular areas of influence included child welfare and elementary education. Photographs show her with luminaries from Eleanor Roosevelt to the pope. The oldest of nine children, and the daughter of a local lawyer and a schoolteacher, she shouldered the responsibilities of rearing her younger siblings after the death of her mother when she was 12. Today the museum illuminates Doña Felisa's life as well as the reverence in which Puerto Ricans hold their most celebrated political matriarch. As such, it's a quirky, intensely personalized monument that combines a strong sense of feminism with Puerto Rican national pride.

Caleta de San Juan 51 at Calle Clara Lair. ☎ 787/723-1897. Free admission. Mon–Fri 9am–4pm. Bus: Old Town Trolley.

Luis Muñoz Marín Foundation A 30-minute drive south of San Juan, this museum offers a chance to visit the former home of the island's most famous governor, Luis Muñoz Marín. As the first elected governor of Puerto Rico, Marín enjoys somewhat the same position in Puerto Rican history that George Washington does for the mainland United States. A documentary acquaints you with the governor's life and achievements. You can walk through Marín's study and library and view his extensive art collection, and later you can relax in his tropical garden and gazebo. There's also an on-site antique automobile exhibition.

Marginal Rd. 877, Km 0.4, Trujillo Alto Expwy. © **787/755-7979.** Admission $2 adults, $1 children. Tours Mon–Fri (reservations required) 10am and 2pm.

Museo de Arte 🏵🏵 Puerto Rico's most important gallery, which opened in 2000 and was constructed at a cost of $55 million, is a state-of-the-art showcase for the island nation's rich cultural heritage, as reflected mainly through its painters. Housed in a former city hospital in Santurce, the museum features both a permanent collection and temporary exhibitions. Prominent local artists are the stars—for example, Francisco Oller (1833–1917), who brought a touch of Cézanne or Camille Pissarro to Puerto Rico (Oller actually studied in France with both of these Impressionists). Another leading star of the permanent collection is José Campeche, a late-18th-century classical painter. The museum is like a living textbook of Puerto Rico, beginning with its early development and going on to showcase camp aspects, such as the poster art created here in the mid–20th century. All the important modern island artists are also presented, including the best known, the late Angel Botello, and also such contemporaries as Rafael Tufiño and Arnaldo Roche Rabell.

Av. José de Diego 299, Santurce. © **787/977-6277.** www.mapr.org. Admission $6 adults, $2.50 seniors, $3 children under age 12. Tues and Thurs–Sat 10am–5pm; Wed 10am–8pm; Sun 11am–6pm. Bus: A5 or B21.

Museo de Arte e Historia de San Juan   Located in a Spanish colonial building at the corner of Calle MacArthur, this cultural center was the city's main marketplace in the mid–19th century. Local art is displayed in the east and west galleries, and audiovisual materials reveal the history of the city. Sometimes major cultural events are staged in the museum's large courtyard. English- and Spanish-language audiovisual shows are presented Tuesday to Friday every hour on the hour from 9am to 4pm.

Calle Norzagaray 150. ⓒ **787/724-1875.** Free admission, but donations accepted. Tues–Fri 9am–4pm; Sat–Sun 10am–4pm. Bus: B21 to Old San Juan terminal; then a trolley from the terminal to the museum.

Museo de las Américas ⓡ   This museum showcases the artisans of North, South, and Central America, featuring everything from carved figureheads from New England whaling ships to dugout canoes carved by Carib Indians in Dominica. It is unique in Puerto Rico and well worth a visit. Also on display is a changing collection of paintings by artists from throughout the Spanish-speaking world, some of which are for sale, and a permanent collection called "Puerto Rican *Santos,*" donated by Dr. Ricardo Alegría.

Cuartel de Ballajá. ⓒ **787/724-5052.** Free admission. Tues–Sun 10am–4pm. Bus: Old Town Trolley.

Museo de Pablo Casals   This museum is devoted to the memorabilia left to the people of Puerto Rico by the musician Pablo Casals. The maestro's cello is here, along with a library of videotapes (which can be played upon request) of some of his festival concerts. This small 18th-century house also contains manuscripts and photographs of Casals. The annual Casals Festival draws worldwide interest and internationally known performing artists; it's held during the first 2 weeks of June.

Plaza San José, Calle San Sebastián 101. ⓒ **787/723-9185.** Admission $1 adults, 50¢ students and children. Tues–Sat 9:30am–4:30pm. Bus: Old Town Trolley.

HISTORIC SIGHTS

In addition to the forts and churches listed above, you might want to see the sites described below.

   San Juan Gate, Calle San Francisco and Calle Recinto Oeste, built around 1635, just north of La Fortaleza, several blocks downhill from the cathedral, was the main point of entry into San Juan if you arrived by ship in the 17th and 18th centuries. The gate is the only one remaining of the several that once pierced the fortifications of the old walled city. For centuries it was closed at sundown to cut off access to the historic old town. Bus: B21 or Old Town Trolley.

   Plazuela de la Rogativa, Caleta de las Monjas, is a little plaza with a statue of a bishop and three women, commemorating one of Puerto Rico's most famous legends. In 1797, from across San Juan Bay at Santurce, the British held the Old Town under siege. That same year they mysteriously sailed away. Later, the commander claimed he feared that the enemy was well prepared behind those walls; he apparently saw many lights and believed them to be reinforcements. Some people believe that those lights were torches carried by women in a *rogativa,* or religious procession, as they followed their bishop. Bus: T1.

   The **city walls** around San Juan were built in 1630 to protect the town against both European invaders and Caribbean pirates. The city walls that remain today were once part of one of the most impregnable fortresses in the New World and even today are an engineering marvel. Their thickness averages 20 feet (6m) at the base and 12 feet (3.7m) at the top, with an average height of 40 feet (12m). At their top, notice the balconied buildings that served for centuries as hospitals and also residences of the island's various governors. Between Fort San Cristóbal and El Morro, bastions were erected at frequent intervals. The walls come into view as you approach from San Cristóbal on your way to El Morro. Bus: C45 and A5.

San Juan Cemetery, on Calle Norzagaray, officially opened in 1814 and has since been the final resting place for many prominent Puerto Rican families. The circular chapel, dedicated to Saint Magdalene of Pazzis, was built in the 1860s. Aficionados of old graveyards can wander among marble monuments, mausoleums, and statues, marvelous examples of Victorian funereal statuary. Because there are no trees, or any other form of shade here, it would be best not to go exploring in the noonday sun. In any case, be careful—the cemetery is often a venue for illegal drug deals and can be dangerous. Bus: Old Town Trolley.

Alcaldía (City Hall)
The City Hall, with its double arcade flanked by two towers resembling Madrid's City Hall, was constructed in stages from 1604 to 1789. Still in use, this building today contains a tourist-information center downstairs plus a small art gallery on the first floor.

Calle San Francisco. ℂ 787/724-7171. Free admission. Mon–Fri 8am–5pm. Closed holidays. Bus: Old Town Trolley.

Casa Blanca
Ponce de León never lived here, although construction of the house—built in 1521, 2 years after his death—is sometimes attributed to him. The work was ordered by his son-in-law, Juan García Troche. The parcel of land was given to Ponce de León as a reward for services rendered to the Crown. Descendants of the explorer lived in the house for about 2½ centuries, until the Spanish government took it over in 1779 for use as a residence for military commanders. The U.S. government also used it as a home for army commanders. On the first floor, the **Juan Ponce de León Museum** is furnished with antiques, paintings, and artifacts from the 16th through the 18th centuries. In back is a garden with spraying fountains, offering an intimate and verdant respite.

Calle San Sebastián 1. ℂ 787/725-1454. Admission $2. Tues–Sat 9am–noon and 1–4:30pm. Bus: Old Town Trolley.

El Arsenal
The Spaniards used a shallow craft to patrol the lagoons and mangroves in and around San Juan. Needing a base for these vessels, they constructed El Arsenal in the 19th century. It was at this base that they staged their last stand, flying the Spanish colors until the final Spaniard was removed in 1898, at the end of the Spanish-American War. Changing art exhibitions are held in the building's three galleries.

La Puntilla. ℂ 787/723-3068. Free admission. Wed–Sun 8:30am–4:30pm. Bus: Old Town Trolley.

La Casa del Libro
This restored 19th-century house shelters a library and museum devoted to the arts of printing and bookmaking, with examples of fine printing, which date back 5 centuries, and some illuminated medieval manuscripts.

Calle del Cristo 255. ℂ 787/723-0354. Free admission. Tues–Sat 11am–4:30pm. Bus: Old Town Trolley.

La Fortaleza
The office and residence of the governor of Puerto Rico is the oldest executive mansion in continuous use in the Western Hemisphere, and it has served as the island's seat of government for more than 3 centuries. Its history goes back even further than that to 1533, when construction began on a fortress to protect San Juan's Spanish settlers during raids by Carib tribesmen and pirates. The original medieval towers remain, but as the edifice was subsequently enlarged into a palace, other modes of architecture and ornamentation were also incorporated, including baroque, Gothic,

neoclassical, and Arabian. La Fortaleza has been designated a national historic site by the U.S. government. Proper attire is required (informal okay).

Calle Fortaleza, overlooking San Juan Harbor. ℂ 787/721-7000, ext. 2211. Free admission. 30-min. tours of the gardens and building (conducted in English and Spanish) given Mon–Fri, every half-hour 9am–3:30pm. Bus: Old Town Trolley

Museo Nuestras Raíces Africanas　Set within the Casa del Contrefueras, this museum documents the African contribution to the sociology of Puerto Rico. You'll find a series of tastefully arranged art objects, including musical instruments, intricately carved African masks, drums, graphics, and maps that show the migratory patterns, usually through the slave trade, from Africa into Puerto Rico. There are graphic depictions of the horrendous disruptions to families and individuals caused by the slave trade during the plantation era.

Plaza San José, Calle San Sebastián. ℂ **787/724-4294.** Admission $2 adults; $1 seniors, children, and students; free for ages 12 and under. Tues–Sat 8:30am–4:30pm. Bus: Old Town Trolley.

Teatro Tapía　Standing across from the Plaza de Colón, this is one of the oldest theaters in the Western Hemisphere, built about 1832. In 1976 a restoration returned the theater to its original appearance. Much of Puerto Rican theater history is connected with the Tapía, named after the island's first prominent playwright, Alejandro Tapía y Rivera (1826–82). Various productions—some musical—are staged here throughout the year, representing a repertoire of drama, dance, and cultural events.

Av. Ponce de León. ℂ **787/721-0180.** Access limited to ticket holders at performances (see "San Juan After Dark," later in this chapter). Bus: B8 or B21.

HISTORIC SQUARES

In Old San Juan, **Plaza del Quinto Centenario (Quincentennial Plaza)** overlooks the Atlantic from atop the highest point in the city. A striking and symbolic feature of the plaza, which was constructed as part of the 1992–93 celebration of the 500th anniversary of the discovery of the New World, is a sculpture that rises 40 feet (12m) from the plaza's top level. The monumental sculpture in black granite and ceramics symbolizes the earthen and clay roots of American history and is the work of Jaime Suarez, one of Puerto Rico's foremost artists. From its southern end, two needle-shaped columns point skyward to the North Star, the guiding light of explorers. Placed around the plaza are fountains, other columns, and sculpted steps that represent various historic periods in Puerto Rico's 500-year heritage.

Sweeping views extend from the plaza to El Morro Fortress at the headland of San Juan Bay and to the Dominican Convent and San José Church, a rare New World example of Gothic architecture. Asilo de Beneficencia, a former indigents' hospital dating from 1832, occupies a corner of El Morro's entrance and is now the home of the Institute of Puerto Rican Culture. Adjacent to the plaza is the Cuartel de Ballajá, built in the mid–19th century as the Spanish army headquarters and still the largest edifice in the Americas constructed by Spanish engineers; it houses the Museum of the Americas.

Centrally located, Quincentennial Plaza is one of modern Puerto Rico's respectful gestures to its colorful and lively history. It is a perfect introduction for visitors seeking to discover the many rich links with the past in Old San Juan.

Once named St. James Square, or Plaza Santiago, **Plaza de Colón** in the heart of San Juan's Old Town is bustling and busy, reached along the pedestrian mall of Calle Fortaleza. The square was renamed Plaza de Colón to honor the 400th anniversary of the explorer's so-called discovery of Puerto Rico. Of course, it is more politically correct today to say that Columbus explored or came upon an already inhabited island. He certainly didn't discover it. But when a statue here, perhaps the most famous on the island, was erected atop a high pedestal, it was clearly to honor Columbus, not to decry his legacy.

PARKS & GARDENS

Jardín Botánico   Administered by the University of Puerto Rico, Jardín Botánico is a lush tropical garden with some 200 species of vegetation. You can pack a picnic lunch and bring it here if you choose. The orchid garden is exceptional, and the palm garden is said to contain some 125 species. Footpaths blaze a trail through heavy forests opening onto a lotus lagoon.

Barrio Venezuela (at the intersection of routes 1 and 847), Río Piedras. © 787/765-1845. Free admission. Daily 6am–6pm. Bus: 19.

Luis Muñoz Marín Park *(Kids* This park is administered by the Park Trust of Puerto Rico, and it is the best-known, most frequently visited children's playground in Puerto Rico—although it has equal appeal to adults. Conceived as a verdant oasis in an otherwise crowded urban neighborhood, it's a fenced-in repository of swings, jungle gyms, and slides set amid several small lakes. Here you'll also find an incomparable view of San Juan. A small-scale cable car carries passengers aloft at 10-minute intervals for panoramic views of the surrounding landscape ($2 per person).

Av. Piñero, at Alto Rey. © 787/751-3353. Free admission for pedestrians; parking $2 or $3. Wed–Sun 8am–6pm. Bus: A1 to Río Piedras, then switch to bus 52.

Muñoz Rivera Park   This park is affiliated with Luis Muñoz Marín Park (see above), with which it is frequently confused. This green space is administered by the **Park Trust of Puerto Rico** (© **787/763-0613**). It's a rectangular, seaward-facing park that was built about 50 years ago to honor Luis Muñoz Rivera, the Puerto Rican statesman, journalist, and poet. It's filled with picnic areas, wide walks, shady trees, landscaped grounds, and recreational areas. Its centerpiece, El Pabellon de la Paz, is sometimes used for cultural events and expositions of handicrafts.

Av. Ponce de León. © 787/724-4430. Free admission. Daily 24 hr. Bus: A1 (or take the Los Américas Expwy. to Av. Piñero, then head west until you reach the entrance).

Parque Central Municipio de San Juan   This mangrove-bordered park was inaugurated in 1979 for the Pan-American Games. It covers 35 acres (14 hectares) and lies southeast of Miramar. Joggers appreciate its labyrinth of trails, tennis players enjoy the courts, and all city dwellers stroll to relieve the pressures of urban life.

Calle Cerra. © 787/722-1646. Free admission for pedestrians; parking $1. Mon–Thurs 6am–10pm; Fri 6am–9pm; Sat–Sun 6am–7pm. Bus: A1.

SIGHTSEEING TOURS

If you want to see more of the island but you don't want to rent a car or manage the inconveniences of public transportation, perhaps an organized tour is for you.

Castillo Sightseeing Tours & Travel Services, 2413 Calle Laurel, Punta La Marias, Santurce (© **787/791-6195**), maintains offices at some of the capital's best-known hotels, including the Caribe Hilton and San Juan Marriott Resort. Using six of their own air-conditioned buses, with access to others if demand warrants it, the company's tours include pickups and drop-offs at hotels as an added convenience.

Tips   **The Best Places to See Puerto Rican Art**

With its dozen or so museums and even more art galleries, Old San Juan is the greatest repository of Puerto Rican arts and crafts. Galleries sell everything from pre-Columbian artifacts to paintings by relatively contemporary artists such as Angel Botello, who died in 1986. **Galería Botello** (p. 151) was his former home. He restored the colonial mansion himself; now his paintings and sculptures are on display there.

The grandest repository of art in San Juan is at the **Museo de Arte** (p. 133), which is a virtual textbook on all the big names in the art world who rose from Puerto Rico often to international acclaim.

Another good place to see Puerto Rican art is the **Museum of History, Anthropology & Art** (© 787/763-3939). Because of space limitations, the museum's galleries can exhibit only a fifth of their vast collection at one time, but the work is always top-notch. The collection ranges from pre-Columbian artifacts to works by today's major painters.

Outside San Juan, the greatest art on the island is at the **Museo de Arte de Ponce** (p. 181). The collection, donated by former governor Luís A. Ferré, ranges from Jan van Eyck's *Salvatore Mundi* to Rossetti's *Daughters of King Lear.* The museum building was designed by Edward Durell Stone, who also designed New York's Museum of Modern Art. Works are displayed in a honeycomb of skylit hexagonal rooms. In addition to such European masters as Reubens, Van Dyck, and Murillo, the museum features works by Latin American artists, including Diego Rivera. Puerto Rican artists who are represented include José Campeche and Francisco Oller.

One of the most popular half-day tours departs most days of the week between 8:30 and 9am, lasts 4 to 5 hours, and costs $45 per person. Leaving from San Juan, it tours along the northeastern part of the island to El Yunque. The company also offers a city tour of San Juan that departs daily around 1pm. The 4-hour trip costs $40 per person and includes a stop at the Bacardi Rum Factory. The company also operates full-day snorkeling tours to the reefs near the coast of a deserted island off Puerto Rico's eastern edge aboard one of two sail- and motor-driven catamarans. With lunch, snorkeling gear, and piña coladas included, the full-day (7:45am–5pm) excursion goes for $80 per person.

Few cities of the Caribbean lend themselves so gracefully to walking tours. You can embark on these on your own, stopping and shopping en route (see "Walking Tour: Old San Juan," below).

ESPECIALLY FOR KIDS

Puerto Rico is one of the most family-friendly islands in the Caribbean, and many hotels offer family discounts. Programs for children are also offered at a number of hotels, including day and night camp activities and babysitting services. Trained counselors at these camps supervise children as young as 3 in activities ranging from nature hikes to tennis lessons, coconut carving, and sand-sculpture contests.

Teenagers can learn to hip-hop dance Latino-style with special salsa and merengue lessons, learn conversational Spanish, indulge in watersports, take jeep excursions, or scuba-dive in some of the best diving locations in the world.

The best kiddies program is offered at **El San Juan Hotel & Casino** (p. 92), where camp activities are presented to children between the ages of 5 and 12. Counselors design activities according to the interests of groups of up to 10 children. Kids Klub members receive a T-shirt, membership card, and three Sand Dollars for use in the game room or at a poolside restaurant. The daily fee of $40 includes lunch.

Another worthy choice is the **Condado Plaza Hotel & Casino** (p. 84), where the daily Camp Taíno offers a regular program of activities and special events for children ages 5 to 12. The hotel also has a toddlers' pool, and the kids' water slide in its main pool starts in a Spanish-style castle turret. For teenagers, the hotel has a video game room, a tennis court, several putting greens, and various organized activities.

Children should love **El Morro Fortress** (see "Forts," earlier in this chapter) because it looks just like the castles they have seen on TV and at the movies. On a rocky promontory, El Morro is filled with dungeons and dank places and also has lofty lookout points for viewing San Juan Harbor.

Luis Muñoz Marín Park (see "Parks & Gardens," above) has the most popular children's playground in Puerto Rico. It's filled with landscaped grounds and recreational areas—lots of room for fun in the sun.

Museo del Niño (Children's Museum) *Kids*   In the late 1990s, the city of San Juan turned over one of the most desirable buildings in the colonial zone—a 300-year-old villa directly across from the city's cathedral—to a group of sociologists and student volunteers. Jointly, they created the only children's museum in Puerto Rico. Through interactive exhibits, children learn simple lessons, such as the benefits of brushing teeth or recycling aluminum cans, or the value of caring properly for pets. Staff members include lots of student volunteers who play either one-on-one or with small groups of children. Nothing here is terribly cerebral, and nothing will necessarily compel you to return. But it does provide a play experience that some children will remember for several weeks.

Calle del Cristo 150. (C) **787/722-3791.** Admission $5; $4 children 14 and younger. Tues–Thurs 9am–3:30pm; Fri 9am–5pm; Sat–Sun 12:30–5pm. Bus: Old Town Trolley.

Time Out Family Amusement Center *Kids*   This is the most popular venue for family outings on Puerto Rico. On weekends, seemingly half the families in the city show up. It has a large variety of electronic games for children and adults alike, but there are no rides.

Plaza de las Américas, Las Américas Expwy. at Av. Roosevelt, Hato Rey. (C) **787/753-0606.** Free admission (prices of activities vary). Mon–Thurs 9:30am–10pm; Fri–Sun 9am–11pm. Bus: B21 from Old San Juan.

WALKING TOUR | **OLD SAN JUAN**

Start:	Plaza de la Marina
Finish:	Fort San Cristóbal
Time:	2 hours (not counting stops)
Best times:	Any sunny day between 7am and 6pm
Worst times:	When several cruise ships are in port simultaneously

The streets are narrow and teeming with traffic, so walk carefully through Old San Juan *(El Viejo San Juan)*. Beneficiary of millions of dollars' worth of restoration since the early 1970s, Old San Juan is one of the world's most potent reminders of the power and grandeur of the Spanish Empire. This tour begins at a point just to the west of San Juan's cruise piers and encircles the perimeter of some of the best-preserved fortifications built by the Spaniards during the 16th and 17th centuries. En route, it passes beneath the governor's historic mansion, La Fortaleza, and encircles Casa Blanca, before ending at a point beyond the entrance of one of the most fiercely guarded fortresses of the colonial age, Fort San Cristóbal.

Begin your walking tour near the post office, amid the taxis, buses, and urban congestion of:

❶ Plaza de la Marina

This sloping, many-angled plaza is at the eastern edge of one of San Juan's showcase promenades, Paseo de la Princesa. The 19th-century paseo was an esplanade where the Spanish colonial gentry once strolled while enjoying the balmy Caribbean air.

Towering royal palms shade the broad esplanade, now paved with brick. On the paseo's west side, overlooking the sea, a large bronze fountain, *Raíces* (Roots), sculpted in 1992 by the Spanish artist Luís Sanguino, depicts the Amerindian, African, and Spanish origins of Puerto Rico as human figures, with dolphins cavorting at their feet. Viewed from afar, the entire ensemble looks like a caravel being steered out to sea by dolphins. On the paseo's east side stand five allegorical pieces on the island's heritage sculpted by José Buscaglia in 1992. This work is said to symbolize the various epochs that Puerto Rico has undergone in the past 5 centuries—from the coming of the Spanish conquistadores to the beginning of Puerto Rico's role as a U.S. protectorate.

A gazebo serves light seafood dishes, salads, and the island's famed rich coffee. Outdoor tables with umbrellas allow parents to keep an eye on their children, who may be enjoying the playground nearby. More than 20 trees were planted to shade the tables. *Criollo* dishes are also available from food carts with colored awnings.

Walk westward along Paseo de la Princesa, past heroic statues and manicured trees, until you reach:

❷ La Princesa

The gray-and-white building on your right, which served for centuries as one of the most feared prisons in the Caribbean, is called La Princesa. Today it houses the offices of the Puerto Rico Tourism Company and an exhibit of work by Puerto Rican artists. Gallery hours are Monday through Friday from 9am to noon and 1 to 4pm, and admission is free. In front of La Princesa stands a sculpture of one of the island's most beloved leaders, Doña Felisa Gautier, mayor of San Juan from 1946 to 1968.

Continue walking westward to the base of the fountain near the edge of the sea. Turn to your right and follow the seaside promenade as it parallels the edge of the:

❸ City Walls

These walls were once part of one of the most impregnable fortresses in the New World. See "Historic Sights," earlier in this chapter.

Continue walking between the sea and the base of the city walls until the walkway goes through the walls at the:

❹ San Juan Gate

This gate was built at Calle San Francisco and Recinto del Oeste, around 1635, as the main point of access from the wharves to the colony's interior. See "Historic Sights," earlier in this chapter.

Walking Tour: Old San Juan

Legend:

Information ⓘ   "Take a Break"   ▬ City Walls

1 Plaza de la Marina
2 La Princesa
3 City walls
4 San Juan Gate
5 La Fortaleza
6 Plazuela de la Rogativa
7 La Casa Rosada
8 Castillo de San Felipe del Morro
9 Antiguo Manicomio Insular
10 Asilo de Beneficencia
11 Casa Blanca
12 Cuartel de Ballajá
13 Plaza del Quinto Centenario
14 Plaza de San José
15 El Convento
16 Catedral de San Juan
17 Centro Nacional de Artes Populares y Artesanías
18 Capilla de Cristo
19 Plaza de Armas
20 Plaza de Colón
21 Fort San Cristóbal

0   1/10 mile
0   100 meters

ATLANTIC OCEAN

ATLANTIC OCEAN

SAN JUAN

area of detail

Castillo de San Felipe del Morro

Cementerio de San Juan

El Campo del Morro

Calle del Morro

Murallas de San Juan

Murallas de San Juan

Fuerte San Cristóbal

finish here

start here

Plaza de Colón

Calle O'Donell
C. J. J. Acosta
C. Tamarindo
C. Capilla
Calle Tanca
Calle Luna
Calle Sol
Calle San Sebastián
Norzagaray
de Valle
Calle San Justo
Calle Cruz
Calle San Jose
Del Cristo
Plaza San José
Plaza de Armas
Calle San Francisco
Calle Fortaleza
Calle Tetuan
Calle Recinto
El Arsenal
Calle Presidio
Calle Puntillo
Paseo de la Princesa
Calle Harding
Calle Gen. Pershing
Calle Braumbaugh
Calle Allen
Calle Marina
Ave. Muñoz Rivera
Ave. Ponce de Leon
Paseo de Covadonga
de Muelle

Muelle (pier) 1
Muelle (pier) 2
Muelle (pier) 3
Muelle (pier) 4
Muelle (pier) 6

25
38
25
20

When you're inside the once-dreaded fortifications, turn immediately right and walk uphill along Calle Recinto del Oeste. The wrought-iron gates at the street's end, which will probably be guarded by a pair of attendants, lead to:

❺ La Fortaleza

The centuries-old residence of the Puerto Rican governor, La Fortaleza is located on Calle Fortaleza. See p. 135.

Now retrace your steps along Calle Recinto del Oeste, walking first downhill and then uphill for about a block, until you reach Caleta de las Monjas. Fork left until you see a panoramic view and a contemporary statue marking the center of:

❻ Plazuela de la Rogativa

The statue on this small square commemorates a time in 1797 when British soldiers mistook a religious procession for the arrival of Spanish reinforcements and fled. See "Historic Sights," earlier in this chapter.

Continue westward, passing between a pair of urn-capped gateposts. You'll be walking parallel to the crenellations of the 17th-century city walls. The cool, tree-shaded boulevard will fork; take the right-hand fork and pass just above the pink walls of:

❼ La Casa Rosada

This graceful villa was built in 1812 for leaders of the Spanish army. It cannot be visited, but you can enjoy the view from outside.

Continue climbing the steeply inclined cobble-covered ramp to its top. Walk westward across the field toward the neoclassical gateway of a fortress believed impregnable for centuries:

❽ Castillo de San Felipe del Morro ("El Morro")

The fortress walls here were designed as part of a network of defenses that made San Juan *La Ciudad Murada* (the Walled City). See p. 129.

After your visit, with El Morro behind you, retrace your steps through the sunlit, treeless field to the point where you stood when you first sighted the fortress. Walk down Calle del Morro past the:

❾ Antiguo Manicomio Insular

In 1854 the Spanish king decreed that this structure be built as an insane asylum.

Converted to a U.S. army barracks after the Spanish-American War, it has functioned since 1965 as the Puerto Rican Academy of Fine Arts. Iron fences of grace and elegance protect a pair of courtyards centered around splashing fountains.

Across the street from Antiguo Manicomio Insular is a stately neoclassical building (painted buff with fern-green trim), the:

❿ Asilo de Beneficencia ("Home for the Poor")

Asilo de Beneficencia, which dates from the 1840s, has two attractive interior patios, an austere dignity, and usually an echoing silence. Today it houses the administrative offices of the Institute of Puerto Rican Culture, with several changing exhibition galleries and an interesting room filled with pre-Columbian artifacts. The galleries are open Wednesday to Sunday from 9am to 4:30pm, with free admission. For more information, call ✆ 787/724-0700.

Continue walking uphill to the small, formal, and sloping plaza at the street's top. On the right side, within a trio of buildings, is:

⓫ Casa Blanca

Casa Blanca was built by the son-in-law of Juan Ponce de León as the great conquistador's island home (he never actually lived here). See p. 135.

After your visit to Casa Blanca, exit by the compound's front entrance and walk downhill, retracing your steps for a half-block, and head toward the massive and monumental tangerine-colored building on your right, the:

⓬ Cuartel de Ballajá

This is the 19th-century military barracks of Ballajá, which once housed troops from Spain along with their wives and children, in a setting evocative of the most austere and massive monasteries of old Spain. It is still the largest edifice in the Americas constructed by Spanish engineers. It was declared a National Historic Monument in 1954. On the building's second floor is the Museo de las Américas (p. 134).

After your visit to Cuartel de Ballajá, exit through the extremely narrow eastern door, where you'll immediately spot one of the most dramatic modern plazas in Puerto Rico, the:

⓭ Plaza del Quinto Centenario

This plaza is a terraced tribute to the European colonization of the New World and one of the most elaborate and formal piazzas in Puerto Rico.

Walk a short block to the southeast to reach the ancient borders of the:

⓮ Plaza de San José

The center of this plaza is dominated by a statue of Juan Ponce de León that was cast from English cannons captured during a naval battle in 1797. Around the periphery of the square, notice three important sites: the Museo de Pablo Casals (p. 134); the Casa de los Contrafuertes (House of the Buttresses), which is adjacent to the Museo de Pablo Casals; and the Iglesia de San José, where the conquistador's coat of arms hangs above the altar. This church is one of the oldest places of Christian worship in the New World.

TAKE A BREAK Plaza de San José is home to several prominent bars and restaurants that serve beer, coffee, and simple meals. They include **El Patio de Sam** (p. 159), where locals occupy virtually every nook and bar stool, especially after sundown. Also appealing is El Boquerón, which is in a narrow storefront midway between the two. Stop at any of these places for some refreshment.

Exit from the plaza's southwestern corner and walk downhill along one of the capital's oldest and best-known streets, Calle del Cristo (also known as Calle Cristo). Two blocks later, at the corner of Calle las Monjas, you'll find the venerable walls of:

⓯ El Convento

El Convento was originally conceived as a convent in the 17th century, but it functioned for many decades as one of the few hotels within the Old City. See p. 80.

Diagonally across the street from El Convento lies the island's most famous church and spiritual centerpiece:

⓰ Catedral de San Juan

This distinguished landmark has in recent years been restored to its original Spanish beauty. See p. 131.

Walk 2 more blocks southward along Calle del Cristo, through one of the most attractive shopping districts in the Caribbean. After passing Calle Fortaleza, look on your left for the:

⓱ Centro Nacional de Artes Populares y Artesanías

This building houses the headquarters of the Institute of Puerto Rican Culture. As such, it is assigned to protect the island's precious heritage in arts, crafts, music, and literature. It no longer sells high-quality crafts on these premises, but it uses an outlet on the same street, next to the Iglesia de San José (see "Shopping," later in this chapter).

Continue to the southernmost tip of Calle del Cristo (just a few steps away), to the wrought-iron gates that surround a chapel no bigger than an oversize newspaper kiosk called:

⓲ Capilla de Cristo

The altar here is dedicated to the "Christ of Miracles." See p. 130.

Retrace your steps north for about a block along Calle del Cristo. Turn right on Calle Fortaleza. One block later, turn left onto Calle de San José, which leads to the site of the capital's most symmetrical and beautiful square:

⓳ Plaza de Armas

This broad and open Spanish-style plaza was the original main square of Old San Juan and the very hub of the city. It has a lovely fountain with 19th-century statues representing the four seasons. In times gone by, families with unmarried daughters would parade around the square. It was a proper way for chaperoned young women to catch the eye of young, available men. Two important buildings

The Cathedral of Rum

Called "the Cathedral of Rum," the **Bacardi Distillery** at Route 888, Km 2.6 at Cataño (℗ **787/788-1500**), is the largest of its kind in the world. Reached by taking a 20-minute ferry ride across San Juan Bay (50¢ each way), the distillery produces 100,000 gallons of rum daily. At the site, you can go to the **Casa Bacardi Visitor Center**, Carretera 165, Cataño (℗ **787/788-8400**), for free 90-minute tours Monday to Saturday from 9am to 4:30pm, Sunday 10am to 3:30pm. You are taken on a visit of seven historical displays, including the Bat Theatre, and the Golden Age of the Cocktail Art Deco bar.

Upon entering the first floor, you'll get a glimpse of what rum production was like a century ago, including oak barrels used in the aging process and an old sugar-cane wagon. On the fifth floor you'll enter the Hall of Rum with a collection of beverages made by the corporation over a period of years. You'll then witness "the birth of rum"—the fermentation processes of molasses (it takes 100 gal. of molasses to produce one barrel of rum).

You'll visit the Bacardi Family Museum, documenting the family's history, and you can watch a short video about the bottling process. At the end of the tour you're taken on a trolley ride to the Hospitality Pavilion where you can pick up a souvenir and have one for the road.

flanking this square are the neoclassical Intendencia (which houses some offices of the U.S. State Department) and San Juan's Alcaldía (see "Historic Sights," earlier in this chapter).

Relax on one of the benches if you like, and then leave the square eastward, along Calle San Francisco.

TAKE A BREAK
La Bombonera, Calle San Francisco 259 (℗ **787/722-0658**), offers take-away baked goods, as well as sandwiches, spicy platters of Puerto Rican food, and richly scented coffee. No one will mind if you just order something to drink, but this is a good place for lunch, as the portions are copious and inexpensive. It's rather informal; the place bustles, and no one goes away hungry.

After your pick-me-up, continue your promenade eastward along the length of Calle San Francisco. It will eventually deposit you beside the traffic, parked cars, and open-air conviviality of the very large:

⑳ Plaza de Colón

This plaza features a stone column topped with a statue of Christopher Columbus (see "Historic Squares," earlier in this chapter). To the side of the square is the Teatro Tapía (p. 136), which has been restored to its original 19th-century elegance.

Continue along Calle San Francisco to the intersection with Calle de Valle, turn left, and follow the signs to:

㉑ Fort San Cristóbal

This fort was built as part of the string of fortifications guarding one of Spain's then-most-valuable colonies. Today, like its twin, El Morro, it is maintained by the National Park Service and can be visited throughout the day. See p. 130.

2 Diving, Fishing, Tennis & Other Outdoor Pursuits

Active vacationers have a wide choice of things to do in San Juan, from beaching to windsurfing. The beachside hotels, of course, offer lots of watersports activities (see chapter 5).

THE BEACHES

Some public stretches of shoreline around San Juan are overcrowded, especially on Saturday and Sunday; others are practically deserted. If you find that secluded, hidden beach of your dreams, proceed with caution. On unguarded beaches you'll have no way to protect yourself or your valuables should you be approached by a robber or mugger, which has been known to happen. For more information about the island's many beaches, call the **Department of Sports and Recreation** at ℭ 787/728-5668.

All beaches on Puerto Rico, even those fronting the top hotels, are open to the public. Public bathing beaches are called *balnearios* and charge for parking and for use of facilities, such as lockers and showers. Beach hours in general are 9am to 5pm in winter, to 6pm off season. Major public beaches in the San Juan area have changing rooms and showers.

Famous with beach buffs since the 1920s, **Condado Beach** 𝒞𝒞 put San Juan on the map as a tourist resort. Backed up by high-rise hotels, it seems more like Miami Beach than any other beach in the Caribbean. From parasailing to sailing, all sorts of watersports can be booked at kiosks along the beach or at the activities desk of the hotels. There are also plenty of outdoor bars and restaurants. Lifeguards are on duty daily from 8:30am to 5pm; and there are outdoor showers and beach chairs to rent. Public toilets are rare along the Condado. People-watching is a favorite sport along these golden strands.

A favorite of Sanjuaneros themselves, **Isla Verde Beach** 𝒞𝒞 is also ideal for swimming, and it, too, is lined with high-rise resorts a la Miami Beach. Many luxury condos are on this beachfront. Isla Verde has picnic tables, so you can pick up the makings of a lunch and make it a day at the beach. This strip is also good for snorkeling because of its calm, clear waters, and many kiosks will rent you equipment. Isla Verde Beach extends from the end of Ocean Park to the beginning of a section called Boca Cangrejos. The best beach at Isla Verde is at Hotel El San Juan. Most sections of this long strip have separate names, such as El Alambique, which is often the site of beach parties, and Punta El Medio, bordering the Ritz-Carlton, also a great beach and very popular, even with the locals. If you go past the luxury hotels and expensive condos behind the Luís Muñoz Marín International Airport, you arrive at the major public beach at Isla Verde. Here you'll find parking, showers, fast-food joints, and watersports equipment. The sands here are whiter than those of the Condado, and they are lined with coconut palms, sea-grape trees, and even almond trees, all of which provide shade from the fierce noonday sun.

One of the most attractive beaches in the Greater San Juan area is **Ocean Park Beach** 𝒞𝒞, a mile (1.6km) of fine gold sand in a neighborhood east of Condado. This beach attracts both young people and a big gay crowd. Access to the beach at Ocean Park is limited, but the best place to enter is from a section called El Ultimo Trolley. This area is ideal for volleyball, paddleball, and other games. The easternmost portion, known as Punta Las Marias, is best for windsurfing. The waters at Ocean Park are fine for swimming, although they can get rough at times. On the downside, there are few amenities.

Rivaling Condado and Isla Verde beaches, **Luquillo Beach** is the grandest in Puerto Rico and one of the most popular. It's 30 miles (48km) east of San Juan, near the town of Luquillo (see chapter 8).

SPORTS & OTHER OUTDOOR PURSUITS

BIKE RENTALS   The best places to bike are along Avenida Ashford (in Condado), Calle Loíza (between Condado and Ocean Park), and Avenida Baldorioty de Castro (in Santurce). Other streets in this area may be too congested. Similarly, because of the traffic, biking in Old San Juan is not recommended.

CRUISES   For the best cruises of San Juan Bay, go to **Caribe Aquatic Adventures** (see "Scuba Diving," below). Bay cruises start at $25 per person.

DEEP-SEA FISHING ⚓   Deep-sea fishing is top-notch here. Allison tuna, white and blue marlin, sailfish, wahoo, dolphin (mahimahi), mackerel, and tarpon are some of the fish that can be caught in Puerto Rican waters, where 30 world records have been broken. Charter arrangements can be made through most major hotels and resorts.

Benitez Fishing Charters can be contacted directly at P.O. Box 9066541, Puerto de Tierra, San Juan, PR 00906 (✆ **787/723-2292** until 6pm). The captain offers a 45-foot (14m) air-conditioned deluxe Hatteras called the *Sea Born.* Fishing tours for parties of up to six cost $490 for a half-day excursion, $550 for a half-day excursion, and $700 for a full day, with beverages and all equipment included.

GOLF   A 45-minute drive east from San Juan on the northeast coast takes you to Palmer and its 6,145-yard (5,619m) **Westin Rio Mar Golf Course** ⚓ (✆ **787/888-6000**). Inexperienced golfers gravitate toward this course, even though trade winds can influence your game along the holes bordering the water, and occasional fairway flooding can present some unwanted obstacles. Greens fees are $165 for hotel guests, $190 for nonguests. A gallery of 100 iguanas also adds spice to your game at Rio Mar. Experienced golfers should head to Dorado (30 min. west of San Juan) for the more challenging (and more famous) courses at the former **Hyatt Dorado Beach Resort & Country Club** ⚓⚓. (*Note:* The Dorado is closing as we go to print, though golf courses and tennis courts are expected to stay open indefinitely). Designed by Robert Trent Jones, Sr., these courses have hosted professional tournaments including the World Cup of Golf (see the "World-Class Golf at the Former Hyatt Dorado" box on p. 171).

HORSE RACING   Great thoroughbreds and outstanding jockeys compete year-round at **El Comandante,** Calle 65 de Infantería, Route 3, Km 15.3, at Canovanas (✆ **787/724-6060**), Puerto Rico's only racetrack, a 20-minute drive east of the center of San Juan. Post time varies from 2:45 to 5:30pm on Monday, Wednesday, Friday, Saturday, and Sunday. Entrance to the clubhouse costs $3; no admission is charged for the grandstand.

RUNNING   The cool, quiet, morning hours before 8am are a good time to jog through the streets of Old San Juan. Head for the wide thoroughfares adjacent to El Morro and then San Cristóbal, whose walls jut upward from the flat ground. You might join Puerto Rico's governor, a dedicated runner, in making several laps around the seafront Paseo de la Princesa at the base of his home, La Fortaleza.

If you don't mind heading out into the island a bit from your base in Old San Juan, you might opt for a run through the palm trees of the Parque Central, near Calle Cerra and Route 2 in Santurce. Condado's Avenida Ashford is a busy site for morning runners as well.

SCUBA DIVING   In San Juan, the best outfitter is **Caribe Aquatic Adventures,** Normandie Hotel San Juan, Calle 19 1062, Villa Nevarez (© **787/281-8858;** www.diveguide.com/p2046.htm). Its dive shop is open daily from 9am to 9pm. This outfitter will take you to the best local dive sites in the Greater San Juan area. Dives begin at $125 per person and a resort course for first-time divers also costs $125. Escorted dive jaunts to the eastern shore are also offered. Snorkeling lessons or tours lasting 1 hour and including basic equipment go for $50. Other activities include deep-sea fishing trips, costing $490 per half-day with a maximum of six fishermen. Another good outfitter is **Ocean Sports,** Av. Ashford 1035 (© **787/723-8513**) on the Condado, offering diving courses and scuba diving, along with an array of watersports such as snorkeling gear ($20 per half-day), or kayak rentals ($20 per half-day). Half-day diving trips in the San Juan area range from $75 to $95 per person, and a NAUI certification course goes for $350.

SNORKELING   Snorkeling is better in the outlying portions of the island than in overcrowded San Juan. But if you don't have time to explore greater Puerto Rico, you'll find that most of the popular beaches, such as Luquillo and Isla Verde, have pretty good visibility and kiosks that rent equipment. Snorkeling equipment generally rents for $15. If you're on your own in the San Juan area, one of the best places is the San Juan Bay marina near the Caribe Hilton.

Watersports desks at the big San Juan hotels at Isla Verde and Condado can generally make arrangements for instruction and equipment rental and can also lead you to the best places for snorkeling, depending on where you are in the sprawling metropolis. If your hotel doesn't offer such services, you can contact **Caribe Aquatic Adventures** (see "Scuba Diving," above), which caters to both snorkelers and scuba divers. You can also rent equipment from **Caribbean School of Aquatics,** Taft No. 1, Suite 10F, San Juan (© **787/728-6606**).

> **Tips   Swimmers, Beware**
>
> You have to pick your spots carefully if you want to swim along Condado Beach. The waters along the Condado Plaza Hotel are calmer than in other areas because of a coral breakwater. The beach near the Marriott is not good for swimming because of rocks and an undertow.

SPAS & FITNESS CENTERS   If a spa figures into your holiday plans, the grandest and largest such facility in San Juan is found at **Ritz-Carlton San Juan Hotel, Spa & Casino** ⊛, Avenida de los Gobernadores 6961, no. 187, Isla Verde (© **787/ 253-1700**). You get it all here: the luxury life, with state-of-the-art massages, body wraps and scrubs, facials, manicures, pedicures, and a salon guaranteed to make you look like a movie star.

In an elegant marble-and-stone setting, there are 11 rooms for pampering, including hydrotherapy and treatments custom-tailored for individual needs. The spa also features a 7,200-square-foot (669-sq. m) outdoor swimming pool.

The Ritz-Carlton facility is the only spa in the Caribbean to offer the exotic and ritualistic treatments known to spa lovers around the world as the Balinese Massage and the Javanese Lulur. The fragrant Balinese Massage uses compression, skin-rolling, wringing, and percussion and thumb-walking to "de-stress" the most uptight guests. The Lulur originated centuries ago in the royal palaces of Central Java as part of a

Finds   La Vida Loca & La Criolla Chic

Puerto Rico's newly acquired Latino chic is putting it closer into competition with the very hip South Miami Beach scene in Florida.

There is no hipper venue in San Juan today than the **Museo de Arte** (p. 133). It took $55 million to turn this 1920s city hospital in Santurce, an eyesore for decades, into this new home for art. The new museum has become a way of life for some Puerto Ricans, many of whom go here at least once a week—perhaps to see a production in the 400-seat theater, named for Raúl Juliá, the late Puerto Rican actor, or perhaps to go for a romantic stroll through the museum's 5-acre (2-hectare) garden. Many chic trendsetters return at night for a nuevo criolla meal at **Pikayo** (p. 115).

The emerging neighborhood for the chic set is called **SoFo,** a sector that lies south of Calle Fortaleza in Old Town. This place is becoming so trendy that it is the first of the Old San Juan neighborhoods to be awarded its own acronym, no doubt inspired by New York's SoHo. The **Parrot Club** (p. 107) is the hot spot of the neighborhood, quickly rivaled by **Trois Cent Onze** (p. 107).

Even beaches attract trendsetters. Students, surfers, gay people, and those on the see-and-be-seen circuit avoid the beaches of Condado and Isla Verde, heading for **Ocean Park Beach** instead.

Tired of chic? To mix with the locals, head for the **Mercado de Río Piedras** (Paseo José de Diego), with its 4 blocks of shops and cheap restaurants. (You can reach this area by taxi or car. From the Condado or Santurce, take Av. Ponce de León south until you come to the intersection with Rte. 47 going east. The route is also called Paseo José de Diego. The market will soon appear on your right.) This vast outdoor mall is scented with everything from recently caught fish to just-picked citrus. When Sanjuaneros want to buy anything, they head here. Open from early morning to late evening (but not on Sun), these stores and markets provide a whiff of local life that's unseen anywhere else in San Juan.

When you're tired of museums and shopping, you can head for the boardwalk at **Parque Lineal Marti Coli,** which stretches for nearly 2 miles (3.2km) along Caño de Martín Peña, from Hato Rey to Parque Central. Eventually this boardwalk will reach a distance of nearly 12 miles (19km), linking Old Town with Río Piedras. Biking, hiking, and jogging pathways are planned; one day bikers will be able to go along the breadth of San Juan without having to encounter traffic. In the meantime, enough trails have been completed for a memorable stroll.

Later you can head for **Rumba** (p. 159) to dance the night away to the sounds of salsa and a bomba with an African beat.

ritual for royal brides-to-be. The Lulur was performed daily to beautify, soften, and "sweeten" the bride's skin. Today women and men alike enjoy it.

The only resort spa that challenges the Ritz-Carlton is the runner-up, the newly launched Olas Spa at the **Carib Hilton,** Calle Los Rosales (© **787/721-0303**). The spa offers everything from traditional massages to more exotic body and water therapies, using such products as honey, cucumber, sea salts, seaweed, or mud baths. You can choose your delight among the massages, including one called "Rising Sun," a traditional Japanese form of massage called shiatsu that uses pressure applied with hands, elbows, and knees on specific body points. Among body wraps is one known as Firm Away, a super-firming, brown and green algae body cocoon therapy for a soft, toned, and smooth skin.

The Hilton Spa has the town's best program for hair treatments, including thinning hair and "tired perm." It also has a state-of-the-art fitness center with Universal and Nautilus weight machines, aerobics and yoga classes, treadmills, aerobicycles, loofah body polishes, and facials.

After the extravaganza of these two spas, it's a bit of a comedown at the other leading resorts. The Plaza Spa at the **Condado Plaza Hotel & Casino,** Av. Ashford 999 (© 787/ 721-1000), features Universal weight-training machines, video exercycles, a sauna, whirlpools, and a spa program of facials and massage. We'd recommend this mainly for people who want only minor spa or fitness-center facilities during their stay, and not for those who want to make a spa the number-one goal of their sojourn in San Juan.

El San Juan Hotel & Casino Resort, Av. Isla Verde 6063 (© 787/791-1000), offers a stunning panoramic view of San Juan that almost competes with the facilities. You'll find full amenities, including fitness evaluations, supervised weight-loss programs, aerobics classes, a sauna, a steam room, and luxury massages. A daily fee for individual services is assessed if you want special treatment or care.

If your hotel doesn't have a gym or health club of its own, consider working the kinks out of your muscles at **International Fitness** ☞, Av. Ashford 1131, Condado (© 787/721-0717). It's air-conditioned, well equipped, and popular with residents of the surrounding high-rent district. Entrance costs $15 per visit, $50 for 5 days, or $55 for a week. Hours are Monday to Thursday 5am to 10pm, Friday 5am to 9pm, Saturday 9am to 7pm, and Sunday 10am to 3pm.

TENNIS   Most of the big resorts have their own tennis courts for the use of guests. There are 12 public courts, lit at night, at **San Juan Central Municipal Park,** at Calle Cerra (exit on Rte. 2; © 787/722-1646), open daily. Fees are $3 per hour from 6am to 5pm, and $4 per hour from 6 to 10pm.

WINDSURFING   The most savvy windsurfing advice and equipment rental is available at **Velauno,** Calle Loíza 2430, Punta Las Marías in San Juan (© 787/728-8716). A 1-day rental costs $75, 3 days $150, and 1 week $225. This is the second-biggest full-service headquarters for windsurfing in the United States. The staff here will guide you to the best windsurfing, which is likely to be the Punta Las Marías in the greater San Juan metropolitan area. Office hours are Monday to Friday 10am to 7pm, Saturday 11am to 7pm. Other spots on the island for windsurfing include Santa Isabel, Guánica, and La Parguera in the south; Jobos and Shacks in the northwest, and the island of Culebra off the eastern coast.

3 Shopping

Because Puerto Rico is a U.S. commonwealth, U.S. citizens don't pay duty on items brought back to the mainland. And you can still find great bargains on Puerto Rico, where the competition among shopkeepers is fierce. Even though the U.S. Virgin Islands are duty-free, you can often find far lower prices on many items in San Juan than on St. Thomas.

Tips **Know When the Price Is Right**

The only way to determine if you're paying less for an item in San Juan than you would at home is to find out what the going rate is in your hometown. Obviously, if you can find items in San Juan cheaper than back home, go for it. But know the prices before you go. Otherwise, you could end up lugging merchandise back on an airplane when the same item was available at about the same price, or less, where you live.

The streets of Old Town, such as Calle San Francisco and Calle del Cristo, are the major venues for shopping. Malls in San Juan are generally open Monday to Saturday 9am to 9pm, Sunday 11am to 5pm. Regular stores in town are usually open Monday to Saturday 9am to 6pm. In Old San Juan many stores are open on Sunday, too.

Native handicrafts can be good buys, including needlework, straw work, ceramics, hammocks, and papier-mâché fruits and vegetables, as well as paintings and sculptures by Puerto Rican artists. Among these, the carved wooden religious idols known as *santos* (saints) have been called Puerto Rico's greatest contribution to the plastic arts and are sought by collectors. For the best selection of santos, head for Galería Botello (see "Art," below), Olé, or Puerto Rican Arts & Crafts (see "Gifts & Handicrafts," below).

Puerto Rico's biggest and most up-to-date shopping mall is **Plaza Las Américas,** in the financial district of Hato Rey, right off the Las Américas Expressway. This complex, with its fountains and modern architecture, has more than 200 mostly upscale shops. The variety of goods and prices is roughly comparable to that of large stateside malls.

Unless otherwise specified, the following stores can be reached via the Old Town Trolley.

ANTIQUES

El Alcazar *Finds*   Established in 1986 by retired career officers with the U.S. Army and the U.S. State Department, this is the largest emporium of antique furniture, silver, and art objects in the Caribbean. The best way to sift through the massive inventory is to begin at the address listed below, on Calle San José between Calle Luna and Calle Sol, and ask the owners, Sharon and Robert Bartos, to guide you to the other three buildings that are literally stuffed with important art and antiques. Each shop lies within a half-block of the organization's headquarters, and each is within a historic building of architectural or historical importance (public areas of several large Puerto Rican hotels contain furnishings acquired here). For antique silver, crystal, delicate porcelain, glittering chandeliers, Russian icons, and objects of religious devotion such as santos, look first at the organization's headquarters. Some of the objects, especially the 1930s-era dining-room sets, whose chair backs are composed of wood medallions held in place by woven canes or wicker, derive from Puerto Rico. The majority of the objects, however, are culled from estates and galleries throughout Europe. Calle San José 103. ✆ 787/723-1229.

ART

Butterfly People   Butterfly People is a gallery and cafe in a handsomely restored building in Old San Juan. Butterflies, sold here in artfully arranged boxes, range from $20 for a single mounting to thousands of dollars for whole-wall murals. The butterflies are preserved and will last forever. The dimensional artwork is sold in limited editions and can be shipped worldwide. Most of these butterflies come from farms around the world, some of the most beautiful hailing from Indonesia, Malaysia, and New Guinea. Tucked away within the same premises is **Malula Antiques.** Specializing in tribal art from the Moroccan sub-Sahara and Syria, it contains a sometimes-startling collection of primitive and timeless crafts and accessories. Calle Cruz 152. ℂ 787/723-2432.

The Canvas Gallery   This is one of the better art galleries we've seen in San Juan, with the kind of paintings you'd expect at a major gallery in Madrid or New York, and very few hints of anything vaguely associated with the tourist trade. Paintings on display here are sometimes moved upstairs to the Sake Sushi Bar, which is separately recommended and which is under the same management, to add to the nightlife ambience there. Paintings at The Canvas Gallery begin at $1,800. Recinto Sur 305. ℂ 787/977-1080.

Galería Botello ℛ   A contemporary Latin American art gallery, Galería Botello is a living tribute to the late Angel Botello, one of Puerto Rico's most outstanding artists. Born after the Spanish Civil War in a small village in Galicia, Spain, he fled to the Caribbean and spent 12 years in Haiti. His paintings and bronze sculptures, evocative of his colorful background, are done in a style uniquely his own. This galería is his former colonial mansion home, which he restored himself. Today it displays his paintings and sculptures, showcases the works of many outstanding local artists, and offers a large collection of Puerto Rican antique santos. Calle del Cristo 208. ℂ 787/723-9987.

Galería Fosilarte   This is a specialty gallery, displaying unique art pieces from limestone and coral that may have existed at the time of the dinosaurs. The work is the creation of Radamés Rivera. One of the gallery's most noted artists is Yolanda Velasquez, who paints in an abstract style. The gallery also showcases the work of some 40 other artists, ranging from Mexico to Cuba. Calle Cristo 200B. ℂ 787/725-4252.

Galería Palomas ℛ   This and the also-recommended Galería Botello are the two leading art galleries of Puerto Rico. Here you can find works by some of the leading painters in Latin America. Prices start at $300, and exhibits are rotated every 4 weeks. The setting is a 17th-century colonial house. Of special note are works by such local artists as Homer, Moya, and Alicea. Calle del Cristo 207. ℂ 787/724-8904.

Galería San Juan   This shop, located at the Gallery Inn, specializes in the sculpture and paintings of Jan D'Esopo, a Connecticut-born artist who has spent a great deal of time in Puerto Rico. Many of her fine pieces are in bronze. In the Gallery Inn, Calle Norzagaray 204. ℂ 787/722-1808.

Sun 'n Sand   This is the best store in San Juan for Haitian art and artifacts. Its walls are covered with framed versions of primitive Haitian landscapes, portraits, crowd scenes, and whimsical visions of jungles where lions, tigers, parrots, and herons take on quasi-human personalities and forms. Most paintings range from $20 to $350, although you can usually bargain them down a bit. Look for the brightly painted wall hangings crafted from sheets of metal. Also look for satirical metal wall hangings, brightly painted, representing the *tap-taps* (battered public minivans and buses) of Port-au-Prince. They make amusing and whimsical souvenirs of a trip to the Caribbean. Calle Fortaleza 152. ℂ 787/722-1135.

BOOKS

Bell, Book & Candle   For travel guides, maps, and beach-reading material, head here. It is a large, general-interest bookstore that carries fiction and classics in both

Fun Fact   Grotesque Masks

The most popular of all Puerto Rican crafts are the frightening **caretas**—papier-mâché masks worn at island carnivals. Tangles of menacing horns, fang-toothed leering expressions, and bulging eyes of these half-demon, half-animal creations send children running and screaming to their parents. At carnival time, they are worn by costumed revelers called *vegigantes*. Vegigantes often wear bat-winged jumpsuits and roam the streets either individually or in groups.

The origins of these masks and carnivals may go back to medieval Spain and/or tribal Africa. A processional tradition in Spain, dating from the early 17th century, was intended to terrify sinners with marching devils in the hope that they would return to church. Cervantes described it briefly in *Don Quijote*. Puerto Rico blended this Spanish procession with the masked tradition brought by slaves from Africa. Some historians believe that the Taínos were also accomplished mask makers, which would make this a very ancient tradition indeed.

The predominant traditional mask colors were black, red, and yellow, all symbols of hellfire and damnation. Today, pastels are more likely to be used. Each vegigante sports at least two or three horns, although some masks have hundreds of horns, in all shapes and sizes. Mask making in Ponce, the major center for this craft, and in Loíza Aldea, a palm-fringed town on the island's northeastern coast, has since led to a renaissance of Puerto Rican folk art.

The premier store selling these masks is **La Calle** (below). Masks can be seen in action at the three big masquerade carnivals on the island: the Ponce Festival in February, the Festival of Loíza Aldea in July, and the Día de las Mascaras at Hatillo in December.

Spanish and English, plus a huge selection of postcards. Av. José de Diego 102, Santurce. © 787/728-5000. Bus: A5.

Libreria Cronopios   This is the leading choice in the Old Town, with the largest selection of titles. It sells a number of books on Puerto Rican culture as well as good maps of the island. Calle San José 255. © 787/724-1815.

CARNIVAL MASKS

La Calle   Every Puerto Rican knows that the best, and cheapest, place to buy brightly painted carnival masks *(caretas)* is in Ponce, where the tradition of making them from papier-mâché originated. But if you can't spare the time for a side excursion to Ponce, this store in Old San Juan stocks one of the most varied inventories of vegigantes in the Puerto Rican capital. Depending on their size and composition (some include coconut shells, gourds, and flashy metal trim), they range from $10 to $2,500 each. Side-by-side with the pagan-inspired masks, you'll find a well-chosen selection of paintings by talented local artists, priced from $25 to $2,800 each. Calle Fortaleza 105. © 787/725-1306.

CIGARS

Club Jibarito   This is the retail outlet of a Puerto Rican–based manufacturer of genuinely excellent cigars. You can select from the Jibarito cigars that are proudly displayed within one of the best-designed humidors in town. Overall it's our favorite cigar emporium in San Juan, with a polite staff and lots and lots of class. Calle Cristo 202. © 787/724-7797.

CLOTHING & BEACHWEAR

Mrs. and Miss Boutique   The most visible article available within this shop is "the magic dress," for $115. Crafted in Morocco of a silky-looking blend of rayon and cotton, it comes in 10 different colors or patterns and can be worn 11 different ways. (A saleswoman will show you how.) The shop also stocks sarongs for $9 and long dresses, sometimes from Indonesia, that begin at only $25. Calle Fortaleza 154. © 787/724-8571.

Nono Maldonado   Named after its owner, a Puerto Rico–born designer who worked for many years as the fashion editor of *Esquire* magazine, this is one of the most fashionable and upscale haberdashers in the Caribbean. Selling both men's and women's clothing, it contains everything from socks to dinner jackets, as well as ready-to-wear versions of Maldonado's twice-a-year collections. Both ready-to-wear and couture are available here. Av. Ashford 1051. © 787/721-0456. Bus: A7.

Polo Ralph Lauren Factory Store *Value*   It's as stylish and carefully orchestrated as anything you'd expect from one of North America's leading clothiers. Even better, its prices are often 35% to 40% less than in retail stores on the U.S. mainland. You can find even greater discounts on irregular or slightly damaged garments, but inspect them carefully before buying. The store occupies two floors of a pair of colonial buildings, with one upstairs room devoted to home furnishings. Calle del Cristo 201. © 787/722-2136.

Suravaya (Serenity)   Come here for unusual and not-very-expensive women's dresses styled and designed by the owner, Adele Rodriguez. Each is made from 100% rayon priced at between $40 and $60 each. Clingy and colorful (the staff here refers to them as "classy and sassy"), they're the most obvious draw into this store. Once you're inside, you'll also be tempted with an array of incense, jewelry, handbags, bellydancing accessories, and CDs with music from around the world. Calle Fortaleza 259. © 787/724-7606.

W. H. Smith   This outlet sells mostly women's clothing, everything from bathing suits and beach attire to jogging suits. For men, there are shorts, bathing suits, and jogging suits. There's also a good selection of books and maps. In the Condado Plaza Hotel, Av. Ashford 999. © 787/721-1000, ext. 2094.

COFFEE & SPICES

Spicy Caribbee   This shop has the best selection of Puerto Rican coffee, which is gaining an increasingly good reputation among aficionados. Alto Grande is the grandest brand. Other favorite brands of Puerto Rican coffee are Café Crema, Café Rico, Rioja, and Yaucono—in that order. The shop also has Old Town's best array of hot spicy sauces of the Caribbean. Calle Cristo 154. © 787/725-4690.

Xian Imports   Set within a jumbled, slightly claustrophobic setting, you'll discover porcelain, sculptures, paintings, and Chinese furniture, much of it antique. Island decorators favor this spot as a source for unusual art objects. Calle de la Cruz 153. © 787/723-2214.

The Coffee of Kings & Popes

Of all the coffees of Puerto Rico, our favorite is **Alto Grande,** which has been a tradition in Puerto Rican households since 1839. Over the years, this super premium coffee has earned a reputation for being the "Coffee of Popes and Kings," and is hailed as one of the top three coffees in the world. A magnificently balanced coffee, Alto Grande is a rare and exotic coffee with a sweet, pointed aroma and a bright sparkling flavor. The bean is grown in the highest mountains of the Lares range. This coffee is served at leading hotels and restaurants in Puerto Rico. Should you develop a taste for it, it is also available at various specialty stores throughout the United States.

DEPARTMENT STORES

Marshalls   This store, part of the U.S. discount chain, is one of our favorite department stores in the whole Caribbean. Thousands of Sanjuaneros also consider it their favorite shopping expedition as well. A few dedicated born-to-shop advocates pop in virtually every day to see what new items have gone on sale. At Plaza de Armas, across from the City Hall, expect to see a massive array—at cut-rate prices—of designer clothes, housewares, home furnishings, and shoes, plus a variety of other merchandise. Calle Rafael Cordero 154. ✆ 787/722-3020.

GIFTS & HANDICRAFTS

Atmosphere   Inventory within this exotic-looking gift and housewares store derives from countries with rich traditions in handicrafts. That includes Indonesia (especially Bali), Turkey, India, Mexico, Peru, and Puerto Rico. Come here with ideas about how to decorate, say, an outdoor veranda for warm-weather hangouts. Calle Cristo 205. ✆ 787/ 977-2225.

Bared & Sons *Value*   Now in its fourth decade, this is the main outlet of a chain of at least 20 upper-bracket jewelry stores on Puerto Rico. It has a worthy inventory of gemstones, gold, diamonds, and wristwatches on the street level, which does a thriving business with cruise-ship passengers. But the real value of this store lies one floor up, where a monumental collection of porcelain and crystal is on display in claustrophobic proximity. It's a great source for hard-to-get and discontinued patterns (priced at around 20% less than at equivalent stateside outlets) from Christofle, Royal Doulton, Wedgwood, Limoges, Royal Copenhagen, Lalique, Lladró, Herend, Baccarat, and Daum. San Justo 206 (at the corner of Calle Fortaleza). ✆ 787/724-4811.

Bóveda   This long, narrow space is crammed with exotic jewelry, clothing, greeting cards with images of life in Puerto Rico, some 100 handmade lamps, antiques, Mexican punched tin and glass, and Art Nouveau reproductions, among other items. Calle del Cristo 209. ✆ 787/725-0263.

Centro Nacional de Artes Populares y Artesanias   This store, a superb repository of native crafts, sells crafts of high-quality work. Centro Nacional scans the islands for artisans who still practice time-treasured crafts and do so with considerable skill. The prices aren't cheap, but the work merits the tab. At Calle del Cristo. ✆ 787/721-6866.

El Artesano   If your budget doesn't allow for an excursion to the Andes, head for this shop. You'll find Mexican and Peruvian icons of the Virgin Mary; charming depictions of fish and Latin American birds in terra cotta and brass; all kinds of woven goods; painted cupboards, chests, and boxes; and mirrors and Latin dolls. Calle Fortaleza 314. © 787/721-6483.

Libreria y Tienda de Artesania del Instituto de Cultura Puertorriqueña
This store, next to the Convento de los Dominicos, has not only a collection of books on Puerto Rico, but a good display of crafts in the Old Town, including santos, Indian artifacts, carnival masks (many from Ponce), and baskets. All pieces are said to be made in Puerto Rico, rather than in places such as Taiwan, as is so often the case. Calle Norzagaray 98. © 787/721-6866.

Olé Browsing this store is a learning experience. Even the standard Panama hat takes on new dimensions. Woven from fine-textured *paja* grass and priced from $20 to $1,000, depending on the density of the weave, the hats are all created the same size, then blocked—by an employee on-site—to fit the shape of your head. Dig into this store's diverse inventory to discover a wealth of treasures—hand-beaten Chilean silver, Peruvian Christmas ornaments, Puerto Rican santos—almost all from Puerto Rico or Latin America. Calle Fortaleza 105. © 787/724-2445.

⟮Tips⟯ Shopping for Santos

The most impressive of the island's crafts are the santos, carved religious figures that have been produced since the 1500s. Craftspeople who make these are called *santeros;* using clay, gold, stone, or cedar wood, they carve figurines representing saints, usually from 8 to 20 inches (20–51 centimeters) tall. Before the Spanish colonization, small statues called *zemi* stood in native tribal villages and camps as objects of veneration, and Puerto Rico's santos may derive from that pre-Columbian tradition. Every town has its patron saint, and every home has its santos to protect the family. For some families, worshipping the santos replaces a traditional Mass.

Art historians view the carving of santos as Puerto Rico's greatest contribution to the plastic arts. The earliest figures were richly baroque, indicating a strong Spanish influence, but as the islanders began to assert their own identity, the carved figures often became simpler.

In carving santos, craftspeople often used handmade tools. Sometimes such natural materials as vegetable dyes and even human hair were used. The saints represented by most santos can be identified by their accompanying symbols; for example, Saint Anthony is usually depicted with the infant Jesus and a book. The most popular group of santos is the Three Kings. The Trinity and the Nativity are also depicted frequently.

Art experts claim that santos–making approached its zenith at the turn of the 20th century, although hundreds of santeros still practice their craft throughout the island. Serious santos collectors view the former craftsmen of old as the true artists in the field. The best collection of santos is found at Puerto Rican Arts & Crafts (p. 156).

Some of the best santos on the island can be seen at the Capilla de Cristo in Old San Juan. Perhaps at some future date, a museum devoted entirely to santos will open in Puerto Rico.

Puerto Rican Arts & Crafts   Set in a 200-year-old colonial building, this unique store is one of the premier outlets on the island for authentic artifacts. Of particular interest are papier-mâché carnival masks from Ponce, whose grotesque and colorful features were originally conceived to chase away evil spirits. Taíno designs inspired by ancient petroglyphs are incorporated into most of the sterling silver jewelry sold here. There's an art gallery in back, with silk-screened serigraphs by local artists. The outlet has a gourmet Puerto Rican food section with items like coffee, rum, and hot sauces for sale. A related specialty of this well-respected store involves the exhibition and sale of modern replicas of the Spanish colonial tradition of santos, which are carved and sometimes polychromed representations of the Catholic saints and the infant Jesus. Priced from $50 to $1,100 each, and laboriously carved by artisans in private studios around the island, they're easy to pack in a suitcase because the largest one measures only 12 inches (31 centimeters) from halo to toe. Calle Fortaleza 204. ✆ 787/725-5596.

JEWELRY

Barrachina's   The birthplace, in 1963, of the piña colada (an honor co-claimed by the staff at the Caribe Hilton), Barrachina's is a favorite of cruise-ship passengers. It offers one of the largest selections of jewelry, perfume, cigars, and gifts in San Juan. There's a patio for drinks where you can order (what else?) a piña colada. There is also a Bacardi rum outlet (bottles cost less than stateside but cost the same as at the Bacardi distillery), a costume jewelry department, a gift shop, and a section for authentic silver jewelry, plus a restaurant. Calle Fortaleza 104 (between Calle del Cristo and Calle San José). ✆ 787/725-7912.

Eduardo Barquet   Known as a leading cost-conscious place to buy fine jewelry in Old San Juan, this shop has 14-karat Italian gold chains and bracelets that are measured, fitted, and sold by weight. You can purchase watches or beautiful gems in modern settings in both 14- and 18-karat gold. The store's collection also includes emerald, ruby, diamond, and pearl jewelry, along with platinum bridal jewelry. Calle Fortaleza 200 (at the corner of Calle La Cruz). ✆ 787/723-1989.

Emerald Isles   This jewelry boutique in the Old Town is smaller than other entities that specialize in colored gemstones, but because of its much lower overheads, its prices can sometimes be more reasonable. It specializes in Colombian emeralds, set into silver or gold settings already, or waiting for you to select one. But as long as you're in the shop, look also at the unusual inventories of contemporary reproductions of pre-Columbian jewelry, some of it gold-plated and richly enameled. Many of these pieces sell for around $50 each, and some of them are genuinely intriguing. Calle Fortalez 105. ✆ 787/977-3769.

Gaston Bared Jewelry   This is an offshoot of the above-recommended Bared & Sons, but with a more contemporary inventory. Calle Fortaleza 154 (at Calle San José). ✆ 787/722-2172.

Joseph Manchini   This shop displays the works of its namesake, the shop's owner. He conceives almost anything you'd want in gold, silver, and bronze. Some of Old Town's most imaginative rings, bracelets, and chains are displayed here. If you don't like what's on sale, you can design your own jewelry, including pieces made from sapphire, emerald, and rubies. Calle Fortaleza 101. ✆ 787/722-7698.

Joyería Riviera   This emporium of 18-karat gold and diamonds is the island's leading jeweler. Adjacent to Plaza de Armas, the shop has an impeccable reputation. Its

A Dying Art: Old Lace

Another Puerto Rican craft has undergone a big revival just as it seemed that it would disappear forever: lace. Originating in Spain, *mundillos* (tatted fabrics) are the product of a type of bobbin lace making. This 5-century-old craft exists today only in Puerto Rico and Spain.

The first lace made in Puerto Rico was called *torchon* (beggar's lace). Early examples of beggar's lace were considered of inferior quality, but artisans today have transformed this fabric into a delicate art form, eagerly sought by collectors. Lace bands called *entrados* have two straight borders, whereas the other traditional style, *puntilla,* has both a straight and a scalloped border.

The best outlet in San Juan for lace is **Linen House** (below).

owner, Julio Abislaiman, stocks his store from such diamond centers as Antwerp, Tel Aviv, and New York. This is the major distributor of Rolex watches on Puerto Rico. Prices in the store range from $150 into the tens of thousands of dollars—at these prices, it's a good thing you can get "whatever you want," according to the owner. Calle Fortaleza 257. ℂ 787/725-4000.

Piercing Pagoda There's nothing Puerto Rican or glamorous about this branch of a large U.S. chain. But if you're in the market for a gold or silver chain, or perhaps a pendant or set of earrings, the sales here could be worth a detour. Be alert that some displays feature 10-karat gold rather than the more preferable, and expensive, 14- or 18-karat. Av. F.D. Roosevelt. ℂ 787/706-0634.

LACE & LINENS

Linen House This unpretentious store specializes in table linens, bed linens, and lace and has the island's best selection. Some of the most delicate pieces are expensive, but most are moderate in price. Inventories include embroidered shower curtains that sell for around $35 each, and lace doilies, bun warmers, place mats, and tablecloths that seamstresses took weeks to complete. Some astonishingly lovely items are available for as little as $30. The aluminum/pewter serving dishes have beautiful Spanish-colonial designs. Prices here are sometimes 40% lower than those on the North American mainland. Calle Fortaleza 250. ℂ 787/721-4219.

LEATHER & EQUESTRIAN ACCESSORIES

Lalin Leather Shop Although it lies in an out-of-the-way suburb (Puerto Nuevo), about 2 miles (3.2km) south of San Juan, this is the best and most comprehensive cowboy and equestrian outfitter in Puerto Rico, probably in the entire Caribbean. Here you'll find all manner of boots, cowboy hats, and accessories. More important, however, is the wide array of saddles and bridles, some from Colombia, some from Puerto Rico, priced from a cost-conscious $159 to as much as $3,100. Even the highest-priced items cost a lot less than their U.S. mainland equivalents, so if you happen to have a horse or pony on the U.S. mainland, a visit here might be worth your while. If you decide to make the rather inconvenient pilgrimage, you won't be alone. Regular clients come from as far away as Iceland, The Bahamas, and New York. Everything can be shipped. Av. Piñero 1617, Puerto Nuevo. ℂ 787/781-5305. No bus.

MALLS

Belz Factory Outlet World   The largest mall of its kind in Puerto Rico, and the Caribbean as well, opened in 2001 in Canóvanas, east of San Juan en route to El Yunque. Totally enclosed and air-conditioned, it re-creates the experience of strolling through the streets of Old San Juan, sans the traffic and heat. Five interconnected buildings comprise the mall, with dozens of stores from Nike to Gap, from Dockers to Levi's to Maidenform, from Samsonite to Guess, and from Papaya and Geoffrey Beene. State Rd. #3 18400, Barrio Pueblo, Canóvanas. © 787/256-7040. No bus.

MARKETS

Plaza del Mercado de Santurce   If you'd like an old-fashioned Puerto Rican market, something likely to be found in a small South American country, visit this offbeat curiosity. In a West Indian structure, the central market is filled with "botanicas" hawking everything from medicinal herbs to Puerto Rican bay rum. Here is your best chance to pick up some patchouli roots. What are they used for? In religious observances and to kill unruly cockroaches. Some little cantinas here offer very typical Puerto Rican dishes, including roast pork, and you can also order the best mango banana shakes on the island. Calle Dos Hermanos at Calle Capitol, Santurce. © 787/723-8022. Bus: B5.

4 San Juan After Dark

San Juan nightlife comes in all varieties. From the vibrant performing-arts scene to street-level salsa and the casinos, discos, and bars, there's plenty of entertainment available almost any evening.

As in a Spanish city, nightlife begins very late, especially on Friday and Saturday nights. Hang out until the late, late afternoon on the beach, have dinner around 8pm (9 would be even more fashionable), and then the night is yours. The true party animal will rock until the broad daylight.

Qué Pasa?, the official visitor's guide to Puerto Rico, lists cultural events, including music, dance, theater, film, and art exhibits. It's distributed free by the tourist office.

THE PERFORMING ARTS

Centro de Bellas Artes   In the heart of Santurce, the Performing Arts Center is a 6-minute taxi ride from most of the Condado hotels. It contains the Festival Hall, Drama Hall, and the Experimental Theater. Some of the events here will be of interest only to Spanish speakers; others attract an international audience. Av. Ponce de León 22. © 787/724-4747, or 787/725-7334 for the ticket agent. Tickets $40–$200; 50% discounts for seniors. Bus: 1.

Teatro Tapía   Standing across from Plaza de Colón and built about 1832, this is one of the oldest theaters in the Western Hemisphere (see "Historic Sights," earlier in this chapter). Productions, some musical, are staged throughout the year and include drama, dances, and cultural events. You'll have to call the box office (open Mon–Fri 9am–6pm) for specific information. Av. Ponce de León. © 787/721-0180. Tickets $20–$30, depending on the show. Bus: B8 or B21.

THE CLUB & MUSIC SCENE

Brava   Modeled after an artist's rendition of the once-notorious city in Mesopotamia, this nightclub is designed in the form of a circle, with a central dance floor and a wraparound balcony where onlookers and voyeurs—a 25- to 45-year-old age group—can observe the activities on the floor below. As one patron put it, "Here's where gringos can shake their bon-bons with San Juan's old guard." Equipped with one of the best sound systems in the Caribbean, its location within the most exciting hotel in San Juan allows guests the chance to visit the hotel's bars, its intricately decorated lobby, and its casino en route. Open Thursday through Saturday from 10pm until 3am. In El San Juan Hotel & Casino, Av. Isla Verde 6063, Isla Verde. ℂ 787/791-1000. Cover $15, free for residents of El San Juan Hotel. Bus: A5.

Club Laser   Set in the heart of the Old Town, this disco is especially crowded when cruise ships pull into town. Once inside, you can wander over the three floors of its historic premises, listening to whatever music happens to be hot in New York at the time, with lots of additional Latino merengue and salsa thrown in as well. Depending on the night, the age of the crowd varies, but in general it's the 20s, 30s, and even 40s set. The club is usually open Thursday through Sunday from 10pm until 4am. Calle del Cruz 251 (near the corner of Calle Fortaleza). ℂ 787/725-7581. Cover $10–$15 (free cover for women before midnight on Sat). Bus: Old Town Trolley.

Houlihan's   This is a casual hangout, a member of the U.S. chain of restaurants, and a good place to hear merengue, Spanish rock music, and salsa. Houlihan's also serves reasonably priced food, with main courses costing $8 to $21. Open Sunday through Thursday 11:30am to 10pm, and Friday through Saturday 11:30am to midnight. Galeria Paseos Mall, Gran Vulevar 100. ℂ 787/723-8600.

Lupi's   You can hear some of the best Spanish rock at this Mexican pub and restaurant. It is currently a hot spot, with typical South of the Border decoration and such familiar dishes as fajitas, nachos, and burritos. A wide range of people of all ages are attracted to the place, although after 10pm patrons in their 20s and 30s predominate. Live rock groups perform after 11pm. In addition to the nightly rock bands, Caribbean music is also played on Friday and karaoke on Sunday. Open daily 11am to 2am. Carretera 187, Km 1.3, Isla Verde. ℂ 787/253-1664. Bus: A5.

Rumba   This club is small and cramped, but so photogenically hip that it was selected as the site for the filming of many of the crowd scenes within *Dirty Dancing: Havana Nights*. Set immediately adjacent to the also-recommended restaurant, Barú, with which it's not associated, it's known within San Juan's underground nightlife circuit as one of the places to hang. Expect beautiful people and a sense of cutting-edge Hispanic hip. Open Tuesday to Sunday 9pm to 4am. Calle San Sebastián 152. ℂ 787/725-4407. Cover $15. Bus: M2, M3, or A5.

THE BAR SCENE

Unless otherwise stated, there is no cover charge at the following bars.

Cigar Bar   The Palm Court Lobby at the elegant Wyndham El San Juan boasts an impressive cigar bar, with a magnificent repository of the finest stogies in the world. Although the bar is generally filled with visitors, some of San Juan's most fashionable men—and women, too—can be seen puffing away in this chic rendezvous while sipping cognac. Open daily 6pm to 3am. El San Juan Hotel & Casino, Av. Isla Verde 6063, Isla Verde. ℂ 787/791-1000. Bus: A5.

El Patio de Sam   Except for the juicy burgers, we're not so keen on the food served here anymore (and neither are our readers), but we still like to visit Old Town's best-known watering hole, one of the most popular late-night joints with a good selection of beers. Live entertainment is presented here Monday to Saturday. This is a fun

The Birth of the Piña Colada

When actress Joan Crawford tasted the piña colada at what was then the Beachcombers Bar in the **Caribe Hilton**, Calle Los Rosales (© **787/721-0303**), she claimed it was "better than slapping Bette Davis in the face."

This famous drink is the creation of bartender Ramon "Monchito" Marrero, now long gone, who was hired by the Hilton in 1954. He spent 3 months mixing, tasting, and discarding hundreds of combinations until he felt he had the right blend. Thus, the frothy piña colada was born. It's been estimated that some 100 million of them have been sipped around the world since that fateful time.

Monchito never patented his formula and didn't mind sharing it with the world. Still served at the Hilton, here is his not-so-secret recipe:

2 ounces light rum
1 ounce coconut cream
1 ounce heavy cream
6 ounces fresh pineapple
½ cup crushed ice
Pineapple wedge and maraschino cherry for garnish

Pour rum, coconut cream, cream, and pineapple juice in blender. Add ice. Blend for 15 seconds. Pour into a 12-ounce glass. Add garnishes.

joint—that is, if you dine somewhere else before coming here. Open daily noon to 1am. Calle San Sebastian 102. © 787/723-1149. Bus: Old Town Trolley.

Maria's   Forget the tacky decorations. This is the town's most enduring bar, a favorite local hangout and a prime target for Old Town visitors seeking Mexican food and sangria. The atmosphere is fun, and the tropical drinks include piña coladas and frosts made of banana, orange, and strawberry, as well as the Puerto Rican beer Medalla. Open daily 10:30am to 3am (closes at 4am Fri–Sat). Calle del Cristo 204. © 787/721-1678. Bus: Old Town Trolley.

Palm Court   This is the most beautiful bar on the island—perhaps in the entire Caribbean. Most of the patrons are hotel guests, but well-heeled locals make up at least a quarter of the business at this fashionable rendezvous. Set in an oval wrapped around a sunken bar area, amid marble and burnished mahogany, it offers a view of one of the world's largest chandeliers. After 7pm on Monday through Saturday, live music, often salsa and merengue, emanates from an adjoining room (El Chico Bar). Open daily 6pm to 3am. In El San Juan Hotel & Casino, Av. Isla Verde 6063, Isla Verde. © 787/791-1000. Bus: A5.

Sake Sushi Bar   Set on the upper floor of an antique building near the cruise-ship docks, this is the most trendy, most appealing, and most hip bar in San Juan. Because there's no area that's specifically designated inside as a dance floor, it defines itself as a "lounge." By that, owner Jancy Rodriguez defines his "living room" as a labyrinth of artfully minimalist rooms with comfortable seating, a changing array of dramatic oil paintings *(olio)* on loan from the art gallery (Canvas) downstairs, and a mixture of bright lights and shadow that makes anyone look years younger. Tucked into an alcove, there's a sushi bar to alleviate those ultra-late-night-hunger pangs; and onyx bartops that are lit from beneath to create zebra-striped but tawny-colored patterns. Music emphasizes trance and house music that's either very loud or so loud that it's almost unbearable, but if you can overlook that (rather silly) quirk, you can have a lot of fun at this place. Although the place opens, at least theoretically, at 10pm, it doesn't begin to jump till after midnight. Open nightly until at least 2am. Recinto Sur 305. © **787/977-1082.** Bus: Old Town Trolley.

Shannon's Irish Pub   Ireland and its ales meet the Tropics at this pub with a Latin accent. A sports bar with TV monitors and high-energy rock 'n' roll, it's the regular watering hole of many university students. There's live music Wednesday through Sunday—everything from rock to jazz to Latin. There are pool tables, and a simple cafe serves inexpensive lunches Monday through Friday. A $3 cover charge is sometimes imposed for a special live performance. Open daily 11:30am to 1am (closes at 2:30am Fri–Sat). Calle Bori 496, Río Piedras. © **787/281-8466.** No bus.

Wet Bar   This chic drinking spot operates out of San Juan's finest boutique hotel, The Water Club. This is the best bar for watching the sun set over San Juan. Lying on the 11th floor, it features jazz music and the Caribbean's only rooftop fireplace for those nippy nights in winter when you want to drink outside. The sensuous decor here includes striped zebra-wood stools, futons, pillowy sofas, and hand-carved side tables. The walls feature Indonesian carved teak panels. Thursday through Saturday the Wet Bar is open 7pm to 1am, with Liquid Bar open 6pm to 1am. In The Water Club, Calle José M. Tartak 2. © **787/728-3666.** Bus: A5.

Zabó   Among San Juan's young, restless, and unattached, this place is more famous for its bar than its restaurant. The bar is divided into two separate spaces, the more popular being a cottage-like outbuilding on the grounds of a turn-of-the-20th-century villa. There's lots of charm here, from the attractive crowd, stiff drinks such as Cosmopolitans and martinis, and live music on a select few Wednesday and Thursday nights from 8 to 11:45pm. Some nights, depending on the operating hours of the restaurant, the bar crowd moves into the restaurant's entrance vestibule, a cozy spot for mingling. Open Tuesday through Wednesday 6 to 10pm; Thursday 6 to 11pm; Friday through Saturday 7 to 11pm. Calle Candina 14 (entrance is via an alleyway on Av. Ashford). © **787/725-9494.** Bus: 21.

> ⌐ **Moments Romantic Sunsets**
>
> There is no better place on a Sunday night from 5:30 to 7pm to watch the sun set over Old San Juan than at Paseo de la Princesa. In this evocative colonial setting, you can hear local trios serenade you as the sun goes down. After such a romantic interlude, the night is yours. Of course, you should take along a lover.

HOT NIGHTS IN GAY SAN JUAN

Straight folks are generally welcome in each of these gay venues, and many local couples show up for the hot music and dancing. Local straight boys who show up to cause trouble are generally ushered out quickly. Unless otherwise stated, there is no cover.

Beach Bar   This is the site of a hugely popular Sunday afternoon gathering, which gets really crowded beginning around 4pm and stretches into the wee hours. There's an open-air bar protected from rain by a sloping rooftop and a space atop the seawall with a panoramic view of the Condado beachfront. Drag shows on Sunday take place on the terrace. Open daily 11am to 1am or later. On the ground floor of the Atlantic Beach Hotel, Calle Vendig 1. © 787/721-6900. Bus: B21.

Cups Set in a Latino tavern, this place is valued as the only place in San Juan that caters almost exclusively to lesbians. Men of any sexual persuasion aren't particularly welcome. The scene reminds many lesbians of a tropical version of one of the bars they left behind at home. Entertainment such as live music or cabaret is presented Wednesday at 9pm and Friday at 10pm. Open Wednesday through Saturday 7pm to 4am. Calle San Mateo 1708, Santurce. © 787/268-3570. Bus: B21.

Eros This two-level nightclub caters exclusively to the city's growing gay population. Patterned after the dance emporiums of New York, but on a smaller scale, the club has cutting-edge music and bathrooms that are among the most creative in the world. Here, wall murals present fantasy-charged, eroticized versions of ancient Greek and Roman gods. Regrettably, only 1 night a week (Wed) is devoted to Latino music; on other nights, the music is equivalent to what you'd find in the gay discos of either Los Angeles or New York City. Open Wednesday to Sunday 10pm to 3am or 5am. Av. Ponce de León 1257, Santurce. © 787/727-1390. Cover $5. Bus: 1.

Junior's Bar Lying on a secluded and poorly lit street in Santurce, about a 5-block walk from the more famous gay mecca Eros (see above), Junior's Bar seems little known to most visitors. It's mainly a place where resident gays go to hang out, talk to each other, and order drinks. Most of the music comes from the jukebox. Drag queens (Sat–Sun) and male strippers (Mon–Fri) are a standard feature. There is no cover, but you are required to fulfill a two-drink minimum. Daily 8pm to 5am. Av. Condado 613 (off Av. Ponce de León), Santurce. © 787/723-9477. Bus: B21.

La Rumba Party Cruise

The trouble with most nightlife venues in San Juan is that the real parties in conventional nightclubs begin at hours so impossibly late that the average visitor will tend to be deep asleep by the time the first dancers begin to rock 'n' roll. So if you love to salsa and merengue, but if you maintain relatively conservative ideas about your bedtime, consider the *La Rumba Party Cruise* as a viable option. It all takes place aboard a neon-lit two-level minicruiser that's moored most of the time to a point near Old San Juan's cruise pier no. 1 (Plaza Darsenas) and the Old San Juan Hotel. Schedules vary according to business, but tend to last 75 minutes each, and depart every Friday and Saturday at 9:30pm, 11:30pm, 1:30am; and every Sunday at 6:30pm, 8:30pm, 10:30pm, and 2:30am. And if you show up about an hour prior to a scheduled departure, you can fit in up to an extra hour's worth of shaking your booty to Latino music as the boat sits in port, music blaring, waiting for other clients. Cruises cost $12 per person, with a cash bar on board selling beer for between $4 and $6 each, depending on the brand. There's a sightseeing benefit to the experience as well: en route, as it chugs out to sea, participants garner sea-fronting views of both of San Juan's 18th-century forts and the coastline of Isla Verde. For reservations and more information, call © 787/375-5211.

Barhopping

More than any other place in the Caribbean, San Juan has a nightlife that successfully combines New York hip with Latino zest and the music of the Spanish Tropics. For a no-holds-barred insight into what this means, try the recommendations here.

First, head for a pair of holes in the wall across the street from the El Convento Hotel. **El Batey,** Calle del Cristo 101 (no phone), and **Don Pablo,** Calle del Cristo 103 (no phone), are battered side-by-side hangouts with a clientele of locals, expatriates, and occasional visitors. (In the 1980s, a Hollywood director selected these spots as the set for a Central American drug den, much to the amusement of the regular clientele.) Whereas El Batey's music remains firmly grounded in the rock-'n'-roll classics of the 1970s, with a scattering of Elvis Presley hits, Don Pablo prides itself on cutting-edge music that's continually analyzed by the counterculture aficionados who hang out here. El Batey is open daily from 2pm to 6am; Don Pablo, daily from 8pm to 4am.

These bars, along with the dark and smoky **Café Bohemia,** just across the street, in the cellar of the El Convento Hotel, Calle del Cristo 100 (✆ **787/723-9020**), are hip hangouts for late-night dialogues. At this hideaway you can often hear live jazz while enjoying fruity cocktails, drinks, and light meals. Older locals mingle with hotel guests, the patronage mainly in the post-35 age group.

You might also stumble into **Carli Café Concierto,** Calle Tetuán 206, off Plazoleta Rafael Carrión (✆ **787/725-4927**). This is one of Old Town's best spots for drinking margaritas and watching the world go by. Owner Carli Muñoz, who earned fame as one of The Beach Boys, plays jazz and piano classics nightly, often with invited guests. There is no cover charge.

Also recommended as a dining option, **Tantra,** Calle Fortaleza 356 (✆ **787/977-8141**), serves creative martinis to crowds of clients till very late (between 4 and 5am) every Tuesday to Saturday. After the mainstream menu ends, a different menu that includes platters of fried prawns and pizzas is made available, along with one of the best selections of martinis in town. Priced at $9 each, they include versions with mango, passion fruit, and a personal favorite, a version with cinnamon and clove. Live belly dancers amuse the crowd on Friday and Saturday nights, and any night of the week, you can rent, for $20, a Mogul-style hookah pipe for every member of your dining table if the idea of playing pasha for a night appeals to you.

Tia Maria's Liquor Store   This is not a liquor store, but a bar that caters to both locals and visitors. As one habitué informed us, "During the day, all the local boys claim they're straight. But stick around until after midnight." The place has a very welcoming and unpretentious attitude, attracting both men and women. Don't come here for entertainment, but to hang out with the locals. Open Monday to Thursday and Sunday 11am to midnight; Friday to Saturday 10am to 2am. Av. José de Diego 326 (near the corner of Av. Ponce de León), Santurce. ✆ **787/724-4011.** Bus: B1.

CASINOS

Many visitors come to Puerto Rico on package deals and stay at one of the posh hotels at the Condado or Isla Verde just to gamble.

Nearly all the large hotels in San Juan/Condado/Isla Verde offer casinos, and there are other large casinos at some of the bigger resorts outside the metropolitan area. The atmosphere in the casinos is casual, but still you shouldn't show up in bathing suits or shorts. Most of the casinos open around noon and close at 2, 3, or 4am. Guest patrons must be at least 18 years old to enter.

The casino generating all the excitement today is the 18,500-square-foot (1,719 sq. m) **Ritz-Carlton Casino,** Avenue of Governors, Isla Verde (② 787/253-1700), the largest casino in Puerto Rico. It combines the elegant decor of the 1940s with tropical fabrics and patterns. This is one of the plushest and most exclusive entertainment complexes in the Caribbean. You almost expect to see Joan Crawford—beautifully frocked, of course—arrive on the arm of Clark Gable. It features traditional games such as blackjack, roulette, baccarat, craps, and slot machines.

One of the splashiest of San Juan's casinos is at the **Old San Juan Hotel & Casino,** Calle Brumbaugh 100 (② 787/721-5100), where five-card stud competes with some 240 slot machines and roulette tables. You can also try your luck at the **El San Juan Hotel & Casino** (one of the most grand), Av. Isla Verde 6063 (② 787/791-1000), or the **Condado Plaza Hotel & Casino,** Av. Ashford 999 (② 787/721-1000). You do not have to flash passports or pay any admission fees.

COCKFIGHTS

A brutal sport not to everyone's taste, cockfights are legal in Puerto Rico. The most authentic are in Salinas, a town on the southern coast with a southwestern ethos, which has *galleras,* or rings, for cockfighting. But you don't have to go all the way there to see a match. About three fights per week take place at the **Coliseo Gallistico,** Av. Isla Verde 6600, Av. Isla Verde, esquina Los Gobernadores. Call ② 787/791-6005 for the schedule and to order tickets, which cost $10, $12, $20, or $35, depending on the seat. The best time to attend cockfights is from January to May, as more fights are scheduled at that time. Hours are Tuesday or Thursday 4 to 10pm and Saturday 2 to 9pm.

8

Near San Juan

Within easy reach of San Juan's cosmopolitan bustle are superb attractions and natural wonders. With San Juan as your base, you can explore the island by day and return in time for a final dip in the ocean and an evening on the town. Other places near San Juan, such as the Westin Rio Mar Beach Golf Resort & Spa (see below), are destinations unto themselves.

About 90 minutes west of San Juan is the world's largest radar/radio-telescope, **Arecibo Observatory.** After touring this awesome facility, you can travel west to nearby **Río Camuy,** for a good look at marvels below ground. Here you can plunge deep into the subterranean beauty of a spectacular cave system carved over eons by one of the world's largest underground rivers.

Just 35 miles (56km) east of San Juan is the Caribbean National Forest, the only tropical rainforest in the U.S. National Park System. Named by the Spanish for its anvil-shaped peak, **El Yunque** receives more than 100 billion gallons of rainfall annually. If you have time for only one side trip, this is the one to take. Waterfalls, wild orchids, giant ferns, towering tabonuco trees, and sierra palms make El Yunque a photographer's and hiker's paradise. Pick up a map and choose from dozens of trails graded by difficulty, including El Yunque's most challenging—the 6-mile (9.7km) El Toro Trail to the peak. At El Yunque is El Portal Tropical Center, with 10,000 square feet (929 sq. m) of exhibit space, plazas, and patios. This facility greatly expands the recreational and educational programs available to visitors. La Coca Falls and an observation tower are just off Route 191.

Visitors can combine a morning trip to El Yunque with an afternoon of swimming and sunning on tranquil **Luquillo Beach.** Soft white sand, shaded by coconut palms and the blue sea, makes this Puerto Rico's best and best-known beach. Take a picnic or, better yet, sample local specialties from the kiosks.

1 Arecibo & Camuy ✶

68 to 77 miles (109–124km) W of San Juan

GETTING THERE

Arecibo Observatory lies a 1¼-hour drive west of San Juan, outside the town of Arecibo. From San Juan head west along four-lane Route 22 until you reach the town of Arecibo. At Arecibo, head south on Route 10; the 20-mile (32km) drive south on this four-lane highway is almost as interesting as the observatory itself. From Route 10, follow the signposts along a roller-coaster journey on narrow two-lane roads. Still following the signposts, you take routes 626 and 623, crossing the lush Valley of Río Tanamá until you reach Route 625, which will lead you to the entrance to the observatory.

On the same day you visit the Arecibo Observatory, you can also visit the Río Camuy caves. The caves also lie south of the town of Arecibo. Follow Route 129 southwest from Arecibo to the entrance of the caves, which are at Km 18.9 along the route, north of the town of Lares. Like the observatory, the caves lie approximately 1½ hours west of San Juan.

EXPLORING THE AREA

Dubbed "an ear to heaven," **Observatorio de Arecibo** ⋇ (© 787/878-2612; www.naic.edu) contains the world's largest and most sensitive radar/radio-telescope. The telescope features a 20-acre (8-hectare) dish, or radio mirror, set in an ancient sinkhole. It's 1,000 feet (305m) in diameter and 167 feet (51m) deep, and it allows scientists to monitor natural radio emissions from distant galaxies, pulsars, and quasars, and to examine the ionosphere, the planets, and the moon using powerful radar signals. Used by scientists as part of the Search for Extraterrestrial Intelligence (SETI), this is the same site featured in the movie *Contact* with Jodie Foster. This research effort speculates that advanced civilizations elsewhere in the universe might also communicate via radio waves. The 10-year, $100-million search for life in space was launched on October 12, 1992, the 500-year anniversary of the New World's discovery by Columbus.

Unusually lush vegetation flourishes under the giant dish, including ferns, wild orchids, and begonias. Assorted creatures like mongooses, lizards, and dragonflies have also taken refuge there. Suspended in outlandish fashion above the dish is a 600-ton platform that resembles a space station.

This is not a site where you'll be launched into a *Star Wars* journey through the universe. You are allowed to walk around the platform, taking in views of this gigantic dish. At the Angel Ramos Foundation Visitor Center, you are treated to interactive exhibitions on the various planetary systems and introduced to the mystery of meteors and educated about intriguing weather phenomena.

Tours are available at the observatory Wednesday through Friday from noon to 4pm, Saturday and Sunday from 9am to 4pm. The cost is $5 for adults, $3 for children and seniors. There's a souvenir shop on the grounds. Plan to spend about 1½ hours at the observatory.

Parque de las Cavernas del Río Camuy (Río Camuy Caves) ⋇⋇⋇ (© 787/898-3100) contains the third-largest underground river in the world. It runs through a network of caves, canyons, and sinkholes that have been cut through the island's limestone base over the course of millions of years. Known to the pre-Columbian Taíno peoples, the caves came to the attention of speleologists in the 1950s; they were led to the site by local boys already familiar with some of the entrances to the system. The caves were opened to the public in 1986. Visitors should allow about 1½ hours for the total experience.

Visitors first see a short film about the caves and then descend into the caverns in open-air trolleys. The trip takes you through a 200-foot-deep (61m) sinkhole and a chasm where tropical trees, ferns, and flowers flourish, along with birds and butterflies. The trolley then goes to the entrance of Clara Cave of Epalme, one of 16 caves in the Camuy caves network, where visitors begin a 45-minute walk, viewing the majestic series of rooms rich in stalagmites, stalactites, and huge natural "sculptures" formed over the centuries.

Tres Pueblos Sinkhole, located on the boundaries of the Camuy, Hatillo, and Lares municipalities, measures 65 feet (20m) in diameter, with a depth of 400 feet (122m)—

Arecibo **7**
Arecibo Observatory **9**
Caguas **15**
Dorado **14**
El Yunque **18**
Guajataca Forest **1**

Gurabo **16**
Karst Country **6**
Lago de Guajataca **5**
Lagos dos Bocas **13**
Lake Caonillas **12**
Lake of Loíza **17**

Lares **3**
Luquillo Beach **19**
Parque Ceremonial
Indígena-Caguaña **10**
Río Abajo Forest **8**
Río Camuy Caves **4**
San Sebastián **2**
Utuado **11**

room enough to fit all of El Morro Fortress in San Juan. In Tres Pueblos, visitors can walk along two platforms—one on the Lares side, facing the town of Camuy, and the other on the Hatillo side, overlooking Tres Pueblos Cave and the Río Camuy.

The caves are open Wednesday through Sunday from 8am to 3pm. Tickets cost $10 for adults, $7 for children 4 to 12, and $5 for seniors. Parking is $2. For more information, phone the park.

WHERE TO DINE

The closest place for food is the **Casa Grande Mountain Retreat** (p. 216) in Utuado, a little mountain town south of Arecibo.

2 The Karst Country ★★

48 miles (77km) W of San Juan

One of the most interesting areas of Puerto Rico to explore is the large **Karst Country,** south of Arecibo. One of the world's strangest rock formations, karst is formed by the process of water sinking into limestone. As time goes by, larger and larger basins are eroded, forming sinkholes. *Mogotes* (karstic hillocks) are peaks of earth where the land didn't sink into the erosion pits. The Karst Country lies along the island's north coast, directly northeast of Mayagüez in the foothills between Quebradillas and Manatí. The region is filled with an extensive network of caves. One sinkhole contains the 20-acre (8-hectare) dish of the world's largest radio/radar telescope at the Arecibo Observatory (see above).

This area was deforested in the late 1940s; alluvial valleys and sinkholes were then used for pastures, shifting cultivation, and coffee plantations. In this region, most of the coffee sites were abandoned in the 1960s, and today most of these sites are covered with secondary forests. The recovery of these forests has been very rapid because of a close seed source—trees left on the steep slopes—and the presence of large populations of dispersers, mainly bats.

GETTING THERE   The only way to explore the Karst Country, which is easy to reach from San Juan, is by car. Leave San Juan on the four-lane highway, Route 22, until you come to the town of Arecibo, a 1½-hour drive, depending on traffic. Once at Arecibo, take Route 10 south, in the direction of Utuado. See "A Driving Tour of the Karst Country" below.

A DRIVING TOUR OF THE KARST COUNTRY

If you'd like a specific goal for exploring in the Karst Country, visit the Arecibo Observatory and the Río Camuy Caves, previewed above. However, you can also spend a day driving at random, exploring lakes and forests at your leisure. If you decide to go this route, make the commercial town of **Arecibo** your base. Although not of tourist interest itself, it is the capital of the Karst Country and the starting point from which you can drive south along many interesting and winding roads. Arecibo is reached after a 1½-hour drive west of San Juan along a four-lane highway, Route 22, one of the best and fastest on the island.

From Arecibo you can take Route 10 south in the direction of Utuado (see chapter 10), which can serve as a refueling stop. Along the way you'll pass **Lagos dos Bocas** ★, one of the most beautiful lakes of the Karst Country. This is a reservoir adjacent to the Río Abajo Forest (see below). Lagos dos Bocas, which lies 12 miles (19km) south of

---

Tips **Get a Good Map**

Arm yourself with the most detailed map you can find at one of the bookstores in San Juan. The free maps dispensed by the tourist office are not sufficiently detailed and do not show the tiny secondary roads you'll need to traverse for a motor tour of the Karst Country.

Arecibo, is in the mountains of Cordillera Central. Along with a nearby lake, **Lake Caonillas,** it forms the major water reservoir for the north-central sector of Puerto Rico.

Take time out at Lagos dos Bocas to ride one of the free government-operated **launches** ⊛ that traverse the lake. Established as a taxi service for residents of the area, these launches can be used by sightseers as well. The launches leave from a dock along Route 123 on the west side of the lake, with departures scheduled every hour unless the weather is bad. On weekends many little "restaurants" (really food shacks) are open to serve visitors. If you don't want to get off and patronize one of these ramshackle joints, you can stay on the launch, enjoying one of the most tranquil and scenic 2-hour rides in all of Puerto Rico. The launch will take you back to your car, and then you can continue your journey.

Once at Utuado, you can cut west along Route 111, which leads to the town of Lares. When you come to Route 621 heading north, you can drive into the **Río Abajo Forest (Bosque Estatal de Río Abajo)** ⊛, a piece of island beauty riddled with old lumber roads and trail paths. Filled with lush growth, this forest reserve is filled with many tropical trees, such as bamboo, West Indian mahogany, balsa, and teak.

After a look at the region, you can drive south and hook up again with Route 111 going west to Lares. You'll almost immediately come to **Parque Ceremonial Indígena-Caguaña (Indian Ceremonial Park at Caguaña).** The site is signposted and need not take up more than 30 minutes of your time. Built by the Taíno Indians some 1,000 years ago, the site was used for both recreation and worship, and it is encircled by mountains near the Tanama River. You can still see the outlines of the ancient *bateyes* (ball courts), which are bordered by carved stone monoliths decorated with petroglyphs. The best-known petroglyph is the much-photographed *Mujer de Caguaña,* squatting in the position of an earth-mother fertility symbol. There is a small and very minor museum of Indian artifacts and skeletons on-site. Charging no admission, the site is open daily from 8am to 4:20pm. For more information, call ⓒ **787/894-7325.**

Along Route 111, **Lares** comes upon you like a frontier town, lying in the western foothills of the Cordillera Central's principal cluster of peaks. Lares stands at the southernmost spur of the Karst Country. On the island, the residents of Lares live as far from the ocean as you can get in Puerto Rico.

Although there is little of tourist interest in Lares, other than the toylike quality of the town itself, you can use it as a refueling stop, as it has a number of little shops and minor dining joints. In the center of town is a Spanish colonial church dating from the 19th century.

From Lares continue northwest to the town of San Sebastián, and then cut sharply east along Route 119, until you'll reach the shores of **Lago de Guajataca** ⊛, one of the most majestic bodies of water on Puerto Rico. In many ways this is our favorite lake for some R & R on the island. It is both a 4-mile-long (6.4km) body of water and a wildlife refuge. For a scenic look at the lake, drive along its north shore, which is a haven for some of the most skilled anglers of Puerto Rico. You can go fishing here, but you have to bring your own equipment. The most sought-after fish is *tucunare,* with which the lake is stocked. At the dam here, you can gaze upon an evocative "lost valley" of conical peaks.

If you'd like to explore the **Bosque Estatal de Guajataca (Guajataca Forest)** 🐟🐟, you can stop in at either **Depto de Recursos Naturales Oficina** (ⓒ **787/896-7640**), at Km 22.1 on Route 119 near Lago de Guajataca or Route 446, Km 9, Barrio Llanadas, daily 7am to 3:30pm. Open from 6am to 6pm Tuesday to Sunday, each office has a stock of detailed hiking routes through the forest reserve. Set in the thick of the Karst Country, Guajataca Forest sprawls across nearly 2,400 acres (971 hectares) of forestland, rising and falling at various elevations, ranging from 500 to 1,000 feet (152–305m) or more.

Reaching the forest from the lake can be difficult. You can return to the town of San Sebastián (see above), following Route 119 until you come to the junction with Route 446 heading north. This road will carry you right into the heart of the forest reserve.

The woodland in the forest is punctuated by mogotes and covered with 25 miles (40km) of hiking trails. It is also home to the endangered Puerto Rico boa (you are unlikely to encounter one) and the habitat of nearly 50 different species of birds. The highlight of the forest is the *Cueva del Viento,* the "Cave of the Wind." The hiking trails have been well marked by park rangers.

At the end of the tour, you can continue north along Route 446, which will hook up with Route 2, continuing to the west coast of Puerto Rico. Otherwise, you can head east via Arecibo to San Juan.

3 Dorado 🌟

18 miles (29km) W of San Juan

Dorado—the name itself evokes a kind of magic—is a world of luxury resorts and villas that unfolds along the north shore of Puerto Rico.

The site was originally purchased in 1905 by Dr. Alfred T. Livingston, a Jamestown, N.Y., physician, who developed it as a 1,000-acre (405-hectare) grapefruit-and-coconut plantation. Dr. Livingston's daughter, Clara, widely known in aviation circles as a friend of Amelia Earhart, owned and operated the plantation after her father's death. It was she who built the airstrip here.

GETTING THERE

If you're driving from San Juan, take Highway 2 west to Route 693 north to Dorado (trip time: 40 min.).

WHERE TO STAY

Lodgings in Dorado are pretty much limited to the Hyatt and the Embassy Suites. The Hyatt is a good choice for families, offering family getaway packages at Camp Coquí, the Puerto Rican version of Camp Hyatt, featuring professionally supervised day and evening programs for children ages 3 to 12. Certified counselors direct programs of educational, environmental, and cultural activities. In the evening, movies, talent shows, and video games occupy the agenda. All this costs $40 a day per kid. Children also receive a 50% discount on meals.

Embassy Suites Dorado del Mar Beach & Golf Resort 🌟   This beachfront property in Dorado lies less than 2 miles (3.2km) from the center of Dorado and within easy access from the San Juan airport. It is the only all-suite resort in Puerto Rico, and it has been a success since its opening in 2001. The property offers two-room suites with balconies and 38 two-bedroom condos.

The suites are spread over seven floors, each spacious and furnished in a Caribbean tropical motif, with artwork and one king-size bed or two double beds. Most of them have ocean views of the water. Each condo has a living room, kitchen, whirlpool, and balcony.

Although the accommodations are suites or condos, one bedroom in a condo can be rented as a double room (the rest of the condo is shut off). Likewise, it's also possible for two people to rent one bedroom in a condo, with the living room and kitchen facilities available (the other bedroom is closed off). Because condos contain two bedrooms, most of them are rented to parties of four.

The hotel attracts many families because of its very spacious accommodations. It also attracts golfers because of its Chi Chi Rodriguez signature par-72 18-hole golf course set against a panoramic backdrop of mountains and ocean.

Dorado del Mar Blvd. 210, Dorado, PR 00646. (C) 787/796-6125. Fax 787/796-6145. www.embassysuitesdorado.com. 212 units. Year-round $160–$250 suite; $260–$485 1-bedroom villa; $360–$560 2-bedroom villa. AE, DC, DISC, MC, V. **Amenities:** 2 restaurants; bar and grill; pool; golf; tennis court; limited room service; massage; laundry service; dry cleaning; rooms for those w/limited mobility. *In room:* A/C, TV, dataport, kitchenette, hair dryer, iron, safe, wet bar.

Hyatt Dorado Beach Resort & Country Club 🏨🏨 *Kids*   Hyatt has spent millions on improvements here at what in the 1950s was Laurance Rockefeller's special getaway for presidents and the Hollywood elite, lying on 1,000 acres (405 hectares). The renovated guest rooms have marble bathrooms and terra-cotta floors throughout. Accommodations are available on the beach or in villas tucked in and around the lushly

---

(*Tips* **World-Class Golf at the Former Hyatt Dorado**

The Hyatt Dorado closed its doors in May 2006 and its future is unclear as we go to print, but luckily its world-class golf courses and country club are slated to remain open indefinitely. The **Hyatt Dorado Beach Resort's professional golf courses** 🏨🏨, designed by Robert Trent Jones, Sr., match the finest anywhere. The two original courses, known as East and West ((C) 787/796-8961 for tee times), were carved out of a jungle and offer tight fairways bordered by trees and forests, with lots of ocean holes. The somewhat newer and less noted North and South courses, now called the Plantation Club ((C) 787/796-8915 for tee times), feature wide fairways with well-bunkered greens and an assortment of water traps and tricky wind factors. Each is a par-72 course. The longest is the South course, at 7,047 yards (6,444m). Fees for North and South courses are $65 to $130, $99 to $185 on the East and West courses. Golf carts are included for all courses, and the two pro shops have both a bar and snack-style restaurant. Both are open daily from 7am until dusk. You can also enjoy a pre- or post-game meal at either of the 2 upscale restaurants slated to remain open at the Hyatt, Hacienda del Sol and Zafra. Call (C) 787/796-1234 for either. *Tip:* Ask about rates for game play that starts after 1:30pm, which is sometimes marked down significantly.

planted grounds. They're fairly spacious and bathrooms have everything from tubs to bathrobes, deluxe toiletries to power showers. The casitas are a series of private beach or poolside houses.

Dinner is served in a three-tiered main dining room where you can watch the surf. Hyatt Dorado chefs have won many awards, and the food at its restaurants is among the most appealing in Puerto Rico.

Important Note: As we go to print, this property is closing down and has no plans for the immediate future, though they note that their country club (including golf courses and tennis courts) will remain open indefinitely, as well as two upscale restaurants (Hacienda del Sol and Zafra). We've previously recommended this hotel for everything from family vacations to honeymoons; it's worth calling the main phone line (which is expected to remain operable) or searching online to find out if the hotel will be open under new management during your visit.

Hwy. 693, Dorado, PR 00646. (C) **800/233-1234** or 787/796-1234. Fax 787/796-2022. www.doradobeach.hyatt.com. 262 units, 17 casitas. Winter $455–$675 double; from $800 casita for 2; off season $200–$325 double, from $450 casita for 2. MAP (mandatory in winter) $72 extra per day for adults, $36 extra per day for children. AE, DC, DISC, MC, V. **Amenities:** 5 restaurants; 3 bars; 3 outdoor pools; 2 18-hole championship golf courses; 5 tennis courts; spa; windsurfing school; children's camp; limited room service; babysitting; laundry service; dry cleaning; nonsmoking rooms; rooms for those w/limited mobility. *In room:* A/C, dataport, minibar, coffeemaker, hair dryer, iron, safe.

DINING

El Di Mari PUERTO RICAN   If you'd like to discover an unpretentious local place that serves good Puerto Rican cuisine, then head here, a simple concrete structure that's minutes away from a small shopping center. It has a cozy family ambience and is especially popular on weekends. Some members of the staff speak English, and the chef is best with fresh seafood. The chef might also prepare a variety of items not listed on the menu. Most of the dishes are at the lower end of the price scale; only the lobster is expensive. On Wednesday and Friday a live band plays and patrons dance.

Rte. 693, Km 8.2, Marginal Costa de Oro. (C) **787/796-1645.** Main courses $8–$34. AE, MC, V. Daily 5–11pm.

4 El Yunque ★★★

25 miles (40km) E of San Juan

The El Yunque rainforest, a 45-minute drive east of San Juan, is a major attraction in Puerto Rico. Part of the Caribbean National Forest, this is the only tropical forest in the U.S. National Forest Service system. The 28,000-acre (11,331-hectare) preserve was given its status by President Theodore Roosevelt. Today the virgin forest remains much as it was in 1493, when Columbus first sighted Puerto Rico.

GETTING THERE

From San Juan, road signs direct you to Route 3, which you follow east to the intersection of Route 191, a two-lane highway that heads south into the forest. Take 191 for 3 miles (4.8km), going through the village of Palmer. As the road rises, you will have entered the Caribbean National Forest. You can stop in at the El Portal Tropical Forest Center to pick up information (see below).

VISITOR INFORMATION

El Portal Tropical Forest Center, Route 191, Rio Grande (C) **787/888-1880**), an $18-million exhibition and information center, has 10,000 square feet (929 sq. m) of exhibition space. Three pavilions offer exhibits and bilingual displays. The actor

Jimmy Smits narrates a documentary called "Understanding the Forest." The center is open daily from 9am to 5pm; it charges an admission of $3 for adults and $1.50 for children under 12.

El Yunque is the most popular spot in Puerto Rico for hiking; for a description of our favorite trails, see "Hiking Trails" below. The **Department of Natural Resources Forest Service** (© 787/724-8774) administers some aspects of the park, although for the ordinary hiker, more useful information may be available at **El Yunque Catalina Field Office,** near the village of Palmer, beside the main highway at the forest's northern edge (© 787/888-1880). The staff can provide material about hiking routes, and, with 10 days' notice, help you plan overnight tours in the forest. If you reserve in advance, the staff will also arrange for you to take part in 2-hour group tours. These tours are conducted Saturday to Monday every hour on the hour from 10:30am to 3:30pm; they cost $5 for adults and $3 for children under 12.

EXPLORING EL YUNQUE

Encompassing four distinct forest types, El Yunque is home to 240 species of tropical trees, flowers, and wildlife. More than 20 kinds of orchids and 50 varieties of ferns share this diverse habitat with millions of tiny tree frogs, whose distinctive cry of *coquí* (pronounced "ko-*kee*") has given them their name. Tropical birds include the lively, greenish blue, red-fronted Puerto Rican parrot, once nearly extinct and now making a comeback. Other rare animals include the Puerto Rican boa, which grows to 7 feet (2.1m). (It is highly unlikely that you will encounter a boa. The few people who have are still shouting about it.)

El Yunque is the best of Puerto Rico's 20 forest preserves. The forest is situated high above sea level, with El Toro its highest peak. You can be fairly sure you'll be showered upon during your visit, since more than 100 billion gallons of rain fall here annually. However, the showers are brief and there are many shelters. On a quickie tour, many visitors reserve only a half-day for El Yunque. But we think it's unique and deserves at least a daylong outing.

HIKING TRAILS   The best hiking trails in El Yunque have been carefully marked by the forest rangers. Our favorite, which takes 2 hours for the round-trip jaunt, is called **La Mina & Big Tree Trail,** and it is actually two trails combined. The La Mina Trail is paved and signposted. It begins at the picnic center adjacent to the visitor center and runs parallel to La Mina River. It is named for gold once discovered on the site. After you reach La Mina Falls, the Big Tree Trail begins (also signposted). It winds a route through the towering trees of Tabonuco Forest until it approaches Route 191. Along the trail you might spot such native birds as the Puerto Rican woodpecker, the tanager, the screech owl, and the bullfinch.

Those with more time might opt for the **El Yunque Trail,** which takes 4 hours round-trip to traverse. This trail—signposted from El Caimitillo Picnic Grounds— takes you on a steep, winding path. Along the way you pass natural forests of sierra palm and *palo colorado* before descending into the dwarf forest of Mount Britton, which is often shrouded in clouds. Your major goal, at least for panoramic views, will be the lookout peaks of Roca Marcas, Yunque Rock, and Los Picachos. On a bright, clear day you can see all the way to the eastern shores of the Atlantic.

DRIVING THROUGH EL YUNQUE   If you're not a hiker but you appreciate rainforests, you can still enjoy El Yunque. You can drive through the forest on Route 191, which is a tarmac road. This trail goes from the main highway of Route 3, penetrating deep into El Yunque. You can see ferns that grow some 120 feet (37m) tall, and at any minute you expect a hungry dinosaur to peek between the fronds, looking for a snack. You're also treated to lookout towers offering panoramic views, waterfalls, picnic areas, and even a restaurant.

WHERE TO STAY

For the location of this parador, see the map "Paradores & Country Inns of Puerto Rico" on p. 53.

Ceiba Country Inn *(Finds)*   If you're looking for an escape from the hustle and bustle of everyday life, this is the place for you. This small, well-maintained bed-and-breakfast is located on the easternmost part of Puerto Rico, near the Roosevelt Road's U.S. naval base (you must rent a car to reach this little haven in the mountains). El Yunque is only 15 miles (24km) away, and San Juan is 40 miles (64km) to the west. The rooms are on the bottom floor of a large, old family home, and each has a private shower-only bathroom. They are decorated in a tropical motif with flowered murals on the walls, painted by a local artist. For a quiet evening cocktail, you might want to visit the small lounge on the second floor.

Road no. 977, Km 1.2 (P.O. Box 1067), Ceiba, PR 00735. ℭ 787/885-0471. Fax 787/885-0471. www.geocities.com/countryinnnoo735. 9 units (shower only). $75 double. Rate includes breakfast. AE, DISC, MC, V. Free parking. **Amenities:** Bar (guests only); patio for outdoor entertainment. *In room:* A/C, fridge, ceiling fan.

WHERE TO DINE

We recommend the dining and drinking facilities at the Westin Rio Mar (see "Luquillo Beach" below), which sits very close to the entrance to El Yunque.

5 Luquillo Beach ⭐⭐⭐

31 miles (50km) E of San Juan

Luquillo Beach is the island's best and most popular public stretch of sand. From here, you can easily explore El Yunque rainforest (see above). "Luquillo" is a Spanish adaptation of *Yukiyu,* the god believed by the Taínos to inhabit El Yunque.

GETTING THERE

If you are driving, pass the San Juan airport and follow the signs to Carolina. This leads to Route 3, which travels east toward the fishing town of Fajardo, where you'll turn north to Las Croabas. To reach the Westin, the area's major hotel, follow the signs to El Yunque, and then the signs to the Westin.

A hotel limousine (ℭ **787/888-6000**) from the San Juan airport costs $225 per carload to the Westin Rio Mar Beach Resort. A taxi costs approximately $70. Hotel buses make trips to and from the San Juan airport, based on the arrival times of incoming flights; the cost is $28 per person, each way, for transport to El Conquistador; $25 per person, each way, to the Westin.

HITTING THE BEACH

Luquillo Beach ⭐⭐⭐, Puerto Rico's finest beach, is palm-dotted and crescent-shaped, opening onto a lagoon with calm waters and a wide, sandy bank. It's very crowded on weekends but much better during the week. There are lockers, tent sites, showers, picnic tables, and food stands that sell a sampling of the island's *frituras* (fried fare), especially cod fritters and tacos. The beach is open daily from 9am to 6pm.

You can also snorkel and skin-dive (see below) among the living reefs with lots of tropical fish. Offshore are coral formations and spectacular sea life—eels, octopuses, stingrays, tarpon, big puffer fish, turtles, nurse sharks, and squid, among other sea creatures.

GREAT GOLF

One of Puerto Rico's newest golf courses is also among the very best. Tom Kite and Bruce Besse designed two 18-hole courses for the **Coco Beach Golf and Country Club,** 100 Club Dr., Rio Grande (© **787/657-2000**) adjacent to the well-recommended Sol Melia Paradisus (see below). You face a spectacular vista of fairways, lakes, and the Atlantic beyond. Four 9-hole loops fan out from the Caribbean's largest clubhouse. Each paspalum-grass course is imbued with its own character, including elevation changes. In the backdrop El Yunque's peaks stare at you. The Palms is a sprawling layout skirting wetlands, with the most difficult par 3 and the longest (571 yards) par 5. Winter fees are $150 per 18 holes or $135 after noon. Off season, the respective charges are $130 and $110. Fees include golf carts. On-site is the Paradise Bay Grill, serving freshly caught lobster and succulent steaks, and the locker rooms feature massages and Jacuzzis.

SCUBA DIVING & SNORKELING

The best people to take you diving are at the **Dive Center** at the Westin Rio Mar Beach Resort and Golf Club (© **787/888-6000**). This is one of the largest dive centers in Puerto Rico, a PADI five-star facility with two custom-designed boats that usually take no more than six to ten divers. Snorkeling and skin diving costs $75 for a half-day. The center also offers a full-day snorkeling trip, including lunch and drinks, for $95 per person. Boat tours are available daily from 9am to 4pm. For scuba divers, a two-tank dive costs $135 to $185.

WHERE TO STAY

Sol Melia Paradisus ✦✦✦ (Kids)   Checking into this pocket of posh on the Miquillo de Rio Grande peninsula is the best reason for heading east of San Juan. An all-suite luxury resort, it has set new standards for comfort, convenience, and amenities along the Atlantic northeastern shoreline. This government-rated five-star resort, set in gardens of 40 acres (16 hectares), opens onto the white sands of the mile-long (1.6km) shoreline of Coco Beach. From watersports to two 18-hole golf courses, the resort has everything on-site, including whirlpool baths and massage tables. Spa treatments revitalize and rejuvenate.

You can also wander the globe in the widely varied six restaurants, ranging from Mexico to Southeast Asia. Naturally, the chefs also prepare locally caught seafood imbued with Creole flavor. One restaurant serves only Caribbean and Puerto Rican cuisine, whereas another offers its take on contemporary California. Yet another serves teppanyaki dinners with an adjoining sushi bar.

This is Puerto Rico's first and only all-inclusive, all-suite resort. Bedrooms and suites are spacious and furnished luxuriously. The signature suites are divided among 20 elegant two-story bungalows. Rich mahogany pieces and elegant fabrics are used throughout. If you can afford it, opt for one of the 96 Royal Service Suites. You can even request one with a private Jacuzzi facing the Atlantic. The marble bathrooms are sumptuous.

Coco Beach Blvd. 1000, Rio Grande, PR 00745. © **866/43-MELIA.** Fax 787/809-1785. www.puertoricoparadisus.com. 582 units. Winter $776–$876 suite for 2; $900–$1,000 Royal Service Suite. Off season $600–$700 suite for 2, $726–$826 Royal Service Suite. Rates inclusive of all meals, beverages (including alcoholic), and use of nonmotorized watersports equipment. AE, DISC, MC, V. **Amenities:** 6 restaurants; 3 bars; 2 outdoor pools; 2 golf courses; 3 lit tennis courts; fitness center; gym; spa; sauna; kids clubs; business center; 24-hr. room service; babysitting; laundry service/dry cleaning; nonsmoking rooms; casino; medical services; rooms for those w/limited mobility. *In room:* A/C, TV, dataport, kitchenette, minibar, beverage maker, hair dryer, iron, safe.

Westin Rio Mar Beach Golf Resort & Spa ✦✦✦   Marking Westin's debut in the Caribbean, this $180-million, 481-acre (195-hectare) resort lies on relatively uncrowded Rio Mar Beach, a 5-minute drive from massively popular Luquillo Beach. It was designed to compete with the Hyatt hotel at Dorado and the El Conquistador, with which it's frequently compared. It's the best property in the area.

Landscaping includes several artificial lakes situated amid tropical gardens. More than 60% of the guest rooms look out over palm trees to the Atlantic. Other units open onto the mountains and forests of nearby El Yunque National Park (just a 15-min. drive away). The style is Spanish hacienda with nods to the surrounding jungle; unusual art and sculpture alternate with dark woods, deep colors, rounded archways, big windows, and tile floors. In the bedrooms, muted earth tones, wicker, rattan, and painted wood furniture add to the ambience. Bedrooms are spacious, with balconies or terraces, and good mattresses, plus tub/shower combinations in the large bathrooms.

The resort encompasses the **Rio Mar Country Club,** site of two important golf courses. The older of the two, the Ocean Course, was designed by George and Tom Fazio as part of the original resort, and has been a staple on Puerto Rico's professional golf circuit since the 1960s. In 1997, Westin opened the property's second 18-holer, the slightly more challenging River Course, the first Greg Norman–designed course in the Caribbean. The resort also has a 6,500-square-foot (604-sq. m) casino.

The only hotel in Puerto Rico with more diverse cuisine is El Conquistador (see chapter 11).

Rio Mar Blvd. 6000, Rio Grande, PR 00745. ✆ **800/WESTIN-1** or 787/888-6000. Fax 787/888-6600. www.starwood hotels.com. 600 units. Winter $370–$405 double; off season $225–$280 double; year-round from $695 suite. Children ages 5–17 staying in parent's room $85, including meals and activities. Free for 4 and under. AE, DC, DISC, MC, V. 19 miles east of Luís Muñoz Marín International Airport, with entrance off Puerto Rico Hwy. 3. **Amenities:** 8 restaurants; 4 bars; outdoor pool; 13 tennis courts; health club and spa; deep-sea fishing; sailing; children's pro-grams; 24-hr. room service; laundry; dry cleaning; nonsmoking rooms; casino; horseback riding nearby; rooms for those w/limited mobility. *In room:* A/C, TV, dataport, beverage maker, hair dryer, iron, safe.

WHERE TO DINE

Brass Cactus *finds* AMERICAN/REGIONAL   On a service road adjacent to Route 3 at the western edge of Luquillo, within a boxy-looking concrete building that's in need of repair, is one of the town's most popular bar/restaurants. Permeated with a raunchy, no-holds-barred spirit, this amiable spot has thrived since the early 1990s, when it was established by an Illinois-born bartender who outfitted the interior with gringo memorabilia. Drinks are stiff and the crowd looks tougher than it is, tending to calm down whenever food and drink are brought out. Menu items include king crab salad; tricolor tortellini laced with chicken and shrimp; several kinds of sand-wiches and burgers; and platters of churrasco, T-bone steaks, chicken with tequila sauce, barbecued pork, and fried mahimahi.

In the Condominio Complejo Turistico, Rte. 3, Marginal. ✆ 787/889-5735. Reservations not necessary. Sandwiches $7.95–$11; main courses $7.95–$26. MC, V. Sun–Thurs 11am–11pm; Fri–Sat 11am–midnight.

Palio ✦ ITALIAN   This richly decorated restaurant is the premier dining outlet of the region's largest and splashiest hotel. The Westin chain has poured time and energy into making this a showcase of the resort's creativity. Although most of the ingredients have to be flown in, the cuisine is excellent. A certain attachment to culinary tradition doesn't preclude a modern approach to the cookery. Dishes we've sampled have a superbly aromatic flavor and are beautifully presented and served. The sophisticated menu includes potato and sage gnocchi; rack of American lamb; fresh Maine lobster; center-cut veal chops stuffed with fresh mozzarella, tomatoes, and avocado and served with grappa-laced mashed potatoes; and baby free-range chicken, spit-roasted and served with rosemary jus.

In the Westin Rio Mar Beach Resort and Golf Club. (℃) 787/888-6000. Reservations recommended. Main courses $28–$40. AE, DC, MC, V. Nov–May daily 6–11pm; June–Oct Tues–Sat 6–11pm.

Sandy's Seafood Restaurant & Steak House ★ *Value* SEAFOOD/STEAKS/ PUERTO RICAN The concrete-and-plate-glass facade is less obtrusive than that of other restaurants in town, and the cramped, Formica-clad interior is far from stylish. Nonetheless, Sandy's is one of the most famous restaurants in northeastern Puerto Rico, thanks to the wide array of luminaries—U.S. and Puerto Rican political figures, mainstream journalists, beauty pageant winners, and assorted slumming rich—who travel from as far away as San Juan to dine here. Set about a block from the main square of the seaside resort of Luquillo, it was founded in 1984 by Miguel Angel, aka Sandy.

Platters, especially the daily specials, are huge—so copious, in fact, that they're discussed with fervor by competitors and clients alike. The best examples include fresh shellfish, served on the half-shell; asopaos; four kinds of steak; five different preparations of chicken, including a tasty version with garlic sauce; four kinds of gumbos; paellas; a dozen preparations of lobster; and even jalapeño peppers stuffed with shrimp or lobster.

Calle Fernandez García 276. (℃) **787/889-5765.** Reservations recommended. Main courses $6–$20; lunch special Mon–Fri 11am–2:30pm $5. AE, MC, V. Wed–Mon 11am–between 9:30 and 11pm, depending on business.

9

Ponce, Mayagüez & San Germán

For those who want to see a less urban side of Puerto Rico, Ponce, on the south shore, and Mayagüez, on the west coast, make good centers for sightseeing. From either Ponce or Mayagüez you can take a side trip to historic San Germán, Puerto Rico's second-oldest city and site of the oldest church in the New World.

Founded in 1692, Ponce is Puerto Rico's second-largest city, and it has received much attention because of its inner-city restoration. It is home to the island's premier art gallery.

Puerto Rico's third-largest city, Mayagüez, is a port city on the west coast. It might not be as architecturally remarkable as Ponce, but it's a fine base for exploring and enjoying some very good beaches.

San Germán and Ponce are home to some of the finest Puerto Rican colonial architecture in the Caribbean.

Mayagüez and Ponce also attract beach lovers. Playa de Ponce, for example, is far less crowded than the beaches along San Juan's coastal strip. The area also lures hikers to Puerto Rico's government national forest reserves, the best of which lie outside Ponce and include Guánica State Forest and the Carite Forest Reserve as well as the Toro Negro Forest Reserve.

One of the biggest adventure jaunts in Puerto Rico, a trip to Mona Island, can also be explored from the coast near Mayagüez.

1 Ponce ★★

75 miles (121km) SW of San Juan

"The Pearl of the South," Ponce was named after Loíza Ponce de León, great-grandson of Juan Ponce de León. Founded in 1692, Ponce is today Puerto Rico's principal shipping port on the Caribbean. The city is well kept and attractive. A suggestion of a provincial Mediterranean town lingers in the air.

Timed to coincide with 1992's 500th anniversary celebration of Christopher Columbus's voyage to the New World, a $440-million renovation brought new life to this once-decaying city. The streets are lit with gas lamps and lined with neoclassical buildings, just as they were a century ago. Horse-drawn carriages clop by, and strollers walk along sidewalks edged with pink marble. Thanks to the restoration, Ponce now recalls the turn of the 20th century, when it rivaled San Juan as a wealthy business and cultural center.

ESSENTIALS

GETTING THERE Flying from San Juan to Ponce five times a day, **Cape Air** (© 800/352-0714; www.flycapeair.com), a small regional carrier, offers flights for $99 to $149 round-trip. Flight time is 25 minutes.

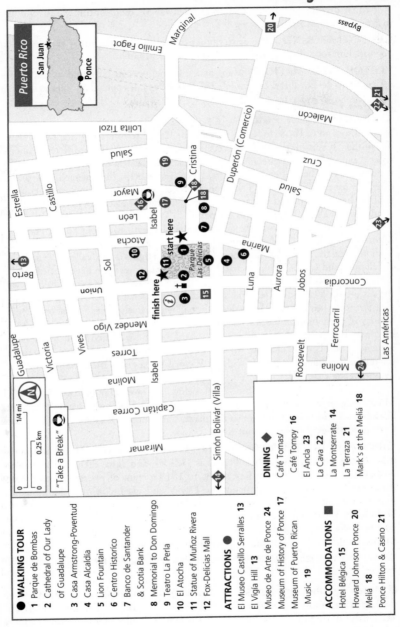

Puerto Rico

San Juan ★

● Ponce

"Take a Break" ☕

0 — 1/4 mi
0 — 0.25 km

● WALKING TOUR

1 Parque de Bombas
2 Cathedral of Our Lady of Guadalupe
3 Casa Armstrong-Poventud
4 Casa Alcaldía
5 Lion Fountain
6 Centro Historico
7 Banco de Santander & Scotia Bank
8 Memorial to Don Domingo
9 Teatro La Perla
10 El Atocha
11 Statue of Muñoz Rivera
12 Fox-Delicias Mall

ATTRACTIONS ●

El Museo Castillo Serralles 13
El Vigía Hill 13
Museo de Arte de Ponce 24
Museum of History of Ponce 17
Museum of Puerto Rican Music 19

ACCOMMODATIONS ■

Hotel Bélgica 15
Howard Johnson Ponce 20
Meliá 18
Ponce Hilton & Casino 21

DINING ◆

Café Tomas/ Café Tompy 16
El Ancla 23
La Cava 22
La Montserrate 14
La Terraza 21
Mark's at the Meliá 18

179

If you're driving, take Route 1 south to Highway 52, then continue south and west to Ponce. Allow at least 1½ hours.

GETTING AROUND   The town's inner core is small enough that everything can be visited on foot. Taxis provide the second-best alternative.

VISITOR INFORMATION   Maps and information can be found at the **tourist office,** Paseo del Sur Plaza, Suite 3 (𝒞 787/841-8044). It's open daily 8am to 4:30pm.

SEEING THE SIGHTS
ATTRACTIONS IN PONCE

Most visitors go to Ponce to see the city's architectural restoration. Calle Reina Isabel, one of the city's major residential streets, is a virtual textbook of the different Ponceño styles, ranging from interpretations of European neoclassical to Spanish colonial. The neoclassical style here often incorporates balconies, as befits the warm climate, and an extensive use of pink marble. The "Ponce Creole" style, a term for Spanish colonial, includes both exterior and interior balconies. The interior balconies have a wall of tiny windows that allows sunlight into the patio.

With partial funding from the governments of Puerto Rico and Spain, Ponce has restored more than 600 of its 1,000 historic buildings. Many are on streets radiating from the stately **Plaza Las Delicias (Plaza of Delights).** On calles Isabel, Reina, Pabellones, and Lolita Tizol, electrical and telephone wires have been buried, replica 19th-century gas lamps have been installed, and sidewalks have been trimmed with the distinctive locally quarried pink marble. Paseo Atocha, one of Ponce's main shopping streets, is now a delightful pedestrian mall with a lively street festival on the third Sunday of every month. Paseo Arias, or Callejon del Amor (Lover's Alley), is a charming pedestrian passage between two 1920s bank buildings, Banco Popular and Banco Santander, on Plaza Las Delicias, where outdoor cafe tables invite lingering. Two monumental bronze lions by Spanish sculptor Victor Ochoa guard the entrance to the old section of the city.

In addition to the attractions listed below, the **weekday marketplace,** open Monday through Friday from 8am to 5pm, at calles Atocha and Castillo is colorful. Perhaps you'll want to simply sit in the plaza, watching the Ponceños at one of their favorite pastimes—strolling about town.

Cathedral of Our Lady of Guadalupe   In 1660 a rustic chapel was built on this spot on the western edge of the Plaza Las Delicias, and since then fires and earthquakes have razed the church repeatedly. In 1919 a team of priests collected funds from local parishioners to construct the Doric- and Gothic-inspired building that stands here today. Designed by architects Francisco Porrato Doría and Francisco Trublard in 1931, and featuring a pipe organ installed in 1934, it remains an important place for prayer for many. The cathedral, named after a famous holy shrine in Mexico, is the best-known church in southern Puerto Rico.

Calle Concordia/Calle Union. 𝒞 787/842-0134. Free admission. Mon–Fri 6am–12:30pm; Sat–Sun 6am–noon and 3–8pm.

El Museo Castillo Serralles ⊛   Two miles (3.2km) north of the center of town is the largest and most imposing building in Ponce, constructed high on El Vigía Hill (see below) during the 1930s by the Serralles family, owners of a local rum distillery. One of the architectural gems of Puerto Rico, it is the best evidence of the wealth produced by the turn-of-the-20th-century sugar boom. Guides will escort you through

the Spanish Revival house with Moorish and Andalusian details. Highlights include panoramic courtyards, a baronial dining room, a small cafe and souvenir shop, and a series of photographs showing the tons of earth that were brought in for the construction of the terraced gardens.

El Vigía 17. *C* **787/259-1774.** Admission $6 adults, $6 seniors over 62, $3 children under 15. Tues–Sun 9:30am–5pm. Free trolley leaving from Plaza Las Delicias de Ponce.

El Vigía Hill   The city's tallest geologic feature, El Vigía Hill (300 ft./91m) dominates Ponce's northern skyline. Its base and steep slopes are covered with a maze of 19th- and early-20th-century development. When you reach the summit, you'll see the soaring Cruz del Vigía (Virgin's Cross). Built in 1984 of reinforced concrete to replace a 19th-century wooden cross in poor repair, this modern 100-foot (30m) structure bears lateral arms measuring 70 feet (21m) long and an observation tower (accessible by elevator), from which you can see all of the natural beauty surrounding Ponce.

The cross commemorates Vigía Hill's colonial role as a deterrent to contraband smuggling. In 1801, on orders from Spain, a garrison was established atop the hill to detect any ships that might try to unload their cargoes tax-free along Puerto Rico's southern coastline.

At the north end of Ponce. Take a taxi from the Plaza Las Delicias; the ride will cost about $4.

Museo de Arte de Ponce 𝕽𝕽𝕽   Donated to the people of Puerto Rico by Luís A. Ferré, a former governor, this museum has the finest collection of European and Latin American art in the Caribbean. The building itself was designed by Edward Durell Stone (who also designed the John F. Kennedy Center for the Performing Arts in Washington, D.C.) and has been called the "Parthenon of the Caribbean." Its collection represents the principal schools of American and European art of the past 5 centuries. Among the nearly 400 works on display are exceptional pre-Raphaelite and Italian baroque paintings. Visitors will also see artworks by other European masters, as well as Puerto Rican and Latin American paintings, graphics, and sculptures. On display are some of the best works of the two "old masters" of Puerto Rico, Francisco Oller and José Campéche. The museum also contains a representative collection of the works of the old masters of Europe, including Gainsborough, Velázquez, Rubens, and Van Dyck. The museum is best known for its pre-Raphaelite and baroque paintings and sculpture—not only from Spain, but from Italy and France as well. Both the Whitney Museum in New York and the Louvre in Paris have borrowed from its collection. Temporary exhibitions are also mounted here.

Av. de Las Américas 23–25. *C* **787/848-0505.** www.museoarteponce.org. Admission $4 adults, $2.50 children under 11. Daily 8:30am–5pm. Follow Calle Concordia from Plaza Las Delicias 1½ miles/2.4km south to Av. de Las Américas.

Museum of Puerto Rican Music   This museum showcases the development of Puerto Rican music, with displays of Indian, Spanish, and African musical instruments that were played in the romantic danza, the favorite music of 19th-century Puerto Rican society, as well as the more African-inspired bomba and plena styles. Also on view are memorabilia of composers and performers.

Calle Isabel 50. *C* **787/848-7016.** Free admission. Dec–Mar Tues–Sat 8:30am–4:30pm; Apr–Nov Tues–Sun 8:30am–4:30pm.

Museum of the History of Ponce (Casa Salazar)   Opened in the Casa Salazar in 1992, this museum traces the history of the city from the time of the Taíno peoples to the present. Interactive displays help visitors orient themselves and locate other attractions. The museum has a conservation laboratory, library, souvenir-and-gift shop, cafeteria, and conference facilities.

Casa Salazar ranks close to the top of Ponce's architectural treasures. Built in 1911, it combines neoclassical and Moorish details, while displaying much that is typical of the Ponce decorative style: stained-glass windows, mosaics, pressed-tin ceilings, fixed jalousies, wood or iron columns, porch balconies, interior patios, and the use of doors as windows.

Calle Reina Isabel 51–53 (at Calle Mayor). (℃ 787/844-7071. Free admission. Tues–Sun 9am–5pm.

Parque de Bombas   Constructed in 1882 as the centerpiece of a 12-day agricultural fair intended to promote the civic charms of Ponce, this building was designated a year later as the island's first permanent headquarters for a volunteer firefighting brigade. It has an unusual appearance—it's painted black, red, green, and yellow. A tourist-information kiosk is situated inside the building (see "Visitor Information," above).

Plaza Las Delicias. (℃ 787/284-4141. Free admission. Daily 8am–5pm.

Teatro la Perla   This theater, built in the neoclassical style in 1864, remains one of the most visible symbols of the economic prosperity of Ponce during the mid–19th century. Designed by Juan Bertoli, an Italian-born resident of Puerto Rico who studied in Europe, it was destroyed by an earthquake in 1918, and rebuilt in 1940 according to the original plans; it reopened to the public in 1941. It is noted for acoustics so clear that microphones are unnecessary. The theater is the largest and most historic in the Spanish-speaking Caribbean. Everything from plays to concerts to beauty pageants takes place here.

At Calle Mayor and Calle Christina. (℃ 787/843-4080.

NEARBY ATTRACTIONS
Hacienda Buena Vista   Built in 1833, this hacienda preserves an old way of life, with its whirring water wheels and artifacts of 19th-century farm production. Once it was one of the most successful plantations on Puerto Rico, producing coffee, corn, and citrus. It was a working coffee plantation until the 1950s, and 86 of the original 500 acres (202 hectares) are still part of the estate. The rooms of the hacienda have been furnished with authentic pieces from the 1850s.

Rte. 123, Barrio Magüeyes, Km 16.8. (℃ 787/812-5027. Tours $7 adults, $4 ages 5–11. Reservations required. 2-hr. tours Wed–Sun at 8:30am, 10:30am, 1:30pm, and 3:30pm (in English only at 1:30pm). A 30-min. drive north of Ponce, in the small town of Barrio Magüeyes, between Ponce and Adjuntas.

Tibes Indian Ceremonial Center   Bordered by the Río Portuguéz and excavated in 1975, this is the oldest cemetery in the Antilles. It contains some 186 skeletons, dating from A.D. 300, as well as pre-Taíno plazas from A.D. 700. The site also includes a re-created Taíno village, seven rectangular ball courts, and two dance grounds. The arrangement of stone points on the dance grounds, in line with the solstices and equinoxes, suggests a pre-Columbian Stonehenge. Here you'll also find a museum, an exhibition hall that presents a documentary about Tibes, a cafeteria, and a souvenir shop.

Rte. 503, Tibes, at Km 2.2. (℃ 787/840-2255. Admission $2 adults, $1 children. Guided tours in English and Spanish are conducted through the grounds. Tues–Sun 9am–4pm. 2 miles/3.2km north of Ponce.

HIKING & BIRD-WATCHING IN GUANICA STATE FOREST 🌟🌟
Heading directly west from Ponce, along Route 2, you reach **Guánica State Forest** 🌟🌟 (℃ 787/724-3724), a setting that evokes Arizona or New Mexico. Here you will find

the best-preserved subtropical ecosystem on the planet. UNESCO has named Guánica a World Biosphere Reserve. Some 750 plants and tree species grow in the area.

The Cordillera Central cuts off the rain coming in from the heavily showered northeast, making this a dry region of cacti and bedrock, a perfect film location for old-fashioned western movies. It's also ideal country for birders. Some 50% of all of the island's terrestrial bird species can be seen in this dry and dusty forest. You might even spot the Puerto Rican emerald-breasted hummingbird. A number of migratory birds often stop here. The most serious ornithologists seek out the Puerto Rican nightjar, a local bird that was believed to be extinct. Now it's estimated that there are nearly a thousand of them.

To reach the forest, take Route 334 northeast of Guánica, to the heart of the forest. There's a ranger station here that will give you information about hiking trails. The booklet provided by the ranger station outlines 36 miles (58km) of trails through the four forest types. The most interesting is the mile-long (1.6km) **Cueva Trail,** which gives you the most scenic look at the various types of vegetation. You might even encounter the endangered bufo lemur toad, once declared extinct but found to still be jumping in this area.

Within the forest, El Portal Tropical Forest Center offers 10,000 square feet (929 sq. m) of exhibition space and provides information.

CARITE FOREST RESERVE ✿

In southeastern Puerto Rico, lying off the Ponce Expressway near Cayey, **Carite Forest Reserve** ✿ is a 6,000-acre (2,428-hectare) reserve with a dwarf forest that was produced by the region's high humidity and moist soil. From several peaks there are panoramic views of Ponce and the Caribbean Sea. On one peak is Nuestra Madre, a Catholic spiritual meditation center that permits visitors to stroll the grounds. Fifty species of birds live in the Carite Forest Reserve, which also has a large natural pool called Charco Azul. A picnic area and campgrounds are shaded by eucalyptus and royal palms. The forest borders lake of the same name. Entrances to the forest are signposted from the town of Cayey, which is reached after an hour's drive east of Ponce. Drive east from Ponce along Route 52, until you near the town of Cayey, where the entrance to the forest reserve is signposted.

TORO NEGRO FOREST RESERVE ✿✿✿ & LAKE GUINEO ✿

North of Ponce via Route 139, **Toro Negro Forest Reserve** ✿✿✿ lies along the Cordillera Central, the cloud-shrouded panoramic route that follows the Cordillera Central as it goes from the southeast town of Yabucoa all the way to Mayagüez on the west coast. This 7,000-acre (2,833-hectare) park, ideal for hikers, straddles the highest peak of the Cordillera Central in the very heart of Puerto Rico. A forest of lush trees, the reserve also contains the headwaters of several main rivers.

The lowest temperatures recorded on the island—some 40°F (4°C)—were measured at **Lake Guineo** ✿, the island's highest lake, which lies within the reserve. The best trail to take here is a short, paved, and wickedly steep path on the north side of Route 143, going up to the south side of Cerro de Punta, which at 4,390 feet (1,338m) is the highest peak on Puerto Rico. Allow about half an hour for an ascent up this peak. Once at the top, you'll be rewarded with Puerto Rico's grandest view, sweeping across the lush interior from the Atlantic to the Caribbean coasts. Other peaks in the reserve also offer hiking possibilities.

WALKING TOUR   PONCE

Start: East side of Plaza Las Delicias
Finish: North side of Plaza Las Delicias
Time: 90 minutes, excluding coffee breaks, museum visits, and shopping stops

The downtown revitalization of Ponce has required more money and generated more publicity than that of any other city in Puerto Rico except San Juan. Your tour of this Caribbean showplace begins on the eastern edge of the town's main square, the Plaza Las Delicias (also known as Plaza Muñoz Rivera). Within the symmetrical borders of this main square, you'll see the red-and-black-striped clapboard facade of the town's most frequently photographed building. (Red and black, incidentally, are the colors of the city's flag.)

As you begin the tour, note the Victorian ginger-bread and the deliberately garish colors of the:

❶ Parque de Bombas (Old Municipal Fire House)

This building housed the fire department before it moved into more modern quarters in another part of the city. You can still see a handful of bright red fire engines parked inside.

On the plaza's opposite side, adjacent to Calle Concordia/Calle Union, is the:

❷ Cathedral of Our Lady of Guadalupe

When you visit, there will almost certainly be parishioners at prayer inside this, the best-known church in southern Puerto Rico. Its alabaster altars were commissioned by an ex-governor of Puerto Rico in the late 1960s in Burgos, Spain.

As you leave the cathedral, notice the many impeccably clipped trees ringing the perimeter of the plaza. Identified as Indian laurels, they were planted between 1906 and 1908 and are one of the botanical triumphs of Ponce. Clipped manually into topiary forms and carefully groomed by a master gardener, they are well worth a second or third glance. The elaborate iron lampposts nearby date from 1916.

Across Calle Concordia from the main entrance to the cathedral is one of Ponce's most famous houses:

❸ Casa Armstrong-Poventud

This paneled and ornately crafted building was once the home of a wealthy Scottish-born banker. The Poventud family moved in after the Armstrongs. Today, it's a cultural center, and it's open Monday through Friday from 8am to noon and 1 to 4:30pm. Admission is free.

Note that at this western border of the Plaza Las Delicias, street signs might identify it as Plaza de Getou. Regardless of what the plaza is called, turn right upon exiting Casa Armstrong-Poventud and walk southward beneath the Indian laurels. On the square's southern edge, you'll see one of the most historic buildings of Ponce, restored to reflect its original function during Spanish colonial days:

❹ Casa Alcaldía (City Hall)

Standing on the site of an 18th-century monastery, this building was erected in 1840 as a general assembly, and then it served as the civic jail until 1905. Speeches by Theodore Roosevelt (in 1906), Herbert Hoover (in 1931), and Franklin D. Roosevelt (in 1934) were delivered from its central second-floor balcony to crowds assembled below. George Bush (I) visited the building in 1987. The clock set into the tower was imported from London in 1877, and a tour of the baronial street-level interior reveals a memorial plaque dedicated to the fallen American dead (Second Wisconsin

Regiment) during the Spanish-American War. A few paces farther, you'll see a galleried courtyard that formerly served as prisoners' cells. The building's main courtyard was used for public executions. In City Hall, other plaques make clear that the city of Ponce was named not after Juan Ponce de León, but rather after de León's great-grandson, Loíza Ponce de León, one of the town's early civic leaders.

Across from the entrance to City Hall (in Plaza Las Delicias), you'll see one of the most beautiful fountains of Puerto Rico, the:

⑤ Lion Fountain (Puente de los Léones)

Crafted from marble and bronze, the Lion Fountain was modeled after a famous fountain in Barcelona, Spain. It was made for the 1939 New York World's Fair and later purchased by the mayor of Ponce.

Continue your walk along the southern edge of the square. Note the way the plaza has "chopped corners" (broadly rounded 45-degree corners rather than 90-degree perpendicular corners). They were designed this way for increased visibility by the Spanish armies as a deterrent to civil unrest and the contraband trade that flourished here during their regime. Ponce is said to have the only large square on Puerto Rico designed with such a feature.

When you reach the corner of Calle Marina and Calle Duperón (Comercio), head south (to your right) for 1 block until you come to the landmark:

⑥ Centro Histórico

Originally built in 1922, this landmark served as the town's casino until it was closed in the mid-1960s. Today it houses government agencies and is not open to the public, although it can be admired from the outside.

After admiring the facade of the Centro Histórico, backtrack along Calle Marina (that is, walk north again) until you again come to the intersection with Calle Duperón (Comercio). On the far right (east) of this intersection loom the:

⑦ Banco de Santander & Scotia Bank

These two banks are both adorned with intricate stained-glass windows, Art Nouveau architectura... rating the two b... lined with African tul... evoke the romantic spirit o... love. This is also the site of pub... certs that are held every Sunday betwee... 8 and 9pm by classical orchestras or dance bands.

Proceed eastward along Calle Cristina. Behind you, you should see the red-and-black-sided fire station at Plaza Las Delicias. At the next cross street, Calle Mayor, diagonal to where you're standing, you'll see the:

⑧ Memorial to Don Domingo

This statue is dedicated to Don Domingo ("Cocolia") Cruz, longtime leader of Ponce's municipal band and one of the best-known musicians from Ponce. He died in 1934.

Turn left on Calle Mayor and admire:

⑨ Teatro La Perla

The neoclassical facade of this, the largest and most historic theater in the Caribbean, is graced by six classical columns (see "Seeing the Sights," above). Depending on the time of day and the season, the lobby of this theater might be open for a quick look at the interior decoration.

Continue walking northward along Calle Mayor to the first intersection (Calle Isabel). To your right stands a Moorish-inspired building known as the Casa Salazar (Salazar House), which accommodates a branch of the Puerto Rican Museum of History.

TAKE A BREAK
Stop for a cup of coffee, an ice cream, or a sandwich at the **Café Tomas/Café Tompy**, Calle Isabel at Calle Mayor (© 787/840-1965). Divided into less formal and more formal sections, it is open daily from 7am to midnight. For more information, see "Where to Dine," later in this chapter.

...eding west along the edge of the square,
...e the:

🔞 Fox-Delicias Mall

Originally built in 1931 as a movie theater, this is one of the city's most alluring watering holes and shopping enclaves. Its pink walls are excellent examples of Art Deco architecture in Puerto Rico. In crumbling disrepair, the theater was transformed into a disco during the 1960s. In 1989 the government of Spain earmarked funds for the restoration of this building to its original celluloid glamour. Today this mall contains an array of shops, nightclubs, and cafes, a good place for refreshment at the end of your stroll.

After exploring the mall, you can walk out and cross Calle Isabel, heading south. You will once again be at Plaza Las Delicias.

After y...   the Plaza Las
Delicias an...   along its northern
edge. Note tha...   confines of the
square is the:

🔞 Statue of Muñoz Rivera

This statue is a memorial to Muñoz Rivera (1898–1980), one of Puerto Rico's best-known politicians. He helped Puerto Ricans become U.S. citizens after a career of political lobbying.

BEACHES & OUTDOOR ACTIVITIES

Ponce is a city—not a beach resort—and should be visited mainly for its sights. There is little here in the way of organized sports, but a 10-minute drive west of Ponce will take you to **Playa de Ponce** 🌟🌟, a long strip of white sand opening onto the tranquil waters of the Caribbean. This beach is usually better for swimming than the Condado in San Juan.

Because the northern shore of Puerto Rico fronts the often-turbulent Atlantic, many snorkelers prefer the more tranquil southern coast, not only off Ponce, but also off **La Parguera** (see section 2, "The Southwest Coast," in chapter 10). On the beaches around Ponce, water lovers can go snorkeling right off the beach, and it isn't necessary to take a boat trip. Waters here are not polluted, and visibility is usually good, unless there are heavy winds and choppy seas.

La Guancha is a sprawling compound of publicly funded beachfront, located 3 miles (4.8km) south of Ponce's cathedral. It has a large parking lot, a labyrinth of boardwalks, and a saltwater estuary with moorings for hundreds of yachts and pleasure craft. A tower, which anyone can climb free of charge, affords high-altitude vistas of the active beach scene. La Guancha is a relatively wholesome version of Coney Island, with a strong Hispanic accent and vague hints of New England. On hot weekends, the place is mobbed with thousands of families who listen to recorded merengue and salsa. Lining the boardwalk are at least a dozen emporiums purveying beer, party-colored drinks, high-calorie snacks, and souvenirs. Weather permitting, this free beach is good for a few hours' diversion at any time of the year.

Although snorkeling is good off the beaches, the best snorkeling is reached by boat trip to the offshore island of **Caja de Muertos,** or **Coffin Island,** an uninhabited key that's covered with mangrove swamps and ringed with worthwhile beaches. A government ferry used to take beach buffs to the wild beaches here, but it was needed for passenger service between Fajardo and Vieques. Today, a private outfitter, **Island**

Adventures, c/o Rafi Vega, La Guancha (© 787/842-8546), will haul day-trippers there for a full-day beachgoers' outing ($20 per person without snorkeling equipment; $35 per person with snorkeling equipment). Advance reservations (which you can make yourself, or leave to the desk staff of whatever hotel you opt for in Ponce) are necessary, as most of this outfit's excursions don't leave unless there are a predetermined number of participants.

The city owns two **tennis complexes,** one at Poly Deportivos, with nine hard courts, and another at Rambla, with six courts. Both are open from 9am to 10pm daily and are lighted for night play. You can play for free, but you must call to make a reservation. For information, including directions on how to get there, call the **Secretary of Sports** at © 787/840-4400.

One of Puerto Rico's finest and newest courses is the **Costa Caribe Golf & Country Club** 🏌🏌 (© 787/848-1000), on the site of the Ponce Hilton & Casino (see below). This 27-hole course charges from $65 to $75 for guests to play 18 holes. The beautifully landscaped holes—with commanding views of the ocean and mountain—are laid out in former sugar-cane fields. The no. 12 hole, one of the most dramatic, calls for a 188-yard carry over water from the back tees. Trade winds add to the challenge. The three 9s can be played in 18-hole combinations, as conceived by golf architect Bruce Besse. The greens are undulating and moderate in speed, averaging 6,000 square feet (557 sq. m). Golf carts are included in the greens fees, and both gas and electric carts are available.

To play golf, you can also go to **Aguirre Golf Club,** Route 705, Aguirre (© 787/853-4052), 30 miles (48km) east of Ponce (take Hwy. 52). This course, open from 7:30am to sunset daily, charges $20 greens fees Monday to Friday, and $30 on weekends and holidays. Another course, **Club Deportivo,** Carretera 102, Km 15.4, Barrio Jogudas, Cabo Rojo (© 787/254-3748), lies 30 miles (48km) west of Ponce. This course is an 18-holer, open daily from 7am to 5pm. Greens fees are $35 during the week and $40 on the weekend.

SHOPPING

If you feel a yen for shopping in Ponce, head for the Fox-Delicias Mall, at the intersection of Calle Reina Isabel and Calle Union, the city's most innovative shopping center. Among the many interesting stores is **Regalitos y Algo Mas** (no phone), located on the upper level. It specializes in unusual gift items from all over Puerto Rico. Look especially for the Christmas tree ornaments, crafted from wood, metal, colored porcelain, or bread dough, and for the exotic dolls displayed by the owners. Purchases can be shipped anywhere in the world.

The best outlet for souvenirs and artisans' work is **El Palacio del Coquí Inc.,** Calle Marina 9227 (© 787/841-0216), whose name means "palace of the tree frog." This is the place to buy the grotesque masks (viewed as collectors' items) that are used at carnival time. Ask the owner to explain the significance of these masks.

Utopía, Calle Isabel 78 (© 787/848-8742), conveniently located in Plaza Las Delicias, has the most imaginative and interesting selection of gift items and handicrafts in Ponce. Prominently displayed are *vegigantes,* brightly painted carnival masks inspired by carnival rituals and crafted from papier-mâché. In Ponce, where many of these masks are made, they sell at bargain prices of between $5 and $500, depending on their size. Other items include cigars, pottery, clothing, and jewelry; gifts imported from Indonesia, the Philippines, and Mexico; and rums from throughout the Caribbean. Julio and Carmen Aguilar are the helpful and enthusiastic owners, who hail from Ecuador and Puerto Rico, respectively.

WHERE TO STAY
EXPENSIVE
Ponce Hilton & Casino 🌀🌀   On an 80-acre (32-hectare) tract of land right on the beach, this is the most glamorous hotel in southern Puerto Rico. At the western end of Avenida Santiago de los Caballeros, it's about a 10-minute drive from the center of Ponce. Designed like a miniature village, with turquoise-blue roofs, white walls, and lots of tropical plants, ornamental waterfalls, and gardens, it welcomes both conventioneers and individual travelers. Accommodations contain tropically inspired furnishings, ceiling fans, and terraces or balconies. All the rooms are medium to spacious, with adequate desk and storage place, tasteful fabrics, good upholstery, and fine linen. The ground-floor rooms are the most expensive. Each is equipped with a generous tiled bathroom with a tub/shower combination.

The food is the most sophisticated and refined on the south coast of Puerto Rico. All the waiters seem to have an extensive knowledge of the menu and will guide you through some exotic dishes—of course, you'll find familiar fare, too.

Av. Caribe 1150 (P.O. Box 7419), Ponce, PR 00716. 📞 800/HILTONS or 787/259-7676. Fax 787/259-7674. www. hilton.com. 153 units. Year-round $180–$325 double; $400 suite. AE, DC, DISC, MC, V. Self-parking $4.50; valet parking $10. **Amenities:** 2 restaurants; 2 bars; lagoon-shaped pool ringed w/gardens; 2 tennis courts; fitness center; bike rentals; playground; children's program; business center; room service (7am–midnight); babysitting; laundry service; dry cleaning; casino; nightclub; rooms for those w/limited mobility. *In room:* A/C, TV, dataport, minibar, coffeemaker, hair dryer, iron, safe.

MODERATE
Howard Johnson Ponce *(Kids)*   This hotel, a 15-minute drive east of Ponce, opened in 1989. Its modest bedrooms are conservative and comfortable, equipped with contemporary furnishings. Each unit has a small tiled bathroom with tub/shower combination. The prices appeal to families.

Turpo Industrial Park 103, Mercedita, Ponce, PR 00715. 📞 787/841-1000. Fax 787/841-2560. www.hojo.com. 120 units. Year-round $97–$127 double; $150 suite. AE, DC, DISC, MC, V. Free parking. East of Ponce on Hwy. 52, opposite the Interamerican University. **Amenities:** Restaurant; bar/disco; pool; children's wading pool; gym; whirlpool; limited room service; laundry service; dry cleaning; rooms for those w/limited mobility. *In room:* A/C, TV, coffeemaker, hair dryer, iron, safe.

Meliá   A city hotel with southern hospitality, the Meliá, which has no connection with the international hotel chain, attracts businesspeople. The location is a few steps away from the Cathedral of Our Lady of Guadalupe and from the Parque de Bombas (the red-and-black firehouse). Although the more expensive Hilton long ago outclassed this old and somewhat tattered hotel, many people who can afford more upscale accommodations still prefer to stay here for its old-time atmosphere. The lobby floor and all stairs are covered with Spanish tiles of Moorish design. The desk clerks speak English. The small rooms are comfortably furnished and pleasant enough, and most have a balcony facing either busy Calle Cristina or the old plaza. Bathrooms are tiny, each with a shower stall. Breakfast is served on a rooftop terrace with a good view of Ponce, and Mark's at the Meliá thrives under separate management (see "Where to Dine," below). You can park your car in the lot nearby.

Calle Cristina 2, Ponce, PR 00731. 📞 800/448-8355 or 787/842-0260. Fax 787/841-3602. www.hotelmeliapr.com. 73 units (shower only). Year-round $90–$120 double; $130 suite. Rates include continental breakfast. AE, MC, V. Parking $3. **Amenities:** Restaurant; bar; outdoor pool; limited room service; rooms for those w/limited mobility. *In room:* A/C, TV, dataport, hair dryer, iron, safe.

INEXPENSIVE

Hotel Bélgica In the hands of a skilled decorator with a l[...]
Spanish colonial mansion from around 1911 could be transforme[...]
bed-and-breakfast. Until then, however, you'll be faced with a combin[...]
charm and modern junkiness, overseen by a brusque staff. You might[...]
conscious spot wonderful or horrible, depending on your point of vi[...]
assignment. The most appealing accommodations are nos. 8, 9, and 10; [...]ooms
are spacious and have balconies that hang over Calle Villa, a few steps from Plaza Las
Delicias. Each unit has a small tiled shower-only bathroom. This venue is for rough-
ing it, backpacker style. The hotel is devoid of the standard amenities, and no meals
are served, but there are several cafes in the area.

Calle Villa 122 (at Calle Union/Concordia), Ponce, PR 00731. ℭ **787/844-3255.** Fax 787/844-3255. www.hotel
belgica.com. 20 units (shower only). Year-round $75 double. MC, V. *In room:* A/C, TV, no phone.

WHERE TO DINE
EXPENSIVE

La Cava ✿✿ INTERNATIONAL This hive of venerable rooms within a 19th-
century coffee plantation is the most appealing and elaborate restaurant in Ponce.
There's a well-trained staff, old-fashioned charm, well-prepared cuisine, and a
champagne-and-cigar bar where the bubbly sells for around $6 a glass. Menu items
change every 6 weeks, but might include duck foie gras with toasted brioche, Parma
ham with mango, cold poached scallops with mustard sauce, a fricassee of lobster and
mushrooms in a pastry shell, and grilled lamb sausage with mustard sauce on a bed of
couscous. Dessert could be a black-and-white soufflé or a trio of tropical sorbets.

In the Ponce Hilton, Av. Caribe 1150. ℭ **787/259-7676.** Reservations recommended. Main courses $26–$30.
AE, DC, DISC, MC, V. Mon–Sat 6:30–10:30pm.

Mark's at the Meliá ✿✿✿ INTERNATIONAL Mark French (isn't that a great
name for a chef?) elevates Puerto Rican dishes into haute cuisine at this eatery. You'd
think he'd been entertaining the celebs in San Juan instead of cooking at what is somewhat of a Caribbean backwater. French was hailed as "Chef of the Caribbean 2000" in
Fort Lauderdale. With his constantly changing menus and his insistence that everything
be fresh, he's still a winner. You'll fall in love with this guy when you taste his tamarind
barbecued lamb with yucca mojo. Go on to sample the grilled lobster with tomato-and-
chive salad or the freshly made sausage with pumpkin, cilantro, and chicken. All over
Puerto Rico you get fried green plantains, but here they come topped with sour cream
and a dollop of caviar. The corn-crusted red snapper with yucca purée and tempura
jumbo shrimp with Asian salad are incredible. The desserts are spectacular, notably the
vanilla flan layered with rum sponge cake and topped with a caramelized banana, as well
as the award-winning bread pudding soufflé with coconut vanilla sauce.

In the Meliá Hotel, Calle Cristina. ℭ **787/284-6275.** Reservations recommended. Main courses $16–$30. AE, MC, V.
Tues–Sat noon–3pm and 6–10:30pm.

MODERATE

El Ancla ✿ PUERTO RICAN/SEAFOOD This is one of Ponce's best restaurants,
with a lovely location 2 miles (3.2km) south of the city center, on soaring piers that
extend from the rocky coastline out over the surf. As you dine, the sound of the sea
rises literally from beneath your feet.

items are prepared with real Puerto Rican zest and flavor. A favorite here is
snapper stuffed with lobster and shrimp, served either with fried plantains or
mashed potatoes. Other specialties are filet of salmon in caper sauce, and a seafood
medley of lobster, shrimp, octopus, and conch. Most of the dishes are reasonably
priced, especially the chicken and conch. Lobster tops the price scale. The side orders,
including crabmeat rice and yucca in garlic, are delectable.

Av. Hostos Final, Playa Ponce. ℭ 787/840-2450. Main courses $13–$36. AE, DC, MC, V. Sun–Thurs 11am–10pm;
Fri–Sat 11am–11pm.

La Montserrate PUERTO RICAN/SEAFOOD   Beside the seafront, in a residential area about 4 miles (6.4km) west of the town center, this restaurant draws a loyal
following from the surrounding neighborhood. A culinary institution in Ponce since
it was established 20 years ago, it occupies a large, airy, modern building divided into
two different dining areas. The first of these is slightly more formal than the other.
Most visitors head for the less formal, large room in back, where windows on three
sides encompass a view of some offshore islands. Specialties, concocted from the catch
of the day, might include octopus salad, several different kinds of asopao, a whole red
snapper in Creole sauce, or a selection of steaks and grills. Nothing is innovative, but
the cuisine is typical of the south of Puerto Rico, and it's a family favorite. The fish
dishes are better than the meat selections.

Sector Las Cucharas, Rte. 2. ℭ 787/841-2740. Main courses $14–$24. AE, DISC, MC, V. Daily 11am–10pm.

La Terraza ℛ INTERNATIONAL   During the design phase of the Ponce Hilton,
a team of architects devoted one of its biggest, sunniest, and most interesting interior
spaces to this dramatic-looking restaurant, where two-story walls of windows sweep
the eye out over the greenery of the hotel's garden. Lunchtimes focus on a well-stocked
buffet that dominates rooms off to the side of the eating area. At nighttime, except for
a sprawling soup-and-salad bar (access to which is included in the price of any main
course), the buffet is eliminated in favor of a la carte dining that's choreographed by
a carefully trained staff. Menu items change with the seasons but are likely to include
grilled grouper with either lemon butter or criolla sauce; T-bone steaks with béarnaise,
red-wine, or mushroom sauce; a succulent chateaubriand that's prepared for two diners at a time; and lobster that's available several different ways.

In the Ponce Hilton, Av. Caribe 1150. ℭ 787/259-7676. Breakfast $5–$19; lunch buffet $22; dinner main courses
$24–$36. AE, DC, DISC, MC, V. Daily 6:30–10:30am, 12:30–4:30pm, and 6:30–10:30pm.

INEXPENSIVE

Café Tomas/Café Tompy (Value) PUERTO RICAN   The more visible and busier
section of this establishment functions as a simple cafe for neighbors and local merchants. At plastic tables often flooded with sunlight from the big windows, you can
order coffee, sandwiches, or cold beer, perhaps while relaxing after a walking tour of
the city.

The family-run restaurant part of this establishment is more formal. The discreet
entrance is adjacent to the cafe on Calle Isabel. Here, amid a decor reminiscent of a
Spanish *tasca* (tapas bar), you can enjoy such simply prepared dishes as salted filet of
beef, beefsteak with onions, four kinds of asopao, buttered eggs, octopus salads, and
yucca croquettes.

Calle Isabel at Calle Mayor. ℭ 787/840-1965. Breakfast $2.25–$4; main courses lunch and dinner $5–$8. AE, MC, V.
Restaurant daily 11:30am–midnight; cafe daily 7am–midnight.

2 Mayagüez (★

98 miles (158km) W of San Juan, 15 miles (24km) S of Aguadilla

The largest city on the island's west coast, Mayagüez is a port whose elegance and charm reached its zenith during the mercantile and agricultural prosperity of the 19th century. Most of the town's stately buildings were destroyed in an earthquake in 1918, and today the town is noted more for its industry than its aesthetic appeal.

Although it's a commercial city, Mayagüez is a convenient stopover for those exploring the west coast. If you want a windsurfing beach, you can head north of Rincón, and if you want a more tranquil beach, you can drive south from Mayagüez along Route 102 to Boquerón. See chapter 10.

Although the town itself dates from the mid–18th century, the area around it has figured in European history since the time of Christopher Columbus, who landed nearby in 1493. Today, in the gracious plaza at the town's center, a bronze statue of Columbus stands atop a metallic globe of the world.

Famed for the size and depth of its **harbor** (the second largest on the island, after San Juan's harbor), Mayagüez was built to control the **Mona Passage,** a route essential to the Spanish Empire when Puerto Rico and the nearby Dominican Republic were vital trade and defensive jewels in the Spanish crown. Today this waterway is notorious for the destructiveness of its currents, the ferocity of its sharks, and the thousands of boat people who arrive illegally from either Haiti or the Dominican Republic, both on the island of Hispaniola.

Queen Isabel II of Spain recognized Mayagüez's status as a town in 1836. Her son, Alfonso XII, granted it a city charter in 1877. Permanently isolated from the major commercial developments of San Juan, Mayagüez, like Ponce, has always retained its own distinct identity.

Today the town's major industry is tuna packing. In fact, 60% of the tuna consumed in the United States is packed here. This is also an important departure point for deep-sea fishing and is the bustling port for exporting agricultural produce from the surrounding hillsides.

ESSENTIALS

GETTING THERE   Cape Air (© 800/352-0714; www.flycapeair.com) flies from San Juan to Mayagüez twice daily (flying time: 40 min.). Round-trip passage is $180 per person.

If you rent a car at the San Juan airport and want to **drive** to Mayagüez, it's fastest and most efficient to take the northern route that combines sections of the newly widened Route 22 with the older Route 2. Estimated driving time for a local resident is about 90 minutes, although newcomers usually take about 30 minutes longer. The southern route, which combines the modern Route 52 with transit across the outskirts of historic Ponce, and final access into Mayagüez via the southern section of Route 2, requires a total of about 3 hours and affords some worthwhile scenery across the island's mountainous interior.

GETTING AROUND   Taxis meet arriving planes. If you take one, negotiate the fare with the driver first because cabs are unmetered here.

There are branches of **Avis** (© 787/832-0406), **Budget** (© 787/832-4570), and **Hertz** (© 787/832-3314) at the Mayagüez airport.

Fun Fact A History of Honeymooning

Mayagüez is still identified by some as "the honeymoon capital of Puerto Rico," partly because of the lush and beautiful vegetation that grows here and partly because of a peculiarly romantic 16th-century legend. It is said that local farmers often kidnapped young Spanish sailors who had stopped at Mayagüez for provisions en route to South America. There was a scarcity of eligible bachelors in Mayagüez, and the farmers kidnapped the young sailors in hopes of providing their daughters with husbands and their farms with overseers. However, it's anyone's guess whether this was good or bad luck.

Many tradition-minded Puerto Rican couples still come here on their honeymoons. But for most international visitors, Mayagüez would rank low as a honeymoon retreat.

VISITOR INFORMATION   Mayagüez doesn't have a tourist-information office. If you're starting out in San Juan, inquire there before you set out (see "Visitor Information" under "Orientation" in chapter 4).

EXPLORING THE AREA: SURFING BEACHES & TROPICAL GARDENS

Along the western coastal bends of Route 2, north of Mayagüez, lie the best **surfing beaches** in the Caribbean. Surfers from as far away as New Zealand come to ride the waves. You can also check out panoramic **Playa Higüero** beach, nearby on Route 413, near Rincón. For more information, see section 1, "Rincón," in chapter 10.

South of Mayagüez is **Boquerón Beach** *✹✹*, one of the island's best, with a wide strip of white sand and good snorkeling conditions.

The chief attraction in Mayagüez is the **Tropical Agriculture Research Station (Estación Experimental Agrícola Federal)** *✹* (© 787/831-3435). It's located on Route 65, between Post Street and Route 108, adjacent to the University of Puerto Rico at Mayagüez campus and across the street from the **Parque de los Próceres (Patriots' Park).** At the administration office, ask for a free map of the tropical gardens, which have one of the largest collections of tropical plant species intended for practical use, including cacao, fruit trees, spices, timbers, and ornamentals. The grounds are open Monday to Friday from 7am to 4pm, and there is no admission fee.

Mayagüez is the jumping-off point for visits to unique **Mona Island,** the "Galápagos of the Caribbean." See the box below for details.

Not far from Mayagüez is **Maricao.** You can reach Maricao from Mayagüez by heading directly east along Route 105, which will take you across mountain scenery and along fertile fields until you reach the village.

From Maricao, you can take Route 120 south to Km 13.8, or from Mayagüez you can take Route 105 east to the **Maricao State Forest** *✹* picnic area, located 2,854 feet (260m) above sea level. The observation tower here provides a panoramic view across the green mountains up to the coastal plains. Trails are signposted here, and your goal might be the highest peak in the forest, Las Tetas de Cerro Gordo, at 2,625 feet (800m). A panoramic view unfolds from here, including a spotting of the offshore island of Mona. Nearly 50 species of birds live in this forest, including the Lesser Antillean pewee and the scaly naped pigeon. Nature watchers will delight to know that there are some 280 tree species in this reserve, 38 of which are found only here.

Mayagüez

ACCOMMODATIONS ■
Mayagüez Resort
& Casino 2
Holiday Inn
& Tropical Casino 1
Hotel Parador El Sol 6
Hotel and Parador
Joyuda Beach 8
Parador Hacienda Juanita 5

DINING ◆
El Castillo 2

ATTRACTIONS ●
Maricao 7
Parque de los Próceres 4
Tropical Agriculture
Research Station 3

NIGHTLIFE ▲
El Casino 2
Veranda Terrace 2

Mona Island: The Galápagos of Puerto Rico

Off Mayagüez, the unique **Isla Mona** 🐊🐊🐊 teems with giant iguanas, three species of endangered sea turtles, red-footed boobies, and countless other seabirds. It features a tabletop plateau with mangrove forests and cacti, giving way to dramatic 200-foot-high (61m) limestone cliffs that rise above the water and encircle much of Mona.

A bean-shaped pristine island with no hotels, Mona is a destination for the hardy pilgrim who seeks the road less traveled. A pup tent, backpack, and hiking boots will do fine if you plan to forego the comforts of civilization and immerse yourself in nature. Snorkelers, spelunkers, biologists, and eco-tourists find much to fascinate them in Mona's wildlife, mangrove forests, coral reefs, and complex honeycomb, which is the largest marine-originated cave in the world. There are also miles of secluded white-sand beaches and palm trees.

Uninhabited today, Mona was for centuries the scene of considerable human activity. The pre-Columbian Taíno Indians were the first to establish themselves here. Later, pirates used it as a base for their raids, followed by guano miners, who removed the rich crop fertilizer from Mona's caves. Columbus landed in Mona during his 1494 voyage, and Ponce de León spent several days here en route to becoming governor of Puerto Rico in 1508. The notorious pirate Captain Kidd used Mona as a temporary hide-out.

Mona can be reached by organized tour from Mayagüez. Camping is available at $10 per night. Everything needed, including water, must be brought in, and everything, including garbage, must be taken out. For more information, call the **Puerto Rico Department of Natural Resources** at ✆ **787/721-5495.**

To reach the island, contact **Tourmarine Adventures,** Route 102, Km 14.1 (✆ **787/375-2625),** Joyuda. Captain Elick Hernández operates boat charters to Mona with a minimum of 10 passengers, each paying $135 for a round-trip day adventure.

Warning: The passage over is extremely rough, and many passengers prone to seasickness take Dramamine the night before the boat ride. There is no bottled water on the island, so bring your own. Also bring food, mosquito repellent, and even toilet paper. Alcoholic drinks are forbidden.

WHERE TO STAY

Holiday Inn & Tropical Casino This six-story hotel competes with the Mayagüez Resort & Casino, though we like the latter better. The Holiday Inn is well maintained, contemporary, and comfortable. It has a marble-floored, high-ceilinged lobby, an outdoor pool with a waterside bar, and a big casino, but its lawn simply isn't as dramatically landscaped as the Mayagüez resort's surrounding acreage. Bedrooms here are comfortably but functionally outfitted in motel style; they've recently been refurbished. Each unit is equipped with a tiled bathroom with a tub/shower combination.

2701 Rte. 2, Km 149.9, Mayagüez, PR 00680-6328. ✆ **888/HOLIDAY** or 787/833-1100. Fax 787/833-1300. www. holiday-inn.com. 142 units. Year-round $115–$147 double; $193 suite. AE, DC, DISC, MC, V. **Amenities:** Restaurant;

2 bars; outdoor pool; casino; gym; business center; limited room service; laundry service; rooms for those w/limited mobility. *In room:* A/C, TV, dataport, coffeemaker, hair dryer, iron, safe.

Hotel Parador El Sol

This parador from around 1970 provides some of the most reasonable and hospitable accommodations in this part of Puerto Rico, although it's far more geared to the business traveler than to the tourist, with no-frills furnishings. All units are nonsmoking and have a small bathroom with tub and shower. This six-floor restored hotel is central to the shopping district and to all highways, 2 blocks from the landmark Plaza del Mercado in the heart of the city. (For the location of this parador, see the map "Paradores & Country Inns of Puerto Rico" on p. 53.)

Calle Santiago Riera Palmer, Este 9, Mayagüez, PR 00680. © 787/834-0303. Fax 787/265-7567. www. hotelelsol.com. 51 units. Year-round $70–$95 double; $85–$95 triple. Rates include continental breakfast. AE, MC, V. Free parking. **Amenities:** Restaurant; pool; 1 room for those w/limited mobility. *In room:* A/C, TV, fridge, hair dryer.

Mayagüez Resort & Casino ✵

Except for the ritzy Horned Dorset Primavera (p. 203), this is the largest and best general hotel resort in western Puerto Rico, appealing equally to business travelers and vacationers. In 1995 local investors took over what was then a sagging Hilton and radically renovated it to the tune of $5 million. The hotel still benefits from its redesigned casino, country-club format, and 20 acres of tropical gardens. The landscaped grounds have been designated an adjunct to the nearby Tropical Agriculture Research Station. Five species of palm trees, eight kinds of bougainvillea, and numerous species of rare flora are set adjacent to the institute's collection of tropical plants, which range from a pink torch ginger to a Sri Lankan cinnamon tree.

The hotel's well-designed bedrooms open onto views of the swimming pool, and many units have private balconies. Guest rooms tend to be small, but they have good beds. The restored bathrooms are well equipped with makeup mirrors, scales, and tub/shower combinations.

For details about El Castillo, the hotel's restaurant, see "Where to Dine," below. The hotel is the major entertainment center of Mayagüez. Its casino has free admission and is open 24 hours a day. You can also drink and dance at the Victoria Lounge.

Rte. 104, Km 0.3 (P.O. Box 3781), Mayagüez, PR 00680. © 888/689-3030 or 787/832-3030. Fax 787/265-3020. www.mayaguezresort.com. 140 units. Year-round $175–$240 double; $285–$325 suite. AE, DC, DISC, MC, V. Parking $4.50. **Amenities:** Restaurant; 3 bars; Olympic-size pool; children's pool; 3 tennis courts; small fitness room; Jacuzzi; steam room; playground; 24-hr. room service; massage; babysitting; laundry service; casino; rooms for those w/limited mobility. *In room:* A/C, TV, dataport, minibar, coffeemaker, iron.

NEARBY PLACES TO STAY

For the location of the paradores described here, see the map "Paradores & Country Inns of Puerto Rico" on p. 53.

Hotel and Parador Joyuda Beach ✵

Built on the beach in scenic Cabo Rojo in 1989, this is little more than an average motel with standard furnishings, but it's a convenient and reasonably priced stopover nevertheless. Each of the simply furnished yet comfortable units (each nonsmoking) has a small tiled bathroom with tub and shower. From here you can easily head to El Combate Beach and the Cabo Rojo Wildlife Refuge. Tennis and golf are just 5 minutes away, and sport-fishing charters, as well as windsurfing and canoeing, can also be arranged. The hotel is often a favorite of Puerto Rican honeymooners.

Rte. 102, Km 11.7, Cabo Rojo, PR 00623. © 787/851-5650. Fax 787/255-3750. www.joyudabeach.com. 41 units. Year-round $70–$120 double. 2 children 11 and under stay free in parent's room. AE, MC, V. Follow Rte. 102 south of Mayagüez to Joyuda. **Amenities:** Restaurant; bar; pool; rooms for those w/limited mobility. *In room:* A/C, TV, dataport.

A Wildlife Refuge for Bird Fanciers

The area around Cabo Rojo, the **Refugio Nacional Cabo Rojo (Red Cape National Refuge;** C 787/851-7297) attracts serious bird-watchers to its government-protected sector. The refuge is on Route 301 at Km 5.1, a mile (1.6km) north of the turnoff to El Combate. At the entrance to the refuge is a visitor center. The only time you can visit the refuge is from 7:30am to 4pm Monday to Friday; admission is free.

Migratory birds, especially ducks and herons but also several species of songbirds, inhabit this refuge. Birders have reported seeing at least 130 species. Trails for bird-watchers have been cut through the reserve. The best time to observe the birds is during the winter months, when they have fled from their cold homelands in the north.

Parador Hacienda Juanita *Æ*   Named after one of its long-ago owners, a matriarch named Juanita, this pink stucco building dates from 1836, when it was a coffee plantation. Situated 2 miles (3.2km) west of the village of Maricao, beside Route 105 heading to Mayagüez, it has a long veranda and a living room furnished with a large-screen TV and decorated with antique tools and artifacts of the coffee industry. Relatively isolated, it's surrounded by only a few neighboring buildings and the jungle. The Luis Rivera family welcomes visitors and serves drinks and meals in their restaurant. There's a swimming pool, billiards table, and Ping-Pong table on the premises. The bedrooms are simple and rural, with ceiling fans, rocking chairs, and rustic furniture, plus small tub-and-shower bathrooms. All are nonsmoking. None of the rooms has air-conditioning (ceiling fans suffice in the cool temperatures of this high-altitude place).

Rte. 105, Km 23.5 (HC01 Box 8200), Maricao, PR 00606. C 787/838-2550. Fax 787/838-2551. www.hacienda juanita.com. 21 units. $130 double with breakfast and dinner. Children 11 and under stay free in parent's room. AE, MC, V. Free parking. **Amenities:** Restaurant; bar; pool; tennis; 1 room for those w/limited mobility. *In room:* TV, dataport, ceiling fan, no phone.

WHERE TO DINE

El Castillo   INTERNATIONAL/PUERTO RICAN   This is the best-managed large-scale dining room in western Puerto Rico, as well as the main restaurant for the largest hotel and casino in the area. The food has real flavor and flair, unlike the typical bland hotel fare so often dished up. Known for its generous lunch buffets, El Castillo serves only a la carte items at dinner, including seafood stew served on a bed of linguine with marinara sauce, grilled salmon with a mango-flavored Grand Marnier sauce, and filets of sea bass with a cilantro, white-wine, and butter sauce. Steak and lobster are served on the same platter, if you want it.

In the Mayagüez Resort & Casino, Rte. 104, Km 0.3. C 787/832-3030. Breakfast buffet $12; Mon–Fri lunch buffet $15; Sun brunch buffet $23; main courses $14–$34. AE, MC, V. Daily 6:30am–midnight.

MAYAGÜEZ AFTER DARK

El Casino   At the completely remodeled casino at the Mayagüez Resort & Casino, with the adjoining Player's Bar, you can try your luck at blackjack, dice, slot machines, roulette, and minibaccarat. Open 24 hours. At the Mayagüez Resort & Casino, Rte. 104. C 787/832-3030, ext. 3301.

Veranda Terrace   On a large and airy covered terrace that opens to a view of a manicured tropical garden, this is a relaxing and soothing place for a cocktail. The bartenders specialize in rum-based concoctions that go well with the hibiscus-scented air. Open daily 11am to 1am. In the Mayagüez Resort & Casino, Rte. 104. ✆ **787/831-7575.**

3 San Germán ⭐⭐

104 miles (167km) SW of San Juan, 34 miles (55km) W of Ponce

Only an hour's drive from Ponce or Mayagüez and the beaches of the southern coast, and just over 2 hours from San Juan, San Germán, Puerto Rico's second-oldest town, is a little museum piece. It was founded in 1512 and destroyed by the French in 1528. Rebuilt in 1570, it was named after Germain de Foix, the second wife of King Ferdinand of Spain. Once the rival of San Juan, San Germán harbored many pirates who pillaged the ships that sailed off the nearby coastline. Indeed, many of today's residents are descended from the smugglers, poets, priests, and politicians who once lived here.

The pirates and sugar plantations are long gone, but the city retains colorful reminders of its Spanish colonial past. Flowers brighten some of the patios here as they do in Seville. Also, as in a small Spanish town, many of the inhabitants stroll through the historic zone in the early evening. Nicknamed *Ciudad de las Lomas* (City of the Hills), San Germán boasts verdant scenery that provides a pleasant backdrop to a variety of architectural styles—Spanish colonial (1850s), criollo (1880s), neoclassical (1910s), Art Deco (1930s), and international (1960s)—depicted in the gracious old-world buildings lining the streets. So significant are these buildings that San Germán is only the second Puerto Rican city (the other is San Juan) to be included in the National Register of Historic Places.

The city's 249 historical treasures are within easy walking distance of one another. Regrettably, you must view most of them from the outside. If some of them are actually open, count yourself fortunate, as they have no phones, keep no regular hours, and are staffed by volunteers who rarely show up. Also, be aware that the signage for the historic buildings can be confusing, and many of the streets in the old town tend to run one-way. Most of the city's architectural treasures lie uphill from the congested main thoroughfare (Calle Luna). We usually try to park on the town's main street (Carretera 102, which changes its name within the borders of San Germán to Calle Luna), and then proceed on foot through the city's commercial core before reaching the architectural highlights described below.

One of the most noteworthy churches in Puerto Rico is **Iglesia Porta Coeli (Gate of Heaven)** ⭐ (✆ **787/892-0160**), which sits atop a knoll at the eastern end of a cobble-covered square, the Parque de Santo Domingo. Dating from 1606 and built in a style inspired by the Romanesque architecture of northern Spain, this is the oldest church in the New World. Restored by the Institute of Puerto Rican Culture, and sheathed in a layer of salmon-colored stucco, it contains a museum of religious art with a collection of ancient *santos,* the carved figures of saints that have long been a major part of Puerto Rican folk art. Look for the 17th-century portrait of St. Nicholas de Bari, the French Santa Claus. Inside, the original palm-wood ceiling and tough ausobo-wood beams draw the eye upward. Other treasures include early choral books from Santo Domingo, a primitive carving of Jesus, and 19th-century Señora de la Monserrate Black Madonna and Child statues. Admission is $1 for adults, free for children under 12. The church is open Wednesday through Sunday from 8:30am to noon and 1 to 4:30pm.

Less than 100 feet (30m) downhill from Iglesia Porta Coeli, at the bottom of the steps that lead from its front door down to the plaza below, is the **Casa Morales** (also known as the **Tomás Vivoni House,** after its architect), San Germán's most photographed and widely recognized house. Designed in the Edwardian style, with wraparound porches, elaborate gables, and elements that might remind you of a Swiss chalet, it was built in 1913, reflecting the region's turn-of-the-20th-century agrarian prosperity. (Note that it is a private residence and can be admired only from the outside.)

The long and narrow, gently sloping plaza that prefaces Iglesia Porta Coeli is the Parque de Santo Domingo, one of San Germán's two main plazas. Street signs also identify the plaza as the Calle Ruiz Belvis. Originally a marketplace, the plaza is paved with red and black cobblestones, and it's bordered with cast-iron benches and portrait busts of prominent figures in the town's history. This plaza merges gracefully with a second plaza, which street signs and maps identify as the Plaza Francisco Mariano Quiñones, the Calle José Julian Acosta, and the Plaza Principal. Separating the two plazas is the unused (and closed to the public) **Viejo Alcaldía (Old Town Hall).** Built late in the 19th century, it's awaiting a new vision, perhaps as a museum or public building.

San Germán's most impressive church—and the most monumental building in the region—is **San Germán de Auxerre** (© **787/892-1027**), which rises majestically above the western end of the Plaza Francisco Mariano Quiñones. Designed in the Spanish baroque style, it was built in 1573 in the form of a simple chapel with a low-slung thatch roof. Its present grandeur is the result of at least five subsequent enlargements and renovations. Much of what you see today is the result of a rebuilding in 1688 and a restoration in 1737 that followed a disastrous earthquake. Inside are three naves, 10 altars, three chapels, and a belfry that was rebuilt in 1939, following an earthquake in 1918. The central chandelier, made from rock crystal and imported from Barcelona in 1866, is the largest in the Caribbean. The pride of the church is the *trompe l'oeil* ceiling, which was elaborately restored in 1993. A series of stained-glass windows with contemporary designs were inserted during a 1999 restoration. The church can be visited daily from 8 to 11am and 1 to 3pm.

A few lesser sights are located near the town's two main squares. **Farmacia Martin,** a modern pharmacy, is incongruously set within the shell of a graceful but battered Art Deco building at the edge of the Parque Santo Domingo (Calle Ruiz Belvis 22; © **787/892-1122**). A cluster of battered and dilapidated clapboard-sided houses line the southern side of the Calle Dr. Ueve, which rambles downhill from its origin at the base of the Iglesia Porta Coeli. The most important house is no. 66, the **Casa Acosta y Fores.** Also noteworthy is **Casa Juán Perichi,** a substantial-looking structure at the corner of Calle Dr. Ueve and Parque Santo Domingo, nearly adjacent to the Iglesia Porta Coeli. Both houses were built around 1917, of traditional wood construction, and are viewed as fine examples of Puerto Rican adaptations of Victorian architecture. Regrettably, both are seriously dilapidated, although that might change as San Germán continues the slow course of its historic renovations.

To the side of the Auxerre church is the modern, cement-sided **Public Library,** Calle José Julia Acosta (© **787/892-3240**), where you might be tempted to duck into the air-conditioned interior for a glance through the stacks and periodical collection. It's open Monday through Thursday from 8am to 8:30pm, Friday from 8am to 6pm, and Saturday from 8am to 1pm and 2 to 4:30pm. Behind the Auxerre church is at least one masonry-fronted town house whose design might remind you of southern Spain (Andalusia), especially when the flowers in the window boxes add splashes of color.

WHERE TO STAY & DINE

For the location of the parador described here, see the map "Paradores & Country Inns of Puerto Rico" on p. 53.

Parador El Oasis Although it's not state of the art, this hotel has a hardworking staff and Spanish colonial charm. As an anchor in this quaint old town, far removed from the beaches, it's a fine place to stay. A three-story building constructed around a pool and patio area, the hotel originated in the late 1700s as a privately owned mansion. With its mint-green walls and white wicker furniture, some of the grace remains. The older rooms, positioned close to the lobby, show the wear and tear of the years but are still preferred by some. More modern rooms, located in the back, are plain and functional yet clean and more spacious than the older units. Three of the units have private balconies, and all units have small shower-only bathrooms.

The in-house restaurant is not the most imaginative choice in town, but it emerges year after year as the most reliable and consistent. It's open Monday to Friday from 11am to 8pm, Saturday 7am to 8pm, and Sunday 7 to 11am. Main courses ($6–$18) include empanadillas, platters of Creole-style corn sticks and cheese balls, tenderloin wrapped in bacon, and combination platters of steak and red snapper.

Calle Luna 72, San Germán, PR 00683. ℂ **787/892-1175.** Fax 787/892-4546. paradoroasis@prtc.net. 52 units (shower only). Year-round $62–$70 double. Children 12 and under stay free in parent's room. Extra person $10. AE, DC, MC, V. Free parking. **Amenities:** Restaurant; bar; outdoor pool; limited room service; babysitting; 1 room for those w/limited mobility. *In room:* A/C, TV, hair dryer.

Villa Del Rey ⚜ *Finds* This is the best place to stay in historic San Germán, although you'll have to drive 15 minutes west to a good beach. The fine country inn is completely modernized and attractively furnished, mostly with picture windows. You're offered a choice of midsize-to-spacious and well-furnished accommodations— single, doubles, or suites. Both the doubles and suites are suitable for families with two children under 12 years old. Each unit comes with a private bathroom with tub and shower. Light meals can be prepared in the suites, each equipped with kitchenette. Guests meet fellow guests at La Veranda, sheltered but in the open air, featuring three meals a day, with a focus on regional dishes.

Rte. 361 Cain Alto Ward, Km 0.8, San Germán, PR 00683. ℂ **787/642-2627.** Fax 787/264-1579. www.villadelrey.net. 19 units. Year-round $90 double; $110 suite. $10 per child in parent's room. MC, V. **Amenities:** Restaurant; bar; outdoor pool; business center. *In room:* A/C, TV.

10

Western Puerto Rico

The scenery of western Puerto Rico varies from a terrain evoking the Arizona desert to a dense blanket of green typical of Germany's Black Forest. The interior has such attractions as the Taíno Indian Ceremonial Park, Río Camuy Cave Park, Arecibo Observatory, and the Karst Country (see chapter 8). Along the west and south coasts, you'll find white sandy beaches, world-class surfing conditions, and numerous towns and attractions. There are modest hotels from which to choose, as well as a few noteworthy paradores, a chain of government-sponsored, privately operated country inns.

The waters of the Atlantic northwest coast tend to be rough—ideal for surfers but not always good for swimming.

Some 8 centuries ago, the Taíno Indians inhabited this western part of Puerto Rico, using it as a site for recreation and worship. Stone monoliths, some decorated with petroglyphs, remain as evidence of that long-ago occupation.

There is a tremendous difference between a holiday on the east coast of Puerto Rico (see chapter 11) and one on the west coast. Nearly all visitors from San Juan head east to explore the El Yunque rainforest (see chapter 8). After that, and perhaps a lazy afternoon on Luquillo Beach, they head back to San Juan and its many resorts and attractions. Others who remain for a holiday in the east are likely to do so because they want to stay at one of the grand resorts such as El Conquistador (p. 223).

Western Puerto Rico, particularly its southwestern sector, is where the Puerto Ricans themselves go for holidays by the sea. The only pocket of posh here is the Horned Dorset Primavera hotel at Rincón (see "Rincón," below). Rincón is also the beach area most preferred by windsurfers.

Other than that, most locals and a few adventurous visitors seeking the offbeat and charming head for the southwestern sector of the island. This is the real Puerto Rico; it hasn't been taken over by high-rise resorts and posh restaurants.

Puerto Rico's west coast has been compared to the old U.S. Wild West. There is a certain truth to that. The cattle ranches on the rolling upland pastures south of the town of Lajas will evoke home for those who come from northwest Texas. Others have compared the peninsula of Cabo Rojo in Puerto Rico to Baja, California.

This western part of Puerto Rico also contains the greatest concentration of paradores, attracting those who'd like to venture into the cool mountainous interior of the west, a wonderful escape from pollution and traffic on a hot day.

1 Rincón

100 miles (161km) W of San Juan, 6 miles (9.7km) N of Mayagüez

North of Mayagüez, on the westernmost point of the island, lies the small fishing village of Rincón, in the foothills of La Cadena mountains. It's not a sightseeing destination unto itself, but surfers from as far away as New Zealand say the area's reef-lined

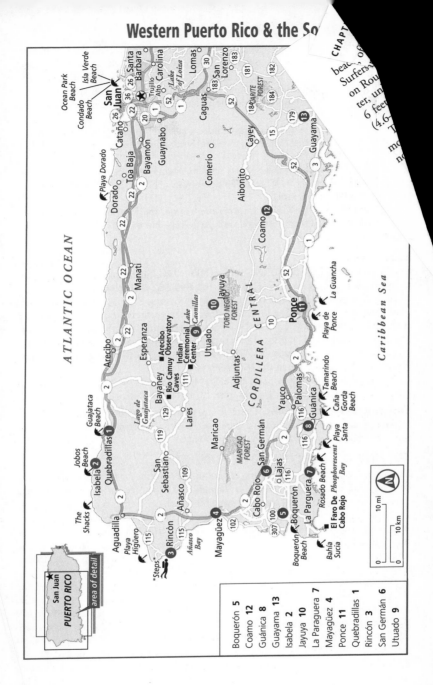

Western Puerto Rico & the Southwest

ATLANTIC OCEAN

Caribbean Sea

PUERTO RICO
San Juan
area of detail

Ocean Park Beach
Condado Beach
Isla Verde Beach
San Juan
Santa Barbara
Trujillo Alto
Carolina
Lomas
Lake of Loíza
San Lorenzo
CARITE FOREST
Caguas
Cayey
Guayama
Cataño
Guaynabo
Bayamón
Playa Dorado
Toa Baja
Dorado
Toa Alta
Comerio
Aibonito
Coamo
Manatí
Esperanza
Arecibo
Bayaney
Arecibo Observatory
Río Camuy Caves
Indian Ceremonial Center
Lake Caonillas
TORO NEGRO FOREST
Jayuya
CORDILLERA CENTRAL
Ponce
Playa de Ponce
La Guancha
Utuado
Adjuntas
Yauco
Palomas
Tamarindo Beach
Guánica
Caña Gorda Beach
Lago de Guajataca
Guajataca Beach
Lares
Maricao
MARICAO FOREST
San Germán
Sabana Grande
Lajas
Playa Santa
Jobos Beach
Isabela
Quebradillas
San Sebastián
Añasco
Mayagüez
Cabo Rojo
Boquerón
La Parguera
Rosado Beach
Playa Santa
The Shacks
Aguadilla
Playa Higüero
Rincón
"Steps"
Añasco Bay
Boquerón Beach
Bahía Sucia
El Faro De Cabo Rojo
Playa Phosphorescent Bay

Boquerón **5**
Coamo **12**
Guánica **8**
Guayama **13**
Isabela **2**
Jayuya **10**
La Parguera **7**
Mayagüez **4**
Ponce **11**
Quebradillas **1**
Rincón **3**
San Germán **6**
Utuado **9**

10 mi
10 km

Route 2 between Mayagüez and Rincón, are the best in the Caribbean. particularly attracted to **Playa Higüero** ✦✦✦, the beach at Punta Higüero, te 413, which ranks among the finest surfing spots in the world. During winnterrupted swells from the North Atlantic form perfect waves, averaging 5 to (1.5–1.8m) in height, with ridable rollers sometimes reaching 15 to 25 feet 7.6m).

he best snorkeling is at a beach gringos have labeled **"Steps."** The waters here are re tranquil than at the beaches attracting surfers. Steps lies right off Route 413, just rth of the center of Rincón.

Endangered humpback whales winter here, attracting a growing number of whalewatchers from December to March. The lighthouse at El Faro Park is a great place to spot these mammoth mammals.

Many nonsurfers visit Rincón for only one reason: the Horned Dorset Primavera Hotel, not only one of the finest hotels in Puerto Rico, but one of the best in the entire Caribbean.

ESSENTIALS

GETTING THERE & GETTING AROUND   Two flights daily go from San Juan to the airport at Mayagüez on **Cape Air** (✆ 800/352-0714; www.flycapeair.com). These flights take 40 minutes, with a round-trip costing $180 per person. From the Mayagüez airport, Rincón is a 30-minute drive to the north on Route 2 (go left or west at the intersection with Rte. 115). Taxis meet planes arriving from San Juan. Because the taxis are unmetered, you should negotiate the fare with your driver at the outset.

There are branches of **Avis** (✆ 787/833-7070), **Budget** (✆ 787/832-4570), and **Hertz** (✆ 787/832-3314) at the Mayagüez airport.

If you're driving from San Juan, either travel west on Route 2 (trip time: 2 hr.) or travel south on scenic Route 52 (trip time: 3½ hr.).

VISITOR INFORMATION   There is no tourist-information office in Rincón. Inquire in San Juan before heading here (see "Visitor Information" under "Orientation" in chapter 4).

SURFING & OTHER OUTDOOR PURSUITS

Despite its claim as the windsurfing capital of the Caribbean, there are very definite dangers in the waters off Rincón. In November 1998 three surfers (two from San Juan, one from the U.S. mainland) drowned in unrelated incidents offshore at Maria's Beach. These deaths are often cited as evidence of the dangerous surf that has misled some very experienced surfers. Local watersports experts urge anyone who's considering surfing at Rincón to ask a well-informed local for advice. When the surf is up and undertows and riptides are particularly strong, losing a surfboard while far offshore seems to be one of the first steps to eventually losing your life.

Windsurfing is best from November to April. The best beaches for surfing lie from Borinquén Point south to Rincón. There are many surfing outfitters along this strip, the best of which is **West Coast Surf Shop,** E. Muñoz Rivera 2 at Rincón (✆ 787/823-3935), open daily 9am to 6pm. A local surfing star, Darren Muschett, is the resident instructor here. Rates for lessons vary, but the outlet rents both long and short boards, charging $25 for 24 hours. The **Hot Wavz Surf Shop,** Maria's Beach (✆ 787/823-3942), also rents long boards, as well as boogie boards, for $15 per day. Some local surfers hang out here, giving lessons that begin at $20 per hour. If you need lessons, place yourself in the hands of Jake Cravey, one of the best windsurfers in the area. He operates the **Buena Vida Surf School** (✆ **787/485-2353**), in a shack adjacent to the Casa Isleña Inn (see below). A 2-hour lesson costs $50 per person.

The windsurfers who hang out here like **Sandy Beach** because it does not have the stone and rocks found on some of the other beaches in the area. Also, from December to February it gets almost constant winds every day. Windsurfers wait on the terrace of Tamboo Tavern (see "Where to Dine," below) for the right wind conditions before hitting the beach.

Oceans Unlimited, Highway 115, Km 12.2, Rincón (✆ **787/823-2340**), is a dive charter operation servicing the entire west coast of Puerto Rico. It offers scuba diving and snorkeling charters to Desecho Island and Mona Island in a 48-foot (15m) vessel. All-inclusive camping and diving charters to Mona Island are offered, along with dive instruction, whale-watching, winter-sunset cruises, and fishing charters.

Another good scuba outfitter is **Taíno Divers,** Black Eagle Marina at Rincón (✆ **787/823-6429**), which offers local boat charters along with scuba and snorkeling trips. Other activities include whale-watching expeditions and sunset cruises. Fees are $99 for a two-tank dive, $625 for a half-day fishing-boat rental, and $50 for snorkeling.

The most visible and sought-after whale-watching panorama in Rincón is **Parque El Faro de Rincón (Rincón's Lighthouse Park),** which lies on El Faro Point peninsula at the extreme western tip of town. Within its fenced-in perimeter are pavilions that sell souvenirs and snack items, rows of binoculars offering 25¢ views, and a stately looking lighthouse built in 1921. The park is at its most popular from December to March for whale-watching and in January and February for surfer gazing. The park is locked every evening between midnight and 7am. Otherwise, you're free to promenade with the locals any time you like.

The park's snack bar is called **Restaurant El Faro,** Barrio Puntas, Carretera 413, Km 3.3 (no phone). Platters of American and Puerto Rican food include mofongos, steaks, and burgers. When is it open? The owner told us, "I open whenever I want to. If I don't want to, I stay home."

Punta Borinquén Golf Club, Route 107 (✆ **787/890-2987**), 2 miles (3.2km) north of Aquadilla's center, across the highway from the city's airport, was originally built by the U.S. government as part of Ramey Air Force Base. Today, it is a public 18-hole golf course, open daily from 6:30am to 6:30pm. Greens fees are $20 per round; a golf cart that can carry two passengers rents for $30 for 18 holes. A set of clubs can be rented for $10. The clubhouse has a bar and a simple restaurant.

WHERE TO STAY
VERY EXPENSIVE
Horned Dorset Primavera ✸✸✸   This is the most sophisticated hotel on Puerto Rico and one of the most exclusive and elegant small properties anywhere in the Caribbean. Set on 8 acres (3.2 hectares), it opens onto a secluded semiprivate beach, and it was built on the massive breakwaters and seawalls erected by a local railroad many years ago. The hacienda evokes an aristocratic Spanish villa, with wicker armchairs, hand-painted tiles, ceiling fans, seaside terraces, and cascades of flowers. Accommodations are in a series of suites that ramble amid lush gardens. The decor is tasteful, with four-poster beds and brass-footed tubs (with showers) in marble-sheathed bathrooms. Rooms are spacious and luxurious, with Persian rugs over tile floors, queen-size sofa beds in the sitting areas, and fine linen and tasteful fabrics on the elegant beds.

The eight-suite Casa Escondida villa, set at the edge of the property, adjacent to the sea, is decorated with an accent on teakwood and marble. Some of the units have private plunge pools; others offer private verandas or sun decks. Each contains high-quality reproductions of colonial furniture by Baker.

The hotel's restaurant, also called Horned Dorset Primavera, is one of the finest on Puerto Rico (see "Where to Dine," below).

Apartado 1132, Rincón, PR 00677. (© **800/633-1857** or 787/823-4030. Fax 787/823-5580. www.horneddorset.com. 55 units. Winter $600–$950 double, $900–$1,490 suite for 2; off season $180–$360 double, $540–$850 suite for 2. Rates include MAP (breakfast and dinner). AE, MC, V. Children under 12 not accepted. **Amenities:** 2 restaurants; bar; 3 outdoor pools (1 infinity); fitness center; kayaking (free); limited room service; massage; laundry service; library. *In room:* A/C, hair dryer, safe.

EXPENSIVE

Rincón Beach Resort   Romantic lovebirds and hipsters in logo T-shirts check into this secluded hideaway. At this beachfront resort, an open-air deck stretches along the coastline at the end of an "infinity pool." It's perhaps the most welcoming place along the western coastline. The staff can help you arrange everything from watersports to golf. Guests meet fellow guests in the lobby bar, and later enjoy a savory Caribbean cuisine in Brasas Restaurant, with its open-air terrace. You're given a choice of ocean-view or poolside-view units, and can also rent well-furnished one- and two-bedroom apartments. The decor is tropical throughout, with vibrant colors.

Route 115, Km 5.8, Añasco, PR 00610. (© **866/598-0009** or 787/589-9000. Fax 787/589-9040. www.rinconbeach.com. 118 units. Winter $230–$280 double, $340 junior suite, $435 1-bedroom suite, $625 2-bedroom suite. Off season $185–$225 double, $290 junior suite, $370 1-bedroom suite, $520 2-bedroom suite. Rates include continental breakfast. AE, DISC, MC, V. **Amenities:** Restaurant; grill; 3 bars; outdoor pool; gym; babysitting; laundry service; nonsmoking rooms; rooms for those w/limited mobility. *In room:* A/C, TV, dataport, kitchenettes in suites, fridge, hair dryer, iron, safe.

MODERATE

Casa Isleña Inn ⭐ (*Finds*)   "Island House" is created from a simple oceanfront former home right on the beach. Behind its gates, away from the water, is a private and tranquil world that offers a series of medium-size and comfortably furnished bedrooms decorated in bright Caribbean colors and designs. Each room has a neatly maintained shower-only bathroom. A natural tidal pool formed by a reef is an 8-minute stroll from the inn. At the tidal pool and from the inn's terraces guests can enjoy views of Aguadilla Bay and Mona Passage. In winter, while standing on the terraces, you can often watch the migration of humpback whales.

Barrio Puntas Carretera Interior 413 Km 4, Rincón, PR 00677. (© **888/289-7750** or 787/823-1525. Fax 787/823-1530. www.casa-islena.com. 9 units (shower only). Year-round $115–$185 double. Extra person $15. MC, V. **Amenities:** Restaurant for breakfast and lunch; bar; 1 room for those w/limited mobility. *In room:* A/C, TV, no phone.

Lemontree Waterfront Suites ⭐ (*Finds*)   Right on a good, sandy beach, these spacious apartments with kitchenettes are for those who don't want to limit themselves to hotel rooms and meals. With the sound of the surf just outside your private back porch, these well-furnished seaside units can provide a home away from home, with everything from ceiling fans to air-conditioning, from paperback libraries to custom woodworking details. The property is well maintained. Families enjoy the three-bedroom, two-bathroom oceanfront suite called "Papaya," and "Mango" and "Pineapple" are ideal for two persons. Each unit contains a midsize shower-only bathroom. The least expensive units, "Banana" and "Coconut," are studio units for those who want a kitchen but don't require a living room. The cottages lie a 10-minute drive west of Rincón.

Rte. 4290 (P.O. Box 3200), Rincón, PR 00677. ℭ **888/418-8733** or 787/823-6452. Fax 787/823-5821. www. lemontreepr.com. 6 units (shower only). Winter $110–$140 double, $165 quad, $175 for 6; off season $95–$125 double, $145 quad, $160 for 6. AE, MC, V. In room: A/C, TV, kitchenette, coffeemaker.

Tres Sirenas Beach Inn ⭐ (Finds)

This B&B opens onto Sandy Bottom Beach, giving you a chance to live in a certain tropical elegant style. It's casual but oh, so tasteful. A boutique hotel, the complex is sometimes rented as a private oceanfront villa to a dozen or so guests. Otherwise you have a choice of two spacious and elegantly furnished bedrooms or else two apartments, all with a certain old Puerto Rican charm. The pool studio would be ideal for families as it accommodates two adults and two children, and features a private balcony. Apartments sleep four and come with a loft and full kitchen.

Sea Beach Dr. 26, Rincón, PR 00677. ℭ **787/823-0558**. www.tressirenas.com. 4 units. Winter $160–$200 double, $280 apt for 4. Off season $145–$180 double, $240 apt for 4. AE, DC, MC, V. **Amenities:** Outdoor pool; hot tub; limited room service; laundry service; nonsmoking rooms. In room: A/C, TV, kitchenette, minibar, beverage maker, hair dryer, iron.

INEXPENSIVE

The Lazy Parrot

Set within an unlikely inland neighborhood, far from any particular view of the sea, this place has a better-than-average restaurant and clean, well-organized bedrooms. Each unit is comfortable, even if not overly large, with light-grained and durable furnishings that might seem appropriate for the bedroom of a high-school senior in a suburb on the U.S. mainland. Bathrooms are simple, functional, and workable, each with a shower, but not at all plush. Lazy Parrot was built as a private home in the 1970s and then transformed into the inn you see today. The place is just as well known for its restaurant as it is for its rooms. Meals are served in an open-sided aerie on the building's uppermost floor.

Rd. 413, Km 4.1, Barrio Puntas, Rincón, PR 00677. ℭ **800/294-1752** or 787/823-5654. Fax 787/823-0224. www. lazyparrot.com. 11 units. Year-round $110–$125 double. Rates include continental breakfast. AE, DISC, MC, V. **Amenities:** Restaurant; bar; pool; limited room service; babysitting. In room: A/C, TV, fridge.

Parador Villa Antonio

Ilia and Hector Ruíz offer apartments by the sea in this privately owned and run parador. The beach outside is nice, but the local authorities don't keep it as clean as they ought to. Surfing and fishing can be enjoyed just outside your front door, and you can bring your catch right into your cottage and prepare a fresh seafood dinner in your own kitchenette (there's no restaurant). This is a popular destination with families from Puerto Rico, who crowd in on the weekends to occupy the motel-like rooms with balconies or terraces. Furnishings are well used but offer reasonable comfort, and the shower-only bathrooms are small.

Rte. 115, Km 12.3 (P.O. Box 68), Rincón, PR 00677. ℭ **787/823-2645**. Fax 787/823-3380. www.villa-antonio.com. 61 units (shower only). $96–$128 studio (up to 2 people); $123–$144 2-bedroom apt (holds up to 4 people); $117 junior suite; $128 suite. AE, DISC, MC, V. **Amenities:** 2 pools; 2 tennis courts; playground; babysitting; laundry service; rooms for those w/limited mobility. In room: A/C, TV, coffeemaker, iron, safe.

Villa Cofresi

Set about a mile (1.6km) south of Rincón's center, this is a clean, family-run hotel with a view of the beach. Thanks to the three adult children of the Caro family, the place is better managed than many of its competitors. Bedrooms are comfortable and airy, with well-chosen furniture that might remind you of something in southern Florida. Each unit has a white tile floor and a small bathroom with a tub and shower. Most rooms have two double beds; some have two twin beds. All are nonsmoking. The two units that tend to be reserved out long in advance are nos. 47 and 55, which have windows opening directly onto the sea.

The in-house restaurant, La Ana de Cofresi, is named after the ship that was captained by the region's most famous 18th-century pirate, Roberto Cofresi. Hand-painted murals highlight some of his adventures. Open Monday through Friday from 5 to 10pm and Saturday and Sunday from noon to 10pm, it charges $8 to $30 for well-prepared main courses that are likely to include fish consommé, four kinds of mofongo, breaded scampi served either with Creole sauce or garlic, and very good steaks, including a 12-ounce New York sirloin.

Rd. 115, Km 12.0, Rincón, PR 00677. © 787/823-2450. Fax 787/823-1770. www.villacofresi.com. 80 units. Winter $125 double, $158 suite; off season $114 double, $125 suite. AE, DC, MC, V. **Amenities:** Restaurant; bar; outdoor pool; room service; rooms for those w/limited mobility. *In room:* A/C, TV, fridge, hair dryer, iron.

WHERE TO DINE
VERY EXPENSIVE
Horned Dorset Primavera ✹✹ FRENCH/CARIBBEAN   This is the finest restaurant in western Puerto Rico—so romantic that people sometimes come from San Juan just for an intimate dinner. A masonry staircase sweeps from the garden to the second floor, where soaring ceilings and an atmosphere similar to that in a private villa awaits you.

The menu, which changes virtually every night based on the inspiration of the chef, might include chilled parsnip soup, a fricassee of wahoo with wild mushrooms, grilled loin of beef with peppercorns, and medallions of lobster in an orange-flavored beurre-blanc sauce. The grilled breast of duckling with bay leaves and raspberry sauce is also delectable. Mahimahi is grilled and served with ginger-cream sauce on a bed of braised Chinese cabbage. It's delicious.

In the Horned Dorset Primavera Hotel, Rte. 429. © 787/823-4030. Reservations recommended. Fixed-price dinner $68 for 5 dishes, $92 for 8 dishes. AE, MC, V. Daily 7–9:30pm.

INEXPENSIVE
Panaderia/Cafeteria Calvache AMERICAN/PUERTO RICAN   The food-service area of this place occupies one end of a store otherwise devoted to the sale of rum, baked goods, and hardware. But it's so friendly and the counter setting is so appropriate for the food (bacon and eggs, spaghetti with sausage, and such local fare as rice with seafood) that we wanted to add it to our listings. In the evening, the staff offers only sandwiches, no hot food. You'll find this Formica-clad heaven about 1½ miles (2.4km) south of the center of Rincón.

Rte. 115, Km 9. © 787/823-6658. Reservations not necessary. Breakfast and sandwiches $2–$6; fixed-price lunch $4. MC, V. Daily 4am–10pm.

Tamboo Tavern AMERICAN   The allure of this place derives from the crowd of surfing enthusiasts who gather here for drinks and fuel before braving the sometimes-treacherous waters at Sandy Beach. The staff prides themselves on knowing the latest surfing conditions. Burgers and sandwiches are the most frequently ordered items, and rum-and-Cokes and piña coladas are enduringly popular, too.

Sandy Beach. © 787/823-8550. Reservations not accepted. Main courses $5–$18 dinner. MC, V. Bar daily noon–2am. Restaurant Thurs–Tues noon–9:30pm.

A NEARBY PLACE TO STAY & DINE IN AGUADA
For the location of the parador described below, see the map "Paradores & Country Inns of Puerto Rico" on p. 53.

J. B. Hidden Village Hotel 🍴   Named using the initials of its owners (Julio Bonilla, his wife, Jinnie, and their son, Julio, Jr.), this is a well-maintained and isolated hotel launched in 1990. Half a mile (.8km) east of Aguada, on a side street that runs off Route 4414, it's nestled in a valley between three forested hillsides, almost invisible from the road. The hotel is a quiet and simple refuge to vacationers who enjoy exploring the area's many beaches. There are two restaurants on the premises (one with a view of a neighboring ravine). Each comfortable bedroom offers views of the pool and has a small tiled bathroom with tub/shower combination.

Carretera 2, Intersection 4416, Km 1, Punta Nueve, Barrio Piedras Blancas, Sector Villarrubia, Aguada, PR 00602. ©️ 787/868-8686. Fax 787/868-8701. 42 units. Year-round $80–$87 double; $125 suite. AE, MC, V. **Amenities:** Restaurant; bar; 2 outdoor pools; rooms for those w/limited mobility. *In room:* A/C, TV, no phone.

RINCON AFTER DARK

Join the surfers for a "sundowner" at **Calypso's Tropical Bar,** Maria's Beach (©️ **787/ 823-1626**), which lies on the road to the lighthouse. Locals gather to watch the sunset in the outdoor courtyard. Happy hour specials are daily 5 to 7pm, when a rum punch costs only $2. Live music is presented on Saturday at 10pm, although the bar is open daily from 11am until the last customer leaves (usually long after midnight). If you decide to hang here for the evening, go for the grilled seafood, with main courses costing from $4 to $12.

One of the best *simpatico* bars is **Rock Bottom,** adjoining Casa Verde Vacation Rentals along Beach Road (©️ **787/605-5351**). It serves burgers and other stateside food. The surfer bar upstairs is decorated with dozens of graffitized surfing boards. Some of the best piña coladas along the coast are served here. The cafe serves daily from 11am to 9pm, with the bar open from 5pm to midnight daily.

2 The Southwest Coast

The true native of Puerto Rico heads not to the fancy resorts along the north coast near San Juan, but instead to the southwestern corner, a region with a distinctly island flavor. Here are some of Puerto Rico's great beaches, notably **Boquerón Beach** 🏖️🏖️, and a lot of mom-and-pop operations that offer nightly rentals and good seafood dinners.

Southern Puerto Rico is increasingly gaining a reputation among **scuba divers,** although the outfitters are a bit lean here and not as well organized or plentiful as in the Cayman Islands. The attraction is the continental shelf that drops off a few miles off the southern coast. Within this watery range is a towering wall that is some 20 miles (32km) long and filled with one of the best assortments of marine life in the West Indies. Diving is possible from the town of La Parguera in the west all the way to Ponce in the east. The wall drops from 60 to 120 feet (18–37m) before it "vanishes" into 1,500 feet (457m) of sea. With a visibility of around 100 feet (30m), divers experience the beautiful formations of some of Puerto Rico's most dramatic coral gardens.

Bird-watchers should head to the **Guánica State Forest,** which is the sanctuary that has the greatest number of birds on the island. For beachcombers, there are many hidden places, such as Gilligan's Island off the coast of the little village of Guánica. For snorkelers, there are miles of coral reefs, awash with tropical fish and coral and marine life. The Cabo Rojo lighthouse, south of Boquerón, offers views of the rocky coastline and a panoramic sweep of the Caribbean.

BOQUERON

Lying 85 miles (137km) southwest of San Juan and 33 miles (53km) west of Ponce is the little beach town of Boquerón. It is just south of Cabo Rojo, west of the historic city of San Germán, and near the western edge of the Boquerón Forest Preserve.

What puts sleepy Boquerón on the tourist map is its lovely public beach, one of the island's finest for swimming. It is also known for the shellfish found offshore. The beach has facilities, including lockers and changing places, plus kiosks that rent watersports equipment. Parking costs $2. On weekends the resort tends to be crowded with families driving down from San Juan.

The outfitter that offers the best scuba diving and snorkeling in the area is **Mona Aquatics,** on Calle José de Diego, directly west of the heart of town (© **787/851-2185**). It can arrange special trips to Mona Island some 50 miles (81km) out to sea, a sanctuary known for its spectacular dive opportunities. The company also rents snorkeling gear and, if enough people are interested, conducts boat tours of the Bahía de Boquerón.

From Boquerón you can head directly south to **El Faro de Cabo Rojo** at the island's southernmost corner. The century-old Cabo Rojo Lighthouse lies on Route 301, along a spit of land between Bahia Sucia and Bahia Salinas. Looking down from the lighthouse, you'll see a 2,000-foot (610m) drop along jagged limestone cliffs. The lighthouse dates from 1881, when it was constructed under Spanish rule. The famous pirate Roberto Cofresi used to terrorize the coast along here in the 19th century and was said to have hidden out in a cave nearby.

WHERE TO STAY

Bahias Salinas Beach Hotel ⭐ *(Finds)*   You live close to nature here. Nature lovers and bird-watchers are drawn to this intimate inn in Cabo Rojo in the far southwestern corner of Puerto Rico. At the tip of the western coast, the sanctuary is bordered by a mangrove reserve and bird sanctuaries. Salt mineral waters, similar to those of the Dead Sea, supply water for the on-site Jacuzzi. Within easy reach are many beautiful white-sand beaches. The place is lovely on weekends, when live music is a feature. Fresh seafood is served in the 25-seat dining room. The bedrooms are midsize to large, and are furnished in the so-called "hacienda" Puerto Rican style, which means wooden colonial-style furniture and four-poster beds. The place is well run and maintained.

Rd. 301, Km 11.5, Sector El Faro, Cabo Rojo, PR 00622. © 787/254-1212. Fax 787/254-1215. www.bahiasalina. com. 22 units. Year-round $80–$125 double. Children under 12 stay free in parent's room. AE, MC, V. **Amenities:** Restaurant; bar; 2 outdoor pools; room service (noon–9pm); rooms for those w/limited mobility. *In room:* A/C, TV.

Cofresi Beach Hotel   Set across from one of the area's best dive shops, this is a choice for clients who can live without maid service and other resort-oriented amenities—there is no full-time reception or concierge staff. The apartments here have kitchens with cutlery, plates, and cooking equipment, durable furniture, and comfortable beds; each has a small tiled bathroom with a tub and shower. It's about as laissez-faire as they come.

Calle Muñoz Rivera 57, P.O. Box 1209, Boquerón, PR 00622. © 787/254-3000. Fax 787/254-1048. www. cofresibeach.com. 12 units. Year-round $119 1-bedroom; $165 2-bedroom; $219 3-bedroom. AE, MC, V. **Amenities:** Pool. *In room:* A/C, TV, kitchenette, coffeemaker, hair dryer, iron.

Parador Boquemar   The pink-walled Parador Boquemar is a late-1980s inn that lies a block or so from Boquerón Beach. Rooms are at the end of long corridors that evoke a college dormitory or an anonymous office building. Despite the small units here, Puerto Rican families like this place a lot, causing readers to complain that children sometimes run up and down the corridors. Rooms are simple, stripped down to the bare essentials, although each has a small tiled shower-only bathroom. The place is a little too rustic and not maintained well enough for our tastes, but the beach somehow compensates. Stay here only if you plan to spend most of your time outside the hotel. Surprisingly, the hotel has one of the best restaurants in the area, Las Cascadas (see "Where to Dine," below).

Carretera 101, Poblado de Boquerón, Cabo Rojo, PR 00622. ✆ 787/851-2158. Fax 787/851-7600. www. boquemar.com. 75 units (shower only). Year-round $75–$85 double; $100 junior suite. AE, DC, MC, V. **Amenities:** Restaurant; bar; outside pool; babysitting; rooms for those w/limited mobility. *In room:* A/C, TV, small fridge.

WHERE TO DINE

For some reason, Boquerón has more shellfish vendors than any other area in western Puerto Rico. They display their bounty on wooden tabletops along the town's main street. Most of the shellfish is not refrigerated, and as such, we cannot vouch for its safety. But if you're adventurous, you might want to give it a try. Most vendors offer a selection of spicy sauces to accompany the shellfish.

Las Cascadas ☆ CREOLE/CONTINENTAL   One of the best restaurants in the area, this popular bar and restaurant is the only *mesones gastronómicos* in Boquerón. On the second floor of Parador Boquemar, it has a waterfall in its interior. The bartenders are the best in the area and seem to know how to whip up any kind of drink. The day begins early here. The chef's breakfast specialty is an omelet Cascada, with ham, tomatoes, onions, peppers, and cheese. At dinner many Creole recipes appear, such as *fomongo de yucca relleno* (stuffed mashed plantains); the plantains can be stuffed with lobster, shrimp, octopus, or conch.

The meats such as filet mignon are imported but tasty. Lobster can be served with five different sauces. Other specialties of the chef include chicken breast stuffed with lobster or shrimp. The tastiest appetizers are fish and cheese balls.

In the Parador Boquemar, Carretera 101, Poblado de Boquerón, Cabo Rojo. ✆ 787/851-2158. Reservations not necessary. Breakfast $4–$5; main courses $13–$22. AE, MC, V. Daily 7:30–11:30am; Thurs–Tues 6–10pm.

Roberto's Fish Net PUERTO RICAN   This is one of two restaurants, both named "Roberto," on the same sleepy street in the center of Boquerón. Both belong to Roberto Aviles and offer roughly equivalent versions of the same food. We prefer this spot to Roberto's Restaurant Villa Playera (✆ 787/254-3163). However, the Villa Playera is still a good choice, particularly on Monday and Tuesday, when the Fish Net is closed. Within the Fish Net's simple environment, a cross between a luncheonette and a bar, you can order tender beefsteaks, well-flavored chicken breasts, or fresh fish, any of which comes with rice and beans. More unusual are the *pilones,* a combination of mashed plantains flavored with your choice of shrimp, conch, or octopus, usually served with salsa, that come in tall wooden cups with old-fashioned mortars.

Calle José de Diego s/n (without number). ✆ 787/851-6009. Reservations not necessary. Main courses $5–$23. AE, DISC, MC, V. Wed–Sun 11am–10pm.

LA PARGUERA ☆

This charming fishing village lies 78 miles (126km) southwest of San Juan and 26 miles (42km) west of Ponce, just south of San Germán. From San Germán, take Route 320 directly south and follow the signposts. Note that this route changes its name several times along the way, becoming Route 101, 116, 315, 305, and then 304 before reaching La Parguera—even though it's all the same highway.

The name of the village comes from *pargos*, meaning snapper. Its main attraction, other than its beaches and diving, is **Phosphorescent Bay**, which contains millions of luminescent dinoflagellates (microscopic plankton). A disturbance causes them to light up the dark waters. For dramatic effect, they are best seen on a moonless night. Boats leave for a troll around the bay nightly from 7:30pm to 12:30am from La Parguera pier, depending on demand. The trip costs $5 per person.

Offshore are some 12 to 15 reefs with a variety of depths. The Beril reef goes down to 60 feet (18m), then drops to 2,000 feet (610m). This wall is famous among divers, and visibility ranges from 100 to 120 feet (30–37m). These reefs also provide some of the best snorkeling possibilities in Puerto Rico. Marine life is both abundant and diverse, including big morays, sea turtles, barracudas, nurse sharks, and manatees. **Paradise Scuba Center,** Hotel Casa Blanca Building, at La Parguera (© **787/899-7611**), offers the best diving and snorkeling. A two-tank dive costs $70; a 3-hour snorkeling jaunt goes for $35 per person. Full equipment can be rented.

WHERE TO STAY

La Jamaka   Set on a low but breezy hillside, a 10-minute hike from the town's congested center, this is a tasteful vacation compound in a verdant setting of bougainvillea and flowering shrubs. Guests here are pulled into the gregarious life of the establishment simply by the warmth of the owners, Elsie Cintron and Carlos Rosado. La Jamaka has a small swimming pool, a communal kitchen, and a garden-style setting for relaxation. Bedrooms are small—almost to the point of being a bit claustrophobic—but they're well maintained and filled in midsummer with vacationers from other parts of Puerto Rico. Each unit has a small, tiled, shower-only bathroom.

Colinas de la Parguera, P.O. Box 303, Lajas, La Parguera PR 00667. ©/fax 787/899-6162. 9 units (shower only). Year-round $69–$89 double. MC, V. From La Parguera, head north on Rte. 304 until you reach the junction with Rte. 116. Continue north on 116 until you see the sign for the resort. **Amenities:** Restaurant; bar; outdoor pool; limited room service. *In room:* A/C, TV, no phone.

Parador Posada Porlamar   Developed by the Pancorbo family in 1967 as one of the first full-service hotels in town, this parador evokes life in a simple fishing village. A horseshoe-shaped compound that overlooks a narrow channel flanked by mangroves, it conducts an ongoing business with dive enthusiasts, thanks to its on-site scuba shop. Bedrooms are plain and neat but don't invite lingering. Some have balconies, minibars, and small sitting rooms, and each has a small, tiled shower-only bathroom. All are nonsmoking. The social center here is a patio overlooking the channel. The restaurants and bars of La Parguera are within a short walk of this centrally located place. On the premises is a rather formal restaurant, La Pared. Specialties include seafood in Creole sauce, lamb chops in Dijon mustard, and sautéed shrimp in soursop-flavored butter sauce.

Rte. 304 (P.O. Box 3113), La Parguera, Lajas, PR 00667. © **787/899-4343.** Fax 787/899-5558. www.parguera puertorico.com. 40 units (shower only). Winter $99–$128 double; off season $80–$99 double. AE, DISC, MC, V. Drive west along Rte. 2 until you reach the junction of Rte. 116; then head south along Rte. 116 and Rte. 304. **Amenities:** Restaurant; bar; pool; rooms for those w/limited mobility. *In room:* A/C, TV, minibar, coffeemaker, hair dryer, safe.

Parador Villa Parguera *Kids*   Although the water in the nearby bay is too muddy for swimming, guests can enjoy a view of the harbor and take a dip in the swimming pool. Situated on the southwestern shore of Puerto Rico, this parador is favored by Sanjuaneros for weekend escapes. It's also known for its seafood dinners (the fish are not caught in the bay), comfortable and uncomplicated bedrooms, and location next to the bay's famous phosphorescent waters. Each unit has either a balcony or a terrace. Bathrooms are rather cramped but well maintained, and each has either a shower or a tub. This place is more gregarious and convivial, and usually more fun, than the Porlamar, a few steps away.

The spacious, air-conditioned restaurant, where the occasionally slow service might remind you of Spain in a bygone era, offers traditional favorites, such as filet of fish stuffed with lobster and shrimp. Nonguests are welcome here, and there's a play area for children.

Because the inn is popular with Puerto Rican families, especially on weekends, there's a special weekend package for a 2-night minimum stay; $385 to $395 (depending on the exposure of your room) covers the price of a double room, welcome drinks, breakfasts, dinners, flowers, and dancing, along with a free show. However, we prefer to stay here during the week, when it's more tranquil.

Main St. 304 (P.O. Box 3400), Carretera 304, Km 303, La Parguera, Lajas, PR 00667. ℂ 787/899-7777. Fax 787/899-6040. www.villaparguera.net. 74 units (all with either shower or tub). Sun–Thurs $100–$120 double; Fri–Sat $107–$150 double. 2 children 9 or under stay free in parent's room. AE, DC, DISC, MC, V. Drive west along Rte. 2 until you reach the junction with Rte. 116; then head south along Rte. 116 and Rte. 304. **Amenities:** Restaurant; bar; pool; babysitting; rooms for those w/limited mobility. *In room:* A/C, TV.

WHERE TO DINE

Besides the following recommendation, **La Jamaka** (see "Where to Stay," above) also serves excellent cuisine.

La Casita SEAFOOD   This is the town's most consistently reliable and popular restaurant. It's flourished here since the 1960s, in a simple wooden building. Inside, lots of varnished pine acts as a decorative foil for platters of local and imported fish and shellfish. Filets of fish can be served in any of seven different styles; lobster comes in five. Even the Puerto Rican starchy staple of mofongo comes in versions stuffed with crab, octopus, shrimp, lobster, and assorted shellfish. Begin with fish chowder, a dozen cheese balls, or fish croquettes. End with coconut-flavored flan. Don't expect grand service or decor, but rather a setting where food is the focus.

Calle Principal 304. ℂ 787/899-1681. Reservations not necessary. All main courses $8. AE, MC, V. Tues–Sun 11am–10:30pm. Closed 2 weeks in Sept.

GUANICA

Guánica, on the Caribbean Sea, lies 73 miles (118km) southwest of San Juan and 21 miles (34km) west of the city of Ponce. Part of the area is a UNESCO-designated world biosphere reserve, adjacent to the famed Guánica dry forest and home to more than 100 species of migratory and resident birds, the largest number in Puerto Rico.

The beach at Guánica is pristine and the crystal-clear water is ideal for swimming, snorkeling, and diving. Directly offshore is the famed Gilligan's Island, plus six of Puerto Rico's best sites for night or day dives.

The area was once known for its leaping bullfrogs. The Spanish conquerors virtually wiped out this species. But the bullfrogs have come back and live in the rolling, scrub-covered hills that surround the 18-acre (7.3-hectare) site of the Copamarina Beach Resort, the area's major hotel (see below.)

Guánica is adjacent to the unique "Dry Forest" and experiences very little rainfall. Nearby mountains get an annual rainfall of 15 feet (4.6m), but Guánica receives only

(Finds) Puerto Rico's Secret Beaches

Some of Puerto Rico's most beautiful and isolated beaches lie on the island's southwestern coast, on the Caribbean Sea, far from major highways. Stretching between Ponce in the east and Cabo Rojo on Puerto Rico's extreme southwestern tip, these beaches flank some of the least densely populated parts of the island. And because the boundaries between them are relatively fluid, only a local resident (or perhaps a professional geographer) could say for sure where one ends and the other begins.

If you consider yourself an aficionado of isolated beaches, it's worth renting a car and striking out for these remote locales. Drive westward from Ponce along Highway 2, branching south along Route 116 to **Guánica**, the self-anointed gateway and capital of this string of "secret beaches."

By far the most accessible and appealing beach is **Caña Gorda** ☆. Set about a quarter-mile (.4km) south of Guánica, at the edge of a legally protected marsh that's known for its rich bird life and thick reeds, Caña Gorda is a sprawling expanse of pale beige sand that's dotted with ramshackle-looking *bohios* (huts) crafted from tree branches and palm fronds. Despite its rusticity, it's a site that's been improved and developed by the local authorities. The centerpiece here is a well-recommended hotel, the **Copamarina** (© 800/468-4553 or 787/821-0505). You can check in for a night or two of sun-flooded R & R (see "Where to Stay," below). Even if you're not staying at the hotel, consider dropping in for a *cuba libre*, a margarita, or a meal.

In the very southwest sector of Puerto Rico are some relatively hidden and very secluded beaches, although getting to them is a bit difficult along some potholed roads. From Boquerón head east on Route 101, cutting south at the junction with Route 301 which will carry you to the one of the most westerly beaches in Puerto Rico, Playa Sucia. The beach opens onto **Bahia Sucia** ☆, whose name rather unappetizingly translates as "Dirty Bay." Actually it isn't dirty; it's a lovely spot.

From Bahia Sucia, you can head east to discover other secret beaches, which are reached along various signposted roads: 324, 304, and 323. The finest beaches, moving toward Ponce, are **Rosado Beach** ☆, **Playa Santa** ☆, and **Playa Tamarindo** ☆.

All these beaches might be hard to reach, but persevere and you'll be met with warm water and long, uncrowded stretches of sand, where towering king palms and salt-tolerant sea grapes provide an idyllic tropical backdrop for sun and surf. Keep in mind that with the exception of Caña Gorda, the beaches mentioned here have virtually no services and public utilities. Pack what you'll need for the day—food, water, sunscreen, and so forth.

about 15 inches (38 centimeters). This is the world's largest dry coastal forest region. The upper hills are ideal for hiking.

Guánica was once the haunt of the Taíno Indians, and it was the place where Ponce de León first explored Puerto Rico in 1508. One of his descendants later founded the nearby city of Ponce in 1692.

SCUBA DIVING, SNORKELING & OTHER OUTDOOR PURSUITS

The best dive operation in Guánica is **Sea Venture Dive Copamarina** (© 787/821-0505, ext. 729), part of the Copamarina Beach Resort. Copamarina has a long pier where fishing is permitted, and a 42-foot (13m) Pro Jet dive boat. Guánica is one of the Caribbean's best areas for day and night dives. A two-tank dive costs $95, with full diving equipment. You can also rent snorkeling gear. Whale-watching excursions can be arranged from January to March at the hotel's tour desk, which also offers ecotours, kayaking, deep-sea fishing, and sunset sails. Horseback riding and sunset biking are also available.

At one of the local beaches, **Playa Santa,** west of town, **Pino's Boat & Water Fun** (© 787/821-6864) will rent you a paddle boat or kayak for $18 to $20 an hour.

One of the most visited sites is **Gilligan's Island,** a series of mangrove and sand cays near the Caña Gorda peninsula. Part of the dry forest reserve, it is set aside for recreational use. A small ferry departs from in front of Restaurant San Jacinto, just past Copamarina Beach Resort, every hour daily from 10am to 5pm, weather permitting; round-trips cost $5.

WHERE TO STAY

Copamarina Beach Resort *Finds* *Value*   In the 1950s Copamarina was the private vacation retreat of the de Castro family, Puerto Rican cement barons. In 1991 it was enlarged and upgraded by talented entrepreneurs. Today, charming, low-key, and discreetly elegant, it stands head and shoulders above everything else along Puerto Rico's western coast, except for the regal Horned Dorset Primavera (its strongest competitor). Situated beside a public beach (the best in the area), amid a landscaped palm grove, the resort is airy and relaxing. A favorite destination of Sanjuaneros, it also draws a well-heeled crowd of clients from Europe and North America, who know good value when they see it.

The accommodations are in one- and two-story wings that radiate from the resort's central core. The attractively decorated units have tile floors, lots of exposed wood, and louvered doors with screens that open onto large verandas or terraces. Everything is airy and comfortable. Bathrooms are larger than you might expect, and up-to-date, some with shower, others with tub.

The resort houses two restaurants, one of which reigns as one of the finest in western Puerto Rico: Alexandra is a destination for clients from as far away as San Juan (see "Where to Dine," below). Less formal, and staffed with a hardworking crowd of young people, is Las Palmas, which is set in the open air beneath a canopy.

The dive facilities here are the best and most varied in western Puerto Rico, attracting divers of all levels of expertise.

Rte. 333, Km 6.5, Caña Gorda (P.O. Box 805), Guánica, PR 00653. © 800/468-4553 or 787/821-0505. Fax 787/821-0070. www.copamarina.com. 106 units. Year-round $165–$270 double; $350–$450 suite. AE, DC, MC, V. From Ponce, drive west along Rte. 2 to Rte. 116 and go south to Rte. 333, then head east. **Amenities:** 2 restaurants; bar; 2 outdoor pools; health club; limited room service; babysitting; laundry service; dry cleaning; rooms for those w/limited mobility. *In room:* A/C, TV, dataport, fridge, coffeemaker, hair dryer, safe.

Mary Lee's by the Sea *Finds* *Finds*   Owned and operated by Michigan-born Mary Lee Alvarez, a former resident of Cuba and a self-described "compulsive decorator," this is an informal collection of cottages, seafront houses, and apartments, located 4 miles (6.4km) east of Guánica. Five California-style houses are subdivided into eight living units, each suitable for one to three couples. Rooms are whimsically decorated in an airy, somewhat bohemian way, with a sense of 1960s comfort and a sometimes sooth-ing sense of clutter. Each unit has a small, tiled bathroom with tub. The entire com-pound, which grew in an artfully erratic way, is landscaped with flowering shrubs, trees, and vines. Overall, the ambience is kind and low-key.

There aren't any formally organized activities here, but the hotel sits next to sandy beaches and a handful of uninhabited offshore cays. The management maintains rental boats with motors, two waterside sun decks, and several kayaks for the benefit of active guests. Hikers and bird-watchers can go north to the Guánica State Forest.

Don't come here looking for nighttime activities or enforced conviviality. The place is quiet, secluded, and appropriate for low-key vacationers looking for privacy. There isn't a bar or restaurant here, but each unit has a modern kitchen and an outdoor barbecue pit. The rooms are serviced weekly, although guests can arrange daily maid service for an extra fee.

Rte. 333, Km 6.7 (P.O. Box 394), Guánica, PR 00653. ✆ **787/821-3600.** Fax 787/821-0744. www.maryleesby thesea.com. 11 units. Year-round $80 double; $100–$140 studio and 1-bedroom apt; $160–$200 2-bedroom apt; $250 3-bedroom house. MC, V. From Ponce, take Rte. 2. When you reach Rte. 116, head south toward Gúanica. The hotel is signposted from the road. **Amenities:** Laundry service. *In room:* A/C, kitchen, coffeemaker, iron, safe, no phone.

WHERE TO DINE
Alexandra ✪ INTERNATIONAL   This is a genuinely excellent restaurant with a kitchen team turning out delectable dishes that include fried red snapper with Creole sauce, filet of mahimahi with pigeon peas, garlic shrimp with local rice, and beef parmigiana with red-wine sauce. The interior is air-conditioned but tropical in its feel, providing a welcome dose of relaxed glamour.

In the Copamarina Beach Resort, Rte. 333, Km 6.5, Caña Gorda (P.O. Box 805), Guánica. ✆ **787/821-0505.** Reser-vations recommended. Main courses $18–$32. AE, DC, DISC, MC, V. Sun–Thurs 6–10:30pm; Fri–Sat 6–11pm.

3 Paradores of Western Puerto Rico

One program that has helped the Puerto Rico Tourism Company successfully promote the commonwealth as "The Complete Island"—the paradores puertorriqueños—will help make your travels even more enjoyable.

The *paradores puertorriqueños* (see chapter 2 for more details about these govern-ment-sponsored inns and a map pinpointing their locations) are a chain of privately owned and operated country inns under the auspices and supervision of the Commonwealth Development Company. These hostelries are easily identified by the Taíno grass hut that appears in the signs and logos of each one. The Puerto Rico Tourism Company started the program in 1973, modeling it after Spain's parador sys-tem, although many of the paradores here are mere shanties compared to some of the deluxe Spanish hostelries. Each parador is situated in a historic or particularly beauti-ful spot. They vary in size, but most share the virtues of affordability, hospitable staffs, and high standards of cleanliness. Most but not all of their rooms are air-conditioned, and each room has a bathroom.

For reservations or further information, contact the **Paradores Puertorriqueños Reservation Office,** P.O. Box 9023960, San Juan, PR 00902 (✆ **800/443-0266**).

JAYUYA
The village of Jayuya, southwest of San Juan and north of Ponce, lies in the middle of the Cordillera Central, a mountain massif. From San Juan, travel west along Highway 22, going past the town of Barceloneta until you come to the junction of Route 140;

Tips Mesones Gastronómicos

Except for those in major hotels, you'll find few well-known restaurants as you tour the western part of the island. However, there are plenty of roadside places and simple taverns. For authentic island cuisine, you can rely on the *mesones gastronómicos* (gastronomic inns). This established dining network, sanctioned by the Puerto Rico Tourism Company, highlights restaurants recognized for excellence in preparing and serving Puerto Rican specialties at modest prices.

Meson gastronómico status is limited to restaurants outside the San Juan area that are close to major island attractions. Membership in the program requires that restaurants have attractive surroundings and comply with strict standards of service. Members must specialize in native foods, but if you order fresh fish, chances are you'll be pleased. Regrettably, there are no maps listing these myriad restaurants, but their signs are easy to spot as you drive around the island.

---

head south to the town of Florida, passing through some of the most dramatic scenery in Puerto Rico. Continue along Route 140 until you come to the junction of Route 141, signposted southwest into Jayuya.

Jayuya is a small town that still retains strong Taíno cultural influences, particularly in the language. At the Jayuya Indian Festival in mid-November, you'll see crafts markets, parades, and displays of Taíno dances. The festival honors the patron saint of the town, Nuestra Señora la Monserrate.

Here you'll also find the Parador Hacienda Gripiñas (see below), a former coffee plantation, where you can glimpse the good old days on Puerto Rico. In 1950 Jayuya received worldwide attention when *independentistas* proclaimed the "Republic of Puerto Rico" and held the town under siege until the National Guard was called in.

WHERE TO STAY & DINE

Parador Hacienda Gripiñas 🏨   A former coffee plantation about 2½ hours from San Juan, Parador Hacienda Gripiñas is reached via a long, narrow, and curvy road. This home-turned-inn is a delightful blend of old-world hacienda and modern conveniences. The plantation ambience is created by ceiling fans, splendid gardens, porch hammocks, and more than 20 acres (8 hectares) of coffee bushes. You'll taste the homegrown product when you order the inn's aromatic brew.

The modest rooms (all nonsmoking) vary in size, and all are kept very tidy. Each unit has a small, tiled shower-only bathroom. For meals, we suggest the restaurant's Puerto Rican dishes rather than the international cuisine. You can swim in the two chilly mountain pools, soak up the sun, or enjoy the nearby sights, such as the Taíno Indian Ceremonial Park at Utuado. Boating and plenty of fishing are just 30 minutes away, at Lake Caonillas. The parador is also near the Río Camuy Caves.

Rte. 527, Km 2.5 (P.O. Box 387), Jayuya, PR 00664. ℂ 787/828-1717. Fax 787/828-1719. 20 units (shower only). Year-round $125 double. Rates include 2 meals a day. AE, MC, V. From Jayuya, head east via Rte. 144; at the junction with Rte. 527, go south 1½ miles/2.4km. **Amenities:** Restaurant; 2 outdoor pools; rooms for those w/limited mobility. *In room:* A/C, TV.

UTUADO

Another good base in the Cordillera Central massif is the little mountain town of Utuado, which lies northwest of Jayuya (see above). This is the heartland of karst, an

Life After Death: Taíno Burial & Ceremonial Sites

The **Taíno Indians** who lived in Puerto Rico before Europeans came here were ruled by *caciques,* or chiefs, who controlled their own villages and several others nearby. The Taínos believed in life after death, which led them to take extreme care in burying their dead. Personal belongings of the deceased were placed in the tomb with the newly dead, and bodies were carefully arranged in a squatting position. Near Ponce, visitors can see the oldest known Indian burial ground in the Antilles, the **Tibes Indian Ceremonial Center** (p. 182).

Even at the time of the arrival of Columbus and the conquistadores who followed, the Taínos were threatened by the warlike and cannibalistic Carib Indians coming up from the south. But though they feared the Caribs, they learned to fear the conquistadores even more. Within 50 years of the Spanish colonization, the Taíno culture had virtually disappeared, the Indians annihilated through either massacres or due to European diseases.

But Taíno blood and remnants of their culture live on. The Indians married with Spaniards and Africans, and their physical characteristics—straight hair, copper-colored skin, and prominent cheekbones—can still be seen in some Puerto Ricans today. Many Taíno words became part of the Spanish language that's spoken on the island even today. Hammocks, the weaving of baskets, and the use of gourds as eating receptacles are part of the heritage left by these ill-fated tribes.

irregular limestone terrain with sinkholes, underground streams, and caverns. This unique landscape was created over several millennia by heavy rainfall (see chapter 8). Utuado is a stronghold of *jíbaro* ("hillbilly") culture, reflecting the mountain life of the island as few other settlements do.

Petroglyphs left over from the Taíno civilization have been found in the area. One depicts an Indian woman with frog legs and an elaborate headdress. From Utuado, you can continue west for 20 miles (32km) on Route 111 to Km 12.3, to reach the Taíno Indian Ceremonial Center (see "Life After Death: Taíno Burial & Ceremonial Sites," below).

WHERE TO STAY & DINE

Casa Grande Mountain Retreat   This parador, situated on 107 lush and steeply inclined acres (43 hectares) of a former coffee plantation in the Caonillas Barrios district, about 1½ hours from San Juan, originated in the 19th century as a hacienda. Thanks to Steve Weingarten, a retired lawyer from New York City, the isolated compound functions today as a simple, eco-sensitive hotel. The cement-sided core of the original hacienda is on view in the lobby and in the likable eatery, Jungle Jane's Restaurant, which serves an array of well-prepared international and Puerto Rican Creole-style dishes. Nonguests can eat here daily from 7:30am to 9:30pm.

Accommodations lie within five wood-sided cottages (four units to a cottage, some of them duplex) scattered throughout the surrounding acreage. Each unit has deliberately simple, spartan-looking decor with exposed wood, airy verandas, a balcony,

Still standing near Utuado, a small mountain town, **Parque Ceremonial Indígena-Caguaña (Indian Ceremonial Park at Caguaña)**, Route 111, Km 12.3 (© 787/894-7325), was built by the Taínos for recreation and worship some 800 years ago. Stone monoliths, some etched with petroglyphs, rim several of the 10 *bateyes* (playing fields) used for a ceremonial game that some historians believe was a forerunner to soccer. The monoliths and petroglyphs, as well as the *dujos* (ceremonial chairs), are existing examples of the Taínos' skill in carving wood and stone.

Archaeologists have dated this site to approximately 2 centuries before Europe's discovery of the New World. It is believed that the Taíno chief Guarionex gathered his subjects on this site to celebrate rituals and practice sports. Set on a 13-acre (5.3-hectare) field surrounded by trees, some 14 vertical monoliths with colorful petroglyphs are arranged around a central sacrificial stone monument. The ball complex also includes a museum, which is open daily from 8:30am to 4pm; admission is $2, free for children under 2.

There is also a gallery called Herencia Indígena, where you can purchase Taíno relics at reasonable prices, including the sought-after *Cemis* (Taíno idols) and figures of the famous little frog, the coquí. The Taínos are long gone, and much that was here is gone, too. This site is of special interest to those with academic pursuits, but of only passing interest to the lay visitor.

hammock, view of the mountains, and a small bathroom with shower. None has TV, phone, or air-conditioning—as such, they're popular with urbanites who want to get back to nature, and some come here to brush up on yoga and meditation skills. A nature trail is carved out of the surrounding forest. Under separate management, a riding stable offers horseback riding a short distance away.

P.O. Box 1499, Utuado, PR 00641. © **888/343-2272** or 787/894-3900. Fax 787/894-3900. www.hotelcasagrande.com. 20 units. Year-round $80–$90 double. AE, DISC, MC, V. From Arecibo, take Rte. 10 south to Utuado, then head east on Rte. 111 to Rte. 140; head north on Rte. 140 to Rte. 612 for ¼ mile/.4km. **Amenities:** Restaurant; bar; pool. *In room:* Ceiling fan, no phone.

QUEBRADILLAS

Quebradillas is one of the sleepy municipalities of northwest Puerto Rico. With its flamboyantly painted houses, narrow streets, and spiritualist herb shops, it is like a town of long ago. Quebradillas lies 70 miles (113km) west of San Juan, only about a 15-mile (24km) trip from the city of Arecibo along Route 2.

The Atlantic waters along the northwest coast of Puerto Rico tend to be rough, with the rugged coastline seemingly plunging right into the ocean. Both snorkelers and scuba divers are drawn to a protected beach area known as **"The Shacks,"** close to the town of Isabela, northwest of Quebradillas. The reefs and coral caverns here are some of the most dramatic in Puerto Rico. Surfers also flock to Isabela's Jobos Beach. Neither beach, however, is ideal for swimming.

Also northwest of Quebradillas lies beautiful **Guajataca Beach,** with its white sands, raging surf, and turbulent, deep waters. This is a fine beach for sunning and collecting shells, but it's a *playa peligrosa* (dangerous beach) unless you're a skilled swimmer. You can also visit **Lago de Guajataca,** another beautiful spot, by heading south for 7 miles (11km) on Route 113. This man-made lake is a lovely place for hiking, and it's the site of two paradores (see below). The staff at these government-sponsored inns will give you advice about jaunts in the **Guajataca Forest Reserve** to the immediate west.

WHERE TO STAY & DINE

Parador El Guajataca *Kids*   You'll find this place on a rolling hillside reaching down to a surf-beaten beach along the north coast. Stay here for the stunning natural setting and don't expect too much, because the hotel itself is somewhat seedy. Each room is rather standard and has its own entrance and private balcony opening onto the turbulent Atlantic. Bathrooms are slightly battered but functional, each with a tub.

Served in a glassed-in dining room where all the windows face the sea, the cuisine isn't much more memorable than the accommodations, with little care going into the preparation of the often-canned ingredients. A local musical group plays for dining and dancing on Friday and Saturday evenings. There are two swimming pools (one for adults, another for children), plus a playground for children.

Rte. 2, Km 103.8 (P.O. Box 1558), Quebradillas, PR 00678. (℃ **800/965-3065** or 787/895-3070. Fax 787/895-3589. www.elguajataca.com. 38 units. Year-round $89–$96 double. AE, MC, V. From Quebradillas, continue northwest on Rte. 2 for 1 mile/1.6km; the *parador* is signposted. **Amenities:** Restaurant; bar; 2 pools; limited room service; laundry service; coin-op laundry; dry cleaning. *In room:* A/C, TV, coffeemaker, iron.

Parador Vistamar   In the Guajataca area, this parador, one of the largest in Puerto Rico, sits like a sentinel surveying the scene from high atop a mountain overlooking greenery and a seascape. There are gardens and intricate paths carved into the side of the mountain, where you can stroll while enjoying the fragrance of the tropical flowers. Or you might choose to search for the calcified fossils that abound on the carved mountainside. For a unique experience, visitors can try their hand at freshwater fishing just down the hill from the hotel (bring your own gear). Flocks of rare tropical birds are frequently seen in the nearby mangroves.

Bedrooms (all nonsmoking) are comfortably furnished in a rather bland motel style. Bathrooms with either shower or tub are functional, but without much decorative zest. There's a dining room with an ocean view where you can have a typical Puerto Rican dinner or choose from the international menu.

A short drive from the hotel will bring you to the Punta Borinquén Golf Course. Tennis courts are just down the hill from the inn itself. Sightseeing trips to the nearby Arecibo Observatory (p. 166)—the largest radar/radio-telescope in the world—and to Monte Calvario (a replica of Mount Calvary) are available. Another popular visit is to the plaza in the town of Quebradillas.

Rte. 113N 6205, Quebradillas, PR 00678. (℃ **787/895-2065.** Fax 787/895-2294. www.paradorvistamar.com. 55 units (each with either shower or tub). Year-round $76–$112 double. Up to 2 children under 12 stay free in parent's room. AE, DISC, MC, V. At Quebradillas, head northwest on Rte. 2, then go left at the junction with Rte. 113 and continue for a mile/1.6km. **Amenities:** Restaurant; bar; pool; limited room service; rooms for those w/limited mobility. *In room:* A/C, TV, coffeemaker (in some).

ISABELA

On the northwestern coast, a 1½-hour drive west of San Juan, the town of Isabela captures the flavor of the west, although it's far less known by visitors than Rincón and

Mayagüez. Its pastel-colored, whitewashed houses border the sea, known for its surf-ing and swimming beaches.

The locals don't survive on tourism, but on such industries as shoemaking and textiles. In spite of manufacturing, many small farms still dot the area.

Tragedy has struck repeatedly in the area because of the geographical location of Isabela, which has made it the victim of both tidal waves and earthquakes since it was first settled.

Isabela enjoys a reputation for horse breeding. This activity is centered around Arenales, south of the town, where a number of horse stables are located.

The area abounds in good beaches, including Jobos Beach, directly west of Isabela on Route 466. The beach is set against a backdrop of cliffs, the most dramatic of which is El Pozo de Jacinto. Nearby at a beach called "The Shacks," both snorkelers and scuba divers enjoy swimming among the reefs, teeming with rainbow-hued fish and the coral caverns.

WHERE TO STAY & DINE

Villas del Mar Hau *Kids*   Opening onto a long private beach, this family-friendly parador complex is peppered with West Indian–style cottages in vivid Caribbean pastels with Victorian wood trim. The location is midway between the west coast cities of Arecibo in the east and Aguadilla in the west, right outside the smaller town of Isabela. Under the shelter of Causuarina pine trees, most guests spend their days lying on Playa Montones. The huge tidal "wading" pool is ideal for children. The place is unpretentious but not completely back-to-nature, as the beachfront cottages are well furnished and equipped, each with a balcony and with capacities for two to six guests. Some have ceiling fans, others have air-conditioning, and all units are equipped with small, tiled, shower-only bathrooms. Since 1960 the Hau family has run this little beach inn. The on-site restaurant is well known in the area for its creative menu featuring fresh fish, shellfish, and meats.

Carretera 466, Km 8.3, Playa Montones, Isabela, PR 00662. ℂ 787/830-8315. Fax 787/830-4988. 42 units (shower only). Year-round $96–$115 for 2; $131–$148 for 4; $150–$250 for 6. AE, MC, V. From the center of Isabella, take Rte. 466 toward Aguadilla. **Amenities:** Restaurant; bar; barbecue area; pool w/snack bar; tennis; beach toy rental; photocopy and fax; convenience store; babysitting; laundry service; horseback riding; volleyball court. *In room:* A/C, TV (in most rooms), kitchenette, coffeemaker.

COAMO

Legend has it that the hot springs in this town, located inland on the south coast about a 2-hour drive from San Juan, were the Fountain of Youth sought by Ponce de León. It is believed that the Taíno peoples, during pre-Columbian times, held rituals and pilgrimages here as they sought health and well-being. Between 1847 and 1958, the site was a center for rest and relaxation for Puerto Ricans and others, some on their honeymoons, others in search of the curative powers of the geothermal springs, which lie about a 5-minute walk from **Parador Baños de Coamo.** Nonguests can come here to use the baths, but the experience is hardly special today. The baths are in poor condition.

WHERE TO STAY & DINE

Parador Baños de Coamo   The spa at Baños de Coamo features this parador, offering hospitality in traditional Puerto-Rican style. The Baños has welcomed many notable visitors over the years, including Franklin D. Roosevelt, Frank Lloyd Wright, Alexander Graham Bell, and Thomas Edison, who came here to swim in the on-site hot springs, said to be the most radioactive in the world. Since those days and since those long-departed visitors, the spa world is now state-of-the-art in many places, including San Juan and some nearby resorts. Such is not the case here; maintenance is poor, and the bathrooms show signs of aging. (Locals sometimes purchase a day pass and use the pool, which leads to noise, confusion, and overcrowding on weekends.)

The buildings range from a lattice-adorned two-story motel unit with wooden verandas to a Spanish colonial pink stucco building, which houses the restaurant. The bedrooms draw a mixed reaction from visitors, so ask to see your prospective room before deciding to stay here. Many of the often-dark rooms are not well maintained, and the bathrooms seem more appropriate for a campsite. Mildew is also evident. The cuisine is both Creole and international, and the coffee Baños-style is a special treat.

P.O. Box 1867, Coamo, PR 00769. © **787/825-2186**. Fax 787/825-4739. www.banosdecoamo.com. 48 units. Year-round $80–$90 double. AE, DC, DISC, MC, V. From Rte. 1, turn onto Rte. 153 at Santa Isabel; then turn left onto Rte. 546 and drive west 1 mile/1.6km. **Amenities:** Restaurant; bar; 2 pools; laundry service; coin-op laundry; dry cleaning; 1 room for those w/limited mobility. *In room:* A/C, TV, iron.

11

Eastern Puerto Rico

The northeast corner of the island, only about 45 minutes from San Juan, contains the island's major attractions, El Yunque rainforest and Luquillo Beach (see chapter 8), as well as a variety of landscapes, ranging from miles of forest to palm groves and beachside settlements.

Here you will find one of the best resorts on the island, El Conquistador Resort.

This is also the site of Fajardo, a preeminent sailor's haven, where you can catch ferries to the islands of Vieques and Culebra (see chapter 12).

1 Las Croabas

35 miles (56km) E of San Juan

Las Croabas, near Fajardo, is the site of the El Conquistador Resort. El Conquistador was the leader in luxury resorts in the Caribbean from the 1960s through the late 1970s. Celebrities Elaine May, Jack Gilford, Celeste Holm (with her husband and two poodles), Elaine Stritch (and her dog), Amy Vanderbilt, Jack Palance, Burt Bacharach, Angie Dickinson, Omar Shariff, Marc Connelly, Maureen O'Sullivan, and Xavier Cugat attended its grand inaugural festivities in 1968. Later, its circular casino, in black and stainless steel, appeared in the James Bond movie *Goldfinger.* The original hotel closed in 1980, but it was reborn in 1993 as the distinctive $250-million El Conquistador we have today.

GETTING THERE

El Conquistador staff members greet all guests at the San Juan airport and transport them to the resort. Guests at the resort can take a taxi or a hotel courtesy car, or they can drive a rental car to Luquillo Beach.

The cost of a taxi from the San Juan airport averages around $60.

If you're driving from San Juan, head east on Route 3 toward Fajardo. At the intersection, cut northeast on Route 195 and continue to the intersection with Route 987, at which point you turn north.

OUTDOOR ACTIVITIES

In addition to the lovely beach and the many recreational facilities that are part of the El Conquistador (p. 223), there are other notable places to play in the vicinity. Don't forget that not far from Las Croabas is **Luquillo Beach,** one of the island's best stretches of sand (see chapter 8).

WATERSPORTS For a cruise, your best bet in Las Croabas is **Erin Go Bragh Charters** (© **787/860-4401**). The 50-foot (15m) ketch is operated by Capt. Bill Henry, who is licensed to carry six passengers. The boat is available for day charters and sunset and evening cruises, and it has equipment for watersports, including

To the Lighthouse: Exploring Las Cabezas de San Juan Nature Reserve

Las Cabezas de San Juan Nature Reserve is better known as El Faro, or "The Lighthouse." Located in the northeastern corner of the island, it is one of the most beautiful and important areas in Puerto Rico. Here you'll find seven ecological systems and a restored 19th-century Spanish colonial lighthouse. From the lighthouse observation deck, majestic views extend to islands as far off as St. Thomas in the U.S. Virgin Islands.

Surrounded on three sides by the Atlantic Ocean, the 316-acre (128-hectare) site encompasses forestland, mangroves, lagoons, beaches, cliffs, offshore cays, and coral reefs. Boardwalk trails wind through the fascinating topography. Ospreys, sea turtles, and an occasional manatee are seen from the windswept promontories and rocky beach.

The nature reserve is open Wednesday through Sunday. Reservations are required; for reservations during the week, call 𝄐 **787/722-5882,** and for reservations on weekends, 𝄐 **787/860-2560** (weekend reservations must be made on the day of your visit). Admission is $7 for adults, $4 for children under 13, and $2.50 for seniors. Guided 2½-hour tours are conducted at 9:30am, 10am, 10:30am, and 2pm (in English at 2pm).

Windsurfers and masks and fins. A full-day tour costs $75 per person, including a barbecue lunch.

For scuba divers, the best deal is offered by the PADI outfit **La Casa del Mar,** at the Puerto del Rey marina, the lowest level of the El Conquistador (𝄐 **787/ 863-1000,** ext. 7917). You can go for ocean dives on the outfitter's boats, a one-tank dive costing $75 or a two-tank dive for $105, including tanks and weight belt. A PADI snorkel program, at $55 per person, is also available.

In Fajardo, the Caribbean's largest and most modern marina, **Puerto del Rey** (𝄐 **787/860-1000**), has facilities for 70 boats, including docking and fueling for yachts up to 200 feet (61m) and haul-out and repair for yachts up to 90 feet (27m). The marina has boat rentals, yacht charters, and watersports, plus shops and a restaurant.

Some of the best snorkeling in Puerto Rico is in and around Fajardo. Its beach, **Playa Seven Seas,** is not as hotsy-totsy as Luquillo Beach, but is an attractive and sheltered strip of sand. The beach lies on the southwestern shoreline of Las Cabezas peninsula and is crowded on weekends. For even better snorkeling, walk along this beach for about half a mile (.8km) to another beach, called **Playa Escondido ("Hidden Beach").** Coral reefs in clear waters lie right off this beach. We'll let you in on a secret: East from Las Cabezas is a marine wildlife refuge known as **La Cordillera,** or "The Spine." Off the mainland of the island, these are the most gin-clear and tranquil waters we have found to date in Puerto Rico. They are teeming with wildlife, including several species of fish such as grouper, but also lobster, moray eels, and sea turtles. On these islets you might even see a rare crested iguana. **East Island Excursion** (𝄐 **787/860-3434**) will take you there.

The following labels appear on the map:

Condado Beach, Ocean Park Beach, Isla Verde Beach, ATLANTIC OCEAN, San Juan, Loiza, Coco Beach, Luquillo Beach, Cabezas de San Juan Nature Reserve, Cataño, Santa Barbara, Las Croabas **7**, Bayamón, **8** Las Croabas **6**, Guaynabo, Trujillo Alto, Carolina, Río Grande, Fajardo **5**, Fajardo Beach, Lake of Loiza, El Yunque **1**, Ceiba, To Culebra, Lomas, Comerio, Caguas, Juncos, Rio Blanco, Daguao, San Lorenzo, La Permina, Naguabo, Naguabo **4**, Naguabo Beach, Punta Santiago, Cayey, CARITE FOREST, Humacao, Cayo Santiago, Playa de Humacao, Palmas del Mar **2**, **3**, To Vieques, Guayama, Yabucoa, Pasaje de Vieques, Caribbean Sea

Map legend:

El Yunque **1**
Fajardo **5**
Humacao **2**
Las Cabezas de San Juan Nature Reserve **7**
Las Croabas **6**
Luquillo Beach **8**
Naguabo **4**
Palmas del Mar **3**

0 — 10 mi
0 — 10 km

TENNIS The seven Har-Tru courts at the **El Conquistador** ✶✶ are among the best tennis courts in Puerto Rico, rivaling those at Palmas del Mar. The staff at the pro shop is extremely helpful to beginning players. Courts are the least crowed during the hottest part of the day, around the lunch hour. If you're a single traveler to the resort and in search of a player, the pro shop will try to match you up with a player of equal skill.

WHERE TO STAY

El Conquistador Resort & Golden Door Spa ✶✶ *Kids* El Conquistador is a destination unto itself. Its array of facilities sits on 500 acres (202 hectares) of forested hills sloping down to the sea. Accommodations are divided into five separate sections united by their Mediterranean architecture and lush landscaping. Most lie several hundred feet above the sea. At the same altitude, a bit off to the side, is a replica of an Andalusian hamlet, Las Casitas Village, which seems straight out of the south of Spain. These pricey units, each with a full kitchen, form a self-contained enclave.

A short walk downhill takes you to a circular cluster of tastefully modern accommodations, Las Olas Village. And at sea level, adjacent to an armada of pleasure craft bobbing at anchor, is La Marina Village, whose balconies seem to hang directly over the water. The accommodations are outfitted with comfortable furniture, tropical colors, and robes. All

Top Caribbean Spa: The Golden Door

Perched atop a stunning 300-foot (91m) bluff overlooking the Caribbean Sea and the Atlantic Ocean, the **Golden Door** ★★, in Las Casitas Village complex at the Wyndham El Conquistador Hotel (© **787/863-1000**), is the most sophisticated, well-managed, and comprehensive spa in the Caribbean, and it is one of the finest in the world. One of only three branches of a spa founded in Escondido, California, and today administered by the Wyndham group, it's devoted to the relaxation and healing of body, soul, and mind. Spa rituals are taken seriously; New Age mysticism is gracefully dispensed within a postmodern setting that's a cross between a Swiss clinic, a state-of-the-art health club, and a Buddhist monastery.

Spa treatments begin at $160 for 80 minutes. You can exercise here for a fee of $15 per day. The spa is open daily from 6:30am to 8:30pm. American Express, MasterCard, and Visa are accepted.

the far-flung elements of the resort are connected by serpentine, landscaped walkways, and by a railroad-style funicular that makes frequent trips up and down the hillside.

One of the most comprehensive spas in the Caribbean, the Golden Door maintains a branch in this resort. The hotel is sole owner of a "fantasy island" (Palomino Island), with caverns, nature trails, horseback riding, and watersports such as scuba diving, windsurfing, and snorkeling. Free private ferries at frequent intervals connect the island, which is about a half-mile (.8km) offshore, to the main hotel. There's also a 25-slip marina. The hotel operates an excellently run Westin Kids Club with activities planned daily.

Av. Conquistador 1000, Las Croabas, Fajardo, PR 00738. © 800/468-5228 or 787/863-1000. Fax 787/863-6500. www.luxuryresort.com. 918 units. Winter $600–$900 double, from $1,500 casita with kitchen for 1–6; off season $399–$540 double, $600–$1,015 casita with kitchen for 1–6. MAP (breakfast and dinner) $96 extra per adult per day, $45 extra per child age 16 and under. Children ages 16 and under stay free in parent's room. AE, DC, DISC, MC, V. Self-parking $10 per day; valet parking $20. **Amenities:** 9 restaurants; 7 bars; nightclub; 7 pools; golf course; 7 Har-Tru tennis courts; health club; spa; 25-slip marina; dive shop; fishing; sailing; children's programs; tour desk; business center; limited room service; massage; laundry service; dry cleaning; nonsmoking rooms; casino; rooms for those w/limited mobility. *In room:* A/C, TV, minibar, fridge, coffeemaker, hair dryer, iron, safe.

WHERE TO DINE
EXPENSIVE

Blossoms ★★ CHINESE/JAPANESE   Blossoms boasts some of the freshest seafood in eastern Puerto Rico. Sizzling delights are prepared on teppanyaki tables, and there's a zesty selection of Hunan and Szechuan specialties. On the teppanyaki menu, you can choose dishes ranging from chicken to shrimp, from filet mignon to lobster. Sushi bar selections range from eel and squid to salmon roe and giant clams.

In the El Conquistador Resort. © 787/863-1000. Reservations recommended. Main courses $20–$49. AE, DC, DISC, MC, V. Daily 6–11:30pm.

Isabela's Grill ★ AMERICAN STEAKHOUSE   Of all the restaurants in El Conquistador Resort, this is the most American. If Ike were to miraculously return, he'd feel comfortable with this 1950s menu. The severely dignified baroque room was inspired by an aristocratic monastery in Spain. The massive gates are among the most spectacular pieces of wrought iron on Puerto Rico. The service is impeccable, the steaks tender, and the seafood fresh.

Special care is taken with the beef dishes, even though the meat is imported frozen. You can begin with the lobster bisque or French soup, then move on to the thick cut of veal chop or the perfectly prepared rack of lamb. Prime rib of beef is a feature, as are the succulent steaks; try the New York strip or the porterhouse.

In the El Conquistador Resort. ℂ 787/863-1000. Reservations required. Main courses $30–$52. AE, DISC, MC, V. Daily 6–10:30pm.

Otello's ℛ NORTHERN ITALIAN   Here you can dine by candlelight either indoors or out. The decor is neo-Palladian. You might begin with one of the soups, perhaps pasta fagioli, or select one of the zesty Italian appetizers, such as an excellently prepared clams Posillipo. Pastas can be ordered as a half portion for an appetizer or as a main dish, and they include homemade gnocchi and fettuccine with shrimp. The chef is known for his superb veal dishes. A selection of poultry and vegetarian food is offered nightly, along with several shrimp and fish dishes. The salmon filet in champagne sauce has beautiful accents, as does the veal chop in an aromatic herb sauce.

In the El Conquistador Resort. ℂ 787/863-1000. Reservations required in winter, recommended off season. Main courses $26–$42. AE, DC, DISC, MC, V. Daily 6–10:30pm.

2 Palmas del Mar

46 miles (74km) SE of San Juan

An hour east of San Juan, the residential resort community of Palmas del Mar lies near Humacao. Here you'll find one of the most action-packed sports programs in the Caribbean, offering golf, tennis, scuba diving, sailing, deep-sea fishing, and horseback riding. Palmas del Mar's location is one of its greatest assets. The pleasing Caribbean trade winds steadily blow across this section of the island, stabilizing the weather and making Palmas del Mar ideal for many outdoor sports.

The resort is no longer what it was in its heyday in the early 1990s. Today it is a real-estate conglomerate that promotes vacation properties to investors, although outsiders can stay here as well. Many of the occupants are residents of San Juan who come here on weekends. Tourists are welcome, but most first-time visitors will find better accommodations up the coast, at the Westin Rio Mar (p. 176) or the El Conquistador (p. 223).

GETTING THERE

Humacao Regional Airport is 3 miles (4.8km) from the northern boundary of Palmas del Mar. It accommodates private planes; no regularly scheduled airline currently serves the Humacao airport. Palmas del Mar Resort will arrange minivan or bus transport from Humacao to the San Juan airport. Two persons can book the van for $40. If five or more passengers book the van, the cost is only $20 per person. The bus can accommodate up to 10 passengers. At night the price goes up to $45 per person for two. That is lowered to $22 per person if five or more share the ride. For reservations, call ℂ 787/285-4323. Call the resort if you want to be met at the airport.

If you're driving from San Juan, take Highway 52 south to Caguas, then take Highway 30 east to Humacao. Follow the signs from there to Palmas del Mar.

BEACHES & OUTDOOR ACTIVITIES

BEACHES   Palmas del Mar Resort has 3 exceptional miles (4.8km) of white-sand beaches (all open to the public). Nonguests pay a $1 charge for parking and 25¢ for a changing room and a locker. The waters here are calm year-round, and there's a watersports center and marina (see "Scuba Diving & Snorkeling," below).

FISHING   Some of the best year-round fishing in the Caribbean is found in the waters just off Palmas del Mar. **Capt. Bill Burleson,** based in Humacao (© 787/850-7442), operates charters on his customized, 46-foot (14m) sport-fisherman, *Karolette,* which is electronically equipped for successful fishing. Burleson prefers to take fishing groups to Grappler Banks, 18 nautical miles away, which lie in the migratory paths of wahoo, tuna, and marlin. A maximum of six people are taken out, costing $680 for 4½ hours, or $840 for 6 hours. Burleson also offers snorkeling expeditions to Vieques at $110 per person for up to 5 hours. He can also take you to other snorkeling locations as well.

GOLF   Few other real-estate developments in the Caribbean devote as much attention and publicity to their golf facilities as the **Palmas del Mar Country Club** ⚜⚜ (© 787/ 285-2256). Today, both the older course, the Gary Player–designed Palm course, and the newer course, the Reese Jones–designed Flamboyant course, have pars of 72 and layouts of around 2,250 yards (2,073m) each. Crack golfers consider holes 11 to 15 of the Palm course among the toughest five successive holes in the Caribbean. The pro shop that services both courses is open daily from 6:30am to 6pm. To play the course costs $85 for guests of Villas at Palmas of Four Points by Sheraton or $150 for nonguests.

HIKING   Palmas del Mar's land is an attraction in its own right. Here you'll find more than 6 miles (9.7km) of Caribbean ocean frontage—3½ miles (5.6km) of sandy beach amid rocky cliffs and promontories. Large tracts of the 2,700-acre (1,093-hectare) property have harbored sugar and coconut plantations over the years, and a wet tropical forest preserve with giant ferns, orchids, and hanging vines covers about 70 acres (28 hectares) near the resort's geographic center.

SCUBA DIVING & SNORKELING   Some of the best dives in Puerto Rico are right off the eastern coast. Two dozen dive sites south of Fajardo are within a 5-mile (8km) radius offshore. See "The Best Scuba Diving" section in chapter 1.

Set adjacent to a collection of boutiques, bars, and restaurants at the edge of Palmas del Mar's harbor, **Palmas Dive Center** ⚜, Anchors Village, 110 Harbor Dr. (© 787/863-3483), owns a 44-foot-long (13m) diveboat with a 16-foot (4.9m) beam to make it stable in rough seas. They offer both morning and afternoon sessions of two-tank dives (for experienced and certified divers only), priced at $99 each. Half-day snorkeling trips, priced at $60 per participant and departing for both morning and afternoon sessions, go whenever there's demand to the fauna-rich reefs that encircle Monkey Island, an offshore uninhabited cay.

TENNIS   The **Tennis Center at Palmas del Mar** ⚜⚜ (© 787/852-6000, ext. 51), the largest in Puerto Rico, features 13 hard courts, two Omni courts, and four clay courts, open to resort guests and nonguests. Fees for guests are $20 per hour during the day and $25 per hour at night. Fees are $25 per hour during the day and $33 per hour at night. Within the resort's tennis compound is a **fitness center,** which has the best-equipped gym in the region; it's open Monday to Friday 6am to 9pm, and Saturday and Sunday 6am to 8pm.

WHERE TO STAY

It's still possible to rent either a studio or villa from the **Villas at Palmas del Mar,** 295 Palmas Inn Way, Suite 6, Carretera no. 3, Km 86.4 Candelero, Humacao, PR 00791 (© **800/468-3331;** fax 787/852-0927). Some 40 studios and villas are available. Renting year-round for $245 to $340 in a double, studios come with one bedroom and a kitchenette, with a full bathroom. Air-conditioning and cable TV are available. Villas rent year-round for $290 to $595, come with anywhere from one to three bedrooms, and each has a full kitchen and dining room. On the grounds are six pools, two golf courses, 20 tennis courts, a fitness center, and dive shop. Fishing, bike or car rentals, babysitting, and horseback riding can be arranged.

Four Points by Sheraton Palmas del Mar Resort ♠ This long-dormant property came alive again in the spring of 2006, with Sheraton as the "helmer." Completely restored and imbued with a post-millennium update, the resort offers bedrooms that are spacious and handsomely furnished. The junior suites are especially comfortable and inviting. A plethora of on-site activities may keep you from ever leaving the premises: championship golf courses, a country club, a casino and pool bar, along with an "infinity pool," are just some of the offerings.

Furnishings are tasteful and exceedingly comfortable, typical of Sheraton's deluxe hotels. Available extras include private balconies, luxury bathrooms, and work desks. The hotel also offers business services for commercial travelers, plus a special pool for kids. The hotel restaurant offers a varied international menu (some dine here every night), and you'll also find a wine and cigar bar.

Candelero Dr. 170, Humacao, PR 00791. © 787/850-6000. Fax 787/850-6001. www.starwoodhotels.com. 107 units. Year-round $220–$240 double. Winter $355 suite; off season $270 suite. AE, MC, V. Self-parking $12; valet parking $15. **Amenities:** Restaurant; 2 bars; outdoor pool; kids' pool; golf; tennis; fitness center; scuba diving; business services; 24-hr. room service; laundry service; dry cleaning; nonsmoking rooms; casino; rooms for those w/limited mobility. *In room:* A/C, TV, dataport, fridge, beverage maker, hair dryer, iron, safe.

WHERE TO DINE

Thanks to the kitchens that are built into virtually every unit in Palmas del Mar, many guests prepare at least some of their meals "at home." This is made relatively feasible thanks to the on-site general store at the Palmanova Plaza, which sells everything from fresh lettuce and sundries to liquor and cigarettes.

Barracuda Bistro ♠ PUERTO RICAN/INTERNATIONAL The most active bar scene in the early evening takes place here, as yachters gather to talk about the adventures of the day. The sautéed mahimahi in tequila-butter and lime sauce alone is worth the trip. Fresh red snapper is sautéed in butter and lemon zest, and you can also count on the chef throwing a T-bone steak on the grill. You can also order both Mexican and Creole specialties, including roast pork and fajitas with either chicken or beef. If you're visiting at lunch or during the afternoon, you can also order fast food, including hot dogs, sandwiches, and burgers.

La Marina. © 787/850-4441. Reservations recommended. Main courses $16–$21. AE, MC, V. Daily noon–10pm.

Blue Hawaiian CHINESE This is the best Chinese restaurant in the region. It combines Polynesian themes (similarly to a toned-down Trader Vic's) with an Americanized version of Chinese food that's flavorful and well suited to Puerto Rico's hot, steamy climate. Menu items include lobster with garlic-flavored cheese sauce; blackened salmon or steaks reminiscent of styles in New Orleans; and a superb house

---

Finds Where the Locals Go for Soul Food

To escape the confines of the resort for the evening, drive over to a local dive, **Trulio's Sea Food** (© 787/850-1840), just off Route 3 on Calle Isidro Andreux Andreu in the hamlet of Punta Santiago. This is strictly no-frills. Though very low in cost, the food is top-notch and even memorable, especially the fried plantain filled with sea conch. The shrimp in garlic sauce will have you asking for more, and you can also order perfectly baked lobster in garlic sauce. Also try the grilled whole red snapper in garlic and onions. You get the point now: Garlic is king here. Puerto Ricans rave about the chef's dessert specialty, which is pound cake soaked in sweet milk. It tastes better than it sounds and is like soul food to the locals because it's just like Mom used to make.

---

version of honey chicken. You'll find the place within the dignified courtyard of the resort's shopping center, with tables for alfresco dining. Your host is Tommy Lo, former chef aboard the now-defunct ocean liner SS *United States*.

In the Palmanova Shopping Center. © 787/852-0897. Reservations recommended. Main courses $13–$39. AE, MC, V. Daily noon–10:30pm.

Chez Daniel ⟨ FRENCH   It's French, and it's the favorite of the folks who tie up their yachts at the adjacent pier. Normandy-born Daniel Vasse, the owner, along with his French Catalonian wife, Lucette, maintain a dining room that is the most appealing in Palmas del Mar. Chez Daniel shows a faithful allegiance to the tenets of classical French cuisine, placing emphasis on such dishes as bouillabaisse, onion soup, and snails as well as lobster and chicken dishes. For dessert, consider a soufflé au Cointreau.

Marina de Palmas del Mar. © 787/850-3838. Reservations required. Main courses $26–$35 at dinner, $7–$12 at lunch, $38 Sun brunch (includes 1st drink). AE, DISC, MC, V. Wed–Mon 6:30–10pm; Fri–Sun noon–3pm. Closed June.

3 Paradores of Eastern Puerto Rico

Most of the government-certified inns called paradores are found in western Puerto Rico (see "Paradores of Western Puerto Rico" in chapter 10), though there are two along the eastern coast that are ideal for escapists. For the locations of these paradores, see the map on p. 53.

The Fajardo Inn ⟨ Finds   A good base for those visiting El Yunque, this inn is ideal for those who are seeking a location in the east and don't want to pay the prices charged at the El Conquistador (p. 223). Lying on a hilltop overlooking the port of Fajardo, this parador evokes a Mediterranean villa with its balustrades and grand staircases. The midsize bedrooms, most of which open onto good views, are spotless, and each has a small shower-only bathroom. The inn and its pool are handsomely landscaped. A few steps from the inn is an older building, The Scenic Inn, which offers access to all of Fajardo Inn's facilities at lower rates—$66 per night—for a double, for those who don't mind a room without phone or view. The Fajardo Inn's restaurant specializes in Creole and Continental cuisine, especially fresh fish, with indoor and outdoor dining.

Parcela Beltrán 52, Fajardo, PR 00740. © 787/860-6000. Fax 787/860-5063. www.fajardoinn.com. 105 units (shower only). Year-round $100–$130 double; $129–$295 suite. AE, DISC, MC, V. A 15-min. walk east of the center of

Fajardo. **Amenities:** 2 restaurants; 2 bars; pool; snorkeling and diving arranged; limited room service; 1 room for those w/limited mobility. *In room:* A/C, TV, hair dryer, iron.

Hotel Parador Palmas de Lucía ⚔ *Finds*   In the southeastern corner of Puerto Rico, where accommodations are scarce, this government-affiliated parador is a knockout discovery. It lies at the eastern end of Ruta Panorámica, a network of scenic, winding roads along which you can take in some of the finest views in the Caribbean before coming to rest at Palmas de Luca, just steps from the pleasant sands of Playa Lucüa. This is one of the newest hotels in eastern Puerto Rico, filling a vast gap in accommodations in this remote part of the island. The Lopez family are your hosts, and their complex combines colonial styling with tropical decoration. Each midsize bedroom is well furnished and has a pool-view balcony and an efficiently organized, tiled shower-only bathroom.

Palmas de Lucía, routes 901 and 9911, Camino Nuevo, Yabucoa, PR 00767. © **787/893-4423.** Fax 787/893-0291. www.palmasdelucia.com. 34 units (shower only). Year-round $84 double; $109 suite. AE, MC, V. From Humacao, take Rte. 53 south to Yabucoa, to the end of the highway, where you connect with Rte. 901 to Maunabo. After a 2-min. drive, turn left at the signposted Carretera 9911, which leads to Playa Lucía. **Amenities:** Restaurant; bar; pool; basketball court. *In room:* A/C, TV.

12

Vieques & Culebra

Vieques and Culebra are where Puerto Ricans go for their own vacations. Sandy beaches and low prices are the powerful attractions of both islands. Culebra still slumbers in the early 1950s, but Vieques is fast becoming one of the hottest tropical destinations in the Caribbean. The unspoiled beaches and stylish inns have created quite a buzz. When you spot Sandra Bernhard on the beach, you know the times are changin'.

Vieques, which has more tourist facilities than Culebra, lies 7 miles (11km) off the eastern coast of the Puerto Rican "mainland." It is visited mainly for its 40-odd white-sand beaches. Vieques was occupied at various times by the French and the British before Puerto Rico acquired it in 1854. The ruins of many

sugar and pineapple plantations testify to its once-flourishing agricultural economy.

The U.S. military took control of two-thirds of the island's 26,000 acres (10,523 hectares) in 1941. The area was used for military training with live-fire maneuvers. After massive protests, the U.S. announced in 2003 that it was shutting down its Roosevelt Roads Naval Station, the site of the Atlantic Fleet Weapons Training Facility.

Culebra, 18 miles (29km) east of the Puerto Rican "mainland" and 14 miles (23km) west of St. Thomas in the U.S. Virgin Islands, is surrounded by coral reefs and edged with nearly deserted, powdery, white-sand beaches. Much of the island has been designated a wildlife refuge by the U.S. Fish and Wildlife Service.

Warning: Dengue fever has returned to Vieques and Culebra. See p. 39.

1 Vieques ★

41 miles (66km) E of San Juan, 7 miles (11km) SE of Fajardo

About 7 miles (11km) east of the big island of Puerto Rico lies Vieques (Bee-*ay*-kase), an island about twice as large as New York's Manhattan, with about 9,300 inhabitants and some 40 palm-lined white-sand beaches.

From World War II until 2003, about two-thirds of the 21-mile (34km) long island was controlled by U.S. military forces. Much of the government-owned land is now leased for cattle grazing.

Unlike the U.S. military, the Spanish conquistadores didn't think much of Vieques. They came here in the 16th century but didn't stay long, reporting that the island and neighboring bits of land held no gold and were, therefore, *las islas inutiles* (the useless islands). The name Vieques comes from the native Amerindian word *bieques* meaning "small island."

The Spaniards later changed their minds and founded the main town, **Isabel Segunda,** on the northern shore. Construction on the last Spanish fort built in the New World began here around 1843, during the reign of Queen Isabella II, for whom the town was named. The fort, never completed, is not of any special interest. The

Vieques & Culebra

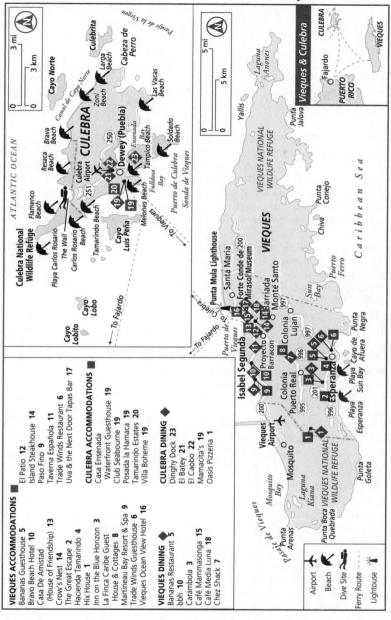

VIEQUES ACCOMMODATIONS ■
Bananas Guesthouse 5
Bravo Beach Hotel 10
Casa De Amistad
(House of Friendship) 13
Crow's Nest 14
The Great Escape 2
Hacienda Tamarindo 4
Hix House 1
Inn on the Blue Horizon 3
La Finca Caribe Guest
House & Cottages 8
Martineau Bay Resort & Spa 9
Trade Winds Guesthouse 6
Vieques Ocean View Hotel 16

El Patio 12
Island Steakhouse 14
Paso Fino 9
Taverna Española 11
Trade Winds Restaurant 6
Uva & the Next Door Tapas Bar 17

CULEBRA ACCOMMODATIONS ■
Casa Ensenada
Waterfront Guesthouse 19
Club Seabourne 19
Posada la Hamaca 19
Tamarindo Estates 20
Villa Boheme 19

VIEQUES DINING ◆
Bananas Restaurant 5
bbh 10
Carambola 3
Café Mammasonga 15
Café Media Luna 18
Chez Shack 7

CULEBRA DINING ◆
Dinghy Dock 23
El Batey 21
El Caobo 22
Mamacita's 19
Oasis Pizzeria 1

231

island's fishermen and farmers conduct much of their business here. The **Punta Mula lighthouse,** north of Isabel Segunda, provides panoramic views of the land and sea.

On the south coast, **Esperanza,** once a center for the island's sugar-cane industry and now a pretty little fishing village, lies near **Sun Bay (Sombe) public beach** 📷. Sun Bay, a government-run, panoramic crescent of sand, is the beach to visit if you have only 1 day to spend on the island. The fenced area has picnic tables, a bathhouse, and a parking lot. A resort, marina, and other facilities add to the allure of the many scalloped stretches of sandy waterfront.

ESSENTIALS

GETTING THERE   Vieques Air Link (📞 787/741-8331; www.vieques-island. com/val), **Isla Nena** (📞 787/741-1577), and **Air Flamenco** (📞 787/724-1818; www.airflamenco.net) fly to Vieques three times daily out of Isla Grand Airport (around $50 one way and $100 roundtrip). You can also fly out of the main Luis Muñoz Marín International Airport on **Cape Air** (📞 800/352-0714 or 787/253-1121; www.flycapeair.com), but you'll pay up to 50% more.

The **Puerto Rico Port Authority** operates two **ferries** a day to Vieques from the eastern port of Fajardo; the trip takes about an hour. The round-trip fare is $4 for adults, $2 for children. Tickets for the morning ferry that leaves Saturday and Sunday sell out quickly, so you should be in line at the ticket window in Fajardo before 8am (it opens at 6:30am) to be certain of a seat on the 9:30am boat. Otherwise, you'll have to wait until the 1 or 4:30pm ferry. For more information about these sea links, call 📞 787/723-2260.

GETTING AROUND   Public cabs or vans called *públicos* transport people around the island. We recommend that you rent a car for at least some of the time, just for the purpose of seeing the layout of the island. To do this, contact **Island Car Rental** (📞 787/741-1666), in the hamlet of Florida, about a 12-minute ride southwest of Isabel Segunda, 5 minutes from the airport. The office is next door to the Crow's Nest hotel (p. 237). The cost of the local vehicles begins at $50 per day, plus another $10 for collision-damage-waiver insurance. American Express, MasterCard, and Visa cards are accepted.

You can also rent a Jeep Wrangler or Cherokee from **Martineau Car Rental,** Km 3.2 Route 200 (📞 787/741-0078), costing $65 to $74 a day. The rental outlet is a 15-minute taxi ride from the airport. There are no car rentals at the airport. You have to call one of the rental agencies and then taxi over to pick up your car.

THE BEST BEACHES

Aficionados of Vieques praise the island for its wide profusion of sandy beaches. Since the pullout of the U.S. Navy, some of the sites that were formerly off-limits have been made accessible to hikers, cyclists, bird-watchers, beachcombers, and other members of the public.

The best beaches are **Red Beach (Bahia Corcha), Blue Beach (Bahia de la Chiva),** and **Playa Plata.** To reach these, take the tarmac-covered road that juts eastward from a point near the southern third of Route 997. Entrance to this part of the island, formerly occupied by the navy, will be identified as **Refugio Nacional de Vida Silvestre de Vieques,** with warnings near its entrance that camping and littering are not allowed. Drive for about a mile (1.6km) along this road, turning right at the sign pointing to Red Beach (Bahia Corcha). En route, you'll have one of the few opportunities in the world to gun your rented car along the battered tarmac of what used to be a landing strip (a very long one) for the navy. Pretend, if you like, however briefly, that you're on a test track for the Indianapolis 500, exercising, naturally, all due caution.

Continue driving to the crescent-shaped, wide-open-to-view expanses of Red Beach, where about a dozen metal-roofed gazebos, many atop cement slabs and accented with picnic tables, provide shelter from the sun, and where "Job Jonnies" (that is, portable chemical toilets) are available. Red Beach, which has picnic tables, is the most family-friendly beach on the island.

At **Blue Beach** the sands are less wide than those of Red Beach. At Blue Beach mangrove and scrub trees grow close to the water's edge. This beach attracts romantic couples or escapists who fantasize they'll happen across a porno shoot. Devotees appreciate the broken sightlines between the bathing spaces, the labyrinth of narrow, rutted dirt roads leading to the individual bathing sites, and the sense of genteel isolation from other sunbathers.

There are signs, within the park, to minor beaches, **Playa Caracas, Caya Melones,** and even **"Playuela,"** but the access roads are blocked off by the Park Service.

We like the myriad coves, one of which is **Playa Chiva,** that pepper the coastline between Blue Beach and the end of the line, Playa Plata, which is as far as a conventional visitor can travel within the park. They're secluded from view, and you'll get the distinct feeling that some of the sunbathers might be making love behind the seagrapes, scrub trees, and palmettos.

The most visible public-works project on Vieques is **Sun Bay Beach.** Its entrance lies off the southern stretch of Route 997. You'll recognize it by a metal sign announcing *Balneario Público Sun Bay.* Just beyond this sign, you'll see a park dotted with trees, an absurdly large number of parking spaces (which no one uses), and a formal entryway to the park, which virtually everybody ignores. (It evokes a public housing project—anonymous and unused and unloved.) Locals, as a means of getting closer to the water and the sands, drive along the access road stretching to the left. It parallels a ¾-mile (1.2km) stretch of tree-dotted beachfront, and they park wherever they find a spot that appeals to them. If you continue to drive past the very last parking spot along Sun Bay Beach, a rutted and winding and very hilly road will lead, after a right-hand fork, to **Media Luna Beach** and **Navio Beach,** both pleasant and isolated. A left-hand fork leads to the muddy and rutted parking lot that services Mosquito Bay (or, Phosphorescent Bay).

Playa Esperanza is one of the most frequented beaches on Vieques. It's best for snorkeling, not for beaching it. The beach opens onto the little fishing village of Esperanza on the south coast.

DIVING & OTHER OUTDOOR PURSUITS

The small scale of Vieques, and the fact that virtually everyone on the island is either related to or linked in some way to everybody else, creates a situation whereby many of the island's watersports outfitters are in constant communication with one another. Therefore, **Blue Caribe Kayaks,** Calle Flamboyan 149 (El Malecón; ✆ 787/741-2522), has evolved into a kind of clearinghouse for the island's watersports outfitters. Consequently, if you're interested in kayaking, snorkeling, water-skiing, scuba-diving, fishing, or swimming in the nighttime waters of Vieques's luminescent bays, the staff here can funnel your request to an appropriate, and competitively priced, outfitter.

Through them, you'll gain access to, and information about, any of the following activities:

Renting a Kayak: The cost is $10 an hour, $25 for 4 hours (a half-day), and $45 for a full day.

Rental of snorkeling equipment: Fins, a mask, and a snorkel rent for $12 for a 24-hour period, upon payment of a $50 fully returnable deposit.

Guided snorkeling tours in a kayak are possible from the harborfront of Esperanza to a sizable island offshore. You can take a kayak at the cost of $30 per person, including guide, to Cayo de Afuera. Snorkelers seek out the island for its gin-clear waters, revealing a stunning collection of antler coral. On some days you can see nurse sharks swim by, and you might even spot the increasingly elusive manatee. Some visitors swim to the island but that takes a lot of stamina.

A 3- to 4-hour spin-casting fishing tour from a kayak, wherein you'll fish for barracuda, grouper, or other reef fish, using segments of squid or octopus as bait: $50 per person. Tours last from around 3pm to sundown daily.

A well-rehearsed outfit that's good at leading newcomers into the island's most savage landscapes is **La Dulce Vida Mountain Bike and Adventure Company,** Route 996, Km 4.5 Barrio Puerto Real (© **787/435-3557;** www.bikevieques.com). Karl Husson and members of his staff lead mountain bikers on half-day ($65 per person) and full-day ($85 per person) tours of obscure trails that are noteworthy for their panoramas and technical difficulties. Use of a mountain bike, usually an aluminum-framed, 28-speed, state-of-the-art model, is included in the price. You can rent one of these bikes, without the services of a trail guide, for $25 per day.

THE LUMINOUS WATERS OF PHOSPHORESCENT BAY &

One of the major attractions on the island is **Mosquito Bay** &, also called **Phosphorescent Bay,** with its glowing waters produced by tiny bioluminescent organisms. These organisms dart away from boats, leaving eerie blue-white trails of phosphorescence. The *Vieques Times* wrote: "By any name the bay can be a magical, psychedelic experience and few places in the world can even come close to the intensity of concentration of the dinoflagellates called pyrodiniums (whirling fire). They are tiny (1/500-in./.13cm) swimming creatures that light up like fireflies when disturbed but nowhere are there so many fireflies. Here a gallon of bay water may contain almost three-quarters of a million." The ideal time to tour is on a cloudy, moonless night. If the moon is shining on a cloudless night, you can save your money as you'll see almost nothing. Some boats go, full moon or not. You should wear a bathing suit because it's possible to swim in these glowing waters.

Island Adventures (© **787/741-0720**) operates trips in Phosphorescent Bay aboard *Luminosa*. These trips are not offered around the time of the full moon. The charge is $25, and most jaunts last about 2 hours. A similar tour on a kayak that also costs $23 is offered by **Blue Caribe Kayak** (© **787/741-2522** for details).

SEEING THE SIGHTS

Fort Conde de Mirasol Museum, Barriada Fuerte at Magnolia 471 (© **787/ 741-1717**), is the major man-made attraction on the island. In the 1840s, Count Mirasol convinced the Spanish government to build a defensive fortress here. Today the carefully restored fort houses a museum of art and history celebrating the story of Vieques. There are Indian relics, displays of the Spanish conquest, and old flags of the Danes, British, and French. The French sugar-cane planters and their African slaves are depicted, and there's even a bust of the great liberator Simón Bolívar, who once visited Puerto Rico. A unique collection of maps shows how the world's cartographers envisioned Vieques. The museum and fort are open Wednesday to Sunday 8:30am to 4:20pm. Admission is $2, or free for ages 11 and under.

WHERE TO STAY
EXPENSIVE
Bravo Beach Hotel ✦✦   In a secluded residential area, this boutique hotel with its Frette linens and Philippe Starck designs comes as a surprise—and a pleasant one. Most of the bedrooms are within only 30 feet (9.1m) of the Atlantic with a good white sandy beach. Units open onto a private terrace facing the sea. It's the little things that count here: an honor bar poolside, those Aveda bath products in the bathroom, or the box lunch the staff will pack for you to take to the beach. Rooms are decorated in a minimalist style, effectively using lots of white, draped plantation-era beds, and wicker furnishings. On-site is a two-bedroom cottage, a vision in white, accented by bamboo and mahogany pieces. You can even check your e-mail poolside, or else enjoy Caribbean-inspired tapas served outdoors.

North Shore Rd. 1, Vieques, PR 00765. ✆ 787/741-1128. www.bravobeachhotels.com. 12 units. Winter $175–$475 double; off season $160–$425 double. AE, DC, MC, V. **Amenities:** Restaurant; bar; 2 outdoor pools; nonsmoking rooms. *In room:* A/C, TV, minibar, beverage maker, hair dryer.

Hix House ✦ *Finds*   No one leaves Hix House without a strong opinion about its value as an eco-sensitive experiment. Angular and avant-garde, and minimalist to the point of looking almost barren, it's one of the most iconoclastic and most admired pieces of eco-sensitive architecture in the Caribbean. It is set on 12 acres (4.9 hectares) of land, formerly used for the cultivation of sugar cane, on a scrub- and tree-covered landscape on a hillside in the center of the island. The inn consists of four separate buildings, designed, respectively, with triangular, circular, or rectangular floor plans. Each of them was created by the celebrated Toronto-based architect John Hix (a "climate and design architect"), who has won awards for the designing of low-maintenance houses in chilly Canada. None of the units has window screens or air-conditioning, and each is—in an aggressive kind of eco-sensitivity that might remind you of a postmodern concrete bunker—outfitted with mosquito netting, low-wattage lighting (brighter lights attract mosquitoes), and virtually indestructible furniture that's crafted either from poured and polished concrete or pressure-treated lumber. And other than yoga classes, priced at $15 per person and conducted 3 mornings a week from 10:30am till noon, there's virtually nothing to do other than the entertainment you create yourself.

Rooms come with refrigerators that are stocked with milk, orange juice, eggs, cereal, freshly baked bread, and fruit. None has a bathtub, and showers are artfully rustic affairs set within open-air concrete alcoves.

Rte. 995, Km 1.5, Vieques, PR 14902. ✆ 787/741-2302. Fax 787/741-2797. www.hixislandhouse.com. 13 units. Winter $220–$295 double; off season $160–$210 double. AE, MC, V. **Amenities:** Outdoor pool. *In room:* Open-air showers, ceiling fans.

Inn on the Blue Horizon ✦✦   Set on the island's southern coastal road, less than a mile (1.6km) west of Esperanza, this is the most charming hotel on Vieques, and it's the one that has repeatedly earned the highest accolades from the international press. In winter, it reigns as the most hip and stylish gathering place in Vieques for the low-key rendezvous of North America's fashion photographers and supermodels. Its centerpiece is an airy seafront house, built in a Mediterranean style in 1975, whose soaring living area opens onto a view of the blue horizon.

In the mid-1990s, the site was transformed into an inn by hotel and restaurant entrepreneur James Weis, a refugee from the New York fashion world. The inn is not stylish or lavish in any way, however. Three of the bedrooms are in the main house; a half-dozen others are in a trio of bungalows, each of which contains two spacious and comfortable units, each with a private balcony and sea view. Airy and clean, they're outfitted with early-19th-century North American antiques and eclectic art from a variety of artists. Two units contain tubs, and the rest are equipped with showers.

Symmetrically positioned arbors are covered with cascades of bougainvillea, with a pool and lawns that slope gracefully down to cliffs at the edge of the sea. The sea adjacent to the hotel has a rocky coastline, but the staff will direct you to the dozens of fine local beaches. The inn's restaurant, Carambola (see "Where to Dine," below) serves the best food on Vieques. Be warned: the place closes down after breakfast and doesn't awaken again until 5pm—that means no lunch or even snacks, so be prepared to do nothing or go wandering.

Rte. 996 (P.O. Box 1556), Km 4.3, Vieques, PR 00765. © 787/741-3318. Fax 787/741-0522. www.innontheblue horizon.com. 10 units (some with shower only). Winter $160–$275 double, $275–$375 suite; off season $125–$205 double, $180–$205 suite. AE, MC, V. Closed Sept–Oct. **Amenities:** Restaurant; cafe/bar; outdoor pool; gym. *In room:* A/C, coffeemaker, hair dryer, no phone.

Martineau Bay Resort & Spa *⭐*   The largest, best-looking, best-accessorized, and most widely visible resort on Vieques opened in 2003. Some visitors accept it as a welcome change from the small-scale, and occasionally small-minded, mentality of some of the other hotels on the island.

Spread out over a desirable tract of beach-fronting land, within a 5-minute drive from the island's airport, it's a carefully designed and very tasteful compound of two- and three-story ocher-colored villas, each richly accessorized and designed with sophisticated decorative accessories that look like something from a photo spread in *Florida Living*. Accommodations are generously sized and very comfortable. Each has bathtubs romantically positioned in theatrical prominence, separate shower stalls, and extremely comfortable furniture.

The centerpiece of the resort is a graceful and airy "Great House," which evokes both an impressive mansion on a South American hacienda and big-windowed, mahogany-trimmed Great House on a plantation in Jamaica. There's a beautiful spa within an outbuilding of this place, rich with an almost Zen spirit of healing and good health and an impressive-looking exercise room. The hotel's bar, cozily nestled within the "Great House" is the most elegant and high-style watering hole on Vieques, offering appropriate preludes for meals within the adjoining (separately recommended) restaurant.

Rte. 200, Km 3.4, Vieques, PR 00765. © 787/741-4100. Fax 787/741-4171. www.martineau.com. 156 units. Winter $407–$780 double, $1,207–$1,447 suite; off season $191–$354 double, $532–$647 suite. AE, DC, DISC, MC, V. **Amenities:** Restaurant; bar; pool bar; outdoor pool; 2 tennis courts; exercise facilities; spa; watersports equipment/ rentals; laundry service; sandy beachfront. *In room:* A/C, TV, dataport, unstocked fridge, hair dryer, iron, safe.

MODERATE
Hacienda Tamarindo *⭐*   Established in the late 1990s on the site of an expanded nightclub, less than a mile (1.6km) west of Esperanza, this inn has lots of flair, style, and pizazz. Vermont-born owners Burr and Linda Vail transformed a thick-walled, rather unimaginative-looking concrete building into a replica of a Spanish colonial hacienda, thanks to Linda's skills as a decorator. The inn was built around a massive

200-year-old tamarind tree, whose branches rise majestically through the hotel's atrium. Its production of fruit (Feb–Mar) is heralded with much excitement. Rooms are stylish, tiled, and spacious. Each contains an eclectic mishmash of art and dark-wood antiques, some of which were brought from Vermont. Bathrooms are modern, clean, and well designed; some contain a tub, others a shower. Although the inn is set about ⅛ mile (.2km) from the sea, there's access to a beach via a footpath, and there's a pool. The restaurant and cafe at the Inn on the Blue Horizon lie within a 5-minute walk.

Rte. 996, Km 4.5, Barrio Puerto Real (P.O. Box 1569), Vieques, PR 00765. ℂ 787/741-0420. Fax 787/741-3215. www.haciendatamarindo.com. 16 units (some with shower only, some with tub only). Winter $170–$200 double, $200–$275 suite; off season $135–$170 double, $170–$225 suite. Rates include breakfast. AE, MC, V. **Amenities:** Bar; pool; babysitting; laundry service; dry cleaning. *In room:* A/C, hair dryer, iron, no phone.

INEXPENSIVE

Bananas Guesthouse   On the island's south shore, on the main tourist strip of Esperanza and best known for its bar and restaurant (see "Where to Dine," below), this guesthouse has eight simple rooms. Each has a ceiling fan; and some rooms are air-conditioned and have screened-in porches. We urge you to consider one of the air-conditioned rooms rather than those without, as a means of cutting down on heat and noise from the outside. Each unit has a bathroom with a tub. The units are unadorned cubicles with little architectural interest; they provide shelter and calm and a basic level of comfort. The ambience is convivial, the staff friendly and accommodating.

Barrio Esperanza (P.O. Box 1300), Vieques, PR 00765. ℂ 787/741-8700. Fax 787/741-0790. www.bananas guesthouse.com. 8 units. Year-round $69–$90 double. AE, MC, V. **Amenities:** Restaurant/bar. *In room:* A/C (in 3 units), ceiling fans, no phone.

Casa de Amistad (House of Friendship)   Until it was radically renovated in 2002 by a likable former resident of Wisconsin and Minnesota, Owen Smith, this boxy-looking, two-story cement building functioned as a battered and run-down boarding-house that focused on cheap mattresses and cheap but bountiful meals for itinerant workers. Today, in far better-maintained premises, something of the same spirit still prevails, albeit in cleaner, more hip, and more convivial circumstances. Owen is a very hands-on manager, who, from the premises of a cottage in back, is always available for advice, counseling, or humor. There's the sense, on the building's ground floor, of something akin to a bohemian commune, thanks to the owner's friendly sense of informality, a tuck-away bar in one corner, a communal kitchen where residents are invited to prepare their own meals, a tiny "lending library" stocked with dog-eared paperback books, and a gift shop where some of Owen's artworks are on sale. Bed-rooms are angular, tawny-colored units that evoke a summer beach hotel in Province-town, Mass., or Fire Island, N.Y.: breezy and airy enclaves with simple but comfortable furniture and a sense of well-intentioned *laissez-faire*. Although any hotel on the island will genuinely welcome gay and lesbian clients, this is the guesthouse that does so most visibly, attracting a clientele that, at least in high season, is about 50% gay. The establishment's social center is within a cement-walled courtyard, around a very small, L-shaped swimming pool sheathed in cerulean-blue tiles.

Calle Benitez Castaño 27, Vieques, PR 00765. ℂ 787/741-3758. www.casadeamistad.com. 7 units. Winter $65–$80 double, $90 suite; off season $55–$65 double, $80 suite. MC, V. **Amenities:** Small outdoor pool; courtyard garden/sun terrace; rooftop sun deck; communal kitchen; TV room; small gift boutique. *In room:* A/C, fan, small unstocked fridge.

Crow's Nest   Set high on 5 acres (2 hectares) of forested hillside, about 1½ miles (2.4km) west/southwest of Isabel Segunda, this inn enjoys northward-facing views

A New Day for Vieques Wildlife Refuge

On May 1, 2003, the U.S. Navy transferred 15,500 acres (6,273 hectares)—often the best beachfront property—to the U.S. Fish & Wildlife Service, which added them to the **Vieques National Wildlife Refuge** 🐾🐾🐾. This is now the largest landmass of its kind in the Caribbean. Refuge lands lie on both the eastern and western ends of Vieques. In 2001, 3,100 acres (1,255 hectares) on the western end were already turned over to the refuge. These tracts of virgin landscape contain several ecologically distinct habitats, including the island's best white sandy beaches along with upland forests and mangrove wetlands, the latter the habitat of some endangered species such as the sea turtle, the manatee, and the brown pelican. Binocular-bearing bird-watchers also flock to the site. The coastal area of the refuge is characterized by coral reef and sea-grass beds. Within the refuge the best beaches are Red Beach and Blue Beach, both open to the public. The refuge is open to the public and also contains a Visitor Center at Vieques Office Park, Rd. 200, Km 0.4 (📞 787/741-2138). The refuge is open 7 days a week during daylight hours (naturally, closings are earlier in winter because of the shorter days).

---

over the Atlantic and a cozy, responsive setting that's favored by many repeat guests. Each of the units has some kind of cooking facilities. Rooms are more upscale-looking than those at either Bananas (which is very basic) or Trade Winds, but they're less elegant and charming than those at Inn on the Blue Horizon. Each unit has a neatly tiled, shower-only bathroom. Like most of the other hotels on the island, this one requires a car ride of around 10 minutes for access to the nearest worthwhile beach.

Rte. 201, Km 1.6, Barrio Florida, Box 1521, Vieques, PR 00765. 📞 787/741-0033. Fax 787/741-1294. www.crowsnestvieques.com. 16 units (shower only). Winter $114–$124 double, $225 suite; off season $90–$100 double, $195 suite. AE, MC, V. **Amenities:** Bar; pool; laundry service; dry cleaning. *In room:* A/C, kitchen, coffeemaker, iron, microwave.

The Great Escape 🐾 *(finds)*   This is the newest bed-and-breakfast on Vieques, and judging by the high-quality furniture, the large size, and the attentive maintenance of the place, one of the most appealing. It occupies a pair of blue-and-white concrete houses, set on the crest of a hill, in a rural neighborhood just north of Esperanza. Your hostess is Danuta Schwartzwald, a Polish émigré who selected Vieques as a place to live after years of self-imposed exile in Switzerland. You might feel just a wee bit isolated here, located as it is behind metal gates, at the end of a long, uphill, and rutted road from Route 201. But the size and solid, surprisingly upscale furnishings—including some mahogany, four-poster beds, tiled floors, upscale bathrooms, and the sense of calm that reigns over the place might eventually persuade you that, indeed, this is a desirable, although uneventful, place to stay. No meals are served other than breakfast, but the staff and managers of this place will offer advice about nearby venues.

Barrio La Llave, directly off Rte. 201, 2 miles (3.2km) northwest of Esperanza, Vieques, PR 14501. 📞 787/741-2927. www.enchanted-isle.com/greatescape. 11 units. Nov–May $125 double; June–Oct $115 double; $200 1-bedroom apts in any season (3-day minimum rental required for all apts). AE, DISC, MC, V. **Amenities:** Pool; bar. *In room:* Ceiling fan.

La Finca Caribe Guest House & Cottages   This bare-bones, eco-sensitive establishment caters to budget-conscious travelers and youthful adventurers. *Finca* means "rustic estate" in Spanish. The centerpiece of the property is a guesthouse with a

spacious porch, outfitted with hammocks and swinging chairs. An admirably maintained garden wraps itself around the scattered components of the compound. The rustic-looking outbuildings include a bathhouse, a communal kitchen, and two self-contained cottages suitable for up to three ("The Casita") or four ("The Cabana") occupants. Both cottages have private decks and kitchens. There's a nonchlorinated pool on the premises (it stays clean through frequent recirculation of water from a mountain stream) and a crew of entrepreneurs that takes clients on bike tours to obscure parts of Vieques (see "Beaches, Diving & Other Outdoor Pursuits," later in this chapter). La Finca is situated on a forested hillside 3 miles (5km) from Sun Bay.

Rte. 995, Km 1.2 (P.O. Box 1332), Vieques, PR 00765. (C) 787/741-0495. Fax 787/741-3584. www.lafinca.com. 6 units (none with bathroom), 2 cottages. Winter $80 double, $700–$1,000 1-week cottage rental for 2–4 occupants; off season $60 double, $525–$750 1-week cottage rental for 2–4 occupants. MC, V. Closed Sept. **Amenities:** Pool; communal kitchen. *In room:* Kitchen (in cottages).

Trade Winds Guesthouse   Along the shore on the south side of the island, in the fishing village of Esperanza, this oceanside guesthouse offers 11 units, four of which are air-conditioned and have terraces. The others have ceiling fans, and some open onto terraces. Bedrooms are white-walled and durable, with absolutely no imagination in terms of decor; the units (all nonsmoking) might remind you of a barracks. They're almost equivalent to the rooms at Bananas, a few buildings away, but they're just a bit better. Each unit has a small, tiled, shower-only bathroom. Because of their low rates, they're usually booked solid, often with divers from the United States or residents of the Puerto Rican mainland who want low rates. This place is well known for its hospitable ambience and its open-air restaurant overlooking the ocean (see "Where to Dine," below).

Calle Flamboyan 107, Barrio Esperanza (P.O. Box 1012), Vieques, PR 00765. (C) **787/741-8666.** Fax 787/741-2964. www.enchanted-isle.com/tradewinds. 11 units (shower only). Winter $70–$75 double; off season $60–$65 double. AE, MC, V. **Amenities:** Restaurant; bar; laundry service; dry cleaning. *In room:* A/C (in 4 units), fan (in some), no phone.

Vieques Ocean View Hotel   Situated in the heart of Isabel Segunda, directly on the coast and a block from the wharf where the ferry lands, this three-story building is one of the tallest on Vieques. Built in the early 1980s, it offers simple rooms with uncomplicated furniture and balconies overlooking either the sea or the town. Most of the rooms are air-conditioned, and each has a small shower-only bathroom. The hotel restaurant serves Chinese and Creole food daily from 11am to 11pm.

Calle Plinio Peterson 57, Isabel Segunda (P.O. Box 124), Vieques, PR 00765. (C) **787/741-3696.** Fax 787/741-1793. 35 units (shower only). Year-round $70–$81 double. AE, MC, V. **Amenities:** Restaurant; bar; pool. *In room:* A/C, TV, no phone.

WHERE TO DINE
EXPENSIVE

Café Media Luna ✮ *Finds* ASIAN/CARIBBEAN/INTERNATIONAL   This laid-back joint grew out of a dumpy building in Isabel Segunda. Today a charming little eatery, it is the domain of Ricardo Betancourt, a photographer turned restaurateur, and his wife, Monica, born in Bombay. Ricardo spent some 15 years in New York, photographing jazz musicians (sometimes for their record covers). Thanks to all the contacts he made, he invites many musicians to Vieques for jazz evenings. If there are two of you, ask to sit on a tiny balcony overlooking the streets. You are likely to catch the action on Saturday evenings. The kitchen turns out a terrific medley of Asian fusion and international dishes. It's good and healthy. The appetizers are freshly made concoctions, based on the best shopping on any given day. We like to arrive here with a party, order several appetizers, and share the goodies. The fresh fish and well-flavored meats round out the main dishes. Ask what is good on any given day; the staff gives good advice. Depending on road conditions, allow 15 to 20 minutes when driving from Esperanza.

Calle Antonio G. Mellado 351, Isabel Segunda. ✆ 787/741-2594. Reservations required. Main courses $24–$27; tasting menu $60–$70. AE, MC, V. May–Aug Thurs–Sun 7–10pm; Oct–Apr Wed–Sun 7–10pm. Closed Sept.

Carambola ✿✿ INTERNATIONAL   In the premises of the Inn on the Blue Horizon (see "Where to Stay," above), this restaurant serves the best food on Vieques. Also on-site is a bar that a team of journalists declared as one of their favorites in the world, so consider starting your evening with a drink or two in the octagonal Blue Moon Bar. Meals are served within the inn's main building or beneath an awning on a seafront terrace lined with plants. It seems an unlikely choice on a Caribbean island, but the chefs make the best New England clam chowder on island. They also deliver the goods with such enticing dishes as lobster ravioli with a spicy sweet-potato cream sauce and even Greek spring rolls known as *Spanakopita*. The menu strikes a good balance between such classics as sautéed soft shell crabs with butter sauce or sautéed frogs' legs with garlic butter and more innovative dishes such as a crispy half duck with a ginger-flavored plum sauce. Expect a crowd of fashion-industry folk, temporarily absent from New York and Los Angeles, and local residents, all mixing in ways that are gregarious, stylish, and usually a lot of fun.

In the Inn on the Blue Horizon, Rte. 996, Km 4.3. ✆ 787/741-3318. Reservations required. Main courses $10–$20. AE, MC, V. 1 mile (1.6km) west of Esperanza. Wed–Sun 6–10pm. Closed Sept–Oct.

Island Steak House INTERNATIONAL   Set in the cool and breezy highlands of Vieques, on a verdant hillside with sweeping views of the island's interior, this restaurant is perched within a gracefully proportioned open-sided building that gives the impression of something midway between a simplified gazebo and a treehouse. It's prefaced with a bar, where the once-a-week happy hour (Tues evenings 5–7pm) is an island-wide event, thanks partly to an ongoing roster of free hors-d'oeuvres. Menu items include up to four different kinds of steak; lamb chops; chicken breasts stuffed with goat cheese and cherry tomatoes; jumbo fried shrimp; and Vieques lobster basted with a sauce made from spiced rum and butter. Burgers are also an option.

In the Crow's Nest hotel. Rte 201, Km 1.6, Barrio Florida. ✆ 787/741-0033. Reservations recommended. Burgers $8–$9; main courses $17–$39. AE, MC, V. Daily 6–10pm. Bar stays open nightly till midnight.

Paso Fino INTERNATIONAL   This is one of the most romantic, and—thanks to thousands of dollars poured into its development by the Wyndham chain—most sophisticated restaurants on Vieques. Set beneath the soaring ceiling of the hotel's baronial centerpiece, with tables that spill out onto an ocean-fronting terrace, the restaurant is charming, slick, and stylish, with attentive and sometimes endearing service. Meals might begin with a cocktail at the mahogany-trimmed bar area, then proceed to settings that are either air-conditioned (in the dining room), or breeze-ventilated (on the terrace) venues. Come here for menu items that might include blackened sea bass with well-seasoned root vegetables, filet mignon in a brandy-flavored cream sauce, shrimp in a spicy barbecue sauce, a succulent version of cream of conch soup, and rich desserts that might include a traditional form of white cake known as *tres leches*.

In the Martineau Bay Resort & Spa, Rte. 200, Km 3.4. ✆ 787/741-4100. Reservations recommended, especially on weekends. Main courses $17–$38. AE, DC, DISC, MC, V. Daily 6–10:30pm.

Uva & the Next Door Tapas Bar ⓖ PUERTO RICAN/ASIAN FUSION
Opened in 2004, this restaurant is trendy and stylish, with a decor that's as urban, hip, and avant-garde as any other restaurant in Vieques. It lies beside a busy street in Isabel Segunda, with separate dining rooms for both its more upscale venue (Uva) and its less expensive venue (the Next Door Tapas Bar). Both areas funnel into a central courtyard with a prominent bohío-style bar and—you guessed it—a fruit-bearing *quenepo* tree whose roots were carefully preserved during the large-scale construction that once surrounded it. Within both venues, you can expect well-prepared grilled meats and fresh fish, though Next Door focuses a bit more on churrasco-style grills, burgers, barbecues, quesadillas, and steaks; Uva's menu offers the cutting-edge, high-style cuisine you might find in an upscale restaurant in San Juan. The best examples, depending on the season, include eggplant stuffed with white beans and chunks of lobster; seviche with ginger, rice, and *jicama* (a local root vegetable) slaw; beef sweetbreads served "lo mein" style with curry sauce; and a salad of smoked venison served with cherry tomatoes and feta cheese. You'll also find seafood with squid-ink pasta; codfish filet served over rice and chickpeas with coconut milk; and lightly glazed and seared sushi-quality tuna with asparagus risotto, prosciutto, and manchego cheese.

Calle Antonio G. Mellado (aka Rte. 200), in Isabel Segunda. ⓒ 787/741-2050. Reservations recommended for Uva. Main courses in Uva, $18–$50. Tapas $8–$13. AE, MC, V. Daily 5pm–midnight.

INEXPENSIVE
Bananas Restaurant INTERNATIONAL   This is an informal and unpretentious restaurant that falls midway between a burger and salad joint and a steakhouse, depending on the kind of food you select. Associated with a simple, also-recommended guesthouse, it's positioned on a narrow veranda, astride the sleepy, seafront boulevard of Esperanza's main drag, behind a screen of verdant plants. There's a definite link here with the Old Town of Key West, Florida, thanks to the establishment's recent acquisition by Glenn Curry (descendant of a family that was prominent there in the late 19th c.) and his Philadelphia-born wife, Wynne. Together, they run a down-to-earth, but not particularly whimsical, establishment with a busy bar trade. Expect a menu that includes Caesar salads, served with or without a garnish of grilled or jerk-marinated chicken; grilled pork chops; grilled fish; steaks; baby back ribs; pizzas; and sandwiches that include BLTs, burgers, and chicken-breast sandwiches. Expect slow service.

Calle Flamboyan (El Malecón), in Esperanza. ⓒ 787/741-8700. Reservations not necessary. Salads and sandwiches $5–$11; main courses $15–$17. MC, V. Daily 11am–10pm.

bbh ⓖⓖ CARIBBEAN/INTERNATIONAL   This is Vieques at its most idyllic. A flawless reception and service are backed up by the island's most imaginative cuisine, which shows the range of Executive Chef Christopher Ellis. The restaurant also offers the largest wine selection on island, the bottles stacked in a walk-in wine-tasting cooler. Tapas by the sea are a special feature of the menu. Our party dug into the Jamaican jerk chicken lettuce wraps with mango, tomato, and herbed sour cream or the seared ahi tuna with a soba noodle salad. Also memorable were those grilled portobello mushrooms with blue cheese and a side of creamy polenta. Roasted beef tenderloin came with a garlic root mash, and other specials included a grilled pork medallion with pineapple relish.

In the Bravo Beach Hotel. North Shore Rd. 1. ⓒ 787/741-1128. Reservations recommended at dinner. Main courses $8–$14. AE, DC, MC, V. Thurs–Sun 11am–3pm and 6–11pm.

Café Mammasonga *Finds* AMERICAN/INTERNATIONAL   Its loyal fans appreciate this luncheonette as a counterculture icon that has defiantly resisted culinary fashion ever since it was established near the piers of Isabel Segunda in the early 1990s. Set across the lane from the also-recommended Al's Mar Azul, it occupies a cement-sided shack that's dominated by the steamy, open-to-view kitchen of German-born Ute Hanna, who was given the affectionate nickname of "Mammasonga" by local fisherman early during her long-term sojourn in Vieques. Today, she's one of the most likable and appealing culinary matriarchs of Vieques, chugging out endless platters of breakfast food (omelets, pancakes, and more); and vast numbers of burgers, nachos, quesadillas, BLT and grilled chicken sandwiches, and steaming bowls of black-bean soup. All of this occurs within a cheerful and completely unpretentious dining room whose windows are always wide open to the energies and social undercurrents of the surrounding neighborhood. Ute, who for many years managed an arts-oriented cabaret (The Blue Angel) in New York City, is assisted in the dining room by her worldly and bemused husband, Irish-born Michael Ellison, a former journalist with London's *The Guardian*. If you're really hungry, ask for a "Mammasonga Sandwich," a gargantuan hero that's piled high with four kinds of sandwich meat, melted cheeses, pickles, lettuce, tomatoes, and whatever condiments you might be able to conceive of. The only thing wrong with this place is that it's never open after 5pm, much to the regret of its ardent fans.

On the Waterfront, adjacent to the piers, in Isabel Segunda. ✆ 787/741-0103. Reservations not needed. Breakfast platters $3.50–$5.50; lunch platters $4.95–$8.95. No credit cards. Wed–Mon 7am–5pm.

Chez Shack INTERNATIONAL   Chez Shack wins, almost without competition, as the most bohemian and countercultural restaurant on Vieques. The setting is exactly what the name implies—a battered wood-sided utility building that evolved from a virtual ruin after it was acquired by a grizzled and outspoken entrepreneur, Hugh Duffy, who was instrumental in the career of the Mamas and the Papas. This group, when still getting its act together, worked at Duffy's Love Shack in St. Thomas, where Mama Cass was said to have been the world's worst waitress. Today, replete with naughty anecdotes that are among the most valuable currency-in-trade on the island, the site is defined as a local monument. Chez Shack opens for business on summer nights even when other restaurants are closed. Menu items include tried-and-true favorites, many of which attract repeat diners who memorized the menu long ago. Examples include baked crab, seafood cocktail, steaks, fish filets, and barbecued ribs. You'll find the place near the edge of the highway, within the closest thing on Vieques to a tropical rainforest. On Monday nights they have a live steel band playing reggae music.

Hwy. 995 (Airport Rd.), north of Esperanza. ✆ 787/741-2175. Reservations recommended. Main courses $24–$34. MC, V. Wed–Sat and Mon 6–10pm; Sun 6:30–10pm. Closed Sept–Oct.

El Patio PUERTO RICAN   This is a simple, uncomplicated, and completely unpretentious Hispanic luncheonette that manages to feed impressive numbers of local residents every day at breakfast and lunch, often with lots of banter about island personalities and politics. It lies beside the western terminus of the road (Rte. 200) that leads eastward from the rest of Vieques into the island's biggest settlement, Isabel Segunda. Expect a cramped and somewhat dusty street-side patio and a Formica-sheathed interior that includes a TV set that drones on throughout the morning and afternoon. But as a breakfast or lunch stopover that's cheap, filling, friendly, and intensely local, we recommend it highly. Gui Sanchez (who was born in Vieques) and Noemi (his wife, who originally came from the Puerto Rico "mainland"), plus extended members of their family, are your hosts. Breakfasts focus on a predictable array of eggs and bacon. Lunches and (early) suppers might include marinated octopus or seafood salads or shrimp, served either buttered, battered, or fried with garlic. There's also *asopao de mariscos* (shellfish stew, with rice); steaks, meat patties served "Parmesan" style with tomato sauce and cheese; and when it's available, cold lobster with mayonnaise.

Calle Antonio G. Mellado 340 (aka Rte. 200, in Isabel Segunda). ℂ 787/741-6381. Reservations not accepted. Breakfast platters $1.50–$6; main courses $6–$20. MC, V. Mon–Fri 6:30am–6pm. Closed Sat–Sun.

Taverna Española SPANISH/PUERTO RICAN   This is the restaurant that every local resident talks about in almost reverential terms. Part of that has to do with the quirky eccentricities of the steely-willed matriarch who owns it, and part of it has to do with the sense of bounty and good flavors that emerge in an endless procession of steaming platters from the cramped kitchens. Don't expect anything fancy. There's something that hints at this boxy-looking place's decidedly unglamorous origins as a warehouse, despite a recent cosmetic overlay. Staff members can become hysterical under pressure, and food is sometimes slung rather than served. But despite that, the place remains a popular staple on the dining scene of Isabel Segunda, thanks to dishes that include breaded shrimp; *pastellitos* (stuffed dumplings) with chicken or beef; *chorizos* (spicy Spanish sausages); fried fish in *mojo* (Creole) sauce; and shellfish stew (*asopao de mariscos*).

Calle Carlos Libron. ℂ 787/741-1175. Reservations recommended on weekends. Main courses $12–$15. AE, MC, V. Daily 5–11pm.

Trade Winds Restaurant STEAK/SEAFOOD   This restaurant is often recommended by hotel owners across the island and therefore manages to feed the residents of a large cross section of island hotels. It lies beside the oceanfront esplanade in the fishing village of Esperanza. A dining experience here often begins with a drink at the open-air Topside Bar. For dinner, the chef's specialties revolve around steak, fish, and lobster, which is often served with butter-flavored rum sauce. The best steak is an 8-ounce filet, cooked just right over the charbroiler and served with a baked potato and a house or Caesar salad; also available is herb-marinated pork loin with mashed potatoes. The fresh fish special varies and is usually a good item to order, as is the jumbo shrimp sautéed with garlic and lemon, or served with curry sauce. Black-bean soup is a good opener.

In Trade Winds Guesthouse, Calle Flamboyan, Barrio Esperanza. ℂ 787/741-8666. Reservations recommended. Main courses $13–$28. AE, MC, V. Dec–May daily 8am–2pm and 6–9:30pm; June–Nov Fri–Sun 6–9:30pm.

SHOPPING

There aren't a lot of shopping possibilities in Vieques; however, you might want to visit **Siddhia Hutchinson Fine Art Studio & Gallery,** Calle 3, A15, Isabel Segunda (ℂ 787/741-8780), located between the lighthouse and the ferry dock. Here you can purchase prints of local seascapes and landscapes, native flowers, fish, and birds. There are also lovely bowls, mugs, and platters for sale.

VIEQUES AFTER DARK

Al's Mar Azul   This is the most successful Anglo-Hispanic bar on Vieques, with a reputation that extends from the waterfront of Isabel Segunda to San Juan, New York City, and some of the capitals of Europe. That's a remarkable achievement for a raffish-looking, cement-built, open-sided bungalow that's perched on a low cliff above the sea, a short uphill walk from the piers where the ferryboats land from the "mainland" (Fajardo). Within a mostly blue environment of fish nets, wide-open views of the harbor, ceiling fans, and nautical memorabilia, within sightlines of a pool table, you'll find a setting that might have been inspired by beachfront venues in either Florida or Southern California. There's a brisk demand for rum punches, frozen piña coladas, and a "Key Lime Pie" that's made from sour mix, milk, and vanilla liqueur. Each is priced at between $4.50 and $5. Open Sunday through Thursday 11am to 1am, and Friday and Saturday 11am to 2:30am. On the Waterfront, adjacent to the ferryboat piers, in Isabel Segunda. ⓒ 787/741-3400.

Bar Plaza   If you travel enough in the Spanish-speaking Caribbean, you'll occasionally stumble across the kind of old-fashioned bar that Hemingway used to celebrate. Macho, unpretentious, and nostalgic, with a history going back to the 1940s, and murals that advertise for products from now-defunct companies, it virtually drips with a sense of frozen time. High-ceilinged, shadowy, and cool, even on the hottest day, it might be a direct transplant from colonial Havana or Madrid during the Spanish Civil War. There's a pool table in the corner, an old-fashioned cement trough that functions as the men's urinal, and a staff and stoic regular patrons that indeed, show their age. No food of any kind is served—only drinks. Beer costs about $3.25. Open daily 9am to 9pm. Plaza del Recreo, in Isabel Segunda. ⓒ 787/741-2176.

2 Culebra ⓐ

52 miles (84km) E of San Juan, 18 miles (29km) E of Fajardo

A tranquil, inviting little island, Culebra lies in a mini-archipelago of 24 chunks of land, rocks, and cays, 18 miles (29km) east of Puerto Rico's main island and halfway to St. Thomas, U.S. Virgin Islands. It's just 7 miles (11km) long and 3 miles (5km) wide and has only 2,000 residents. The landscape is dotted with everything from scrub and cacti to poincianas, frangipanis, and coconut palms.

Today vacationers and boaters can explore the island's beauties, both on land and underwater. Culebra's white-sand beaches (especially Flamenco Beach), its clear waters, and its long coral reefs invite swimmers, snorkelers, and scuba divers.

Culebra, in what was once called the Spanish Virgin Islands, was settled as a Spanish colony in 1886, but like Puerto Rico and Vieques, it became part of the United States after the Spanish-American War in 1898. In fact, Culebra's only town, a fishing village called **Dewey,** was named for Admiral George Dewey, a U.S. hero of that war, although the locals defiantly call it **Puebla.**

Both illustrious and notorious characters visited Culebra in the past. It is believed that Columbus spotted the island on his second voyage to the New World in 1493. When the Spanish started colonizing Puerto Rico, many of the Taíno Indians fled to Culebra as a last refuge. It wasn't many decades later that the swashbuckling Sir Henry Morgan and other notorious pirates used Culebra as a hide-out. The island supposedly still shelters their buried loot.

From 1909 to 1975, the U.S. Navy used Culebra as a gunnery range and as a practice bomb site in World War II. Today the four tracts of the **Culebra Wildlife Refuge,** plus 23 other offshore islands, are managed by the U.S. Fish and Wildlife Service. The refuge is one of the most important turtle-nesting sites in the Caribbean, and it also houses large seabird colonies, notably terns and boobies.

Culebrita, a mile-long (1.6km) coral-isle satellite of Culebra, has a hilltop lighthouse and crescent beaches.

ESSENTIALS

GETTING THERE   Vieques Air-Link (℃ 787/741-8331) and **Air Flamenco** (℃ 787/724-1818; www.airflamenco.net) fly to Culebra several times a day from San Juan's Isla Grande Airport. One-way transit costs $28; round-trip is $54.

The **Puerto Rico Port Authority** operates one or two **ferries** per day (depending on the day of the week) from the mainland port of Fajardo to Culebra; the trip takes about an hour. The round-trip fare is $5 for adults, $2.25 for children 3 to 12 (free for 2 and under). For reservations, call ℃ 787/863-4560.

GETTING AROUND   With no public transportation, the only way to get to Culebra's beaches is by bike or rental car.

There are a number of little **car-rental** agencies on the island, although they seem to open and close when the spirit moves them. **Carlos Jeep Rental,** Parcela 2, Barriada Clark, Dewey (℃ 787/742-3514), lies a 3-minute ride from the airport. The outfitter rents Jeeps for $45 to $79 per day. If you give them notice, they will meet you at the airport. When you drop off your rental, the staff will also drive you back to the airport. Charging exactly the same prices is another reliable operator, **Coral Reef,** Carretera Pedro Marquez 3, Dewey (℃ 787/742-0055). A final option for vehicles is **Willie's Jeep Rental,** Calle Escudero, Barriada Clark, Dewey (℃ 787/742-3537), lying a 5-minute walk from the airport. Vehicles here begin at $45 per day.

Bike riding is a popular means of getting around the island's hills, dirt trails, and bad roads. You can rent mountain bikes at **Dick and Cathy** (℃ 787/742-0062) for $15 for 24 hours. To rent from them, call them, and one of them will come by your hotel with your bike.

BEACHES, DIVING & OTHER OUTDOOR PURSUITS

The island's most popular and best beach is **Flamenco Beach** 🐾, a mile-long (1.6km) horseshoe-shaped cove on the northwestern edge. It's popular partly because of its nearness to Dewey, partly because of its soft sands. If you find Flamenco too crowded, all you need do is walk over the hill to **Playa Carlos Rosario** 🐾. The sands here aren't quite as good as those at Flamenco, but the snorkeling is even better in these clear waters. A barrier reef protects this beach, so you are almost guaranteed tranquil waters. Snorkelers can also walk south from Playa Carlos Rosario for ¼ mile (.4km) to a place called "The Wall" 🐾. There are 40-foot (12m) drop-offs into the water where you are likely to see schools of fish gliding by.

The isolated **Zoni Beach** is a 1-mile (1.6km) strip of sand flanked by large boulders and scrub. Located on the island's northeastern edge, about 7 miles (11km) from Dewey (Puebla), it's one of the most beautiful beaches on the island. Snorkelers, but not scuba divers, find it particularly intriguing, despite the surf that makes underwater visibility a bit murky during rough weather.

Known for its beautiful corals, unspoiled underwater vistas, and absence of other divers, Culebra is what the Caribbean used to be before crowds of divers began exploring the sea. At least 50 dive sites, all around the island, are worthwhile. **Culebra Divers,** Calle Escobar 138 (℃ 787/742-0803), offers a resort course for novice divers, including training in a sheltered cove and a tank dive in 15 to 20 feet (4.5–6m) of water ($90). Full PADI certification costs $550 and requires 4 days of participation in both classroom and ocean experience. Certified divers pay $85 for a two-tank open-water dive. The outfitter provides all the equipment you need for any of the dive experiences. It's rare that more than six divers go out in one of these boats on any day.

Kayak trips are offered by **Jim Petersen's Oceans Safaris,** Calle Escudero 189, Dewey (© **787/379-1973**). Kayaks can be rented for $30 per half-day, and Jim will tell you the best spots to enjoy this sport. He also offers a full-day tour for $75, taking you to such remote islets as Isla Culebrita or Cayo Luis Peña.

WHERE TO STAY

If you operate happily within a rented villa, preparing your own meals, consider making a call to **Culebra Island Realty** (© **787/742-0052;** www.culebraislandrealty.com). Jim Galasso, the rental agent, knows what's happening with most of the island's rental villas and can probably come up with something that's appropriate for your needs.

MODERATE

Club Seabourne   About an 8-minute drive from the center of town, this concrete-and-wood structure is set in a garden of crotons and palms, at the mouth of one of the island's best harbors, Ensenada Bay. It offers scattered villas and four rooms inside the clubhouse. Each unit has a small, tiled, shower-only bathroom.

Overlooking Fulladosa Bay, the club's dining room serves some of the best food on Culebra, with fresh lobster, shrimp, snapper, grouper, and conch, as well as steaks. The hotel also has a patio bar with a nightly happy hour, plus one of two pools on the island. Dive packages and day sails can be arranged at the office.

Fulladosa Rd. (P.O. Box 357), Culebra, PR 00775. © **787/742-3169.** Fax 787/742-0210. www.clubseabourne.com. 12 units (shower only). Winter $199 double, $245 villa; off season $175 double, $255 villa. Rates include continental breakfast. AE, MC, V. From Dewey (Puebla), follow Fulladosa Rd. along the south side of the bay for 1½ miles (2.4km). **Amenities:** Restaurant; bar; pool; 1 room for those w/limited mobility. *In room:* A/C, fridge, safe, no phone.

Tamarindo Estates ★ *(Finds*   On 60 lush acres (24 hectares) beside a private bay, this is a small, intimate Puerto Rican beachfront resort of kitchen-equipped cottages. Living here is like occupying your second home, with laid-back island living. There is a simple, even pristine, aura here, but comfort nonetheless with panoramic views from the roofed verandas. Each unit has either one or two bedrooms, and when *Travel + Leisure* staffers visited, they named this property one of the 20 great and affordable gateways in the Caribbean. The mecca of this nicely secluded place is a swimming pool with an ocean view and a roofed deck. There is easy access to shoreline snorkeling in gin-clear waters. The resort lies a 10-minute drive from town, and all cottages are screened and have ceiling fans. Each cottage has a shower-only bathroom. Housekeeping is not provided.

Tamarindo Beach Rd., Culebra, PR 00775. © **787/742-3343.** Fax 787/742-3342. www.tamarindoestates.com. 12 cottages (shower only). Winter $190 double, $335 quad; off season $140 double, $240 quad. AE, MC, V. **Amenities:** Pool; beach house. *In room:* A/C, TV, kitchen, coffeemaker.

INEXPENSIVE

Casa Ensenada Waterfront Guesthouse   This is a laid-back, tropical-looking house with relatively humble but clean and comfortable bedrooms. Many guests begin their day by taking a kayak over to the Dinghy Dock restaurant (see "Where to Dine," below) for breakfast and later return to sunbathe on the patio. In the evening, guests gather again on the patio for drinks and for barbecue—the catch of the day on the grill. Each unit is midsize and has a tiled, shower-only bathroom. All are nonsmoking. You can rent the Pequeño unit, which sleeps two in a double bed, or the Grande unit for four (two in a king-size bed in the master bedroom and two on a double futon in the living room). The on-site Estudio unit sleeps four, in twin beds and a double futon.

Calle Escudero 142, Dewey, Culebra, PR 00775. © **866/210-0704** or 787/742-3559. Fax 787/742-0278. www. casaensenada.com. 3 units (shower only). Winter $115–$170; off season $75–$140. MC, V. **Amenities:** Kayaking; scuba diving; snorkeling; bikes; laundry service; library. *In room:* A/C, kitchenette, coffeemaker.

Posada la Hamaca *Value* This was one of Culebra's original guesthouses, lying in town next to the Dewey Bridge. Although much competition has opened to challenge it, this place is still going strong. The rooms are housed in a modest island home. Although simply furnished, each of the accommodations is well maintained and tidily kept, each with a private bathroom with shower. Beach towels, coolers, and free ice are provided for beach outings. You'll also find an exterior shower to wash sand off your body before you enter. Room no. 8 is the coziest nest and is often rented by honeymooners. Some units are large enough to accommodate four guests, making them suitable for families. One apartment is spacious enough to accommodate eight to 12 guests.

Calle Castalar 68, Culebra, PR 00775. © **787/742-3516**. www.posada.com. 10 units. Year-round $85 double; $99 studio; $139–$179 apt. MC, V. **Amenities:** Laundry service. *In room:* A/C, TV, kitchenette (in some), beverage maker (in some).

Villa Boheme This modest guesthouse opens onto views of Ensenada Bay, and its hosts invite you to explore their little island in kayaks or bikes. Out back is a great terrace with hammocks that invite you to lead the life of leisure. The best units are a trio of large efficiencies; they are better equipped than the other units here. Each of another three rooms has a small kitchen with a large refrigerator. Occupants of the rest of the rooms share a fully equipped modern kitchen that is located in the patio area. Beds range from queen-size to twins to king-size. Room nos. 2 and 12 can house up to six guests comfortably.

Calle Fulladosa 368, Dewey, Culebra, PR 00775. ©/fax **787/742-3508**. www.villaboheme.com. 11 units. Year-round $95–$136 double. $16 per extra person. AE, MC, V. **Amenities:** Communal kitchen; water taxi. *In room:* A/C, kitchen (in some), fridge (in some), no phone.

WHERE TO DINE
MODERATE

Dinghy Dock AMERICAN/CARIBBEAN/PUERTO RICAN For the best preview of laid-back tropical Culebra, head here. The hangout lies on the banks of Ensenada Honda, just south of the Dewey drawbridge, and it has a dock where dinghies and other boats anchor. Come here for the bar or the restaurant—or perhaps both—and meet the locals along with visiting boaters from the Puerto Rican mainland. We like to come here to enjoy margaritas or Puerto Rico's own Medalla beer and watch the sunsets. You can visit three times a day if you wish: tropical fruit-flavored waffles for breakfast, freshly grilled tuna for lunch, and a lobster and rice dish for dinner.

Punta del Soldado Rd., outside Dewey. © **787/742-0233**. Reservations not necessary. Breakfast $3–$8; main courses $5–$13 lunch, $13–$29 dinner. AE, MC, V. Daily 7:30–11am, noon–2pm, and 6:30–9:30pm.

INEXPENSIVE

El Batey DELI Across from the harbor and cooled by its breezes, this large, clean establishment maintains a full bar and prepares an array of deli-style sandwiches. They'll hand you a cold beer when the afternoon sun is out, and the pool tables make the place lively, especially on weekends, when many locals come here. Disco reigns on Friday and Saturday night. Weekdays, it's much calmer.

Parque de Pelota 250, Carretera. © **787/742-3828**. Sandwiches $3–$5. No credit cards. Wed–Sun noon–midnight (till 2am Fri–Sat).

El Caobo PUERTO RICAN   Locals call this place Tina's and view it as one of their favorite food joints on the island. We were told that Tina cooks for the local taste, which means "lot of chickens or roasted garlic, pork, and plenty of rice and beans." Try her grilled chicken or grilled pork cutlet. Tina will also fry these cuts of meat. If the catch came in, she might even grill you some fresh fish.

Calle Luís Muñoz Marín, La Carriada Clark. © **787/742-0505**. Reservations not necessary. Main courses $7.75–$15. No credit cards. Mon–Sat 9am–10:30pm; Sun 8:30am–4:30pm.

Mamacita's ✦ PUERTO RICAN   It is highly likely that this pink- and purple-tinged bar and restaurant, located by the bay in the town of Dewey, will become your favorite hangout during your stay on Culebra. You can even room here, but it's noisy at night, especially on Saturday when the conga drummers rattle the joint. The island food is good and affordable, enough so to attract expats, locals, and visitors.

Lunch fare is simple, mostly rice and beans type fare, but at night the menu improves considerably, especially if you opt for the locally caught and perfectly grilled seafood. The steaks are imported but satisfy a hearty appetite. The house drink special is an Iguana Colada; you might want to just drink it before you ask what's in it.

If you're a night owl and don't want to stray far from the party, you can rent one of the simply furnished bedrooms, 10 in all, each with a private bathroom with shower. Rooms are colorfully decorated, and older units have murals. Two are suites with kitchenettes, but our favorite is the Crow's Nest on the top floor, opening onto a panoramic view. Rates are $95 double, or $105 to $135 suite.

Calle Castelar 64–66, Dewey. © **787/742-0090**. Reservations not required. Lunch main dishes $6.50–$8.50. Dinner main dishes $12–$22. MC, V. Daily 8am–2:30pm and 6–9pm. Bar Mon–Thurs and Sun 8am–10pm; Fri–Sat 8am–11pm.

Heather's Pizzeria PIZZA   This is the best place to go for pizza on the island. With its funky decor, it is a popular hangout for local expatriates. In addition to those piping-hot pies, the kitchen also turns out an array of freshly made salads, pastas, and well-stuffed sandwiches. The food here is quite good.

Calle Marques 14, Dewey. © **787/742-3175**. Reservations not necessary. Pizzas, sandwiches, and platters $9–$22. No credit cards. Wed–Sun 6–11pm. Closed first 2 weeks of Oct.

Appendix:
Puerto Rico in Depth

"It's heaven and hell—all rolled into one tiny island," a Trenton, N.J., woman said to us about Puerto Rico on a flight from San Juan to Miami. "My husband loved it. I couldn't wait to get back home. But then he's a golfer and a fisherman, and while he was doing that, there were only so many crafts I could buy."

Ever since Castro in the early 1960s started chasing the gringos out of Havana, Puerto Rico has blossomed as a tourist destination, with its towering mountains, rainforests, long beaches, and vibrant Spanish culture.

The woman we talked to saw only the island's crime, unemployment, bad traffic, and what to her was "poor food." But in spite of its many critics, Puerto Rico must be doing something right. Of course, you can get bad food here, but in many places the island's cuisine, an adaptation of many cooking styles, is the finest in the Caribbean.

History buffs will get more ancient buildings and monuments here than anywhere else in the Caribbean, many of them dating back some 500 years, to the Spanish conquistadors. Add some of the best golf and tennis in the West Indies, posh beach resorts, tranquil and offbeat (though not luxurious) government *paradores* (country inns or guesthouses), and lots of Las Vegas–type gambling, glitter, and extravagant shows, and you've got a formidable attraction.

There are problems here. As in many major cities, you could be mugged or have your car stolen or even hijacked. Service personnel are often gruff and unhelpful. Although there are country retreats where you can escape the masses, San Juan and most of the rest of the island are simply overcrowded.

There is also some anti–United States sentiment here. Not all locals passionately embrace Uncle Sam. When we were seeking some real lowdown salsa joints away from the tourist hordes, a taxi driver told us, "I can take you to a club—maybe several clubs—but I'm not sure you'd get back in one piece."

Despite its drawbacks, we still rate Puerto Rico as one of the top Caribbean destinations, right up there with Aruba, St. Thomas, Jamaica, and Barbados.

1 The Natural Environment: Beaches, Mountains, the Rainforest, Off-Island Islands & More

Roughly half the size of New Jersey, this U.S. commonwealth with 272 miles (438km) of Atlantic and Caribbean coastline sits strategically some 1,000 miles (1,610km) southeast of Florida at the hub of the Caribbean chain of islands. You'll probably fly in and out of San Juan at least once if you're doing much touring in the region. And with a 2-year, $2.8-million project that restored its waterfront, this oldest capital city under the U.S. flag is also the world's second-largest home port for cruise-ship passengers.

Puerto Rico has experienced many political changes since the days of its first Spanish governor, Juan Ponce de León, the conquistador who sailed with Columbus and who tried in vain to find a fountain of youth in Florida. With nearly 500 years reflected in its restored Spanish colonial architecture, Old San Juan is the Caribbean's greatest historic center.

Puerto Rico is the most easterly and the smallest of the four major islands that form the Greater Antilles. The other three are Cuba, Jamaica, and Hispaniola (which is home to two nations, Haiti and the Dominican Republic). Surrounded by the Atlantic Ocean to the north and the Caribbean Sea to the south, Puerto Rico is flanked by a trio of smaller islands—Vieques and Culebra to the east and Mona to the west—which are its political and geologic satellites.

The island's terrain ranges from palm-lined beaches on four coastlines to rugged mountain ranges, gently rolling hills, and dry desert-like areas. There are 20 designated forest reserves in Puerto Rico.

BEACHES

The island has dozens of miles of sandy beaches, some long and straight, others broken into coves by headlands. On the northern coast, the Atlantic waters are often more turbulent than those along the more tranquil southern coast. (For a more detailed discussion of Puerto Rican beaches, see "Beaches" under "The Active Vacation Planner" in chapter 2. For even more strips of sand, refer to the previews of beaches given in the individual chapters of this book.)

TOWERING MOUNTAINS

Besides the beaches, the island's most noteworthy geological feature is the **Cordillera**—the towering mountains that rise high above its central region. Geologists have identified the island's summits as the high parts of a chain of mountains whose mass is mostly submerged beneath the sea. These mountains are some of the oldest of the many landmasses in the West Indies.

What makes the mountain altitudes even more impressive is the existence, about 75 miles (121km) to the island's north, of one of the deepest depressions

in the Atlantic, the Puerto Rico Trough. Running more or less parallel to the island's northern shoreline, it plunges to depths of up to 30,000 feet (9,000m). Although not as obvious as this trench, the sea floor a few miles from the island's southern coast also drops off, to nearly 17,000 feet (5,100m) below sea level. Geologists have calculated that if the base of this mountain chain were at sea level, it would be one of the highest landmasses in the world. Puerto Rico's highest summit—Cerro de Punta, at 4,389 feet (1,317m)—would exceed in altitude Mount Everest, the world's tallest peak.

Most of Puerto Rico's geology, especially its mountain peaks, resulted from volcanic activity that deposited lava and igneous rock in consecutive layers. To a lesser degree, the island is also composed of quartz, diomites, and, along some of its edges, coral limestone.

EL YUNQUE & THE OTHER FOREST PRESERVES

The mountains are home to the island's greatest natural attraction, **El Yunque** (© **787/888-1810** or 787/888-5646 for information), a 45-minute drive east of San Juan. Given national-park status by President Theodore Roosevelt, this 28,000-acre (11,200-hectare) preserve is the only tropical rainforest on U.S. soil and is protected by the U.S. Forest Service.

Today, El Yunque offers visitors close encounters of the natural kind, from picnics amid rare flora and fauna to hikes along scenic trails. Encompassing four distinct forest types, it is home to 240 species of tropical trees; flowers, including more than 20 kinds of orchids; and other wildlife, including millions of tiny tree frogs whose distinctive cry of *coquí* (pronounced "ko-*kee*") has given them their name. For details on touring this unique attraction, see chapter 8.

Puerto Rico also has 19 other forest preserves. Directly east of San Juan lies

Piñones Forest, which contains the island's largest mangrove forest. West of Ponce, **Guánica Forest** borders several white-sand beaches and the historic bay where U.S. troops first landed in 1898 during the Spanish-American War. **Cambalache Forest,** east of Arecibo, contains plantations of eucalyptus, teak, and mahoe trees. The driest vegetation and expansive views to the west coast are found in **Maricao Forest.** Few visitors will have time for a forest preserve other than El Yunque. If you do, make it **Toro Negro Forest Reserve,** which straddles the peaks of the Cordillera in the center of the island and boasts the island's tallest peak, with stunning drops to the Caribbean and the Atlantic. For more details on exploring Toro Negro, see the "Ponce" section of chapter 9. All of these forests are open to visitors, and several have picnic areas and campsites.

THE KARST COUNTRY & RIO CAMUY CAVES

One of the most mysterious areas of Puerto Rico is the **Karst Country.** One of the world's strangest rock formations, *karst* is formed by the process of water sinking into limestone. As time goes by, large basins are eroded, forming sinkholes. *Mogotes,* or karstic hillocks, are peaks of earth where the land didn't sink into the erosion pits. The Karst Country lies along the island's north coast, northeast of Mayagüez, in the foothills between Quebradillas and Manatí. The region is filled with an extensive network of caves. One sinkhole contains the 20-acre (8-hectare) dish of the world's largest radio/radar telescope at the Arecibo Observatory.

Reached by Route 446, the **Guajataca Forest Reserve** is found here, offering some 25 miles (40km) of trails that take you through some of the most rugged parts of this country.

Eons ago, one of the world's largest underground rivers carved the **Río Camuy**

Caves in northwest Puerto Rico, which experts today consider to be among the most spectacular caves on earth. The Río Camuy Caves contain evidence of occupation long before the island was sighted by Columbus in 1493. The first professional explorers of the system were led to the site by local boys already familiar with some of the entrances.

For a journey through this foreboding landscape, see chapter 8.

OFF-ISLAND ISLANDS

Three offshore islands—Mona, Vieques, and Culebra—are well worth exploring.

Despite bad publicity generated by U.S. Naval bombing exercises, **Vieques** is the most developed of the offshore islands from a tourist prospective. Shaped like a long fish, its spine is a mountain range that separates it lengthwise from west to east. At 21 miles (34km) in length and 5 miles (8km) in width, Vieques is the largest landmass of the Spanish Virgin Islands.

Although the Spanish referred to both Vieques and Culebra as *las islas inútiles* (the useless islands) because there was no gold to be mined there, they are islands *bonito* for the visitor. Offering the lazy life, Vieques has top-notch inns and excellent and relatively undiscovered dining. Most visitors come here to escape and to enjoy the gorgeous beaches.

Even sleepier than Vieques is the smaller and less developed island of **Culebra.** It's a place where you have to drive carefully to let Mother Hen cross the road. At a distance of some 17 miles (27km) east of the Puerto Rican port of Fajardo, Culebra, from the geologist's point of view, is closer to the U.S. Virgin Islands than "mainland" Puerto Rico. St. Thomas lies only 12 miles (19km) to the east.

With its rugged peaks, sandy beaches, and offshore caves, Culebra can quickly bring out the beach bum in you. Many visitors, in fact, have settled there. As two *culebrenses* (the name of the islanders) confided to us, "If you come here with gringo uptightness, you'll lose it in a few days."

Much of Culebra is a national wildlife refuge—so much so that in summer many of the beaches are closed by the U.S. Fish and Wildlife Service because they are nesting grounds for endangered sea turtles.

For touring details on the Vieques and Culebra, see chapter 12.

A unique environment can be found on **Mona Island,** 50 miles (81km) west of Puerto Rico. Like the Galápagos Islands, this untouched island has species that are not found elsewhere. Mona is a protected island, under the management of the U.S. National Park Service and the Puerto Rican Natural Resources Department. Accessible by a sometimes difficult, long, boat ride, the island is available for sport diving to those who are willing to rough it. See chapter 9.

2 Puerto Rico Today

As the commonwealth moves more deeply into the new millennium, Puerto Rico continues to make headlines in mainland newspapers. Sometimes the news is good; at other times, troubling.

First the good. Puerto Rico's tourism figures have been rising annually since the beginning of the 21st century; the island's aggressive hotel and marketing promotion seems to be paying off. Travelers from the United States are the major visitors, and their numbers rose steadily throughout the early 2000s. Canadian tourism is also on the rise, and the greatest increase is in Latin American visitors.

The island's 3.88 million people—1 million of whom live in the San Juan metropolitan area—have forged ahead economically and made rapid strides. Their annual income is now the highest in Latin America, and their average life expectancy has risen to 73.8 years. And with the island's economy evolving from agriculture to manufacturing and tourism, a demand for an educated workforce has resulted in the ordinary worker having at least 12 years of schooling.

Tourism represents about 6% of the gross national product. Puerto Rico's present governor, and its first woman governor, Sila M. Calderón, has challenged both the private and public sectors of the tourism industry to double that

contribution to the GNP within the next decade. At once both labor-intensive and environmentally friendly, tourism is seen as the island's best alternative to continued heavy industrialization in pursuit of new jobs for its people.

Even in the now-prosperous tourism industry, storm clouds loom. The unspoken fear among developers of megaresorts is the possible impact of Cuba reopening to the American tourism market. Before Fidel Castro took over Cuba in 1959, Americans by the thousands flocked to Havana, and Puerto Rico was a mere dot on the tourist map. The island's growth was fueled enormously by the embargo imposed on Castro's communist government.

Now the bad: As part of legislation raising the U.S. minimum wage in 1996, President Bill Clinton vetoed a set of tax breaks for U.S. companies operating on the island. That ended 75 years of federal incentives that attracted stateside industries and helped make Puerto Rico the industrial powerhouse in the West Indies. For example, it produces about half the prescription drugs sold in the United States.

Even with the tax breaks, Puerto Rico struggles with a 12.5% unemployment rate and a per capita income of $8,509, about half the level of the poorest U.S. state, Mississippi.

Mirroring the U.S. mainland, rising crime, drugs, AIDS, unemployment, overpopulation, and more troubles plague Puerto Rico. The island has America's third-highest AIDS rate and the dubious distinction of being a major gateway into the United States for drugs from Latin America. The violence and social ills associated with drugs have beset the island. Although the drug issue is of epidemic proportions, you can visit Puerto Rico and be completely unaware that all this criminal activity is going on around you, especially if you're heading to one of the big, self-sufficient resorts. And efforts are being made to solve the drug problem. Since the mid-1990s, the government has increased the number of police officers, enacted harsher prison sentences for drug dealers, and conducted arms and drug raids—part of a battle to stop the flow of illegal drugs into the United States.

The New Progressive Party wants to make Puerto Rico the 51st state, but the opposition is strong, both on the island and in Congress. A nonbinding reference in 1998 resulted in a defeat of statehood.

3 History 101

IN THE BEGINNING

Although the Spanish occupation was the decisive factor defining Puerto Rico's current culture, the island was settled many thousands of years ago by Amerindians. The oldest archaeological remains yet discovered were unearthed in 1948. Found in a limestone cave a few miles east of San Juan, in Loíza Aldea, the artifacts consisted of conch shells, stone implements, and crude hatchets deposited by tribal peoples during the first century of the Christian Era. These people belonged to an archaic, seminomadic, cave-dwelling culture that had not developed either agriculture or pottery. Some ethnologists suggest that these early inhabitants originated in Florida, immigrated to Cuba, and from there began a steady migration along the West Indian archipelago.

Around A.D. 300, a different group of Amerindians, the Arawaks, migrated to Puerto Rico from the Orinoco Basin in what is now Venezuela. Known by ethnologists as the Saladoids, they were the first of Puerto Rico's inhabitants to make and use pottery, which they decorated with exotic geometric designs in red and white. Subsisting on fish, crabs, and whatever else they could catch, they populated the big island as well as the offshore island of Vieques.

By about A.D. 600, this culture had disappeared, bringing to an end the island's historical era of pottery making. Ethnologists' opinions differ as to whether the tribes were eradicated by new invasions from South America, succumbed to starvation or plague, or simply evolved into the next culture that dominated Puerto Rico—the Ostionoids.

Much less skilled at making pottery than their predecessors but more accomplished at polishing and grinding stones for jewelry and tools, the Ostionoids were the ethnic predecessors of the tribe that became the Taínos. The Taínos inhabited Puerto Rico when it was explored and invaded by the Spanish beginning in 1493. The Taínos were spread throughout the West Indies but reached their greatest development in Puerto Rico and neighboring Hispaniola (the island shared by Haiti and the Dominican Republic).

Taíno culture impressed the colonial Spanish, and it continues to impress modern sociologists. This people's achievements included construction of ceremonial ballparks whose boundaries

Ponce de León: Man of Myth & Legend

For an explorer of such myth and legend, Juan Ponce de León still remains an enigma to many historians, his exploits subject to as much myth as fact.

It is known that he was born around 1460 in San Tervas de Campos, a province of Valladolid in Spain, to a noble Castilian family. The red-haired youth grew into an active, aggressive, and perhaps impulsive young man, similar in some respects to Sir Francis Drake in England. After taking part in Spain's Moorish wars, Ponce de León sailed to America with Columbus on his second voyage, in 1493.

In the New World, Ponce de León served as a soldier in the Spanish settlement of Hispaniola, now the island home of Haiti and the Dominican Republic. From 1502 to 1504, he led Spanish forces against Indians in the eastern part of the island, finally defeating them.

In 1508 he explored Puerto Rico, discovering gold on the island and conquering the native tribes within a year. A year later, he was named governor of Puerto Rico and soon rose to become one of the most powerful Europeans in the Americas. From most accounts, Ponce de León was a good governor of Puerto Rico before his political rivals forced him from office in 1512.

At that time he received permission from King Ferdinand to colonize the island of Bimini in the Bahamas. In searching for Bimini, he came upon the northeast coast of Florida, which he at first thought was an island, in the spring of 1513. He named it La Florida because he discovered it at the time of Pascua Florida or "Flowery Easter." He was the first explorer to claim some of the North American mainland for Spain.

The following year he sailed back to Spain, carrying with him 5,000 gold pesos. King Ferdinand ordered him back to Puerto Rico with instructions to colonize both Bimini and Florida. Back in Puerto Rico, Ponce de León ordered the building of the city of San Juan. In 1521 he sailed to Florida with 200 men and supplies to start a colony. This was to be his downfall. Wounded by a poison arrow in his thigh, he was taken back to Cuba in June 1521 and died there from his wound.

Legend says Ponce de León searched in vain for the so-called Fountain of Youth, first in Bimini and later in Florida. He never once mentioned it in any of his private or official writings—at least those writings that still exist—and historians believe his goal was gold and other treasures (and perhaps to convert the natives to Catholicism).

His legacy lives on at the Casa Blanca in Old San Juan (p. 135). Casa Blanca is the oldest continuously occupied residence in the Western Hemisphere and the oldest of about 800 Spanish colonial buildings in Old San Juan's National Historic Zone. In 1968 it became a historic national monument. Today the building is the site of the Juan Ponce de León Museum. The conquistador's carved coat of arms greets visitors at the entrance.

were marked by upright stone dolmens, development of a universal language, and creation of a complicated religious cosmology. They believed in a hierarchy of deities who inhabited the sky. The god Yocahu was the supreme creator. Another god, Juracán, was perpetually angry and ruled the power of the hurricane. Myths and traditions were perpetuated through ceremonial dances *(areytos)*, drumbeats, oral traditions, and a ceremonial ballgame played between opposing teams (10–30 players per team) with a rubber ball; winning this game was thought to bring a good harvest and strong, healthy children. Skilled at agriculture and hunting, the Taínos were also good sailors, canoe makers, and navigators.

About 100 years before the Spanish invasion, the Taínos were challenged by an invading South American tribe—the Caribs. Fierce, warlike, sadistic, and adept at using poison-tipped arrows, the Caribs raided Taíno settlements for slaves (especially female) and bodies for the completion of their rites of cannibalism. Some ethnologists argue that the preeminence of the Taínos, shaken by the attacks of the Caribs, was already jeopardized by the time of the Spanish occupation. In fact, it was the Caribs who fought most effectively against the Europeans; their behavior led the Europeans to unfairly attribute warlike tendencies to all of the island's tribes. A dynamic tension between the Taínos and the Caribs certainly existed when Christopher Columbus landed on Puerto Rico.

To understand Puerto Rico's prehistoric era, it is important to know that the Taínos, far more than the Caribs, contributed greatly to the everyday life and language that evolved during the Spanish occupation. Taíno place names are still used for such towns as Utuado, Mayagüez, Caguas, and Humacao. Many Taíno implements and techniques were copied directly by the Europeans, including the *bohío* (straw hut), the *hamaca* (hammock), the musical instrument known as the maracas, and the method of making bread from the starchy cassava root. Also, many Taíno superstitions and legends were adopted and adapted by the Spanish and still influence the Puerto Rican imagination.

SPAIN, SYPHILIS & SLAVERY

Christopher Columbus became the first European to land on the shores of Puerto Rico, on November 19, 1493, near what would become the town of Aguadilla, during his second voyage to the New World. Giving the island the name San Juan Bautista, he sailed on in search of shores with more obvious riches for the taking. A European foothold on the island was established in 1508, when Juan Ponce de León, the first governor of Puerto Rico, imported colonists from the nearby island of Hispaniola. They founded the town of Caparra, which lay close to the site of present-day San Juan. The town was almost immediately wracked with internal power struggles among the Spanish settlers, who pressed the native peoples into servitude, evangelized them, and frantically sought for gold, thus quickly changing the face of the island.

Meanwhile, the Amerindians began dying at an alarming rate, victims of imported diseases such as smallpox and whooping cough, against which they had no biological immunity. The natives paid the Spanish back, giving them diseases such as syphilis against which they had little immunity. Both communities reeled, disoriented from their contact with one another. In 1511 the Amerindians rebelled against attempts by the Spanish to enslave them. The rebellion was brutally suppressed by the Spanish forces of Ponce de León, whose muskets and firearms were vastly superior to the hatchets and arrows of the native peoples. In desperation, the Taínos joined forces with their traditional enemies, the Caribs, but even that union did little to check the growth of European power.

Because the Indians languished in slavery, sometimes preferring mass suicide to imprisonment, their work in the fields and mines of Puerto Rico was soon taken over by Africans who were imported by Spanish, Danish, Portuguese, British, and American slavers.

By 1521 the island had been renamed Puerto Rico ("Rich Port") and was one of the most strategic islands in the Caribbean, which was increasingly viewed as a Spanish sea. Officials of the Spanish Crown dubbed the island "the strongest foothold of Spain in America" and hastened to strengthen the already impressive bulwarks surrounding the city of San Juan.

PIRATES & PILLAGING ENGLISHMEN

Within a century, Puerto Rico's position at the easternmost edge of what would become Spanish America helped it play a major part in the Spanish expansion toward Florida, the South American coast, and Mexico. It was usually the first port of call for Spanish ships arriving in the Americas; recognizing that the island was a strategic keystone, the Spanish decided to strengthen its defenses. By 1540, La Fortaleza, the first of three massive fortresses built in San Juan, was completed. By 1600, San Juan was completely enclosed by some of the most formidable ramparts in the Caribbean, whereas, ironically, the remainder of Puerto Rico was almost defenseless. In 1565 the king of Spain ordered the governor of Puerto Rico to provide men and materials to strengthen the city of St. Augustine, Florida.

By this time, the English (and to a lesser extent, the French) were seriously harassing Spanish shipping in the Caribbean and north Atlantic. At least part of the French and English aggression was in retaliation for the 1493 Papal Bull

dividing the New World between Portugal and Spain—an arrangement that eliminated all other nations from the spoils and colonization of the New World.

Queen Elizabeth I's most effective weapon against Spanish expansion in the Caribbean wasn't the Royal Navy; rather, it was buccaneers such as John Hawkins and Sir Francis Drake. Their victories included the destruction of St. Augustine in Florida, Cartagena in Colombia, and Santo Domingo in what is now the Dominican Republic, and the general harassment and pillaging of many Spanish ships and treasure convoys sailing from the New World to Europe with gold and silver from the Aztec and Inca empires. The Royal Navy did play an important role, however, as its 1588 defeat of the Spanish Armada marked the rise of the English as a major maritime power. The Spanish then began to aggressively fortify such islands as Puerto Rico.

In 1595, Drake and Hawkins persuaded Queen Elizabeth to embark on a bold and daring plan to invade and conquer Puerto Rico. An English general, the Earl of Cumberland, urged his men to bravery by "assuring your selves you have the maydenhead of Puerto Rico and so possesse the keyes of all the Indies." Confident that the island was "the very key of the West Indies which locketh and shutteth all the gold and silver in the continent of America and Brasilia," he brought into battle an English force of 4,500 soldiers and eventually captured La Fortaleza.

Although the occupation lasted a full 65 days, the English eventually abandoned Puerto Rico when their armies were decimated by tropical diseases and the local population, which began to engage in a kind of guerrilla warfare against the English. After pillaging and destroying much of the Puerto Rican countryside, the English left. Their short but abortive victory compelled the Spanish king, Philip III, to continue construction of the island's defenses. Despite these efforts, Puerto Rico retained a less-than-invincible aspect as Spanish soldiers in the forts often deserted or succumbed to tropical diseases.

A DUTCH TREAT

In 1625 Puerto Rico was covetously eyed by Holland, whose traders and merchants desperately wanted a foothold in the West Indies. Spearheaded by the Dutch West India Company, which had received trading concessions from the Dutch Crown covering most of the West Indies, the Dutch armies besieged El Morro Fortress in San Juan in one of the bloodiest assaults the fortress ever sustained. When the commanding officer of El Morro refused to surrender, the Dutch burned San Juan to the ground, including all church and civil archives and the bishop's library, by then the most famous and complete collection of books in America. Fueled by rage, the Spanish rallied and soon defeated the Dutch.

In response to the destruction of the strongest link in the chain of Spanish defenses, Spain threw itself wholeheartedly into improving and reinforcing the defenses around San Juan. King Philip IV justified his expenditures by declaring Puerto Rico the "front and vanguard of the Western Indies and, consequently, the most important of them and most coveted by the enemies of Spain."

Within 150 years, after extravagant expenditures of time and money, San Juan's walls were considered almost impregnable. Military sophistication was added during the 1760s, when two Irishmen, Tomas O'Daly and Alejandro O'Reilly, surrounded the city with some of Europe's most up-to-date defenses. Despite the thick walls, however, the island's defenses remained precarious because of the frequent tropical epidemics that devastated the ranks of the soldiers; the chronically late pay, which weakened the soldiers' morale; and the belated and often wrong-minded priorities of the Spanish monarchy.

A CATHOLIC CRUSADE

From the earliest days of Spanish colonization, an army of priests and missionaries embarked on a vigorous crusade to convert Puerto Rico's Taínos to Roman Catholicism. King Ferdinand himself paid for the construction of a Franciscan monastery and a series of chapels, and he required specific support of the church from the aristocrats who had been awarded land grants in the new territories. They were required to build churches, provide Christian burials, and grant religious instruction to both Taíno and African slaves.

Among the church's most important activities were the Franciscan monks' efforts to teach the island's children how to read, write, and count. In 1688 Bishop Francisco Padilla, who is now included among the legends of Puerto Rico, established one of the island's most famous schools. When it became clear that local parents were too poor to provide their children with appropriate clothing, he succeeded in persuading the king of Spain to pay for their clothes.

Puerto Rico was declared by the pope as the first *see* (ecclesiastical headquarters) in the New World. In 1519 it became the general headquarters of the Inquisition in the New World. (About 70 years later, the Inquisition's headquarters was transferred to the well-defended city of Cartagena, Colombia.)

FROM SMUGGLING TO SUGAR

The island's early development was shackled by Spain's insistence on a centrist economy. All goods exported from or imported to Puerto Rico had to pass through Spain itself, usually through Seville. In effect, this policy prohibited any official trade between Puerto Rico and its island neighbors.

In response, a flourishing black market developed. Cities such as Ponce became smuggling centers. This black market was especially prevalent after the Spanish colonization of Mexico and Peru, when many Spanish goods, which once would have been sent to Puerto Rico, ended up in those more immediately lucrative colonies instead. Although smugglers were punished if caught, nothing could curb this illegal (and untaxed) trade. Some historians estimate that almost everyone on the island—including priests, citizens, and military and civic authorities—was actively involved in smuggling.

By the mid-1500s, the several hundred settlers who had immigrated to Puerto Rico from Spain heard and sometimes believed rumors of the fortunes to be made in the gold mines of Peru. When the island's population declined because of the ensuing mass exodus, the king enticed 500 families from the Canary Islands to settle on Puerto Rico between 1683 and 1691. Meanwhile, an active trade in slaves—imported as labor for fields that were increasingly used for sugar-cane and tobacco production—swelled the island's ranks. This happened despite the Crown's imposition of strict controls on the number of slaves that could be brought in. Sugar cane earned profits for many islanders, but Spanish mismanagement, fraud within the government bureaucracy, and a lack of both labor and ships to transport the finished product to market discouraged the fledgling industry. Later, fortunes were made and lost in the production of ginger, an industry that died as soon as the Spanish government raised taxes on ginger imports to exorbitant levels. Despite the arrival of immigrants to Puerto Rico from many countries, diseases such as spotted fever, yellow fever, malaria, smallpox, and measles wiped out the population almost as fast as it grew.

MORE SMUGGLING

As the philosophical and political movement known as the Enlightenment swept both Europe and North America during the late 1700s and the 1800s, Spain moved to improve Puerto Rico's economy through its local government. The island's defenses were beefed up, roads and bridges were built, and a public education program was launched. The island remained a major Spanish naval stronghold in the New World. Immigration from Europe and other places more than tripled the population. It was during this era that Puerto Rico began to develop a unique identity of its own, a native pride, and a consciousness of its importance within the Caribbean.

The heavily fortified city of San Juan, the island's civic centerpiece, remained under Spain's rigid control. Although it was the victim of an occasional pirate raid, or an attack by English or French forces, the outlying countryside was generally left alone to develop its own local power centers. The city of Ponce, for example, flourished under the Spanish Crown's lax supervision and grew wealthy from the tons of contraband and the high-quality sugar that passed through its port. This trend was also encouraged by the unrealistic law that declared San Juan the island's only legal port. Contemporary sources, in fact, cite the fledgling United States as among the most active of Ponce's early contraband trading partners.

RISING POWER

During the 18th century, the number of towns on the island grew rapidly. There were five settlements in Puerto Rico in 1700; 100 years later, there were almost 40 settlements, and the island's population had grown to more than 150,000.

Meanwhile, the waters of the Caribbean increasingly reflected the diplomatic wars unfolding in Europe. In

1797 the British, after easily capturing Trinidad (which was poorly defended by the Spanish), failed in a spectacular effort to conquer Puerto Rico. The *criollos,* or native Puerto Ricans, played a major role in the island's defense and later retained a growing sense of their cultural identity.

The islanders were becoming aware that Spain could not enforce the hundreds of laws it had previously imposed to support its centrist trade policies. Thousands of merchants, farmers, and civil authorities traded profitably with privateers from various nations, thereby deepening the tendency to evade or ignore the laws imposed by Spain and its colonial governors. The attacks by privateers on British shipping were especially severe because pirates based in Puerto Rico ranged as far south as Trinidad, bringing dozens of captured British ships into Puerto Rican harbors. (Several decades earlier, British privateers operating out of Jamaica had endlessly harassed Spanish shipping; the tradition of government-sanctioned piracy was well established.)

It was during this period that coffee—which would later play an essential role in the island's economy—was introduced to the Puerto Rican highlands from the nearby Dominican Republic.

Despite the power of San Juan and its Spanish institutions, 18th-century Puerto Rico was predominantly rural. The report of a special emissary of the Spanish king, Marshal Alejandro O'Reilly, remains a remarkably complete analysis of 18th-century Puerto Rican society. It helped promote a more progressive series of fiscal and administrative policies that reflected the Enlightenment ideals found in many European countries.

Puerto Rico began to be viewed as a potential source of income for the Spanish Empire rather than a drain on income. One of O'Reilly's most visible legacies was his recommendation that people live in towns rather than be scattered about the countryside. Shortly after this, seven new towns were established.

As the island prospered and its bourgeoisie became more numerous and affluent, life became more refined. New public buildings were erected; concerts were introduced; and everyday aspects of life—such as furniture and social ritual—grew more ornate. Insights into Puerto Rico's changing life can be seen in the works of its most famous 18th-century painter, José Campeche.

THE LAST BASTION

Much of the politics of 19th-century Latin America cannot be understood without a review of Spain's problems at that time. Up until 1850, there was political and military turmoil in Spain, a combination that eventually led to the collapse of its empire. Since 1796, Spain had been a military satellite of postrevolutionary France, an alliance that brought it into conflict with England. In 1804 Admiral Horatio Lord Nelson's definitive victory for England over French and Spanish ships during the Battle of Trafalgar left England in supreme control of the international sea lanes and interrupted trade and communications between Spain and its colonies in the New World.

These events led to changes for Spanish-speaking America. The revolutionary fervor of Simón Bolívar and his South American compatriots spilled over to the entire continent, embroiling Spain in a desperate attempt to hold on to the tattered remains of its empire. Recognizing that Puerto Rico and Cuba were probably the last bastions of Spanish Royalist sympathy in the Americas, Spain liberalized its trade policies, decreeing that goods no longer had to pass through Seville.

The sheer weight and volume of illegal Puerto Rican trade with such countries as Denmark, France, and—most important—the United States, forced Spain's hand in establishing a realistic set of trade reforms.

A bloody revolution in Haiti, which had produced more sugar cane than almost any other West Indies island, spurred sugar-cane and coffee production in Puerto Rico. Also important was the introduction of a new and more prolific species of sugar cane, the Otahiti, which helped increase production even more.

By the 1820s the United States was providing ample supplies of such staples as lumber, salt, butter, fish, grain, and foodstuffs, and huge amounts of Puerto Rican sugar, molasses, coffee, and rum were consumed in the United States. Meanwhile, the United States was increasingly viewed as the keeper of the peace in the Caribbean, suppressing the piracy that flourished while Spain's navy was preoccupied with its European wars.

During Venezuela's separation from Spain, Venezuelans loyal to the Spanish Crown fled en masse to the remaining Royalist bastions in the Americas— Puerto Rico and, to a lesser extent, Cuba. Although many arrived penniless, having forfeited their properties in South America in exchange for their lives, their excellent understanding of agriculture and commerce probably catalyzed much of the era's economic development in Puerto Rico. Simultaneously, many historians argue, their unflinching loyalty to the Spanish Crown contributed to one of the most conservative and reactionary social structures anywhere in the Spanish-speaking Caribbean. In any event, dozens of Spanish naval expeditions that were intended to suppress the revolutions in Venezuela were outfitted in Puerto Rican harbors during this period.

A REVOLT SUPPRESSED & SLAVERY ABOLISHED

During the latter half of the 19th century, political divisions were drawn in Puerto Rico, reflecting both the political instability in Spain and the increasing demands of Puerto Ricans for some form of self-rule. As governments and regimes in Spain rose and fell, Spanish policies toward its colonies in the New World changed, too.

In 1865 representatives from Puerto Rico, Cuba, and the Philippines were invited to Madrid to air their grievances as part of a process of liberalizing Spanish colonial policy. Reforms, however, did not follow as promised, and a much-publicized and very visible minirevolt (during which the mountain city of Lares was occupied) was suppressed by the Spanish governors in 1868. Some of the funds and much of the publicity for this revolt came from expatriate Puerto Ricans living in Chile, St. Thomas, and New York.

Slavery was abolished in March 1873, about 40 years after it had been abolished throughout the British Empire. About 32,000 slaves were freed following years of liberal agitation. Abolition was viewed as a major victory for liberal forces throughout Puerto Rico, although cynics claim that slavery was much less entrenched in Puerto Rico than in neighboring Cuba, where the sugar economy was far more dependent on slave labor.

The 1895 revolution in Cuba increased the Puerto Rican demand for greater self-rule; during the ensuing intellectual ferment, many political parties emerged. The Cuban revolution provided part of the spark that led to the Spanish-American War, Cuban independence, and U.S. control of Puerto Rico, the Philippines, and the Pacific island of Guam.

THE YANKS ARE COMING, THE YANKS ARE COMING!

In 1897, faced with intense pressure from sources within Puerto Rico, a weakened Spain granted its colony a measure of autonomy, but it came too late. Other events were taking place between Spain and the United States that would forever change the future of Puerto Rico.

On February 15, 1898, the U.S. battleship *Maine* was blown up in the harbor of Havana, killing 266 men. The so-called yellow press in the United States, especially the papers owned by the tycoon William Randolph Hearst, aroused Americans' emotions into a fever pitch for war, with the rallying cry "Remember the *Maine*."

On April 20 of that year, President William McKinley signed a resolution demanding Spanish withdrawal from Cuba. The president ordered a blockade of Cuba's ports, and on April 24, Spain, in retaliation, declared a state of war with the United States. On April 25, the U.S. Congress declared war on Spain. In Cuba, the naval battle of Santiago was won by American forces, and in another part of the world, the Spanish colony of the Philippines was also captured by U.S. troops.

On July 25, after their victory at Santiago, U.S. troops landed at Guánica, Puerto Rico, and several days later they took over Ponce. U.S. Navy Capt. Alfred T. Mahan later wrote that the United States viewed Puerto Rico, Spain's remaining colonial outpost in the Caribbean, as vital to American interests in the area. Puerto Rico could be used as a military base to help the United States maintain control of the Isthmus of Panama and to keep communications and traffic flowing between the Atlantic and the Pacific.

Spain offered to trade other territory for Puerto Rico, but the United States refused and demanded Spain's ouster from the island. Left with little choice against superior U.S. forces, Spain capitulated. The Spanish-American War ended on August 31, 1898, with the surrender of Spain and the virtual collapse of the once-powerful Spanish Empire. Puerto Rico, in the words of McKinley, was to "become a territory of the United States."

Although the entire war lasted just over 4 months, the invasion of Puerto Rico took only 2 weeks. "It wasn't much of a war," remarked Theodore Roosevelt, who had led the Rough Riders cavalry outfit in their charge up San Juan Hill, "but it was all the war there was." The United States had suffered only four casualties while acquiring Puerto Rico, the Philippines, and the island of Guam. The Treaty of Paris, signed on December 10, 1898, settled the terms of Spain's surrender.

A DUBIOUS PRIZE

Some Americans looked on Puerto Rico as a "dubious prize." One-third of the population consisted of mulattoes and blacks, descended from slaves, who had no money or land. Only about 12% of the population could read or write. About 8% were enrolled in school. It is estimated that a powerful landed gentry—only about 2% of the population—owned more than two-thirds of the land.

Washington set up a military government in Puerto Rico, headed by the War Department. A series of governors-general were appointed to rule the island, with almost the authority of dictators. Although ruling over a rather unhappy populace, these governors-general brought about much-needed change, including tax and public health reforms. But most Puerto Ricans wanted autonomy, and many leaders, including Luís Muñoz Rivera, tried to persuade Washington to compromise. However, their protests generally fell on deaf ears.

Tensions mounted between Puerto Ricans and their new American governors. In 1900, U.S. Secretary of War Elihu Root decided that military rule of the island was inadequate; he advocated a program of autonomy that won the endorsement of President McKinley.

The island's beleaguered economy was further devastated by an 1899 hurricane that caused millions of dollars' worth of property damage, killed 3,000 people, and left one out of four people homeless. Belatedly, Congress allocated the sum of

$200,000, but this did little to relieve the suffering.

Thus began a nearly 50-year colonial protectorate relationship, as Puerto Rico was recognized as an unincorporated territory with its governor named by the president of the United States. Only the president had the right to override the veto of the island's governors. The legislative branch was composed of an 11-member executive committee appointed by the president, plus a 35-member chamber of delegates elected by popular vote. A resident commissioner, it was agreed, would represent Puerto Rico in Congress, "with voice but no vote."

As the United States prepared to enter World War I in 1917, Puerto Ricans were granted U.S. citizenship and, thus, were subject to military service. The people of Puerto Rico were allowed to elect their legislature, which had been reorganized into a Senate and a House of Representatives. The president of the United States continued to appoint the governor of the island and retained the power to veto any of the governor's actions.

FROM HARVARD TO REVOLUTION

Many Puerto Ricans continued, at times rather violently, to agitate for independence. Requests for a plebiscite were constantly turned down. Meanwhile, economic conditions improved, as the island's population began to grow dramatically. Government revenues increased as large corporations from the U.S. mainland found Puerto Rico a profitable place in which to do business. There was much labor unrest, and by 1909, a labor movement demanding better working conditions and higher wages was gaining momentum.

The emerging labor movement showed its strength by organizing a cigar workers' strike in 1914 and a sugar-cane workers' strike the following year. The 1930s proved to be disastrous for Puerto Rico, which suffered greatly from the worldwide depression. To make matters worse, two devastating hurricanes—one in 1928 and another in 1932—destroyed millions of dollars' worth of crops and property. There was also an outbreak of disease that demoralized the population. Some relief came in the form of food shipments authorized by Congress.

As tension between Puerto Rico and the United States intensified, there emerged Pedro Albizu Campos, a graduate of Harvard Law School and a former U.S. Army officer. Leading a group of militant anti-American revolutionaries, he held that America's claim to Puerto Rico was illegal, since the island had already been granted autonomy by Spain. Terrorist acts by his followers, including assassinations, led to Albizu's imprisonment, but terrorist activities continued.

In 1935 President Franklin D. Roosevelt launched the Puerto Rican Reconstruction Administration, which provided for agricultural development, public works, and electrification. The following year, Sen. Millard E. Tidings of Maryland introduced a measure to grant independence to the island. His efforts were cheered by a local leader, Luís Muñoz Marín, son of the statesman Luís Muñoz Rivera. In 1938 the young Muñoz founded the Popular Democratic Party, which adopted the slogan "Bread, Land, and Liberty." By 1940 this party had gained control of more than 50% of the seats of both the upper and lower houses of government, and the young Muñoz was elected leader of the Senate.

Roosevelt appointed Rexford Guy Tugwell governor of Puerto Rico; Tugwell spoke Spanish and seemed to have genuine concern for the plight of the islanders. Muñoz met with Tugwell and convinced him that Puerto Rico was capable of electing its own governor. As a step in that direction, Roosevelt appointed Jesús Piñero as the first resident commissioner of the island. In 1944 the U.S. Congress approved a bill granting Puerto Rico the right to elect its own governor. This was the beginning of the famed Operation Bootstrap, a pump-priming fiscal and economic aid package designed to improve the island's standard of living.

SHOOTING AT HARRY

In 1946 President Harry S. Truman appointed native-born Jesús Piñero as governor of Puerto Rico, and the following year the U.S. Congress recognized the right of Puerto Ricans to elect their own governor. In 1948, Luís Muñoz Marín became the first elected governor and immediately recommended that Puerto Rico be transformed into an "associated free state." Endorsement of his plan was delayed by Washington, but President Truman approved the Puerto Rican Commonwealth Bill in 1950, providing for a plebiscite in which voters would decide whether they would remain a colony or become a U.S. commonwealth. In June 1951, Puerto Ricans voted three to one for commonwealth status, and on July 25, 1952, the Commonwealth of Puerto Rico was born.

This event was marred when a group of nationalists marched on the Governor's Mansion in San Juan, resulting in 27 deaths and hundreds of casualties. A month later, two Puerto Rican nationalists made an unsuccessful attempt on Truman's life in Washington, killing a police officer in the process. And in March 1954, four Puerto Rican nationalists wounded five U.S. Congressmen when they fired down into the House of Representatives from the visitors' gallery.

Despite this violence, during the 1950s Puerto Rico began to take pride in its culture and traditions. In 1955 the Institute of Puerto Rican Culture was established, and 1957 saw the inauguration of the Pablo Casals Festival, which launched a renaissance of classical music and a celebration of the arts. In 1959 a wealthy industrialist, Luís A. Ferré, donated his personal art collection toward the establishment of the Museo de Arte de Ponce.

GIVE ME LIBERTY OR GIVE ME STATEHOOD

Luís Muñoz Marín resigned from office in 1964, but his party continued to win subsequent elections. The Independent Party, which demanded complete autonomy, gradually lost power. An election on July 23, 1967, reconfirmed the desire of most Puerto Ricans to maintain commonwealth status. In 1968 Luís A. Ferré won a close race for governor, spearheading a pro-statehood party, the New Progressive Party. It staunchly advocated statehood as an alternative to the island's commonwealth status, but in 1972, the Partido Popular Democrático returned to power; by then, the island's economy was based largely on tourism, rum, and industry. Operation Bootstrap had been successful in creating thousands of new jobs, although more than 100,000 Puerto Ricans moved to the U.S. mainland during the 1950s, seeking a better life. The island's economy continued to improve, although perhaps not as quickly as anticipated by Operation Bootstrap.

Puerto Rico grabbed the world's attention in 1979 with the launching of the Pan-American Games. The island's culture received a boost in 1981 with the opening of the Center of the Performing Arts in San Juan, which attracted world-famous performers and virtuosos. The international spotlight again focused on Puerto Rico at the time of the first papal visit there in 1986. John Paul II (or Juan Pablo II, as he was called locally) kindled a renewed interest in religion, especially among the Catholic youth of the island.

In 1996, Puerto Rico lost its special tax-break status, which had originally lured U.S. industry to the island. Down the road, some dire consequences to the island's economy are predicted as a result of this loss.

A flare-up between the U.S. Navy and Puerto Ricans, especially the islanders of Vieques, burst into the headlines in 1999. Islanders vehemently protested the Navy's use of Vieques for the testing of bombardments.

In 2001, Sila M. Calderón was inaugurated as Puerto Rico's first female governor. The daughter of a rich entrepreneur whose holdings include ice-cream factories and hotels, she was raised to a life of privilege. As head of the Popular Democratic Party, she took office and immediately angered Washington by advocating that the U.S. Navy halt bombing on Vieques. She also opposes statehood for Puerto Rico. "When I was a little girl everybody who had power were men," the new governor told the press. "Now girls know that it is very normal for power to be shared by men and women."

In 2003, the U.S. Navy closed its Roosevelt Roads Naval Station on the island of Vieques in the wake of massive protests. With the closing, more than 6,000 people lost their jobs and the island itself suffered a falloff of $300 million a year in income. Puerto Rican leaders are hoping to fill the economic gap with tourism.

The navy since 1947 had used parts of the island for test bombing. The former naval base has been turned over to the U.S. Fish and Wildlife Service for use as a nature refuge, as the landmass is the home to several endangered species.

In December 2005 the Bush administration asked Congress to set another vote to allow the citizens of the overpopulated island to decide on their future: to opt for statehood or else full independence. Statehood would bring the right to vote in U.S. elections, and full independence would require some islanders to relinquish their American citizenship.

Because of the possible disastrous economic consequences of full independence, only a small, somewhat militant group backs full independence. As a state, Puerto Rico might alter the balance of power between Democrats and Republicans.

Of course, one option still remains on the table and that is for Puerto Rico to continue as a commonwealth of the U.S. At present, Puerto Rico has no voting representation in Congress. On the other hand, islanders pay no federal income taxes.

4 A Portrait of the Puerto Ricans

The people of Puerto Rico represent a mix of races, cultures, languages, and religions. They draw their heritage from the original native population, from Spanish royalists who sought refuge here, from African slaves imported to work the sugar plantations, and from other Caribbean islanders who have come here seeking jobs. The Spanish they speak is a mix, too, with many words borrowed from the pre-Columbian Amerindian tongue as well as English. Even the Catholicism they practice incorporates some Taíno and African traditions.

THE ISLANDERS

Some 3.88 million people inhabit the main island of Puerto Rico, making it one of the most densely populated islands in the world. It has an average of about 1,000 people per square mile, a ratio higher than that of any of the 50 states. It is estimated that if the 2 million Puerto Ricans who have migrated to the United

States (more Puerto Ricans are said to live in New York City than in San Juan) were to return home, the island would be so crowded that there would be virtually no room for them to live.

When the United States acquired the island in 1898, most Puerto Ricans worked in agriculture; today most jobs are industrial. One-third of Puerto Rico's population is concentrated in the San Juan metropolitan area.

When the Spanish forced the Taíno peoples into slavery, virtually the entire indigenous population was decimated, except for a few Amerindians who escaped into the remote mountains. Eventually they intermarried with the poor Spanish farmers and became known as *jíbaros*. Because of industrialization and migration to the cities, few jíbaros remain.

Besides the slaves imported from Africa to work on the plantations, other ethnic groups joined the island's racial mix. Fleeing Simón Bolívar's independence movements in South America, Spanish loyalists headed to Puerto Rico—a fiercely conservative Spanish colony during the early 1800s. French families also flocked here from both Louisiana and Haiti, as changing governments or violent revolutions turned their worlds upside down. As word of the rich sugar-cane economy reached economically depressed Scotland and Ireland, many farmers from those countries also journeyed to Puerto Rico in search of a better life.

During the mid–19th century, labor was needed to build roads. Initially, Chinese workers were imported for this task, followed by workers from countries such as Italy, France, Germany, and even Lebanon. American expatriates came to the island after 1898. Long after Spain had lost control of Puerto Rico, Spanish immigrants continued to arrive on the island. The most significant new immigrant population arrived in the 1960s,

when thousands of Cubans fled from Fidel Castro's communist state. The latest arrivals in Puerto Rico have come from the economically depressed Dominican Republic.

THEIR LANGUAGES

Spanish is the language of Puerto Rico, although English is widely spoken, especially in hotels, restaurants, shops, and nightclubs that attract tourists. In the hinterlands, however, Spanish prevails.

If you plan to travel extensively in Puerto Rico but don't speak Spanish, pick up a Spanish-language phrase book. The most popular is *Berlitz Spanish for Travelers*, published by Collier Macmillan. The University of Chicago's *Pocketbook Dictionary* is equally helpful. If you have a basic knowledge of Spanish and want to improve your word usage and your sentence structure, consider purchasing a copy of *Spanish Now*, published by Barron's.

Many Amerindian words from pre-Columbian times have been retained in the language. For example, the Puerto Rican national anthem, titled "La Borinqueña," refers to the Arawak name for the island Borinquén, and Mayagüez, Yauco, Caguas, Guaynabo, and Arecibo are all pre-Columbian place names.

Many Amerindian words were borrowed to describe the phenomena of the New World. The natives slept in *hamacas*, and today Puerto Ricans still lounge in hammocks. The god Juracán was feared by the Arawaks just as much as contemporaries fear autumn hurricanes. African words were also added to the linguistic mix, and Castilian Spanish was significantly modified.

With the American takeover in 1898, English became the first Germanic language to be introduced into Puerto Rico. This linguistic marriage led to what some scholars call Spanglish, a colloquial dialect blending English and Spanish into forms not considered classically correct in either linguistic tradition.

The bilingual confusion was also greatly accelerated by the mass migration to the U.S. mainland of thousands of Puerto Ricans, who quickly altered their speech patterns to conform to the language used in the urban Puerto Rican communities of cities such as New York.

THEIR RELIGIONS

The majority of Puerto Ricans are Roman Catholic, but religious freedom for all faiths is guaranteed by the Commonwealth Constitution. There is a Jewish Community Center in Miramar, and there's a Jewish Reformed Congregation in Santurce. There are Protestant services for Baptists, Episcopalians, Lutherans, and Presbyterians, and there are other interdenominational services.

Although it is predominantly Catholic, Puerto Rico does not follow Catholic dogma and rituals as assiduously as do the churches of Spain and Italy. Because the church supported slavery, there was a long-lasting resentment against the all-Spanish clergy of colonial days. Island-born men were excluded from the priesthood. When Puerto Ricans eventually took over the Catholic churches on the island, they followed some guidelines from Spain and Italy but modified or ignored others.

Following the U.S. acquisition of the island in 1898, Protestantism grew in influence and popularity. There were Protestants on the island before the invasion, but their numbers increased after Puerto Rico became a U.S. colony. Many islanders liked the idea of separation of church and state, as provided for in the U.S. Constitution. In recent years, Pentecostal fundamentalism has swept across the island. There are some 1,500 Evangelical churches in Puerto Rico today.

As throughout Latin America, the practice of Catholicism in Puerto Rico blends native Taíno and African traditions with mainstream tenets of the faith. It has been said that the real religion of Puerto Rico is *espiritismo* (spiritualism), a quasi-magical belief in occult forces. Spanish colonial rulers outlawed spiritualism, but under the U.S. occupation it flourished in dozens of isolated pockets of the island.

Students of religion trace spiritualism to the Taínos, and to their belief that *jípia* (the spirits of the dead—somewhat like the legendary vampire) slumbered by day and prowled the island by night. Instead of looking for bodies, the jípia were seeking wild fruit to eat. Thus arose the Puerto Rican tradition of putting out fruit on the kitchen table. Even in modern homes today, you'll often find a bowl of plastic, flamboyantly colored fruit resting atop a refrigerator.

Many islanders still believe in the "evil eye," or *mal de ojo*. To look on a person or a person's possessions covetously, according to believers, can lead to that individual's sickness or perhaps death. Children are given bead charm bracelets to guard against the evil eye. Spiritualism also extends into healing, folk medicine, and food. For example, some spiritualists believe that cold food should never be eaten with hot food. Some island plants, herbs, and oils are believed to have healing properties, and spiritualist literature is available throughout the island.

Index

See also Accommodations and Restaurant indexes, below.

ACCOMMODATIONS

RESTAURANTS

THE NEW TRAVELOCITY GUARANTEE

EVERYTHING YOU BOOK WILL BE RIGHT, OR WE'LL WORK WITH OUR TRAVEL PARTNERS TO MAKE IT RIGHT, RIGHT AWAY.

*To drive home the point,
we're going to use the word "right" in every single sentence.*

Let's get right to it. Right to the meat! Only Travelocity guarantees everything about your booking will be right, or we'll work with our travel partners to make it right, right away. Right on!

Here's a picture taken smack dab right in the middle of Antigua, where the guarantee also covers you.

The guarantee covers all but one of the items pictured to the right.

Now, you may be thinking, "Yeah, right, I'm so sure." That's OK; you have the right to remain skeptical. That is until we mention help is always right around the corner. Call us right off the bat, knowing that our customer service reps are there for you 24/7. Righting wrongs. Left and right.

For example, what if the ocean view you booked actually looks out at a downright ugly parking lot? You'd be right to call – we're there for you. And no one in their right mind would be pleased to learn the rental car place has closed and left them stranded. Call Travelocity and we'll help get you back on the right track.

Now if you're guessing there are some things we can't control, like the weather, well you're right. But we can help you with most things – to get all the details in righting,* vi travelocity.com/guarantee

*Sorry, spelling things right is one of t
few things not covered under the gu

I'd give my right arm for a guarantee like this, although I'm glad I don't have to.